Questions and Answers in Attitude Surveys

Experiments on Question Form, Wording, and Context

Questions and Answers in Attitude Surveys

Experiments on Question Form, Wording, and Context

HOWARD SCHUMAN
University of Michigan

STANLEY PRESSER
University of Maryland

SAGE PUBLICATIONS
International Educational and Professional Publisher
Thousand Oaks   London   New Delhi

For information address:

SAGE Publications, Inc.
2455 Teller Road
Thousand Oaks, California 91320
E-mail: order@sagepub.com

SAGE Publications Ltd.
6 Bonhill Street
London EC2A 4PU
United Kingdom

SAGE Publications India Pvt. Ltd.
M-32 Market
Greater Kailash I
New Delhi 110 048 India

Printed in the United States of America

Library of Congress Cataloging-in-Publication Data

Schuman, Howard.
    Questions and answers in attitude surveys: Experiments on
question form, wording, and context / Howard Schuman, Stanley
Presser.
        p.   cm.
    Originally published: New York: Academic Press, 1981.
    Includes bibliographical references (pp. 351–362) and index.
    ISBN 0-7619-0359-3 (pbk.: alk. paper)
    1. Social surveys.   2. Social sciences—Research.   I. Presser,
Stanley, 1950–   .   II. Title.
HN29.S338   1996
300'.723—dc20   95-48479

This book is printed on acid-free paper.

        99 10 9 8 7 6 5 4

Production Editor: Diane S. Foster

Contents

Revised Preface

The combination of language with its intellectual content, its meaning, is as close a union as can well be imagined.

—A. E. Housman

There are several reasons why this book, first published in 1981, remains relevant today. First, *Q&A*, as we have come to call it, stimulated a considerable amount of later research on the question-answer process in surveys. It focused attention on a number of now common concepts such as "the subtraction effect," "part-whole consistency," "form-resistant correlations," and "don't know filters"; introduced some well-known experimental items ("the Agricultural Trade Act," "the abortion context effect"); and raised still broader issues like the impact of attitude intensity on question effects and the difference between general and specific attitudes. By providing a theoretically organized approach to survey questioning and stressing associations among variables rather than single variable effects, the book reinvigorated a tradition of experimentation in surveys that had languished since the days of Cantril, Gallup, Hyman, and others.

Second, the experiments we report in the following pages are almost all based on carefully designed probability samples of the U.S. national population. Current theory in the areas we deal with, including developments under the now common heading of "cognitive research," must be able to encompass the results from such general population studies. Thus our findings continue to provide "data" for those interested in exploring the question-answer process, and in that sense this remains a sourcebook for those wishing to explain effects due to question form, wording, or context. There have already been a number of reanalyses of our experiments, made easier because the original data are available through the Inter-university Consortium for Political and Social Research, and we hope others will see ways of looking at this evidence that go beyond our own analyses.

Moreover, it becomes increasingly possible to repeat earlier experiments with an eye to change over time. Some of our most interesting findings occurred when we replicated research carried out by others three or four decades before we came on the scene. Thus, in Chapter 2 we show how questionnaire order effects themselves changed over time depending on whether the context emphasized the object of an attitude ("communists") or a more general norm of reciprocity that governed answering. In Chapter 11 we report a series of replications of a classic experiment from 1940 on the difference between "forbidding" and "allowing" speeches, which demonstrated that the original response effect was robust but also that both versions of the question shifted to the same degree over time and thus allowed conclusions about change that transcended the effect due to tone of wording. No doubt many of our own experiments can now be treated as earlier time points for new replications that investigate the impact of social and linguistic change on question wording effects. Experiments in survey research—as in all social research—can never be timeless but must always allow for changes in the meaning of questions to new generations.

Finally we think that the method pursued here is also instructive. Rather than the one-shot experiment, we were able to replicate and develop results from one experiment to another. This frequently showed that earlier findings were not reliable or were inadequately interpreted. Our experience has made us skeptical of the quickly published finding that is intuitively (or even counterintuitively) persuasive but has not been tested in realistic surveys through both literal and construct replication.

We continue to find questions about questions a fascinating area for research, one that is important to survey methodologists, to cognitive and attitude theorists, and to both producers and users of survey results. Having returned to this book on numerous occasions in our own later research, we hope it will continue to be of value to others as well.

Preface

This book reports a set of investigations into the nature of attitude survey questions. It records ideas developed and experiments carried out systematically over more than 6 years.

The book consists of an introductory chapter that explains what we are about, 10 substantive chapters that present problems and results, and a final chapter that draws together some of the more important conclusions cross-cutting two or more chapters. Readers are urged to look at the introductory chapter first, but from there on it is not crucial to follow the organizing scheme that seemed to us most logical. Although certain pairs of chapters are closely linked (especially Chapters 4 and 5, Chapters 7 and 8, and Chapters 9 and 10), almost all can stand more or less independent of the others, and of course some cross-referencing is provided. Appendixes A and B also discuss general problems that should be of considerable interest to survey methodologists; Appendixes C and D contain supplementary questions and codes.

Parts of the book have appeared in earlier versions as journal articles, but in no case is a chapter simply a reprinting of a previous article. In addition to some reorganization and rewriting of these earlier versions, in several important cases (especially in Chapters 4 and 5) further experimentation was carried out subsequent to the original article, leading to new evidence and new conclusions. For these reasons, the book largely supercedes our previously published articles on these problems. Other parts of the book—almost all of Chapters 1, 2, 7, 8, 10–12, and the appendixes—have not been published before in any form.[1] Because we have often found our hypotheses to be wrong and our conclusions in need of amendment, we are well aware that some of the findings and interpretations offered here may turn out to need more than minor adjustment. But data analysis, like psychoanalysis, can go on forever, and it came time to report what we think we have learned thus far. No doubt others, and perhaps we ourselves, will improve on what is offered here.

It is satisfying at this point to be able to thank the organizations and individuals who helped make the research and the book possible, though the usual disclaimer regarding their responsibility for its conclusions and limitations certainly holds. One major debt is to the National Science Foundation (Grant No. Soc76–15040 and Grant No. Soc78–04021) and the National Institute of Mental Health (Grant No. MH–24266) for the funds that supported most of the work. A comprehensive series of experiments in national surveys is expensive, but if methodological understanding of surveys is to make headway, we are convinced that sustained programmatic work is essential—not simply the addition of an occasional methodological tail to a larger substantive study.

Jean M. Converse collaborated with us over the first half of the project. Her role in the early stages of the research was crucial, and her good ideas and good judgment have continued to bear fruit. Jacob Ludwig was our sole research assistant over the past 3 years, skillfully carrying out a wide range of computing and statistical functions with an extremely complex data set, and providing many useful suggestions. Margaret Grillot typed the many visions and revisions of this manuscript with efficiency and patience, often catching errors of our own that we might have missed. Sonya Kennedy contributed expert editorial advice that clarified both text and tables. Jo Miles Schuman prepared the figures in Chapters 9, 10, and 11 and helped at a number of other points.

[1]The data on which the book is based are available to others who may wish to carry out further analysis. Inquiries about costs and other pertinent matters should be directed to the appropriate survey organization, giving the year and the month of the survey desired.

For the original DAS data: The Detroit Area Study, Department of Sociology, University of Michigan, Ann Arbor MI 48109.

For the original NORC data: The Roper Center, University of Connecticut, Storrs CT 06268.

For the original SRC data: Surveys of Consumer Attitudes, Institute for Social Research, Box 1248, Ann Arbor MI 48106.

The original SRC, NORC, and DAS surveys include much data not directly related to our experiments. A computer tape and code book containing only the survey data that are the basis for the present book is being prepared by the Inter-University Consortium for Political and Social Research, Institute for Social Research, P.O. Box 1248, Ann Arbor, MI 48106.

Over the course of the work we have consulted many people. A number were acknowledged in earlier articles or are noted in chapter footnotes, but we would like here to thank the following persons who helped solve problems or provided advice at several points along the way: Philip E. Converse, Otis Dudley Duncan, Jane Fountain, James House, Alex Inkeles, Mary Jackman, Graham Kalton, Daniel Katz, William H. Kruskal, Elizabeth Martin, William M. Mason, and J. E. Keith Smith. Drs. Duncan, Kalton, Kruskal, and Martin each read several chapter drafts and gave us detailed suggestions. We wish that our abilities and resources had allowed us to follow more of their advice than proved possible, but the book is certainly better for their generous help.

Otis Dudley Duncan worked with the senior author on the design of context and wording experiments in the 1971 Detroit Area Study; these helped prepare for the present program of research, and provided some of the data for Chapter 2. James A. Davis allowed space in the 1974 NORC General Social Survey (GSS) for the first of our main set of experiments, and both he and Tom W. Smith helped make the GSS an important resource for our work. Richard Curtin and his staff were most cooperative in providing the flexibility necessary for our many experiments in the Survey Research Center's monthly telephone surveys. Robert Groves and Robert Kahn allowed us to include several experiments in their larger comparison of telephone and face-to-face interviewing in 1976, and Dr. Groves later provided advice on our use of these data. Many other people at The University of Michigan's Institute for Social Research (ISR) aided the development of the research, and ISR itself was an ideal setting for our work. We were also fortunate to be able to draw on the resources of the University of Michigan's Detroit Area Study, and on the University of North Carolina's Institute for Research in Social Science.

We dedicate the book to the memory of Samuel Stouffer. Stouffer had a firm belief in the value of survey research, but at the same time a commitment to understanding its limitations and developing its potential so that it could be used more wisely for both practical and theoretical ends. We have tried to keep these as our goals also.

CREDITS

Pages 3–5 in Chapter 1 are adapted from Schuman and Presser, "Question Wording as an Independent Variable in Survey Analysis," in *Sociological Methods and Research*, 1977, 6: 151–170 (Sage Publications).

Pages 36–39 in Chapter 2 are adapted from Schuman, Presser, and Ludwig, "Context Effects on Survey Responses to Questions About Abortion," in *Public Opinion Quarterly*, 1981, 45: 216–223.

Chapter 3 has been adapted from Schuman and Presser, "The Open and Closed Question," in the *American Sociological Review*, 1979, 44: 692–712.

Pages 113–141 in Chapter 4 are adapted from Schuman and Presser, "The Assessment of 'No Opinion' in Attitude Surveys," in *Sociological Methodology 1979*, Karl Schuessler (ed.), Jossey-Bass, 1978.

Pages 147–157 in Chapter 5 are adapted from Schuman and Presser, "Public Opinion and Public Ignorance: The Fine Line Between Attitudes and Non-Attitudes," in the *American Journal of Sociology*, 1980, 85: 1214–1225.

Chapter 6 is adapted from Presser and Schuman, "The Measurement of a Middle Position in Attitude Surveys," in *Public Opinion Quarterly*, 1980, 44: 70–85.

Pages 234–243 in Chapter 9 are adapted from Schuman and Presser, "The Attitude-Action Connection and the Issue of Gun Control," *The Annals of the American Academy of Political and Social Science*, 1981, 455: 40–47.

1
Scope and Method

She said to me early in the afternoon,
"What is the answer?" I was silent.
"In that case," she said,
"What is the question?"
  —Alice B. Toklas, *What Is Remembered*

Despite repeated criticisms, polls and surveys continue to flourish in number and influence. The reason for their success is simple. They combine two things: the ancient but extremely efficient method of obtaining information from people by asking questions; and modern random sampling procedures that allow a relatively small number of such people to represent a much larger population. When the speed of computer processing and the power of multivariate analysis are added to the more basic ingredients of questions and samples, the whole can yield information and insights impossible to obtain in any other way about a large population. Yet all the technical developments of sampling theory, computing, and analysis are meaningful only as they facilitate use of inquiries not fundamentally different in nature from our most ordinary attempts to satisfy curiosity by asking someone something.

This book reports an extensive investigation of the kinds of questions asked in surveys, especially surveys dealing with what Turner and Krauss (1978) refer to as "subjective phenomena." Although this focus means that we will ordinarily not treat questions about "facts" as problematic, it is well to keep in mind that many questions commonly regarded as factual have a large subjective component. In Chapter 2 we cite evidence that reports to Census interviewers about past experiences ("facts") vary with question context, and it is also evident that Census measures of unemployment status, marital separation, and racial and ethnic identity are open to many of the same problems that characterize the assessment of attitudes. Thus, although our main concern in this volume is with questions dealing with attitudes, opinions, beliefs, values, preferences, and so on—for shorthand we shall often refer to all of these as attitude questions—the research has implications for virtually all questions asked in polls and surveys.

Our main goal is to determine how the ways in which attitude questions are asked in surveys affect the results derived from these same surveys. Such results may be in the form of simple response distributions, as with the overall percentages saying "favor" and "oppose" on an issue, or they may involve associations between responses to two or more questions. The latter are particularly important when surveys are used as research tools, and much of our effort has gone into investigating the effects of question form on associations. Changes in single variables are also of interest, however, and we shall be concerned with these as well.

Questions can be asked in infinitely varied ways about an infinite number of subjects. It is not possible, except in a purposive or else purely metaphoric way, to sample the universe of all survey questions. Instead, our strategy has been to identify a small number of important ways in which questions vary in form, and investigate whether these variations have systematic effects that are detectable regardless of exact wording or subject matter. For example, almost any attitude question can include an explicit "don't know" alternative, but most survey questions do not provide this option for the respondent. In Chapter 4, we look at how this apparently simple variation—offering or not offering a don't know option—affects results for a number of different survey questions. At a later point in the present chapter we will outline all the major variations in question form that we have investigated. Of course, the assumption that there are important formal ways in which questions vary is itself tested throughout the entire volume.

Our primary way of proceeding has been to carry out experiments within surveys. Since our concern is to throw light on large-scale surveys, we have generally not used student or other special samples, but rather have worked with probability samples drawn from the national population, or, in a few cases, from the population of metropolitan Detroit. Within these surveys we ordinarily employ a between-subjects experimental design, randomly dividing the total sample into two or more subsamples, each of which is administered one form of a question. In public opinion research this method has traditionally been called the "split-ballot experiment," and we sometimes use that term below. In certain cases we also employ "panel data," a form of within-subjects design where the same respondents are interviewed on two or more occasions. Whichever design was used, our aim was to combine the testing of causal hypotheses through experimental manipulation and randomization ("internal validity") with the ability to generalize to the national population ("external validity").

There is one other characteristic of our work that distinguishes it from most reports using survey data. Rather than testing many hypotheses once in a single effort, we have developed our ideas step by step, starting with a relatively few experiments, then attempting to profit from the results (and our mistakes) to design a new set of experiments, and so on. Altogether we have worked within more than 30 separate surveys over a 6-year period. Furthermore, we have frequently used replication to test the reliability of results, especially those that are unusual or counterintuitive. Although most social scientists recognize that statistical significance testing is of uncertain meaning in the context of extensive analysis of a single data set (Kish, 1959), the great cost and effort of carrying out a major survey usually precludes systematic replication. Our own approach, which involved buying small blocks of time in ongoing surveys, together with assumptions and experiences that emphasized the importance of replicability, led us in the opposite direction.

This then is the basic nature of the research to be reported. There are many important problems and results not hinted at, but the broadest outlines of the research have been laid out. The remainder of this chapter briefly recounts the history of prior work on survey questions, outlines the main variations in question form that occupy our attention throughout most of the book, and describes sources of data and methods of analysis.

PAST RESEARCH ON QUESTION EFFECTS

During the 1940s a number of experiments on attitude-question wording and form were carried out by both academic and commercial survey researchers seeking to determine whether different ways of asking the same attitude item led to different results. These experiments became most widely known through the collection of papers in Cantril (1944) on *Gauging Public Opinion* and the useful book by Payne (1951) on *The Art of Asking Questions*. An example of such experiments was a pair of questions on freedom of speech reported by Rugg in 1941. One national sample was asked: *Do you think the United States should allow public speeches against democracy?* A comparable sample was asked: *Do you think the United States should forbid public speeches against democracy?* Approximately 20% more people were willing to "not allow" such speeches than were willing to "forbid" them—a difference suggesting that a seemingly innocuous change in one word can shift responses substantially. (The 1941 results, plus our recent replications and extensions, are reported in Chapter 11.)

By the early 1950s such question-wording experiments had largely disappeared from major surveys. We think there were several reasons for their demise. First, the basic fact that the overall response distribution to a question (i.e., the item "marginals") are in part a function of question wording was by then recognized, at least in theory, by virtually all serious survey researchers. Beyond repeatedly demonstrating the phenomenon, further experiments seemed to serve no particular purpose, as McNemar observed in his extended review of "Opinion–Attitude Methodology" in 1946. Of even greater importance, we believe, was the fact that almost all these early reports of experiments were restricted to univariate results, while survey *analysis* is typically concerned with relationships between variables. The assumption developed among investigators that marginals cannot be trusted owing to question-wording uncertainties, but that associations between variables are not subject to this same sort of instability. Exactly this assumption is made, for example, by Stouffer and DeVinney in *The American Soldier* (1949: 168):

> One must be careful to focus attention on differences in percentages among different categories of men with favorable attitudes on a given item, not on absolute percentages. The fact that the percentages saying the army was run pretty well or very well are large does not mean, necessarily, that so many men were actually favorable to the Army—such percentages are artifacts of question wording and of the checklist categories arbitrarily selected as "favorable." . . . But when we focus on *differences* in percentages responding favorably to the same questions, among men in different categories, the differences can be meaningful in a sense in which the absolute values cannot [emphasis in original; copyright © 1949 by Princeton University Press, reprinted by permission of Princeton University Press].

What Stouffer and DeVinney state explicitly appears, in the absence of warnings to the contrary, to have been taken for granted by many other survey methodologists and practitioners. (For one exception, see Hyman, 1944; no doubt there were others.)

This assumption of "form-resistant correlations," as we will call it, was further bolstered as academic survey analysts came to stress the use of multi-item attitude scales. On the one hand, this steered the analyst away from single-item percentage results, with their illusion of absolute proportions for and against specific social objects or positions. On the other hand, attitude scaling is intended to reduce idiosyncratic effects of individual items, though how this will necessarily eliminate *systematic* form effects is not so clear. If, for example, some respondents show a propensity to say "don't know" when it is offered but not when it must be volunteered, then a scale constructed from a set of similarly formatted items will simply cumulate this potential source of bias. Moreover, where multiple items are used for an issue, they frequently do not scale adequately in a unidimensional sense. When they are simply added together to form a reliable summary index, the individual items can turn out to reveal important differential relations with other variables (including time) that would be lost were only total index scores analyzed (Converse, 1972; Duncan, 1979; Wendt, 1979; Piazza, 1980). Perhaps the main difficulty here lies in the assumption that a set of attitude items is like a set of words in a spelling or vocabulary test. The latter can be thought of as a sample of more or less interchangeable elements from a population, even if the population cannot be readily enumerated. But attitude questions, especially those dealing with public issues, are much less interchangeable. Each one is apt to have unique meaning, so that its distinctive determinants are of importance in themselves, and not merely because they tap a single concept (for example, "authoritarianism") that is of interest to the social scientist. For all these reasons, plus the important practical constraint that even in the best surveys lack of time or anticipation prevents detailed measurement of every construct of interest, we do not regard the scaling approach as having solved the question wording problem.

Another reason for the decline of question-wording experiments lay in the ad hoc character of much of the early work. Even in terms of univariate results, larger theoretical issues of question construction and typology were seldom addressed in a sustained way, and there was little concern to replicate findings or to estimate the frequency, magnitude, or underlying nature of question-wording effects. For this reason, wording experiments have come to be treated anecdotally, reported as illustrative warnings in survey methods books, but not further developed theoretically or empirically. Our present research returns to the question wording experiments of four decades ago, but does so with a different focus, a more systematic concern with types of variations in survey questions, and improvements in methodological procedure and analysis.[1]

---

[1]In addition to our own research, which began unofficially in 1971 and more formally as a funded project in 1974, at least two other teams of investigators have recently begun similar research, one led by George Bishop, the other by Graham Kalton. We refer to their work at relevant points below. We would also like to acknowledge one little known early attempt at a systematic approach to question form, Tamulonis (1947). Although the results of her analysis are not readily usable, her organization of question-form variations was helpful to our early thinking.

A SYSTEMATIC APPROACH TO
QUESTION EFFECTS

Although our work draws on early question wording research, our goals differ from it in two important ways: We are concerned with associations as much as or more than with marginal effects, and we attempt to deal comprehensively with general features of question form, rather than with variations in particular words.

Marginals versus Relationships

Our investigation distinguishes sharply between two ways in which question variations may influence survey results. First, changes in question wording may affect univariate or marginal distributions. As noted before, this type of effect is commonly assumed in survey research, and sometimes leads investigators to place little credence in the absolute percentage giving any particular response. Reports of polls, however, often do present the marginals for a single question at a single point in time as though they have some absolute meaning, and it would be useful to have a better understanding of the likely sources and ranges of variation in such reports. Moreover, for one increasingly important use of surveys—charting trends in attitudes over time—changes in univariate distributions are at the center of interest.

Second, changes in question wording may affect the size or even the direction of relationships. As noted earlier, this type of effect is seldom addressed by investigators, and our reading of the survey literature suggests that most social scientists discount it. Although question marginals are often treated as unstable, relationships among attitude questions or between attitude questions and such background variables as education are almost always reported as though they are unlikely to change importantly with alterations in question wording.

Where question wording does alter marginals appreciably, it seemed to us likely that the persons who shifted would be distinctive in other ways as well. Our initial reasoning was that those most easily affected by variations in question form should tend to be less educated, as well as less interested or involved in the particular issues asked about. We thought better educated and more-informed respondents would more readily grasp the general point of a question and be less easily affected by emotionally colored words, though they should also be more sensitive to precise verbal distinctions where that is appropriate. Moreover, in several of the question variations studied, one form of the item can be seen as providing a new argument that less informed respondents might not have thought of independently and therefore one they might find persuasive, as Newcomb, Turner, and Converse (1965) suggest in a discussion of lack of information as a factor in attitude change. It also seemed likely that better educated respondents would be less deferential toward the interviewer and the questionnaire, and therefore more likely to insist on giving a sensible alternative answer (e.g., a midpoint between two polar positions) where it was not provided by the question. For these reasons, plus the general importance of years of schooling as both a cognitive and a status indicator, education is our most frequently used background variable. (Questions used to obtain education are shown in Appendix C, along with questions employed to measure information on issues.)

We also consider such other standard background factors as age and sex at most points, and we look systematically at the effects of question form on associations between attitude items themselves. Finally, the impact of attitude strength is investigated at a number of points, as well as being our main concern in Chapters 9 and 10.

A Typology of Question Forms

We decided at the beginning of our project to avoid a focus on isolated wording effects. A few interesting examples of this type are reported in Chapter 11, but our main goal has been to develop a typology of question forms that would classify all attitude items in terms of a relatively small number of important formal variations, so that samples of questions within each type could be selected or constructed. To the extent that the types reflect generic features of questions, findings based on experiments with these samples should have some generality.

In attempting to conceptualize general question forms, we took the standpoint of the survey investigator designing a questionnaire. Such investigators are confronted at each stage—whether or not they realize it—with a series of decisions about alternative forms for each question. These decisions are introduced next in roughly the order in which they occur, and are treated in detail in the chapters indicated.

Open versus Closed Questions

Perhaps the most basic decision an investigator must make is whether to leave a question open, or to close it by providing a set of fixed alternatives from which respondents can choose. On the one hand, the open form does not limit respondents to alternatives within the investigator's frame of reference, and it also avoids suggesting or imposing answers the respondent may not have considered. On the other hand, the closed form restricts responses to those germane to the researcher's aims and provides data in a form that is a great deal easier to code and analyze. The issue here, however, is whether the two forms yield basically the same results, and if not, why not. Given the antiquity of the controversy (see Lazarsfeld, 1944, for an early but still widely read statement), the general absence of split-ballot comparisons of the two forms is surprising.

Of course, here as with most decisions to be discussed, not every investigator relives past controversies and considers carefully the pros and cons of the decision for each question. The National Opinion Research Center's General Social Survey (GSS), for example, excludes all open questions on principle, probably because the GSS is geared to rapid and efficient distribution of data. The Institute for Social Research's Election Studies, by contrast, have maintained a fairly large number of open questions, despite their expensive and cumbersome nature. In our experience, most contemporary surveys are closer to the former than to the latter model. In any case, whether explicitly or implicitly, almost every survey item constructed or selected has involved an "open–closed" decision at some stage; we deal with this problem in Chapter 3.

The Don't Know Problem

On many issues, it seems likely that some people have no opinion. Although most survey investigators are willing to allow a don't know (DK) response to a question, they usually do so with considerable reluctance, since it reduces the effective sample size and representativeness for the item. Training manuals often urge interviewers not to accept DK too easily, on the assumption that it may represent only momentary hesitancy, and questionnaires frequently do not provide a DK option for interviewers to check. At the other extreme, some investigators include a DK alternative as an explicit part of the question, or even precede the question with a "DK filter" that asks whether the issue is one on which the respondent has an opinion. In Chapter 4 we examine the effects of encouraging or discouraging DK responses.

The problem of how to assess which respondents have no opinion about the object of an attitude question raises the more general issue of how respondents deal with subjects they know little or nothing about. In Chapter 5 we expand our investigation of the DK response into an exploration of the general concept of "nonattitudes" (Converse, 1970) by examining survey results for two issues unfamiliar to all respondents.

Middle Positions

In many cases a question has a logical "middle alternative": for example, *Do you think laws against the use of marijuana are too strict, too lenient, or about right?* Some investigators prefer to omit the middle alternative "about right," on the grounds that almost everyone really leans in one direction or the other on most issues, and that a middle alternative invites evasion. In Chapter 6 we consider the consequences of including or omitting middle alternatives in questions. An example of a longer scale (five categories) is also employed in these experiments.

Unbalanced Questions versus Balancing Attempts

Some questions can be considered unbalanced because they state only the affirmative side of the issue: for example, *Do you favor capital punishment?* A purely formal method of balancing is simply to include the negative: *Do you favor or oppose . . . ?* Some investigators feel that *either* of these questions on capital punishment is inherently imbalanced in a positive direction and that fairness requires the addition of a counterbalancing argument against the death penalty. We deal with these issues of balance and counterargument in Chapter 7.

Agree–Disagree Items

Statements read to (or by) respondents, which they can agree or disagree with, provide a rapid way of asking questions in surveys, as well as in self-administered questionnaires. Such propositions, however, are often viewed as involving a special form of imbalance, referred to by such varying terms as agreeing-response bias, acquiescence, or yeasaying. Large literatures in both psychology and sociology have developed over this single type of item and its presumed biasing effects. Chapter 8 discusses the general issue, presents experiments dealing with agree–disagree statements, and wrestles with the problem of what agreement with one-sided statements represents. In terms of results, this is a difficult chapter and it suggests that the acquiescence phenomenon is not as straightforward as has often been assumed.

Attitude Strength

It is widely recognized that simple pro and con positions tell us only a limited amount about attitudes and that one useful supplement is a measure of the strength or indeed passion with which attitudes are held. There are several distinguishable ways of conceptualizing this attribute: for example, "centrality," "intensity," and "extremity" (Scott, 1968). Moreover, the problem can be approached in other ways, such as attempting to gather evidence on actual behavior (e.g., *Have you ever donated money to the cause you favor?*). We will consider in Chapter 9 several experiments that explore the gain in understanding that comes from adding different types of strength measures to inquiries about attitudes.

Attitude Crystallization

In Chapter 10, the attitude-strength measures developed in the preceding chapter are related to the problems of item reliability over time and of interitem correlations. The term *attitude crystallization*, often used as an undefined metaphor in survey writings, is given an explicit definition (with reliability as one important component) and the relation between attitude strength and crystallization is discussed conceptually and tested empirically.

Tone of Wording

Although we concentrated most of our effort on systematic variations in question form, we did include several experiments on changes in more specific words. For example, we repeated and developed the forbid–allow experiment first reported by Rugg in 1941, and this is of interest not only as a replication more than three decades later, but also because political and moral issues are often cast in forbid or allow terms in survey questions. These "tone of wording" and some closely related experiments are reported in Chapter 11.

QUESTION FORM VERSUS QUESTION CONTENT

A basic issue needs to be confronted at this point. Some investigators might argue that *any* change in the wording of a question results in a uniquely new question. We do not accept this notion, and feel that it is useful to distinguish between certain formal features of question wording and the specific words used in any particular question. But the more practical and relevant side of the issue arises from the opposite direction, from changes in question content that are mistaken for "mere" changes in wording. Many of us tend to speak of public issues at a fairly high level of abstraction: the gun control issue, the abortion issue, and so forth. Yet it is clear that the general public, at least in the aggregate form represented by question marginals, often responds in terms of more concrete phrasing of issues, as indeed it should on an intelligent basis. Support for compulsory registration of guns is considerably greater than support for the banning of guns (Schuman and Presser, 1977–1978), hence "gun control" may not be a meaningful term to use in summary fashion, even though it may represent a theoretical construct or scale of interest to an investigator. Again, many more people believe in legalized abortion in the case of a defective fetus than believe in legalization of abortion on demand (NORC,1980), so there is no single public opinion on abortion as such. It is a serious mistake to see such differences in marginals as due only to alterations in question wording. Fundamentally different issues are involved and it is naïve for a reporter of results— whether a journalist or an academician—to talk generally in terms of opinion on abortion or gun control, ignoring the specificity of the actual items answered.

There are of course gray areas. Consider the following question (discussed in Chapter 11):

> *If a situation like Vietnam were to develop in another part of the world, do you think the United States should or should not send troops to stop a Communist takeover?*

Does the phrase "to stop a Communist takeover" constitute a specification of the issue, in which case it is a necessary part of the question? Or does it involve only a rhetorical device, a bugle call before the charge, aimed at influencing those who know nothing about Vietnam but respond to an anti-Communist appeal? This dilemma is probably impossible to resolve, and the true meaning may in fact differ for different respondents. Clearly there are alterations in question wording that are ambiguous with regard to whether the substantive question is altered in character or only in some secondary feature—reminiscent of the debates between philosophers over primary and secondary qualities of objects (Whitehead, 1925). We have tried to avoid this ambiguity by focusing on formal features of questions that are quite general, such as offering or not offering a DK alternative, though it will be obvious that at some points we were unsuccessful in maintaining this level of abstraction and became inextricably immersed in the gray area where changes in the wording of a question tend to become changes in the issue itself.

ORDER EFFECTS AND OTHER PROBLEMS

Questions do not, of course, appear in isolated form in surveys, but are always part of a larger sequence of questions, a questionnaire. A worrisome problem is whether answers to a given item are influenced by the particular question or questions that precede it. If such influence is pervasive, we can never talk of question effects—or indeed of any survey results—divorced from the context in which the questions were asked. Obviously the issue affects our research profoundly, as it does all attempts to generalize from survey data. We will refer to this problem as that of *question order,* and include within it both contextual factors of meaning and more mechanical sequence factors such as possible "fatigue effects."

A problem somewhat analogous to that of question order occurs within any closed item: the order of alternatives offered to a respondent. The *response-order* problem, as we will term it, is usually whether there is a *primacy* or *recency* effect, that is, whether there is a systematic tendency for respondents to choose the first or last alternative in a set. We shall deal with the problems of both response order and question order in Chapter 2, since they logically precede issues of specific types of questions.

There were certain additional problems that we would perhaps have preferred to avoid studying, since our research was already complex, yet which arose because of factors or events beyond our control. Thus some of the surveys we used were carried out by telephone interviewing and some by face-to-face interviewing, and in most instances this was not a matter of choice, nor (except in one survey) a matter under experimental control. Again, the surveys differ in response rates, and this unwanted difference may have affected our results. We do not have fully adequate evidence on either of these problems, and have not tried to focus on them in depth, but we do need to alert readers to the main issues and to present the evidence that is available. These and certain other related methodological problems are discussed in Appendix B.

THE PRINCIPLE OF QUESTION SELECTION

When scrutinized, almost every survey question is subject to criticism. Both in our own presentations and those of others, we have noted time and again the reaction that results should not be taken too seriously because the questions are flawed. Sometimes terms are ambiguous, sometimes the wording seems biased—there is no end to problems when one looks carefully at questionnaire items. Even the masters of survey research sometimes write questions that in retrospect seem questionable. Consider the following item by Stouffer (1955), one of the most highly respected of all survey investigators:

> *There are always some people whose ideas are considered bad or dangerous by other people. For instance, somebody who is against all churches and religion. If such a person wanted to make a speech in your (city/town/community) against churches and religion, should he be allowed to speak, or not?*

Why did Stouffer feel it necessary to begin this question by suggesting that atheists are considered "bad or dangerous?" It seems gratuitous and possibly biasing, although results of an experiment with the item (see Chapter 11) do not show clear effects of the phrase.

We naturally wanted to avoid using defective items, except as deliberate versions in an experiment, but we despaired of being able to construct questions immune from serious criticism. Moreover, an additional danger in constructing our own questions lay in developing a rarefied set of examples substantially different from those employed in standard surveys. Just as we needed to gather data from the same national population sampled in most surveys, so we needed, in an admittedly rough sense, to work from questionnaire items similar to those commonly used in survey research. These considerations led to our trying wherever possible to begin experiments with a question that had already been employed in an important survey, and only then to devise variations from it as part of the experiments. Thus many of the questions reported below come from surveys carried out by the Institute for Social Research (ISR), the National Opinion Research Center (NORC), Gallup, Harris, or other major survey organizations, and the reader who feels that the questions are imperfect should keep in mind that they are fairly typical survey items.

We have not stuck rigidly to the principle of prior use. In some cases questions were adapted or (we think) improved. In other cases it was necessary to construct entirely new questions, because we could not locate suitable existing items for the specific purpose at hand. For the majority of experiments reported in this book, however, one form of the question is taken exactly or adapted in only minor ways from a previous questionnaire that had been developed as part of a substantive investigation by others. The source is normally given when the question is first presented.

THE SOURCES OF OUR EXPERIMENTAL DATA

Our data come from over 200 experiments that we conducted over the past decade in more than 30 different surveys. Basic information on these surveys is given in Table 1.1. This table also contains a key to the abbreviations used throughout the book in referring to particular surveys (e.g., SRC–74 Fall designates the survey described in the third row of Table 1.1).

The surveys themselves are diverse in several respects. Prior to the actual beginning of the project, several experiments were designed for the 1971 Detroit Area Study (DAS) and later for the 1974 NORC General Social Survey. Our first attempt at systematic experimentation used the 1974 Survey Research Center (SRC) national Omnibus Survey. Most of the respondents from this SRC–74 Fall face-to-face survey were reinterviewed a few months later as part of a 1975 telephone survey and this allowed us to collect much of the panel data employed in the book. After 1975 we moved, for reasons of cost and speed, mainly to ongoing SRC national telephone surveys. As Table 1.1 shows, there have been a large number of these, most involving only a few experiments. In 1976, we were able to include three experiments in a study by Groves and Kahn (1979) that was itself an experimental comparison of face-to-face and telephone modes of interviewing. Also in 1976 a large set of experiments was included in the Detroit Area Study; in addition to replications and extensions of earlier work, our first experiments with open and closed questions were developed at that point. And in 1978 we had a further opportunity to build three experiments into the NORC General Social Survey. Altogether we draw on experiments from 34 different surveys.

METHOD OF ANALYSIS

Most of our results appear in the form of cross-classifications. The form of the question, assigned randomly to respondents, is the experimental factor, and is treated as an independent variable.[2] Responses to

---

[2]Questionnaire forms were randomized by cover-sheet instructions so that the randomization operates not only over the sample as a whole, but within sample clusters and within interviewers as well. Where only two random subsamples were created, their N's should be approximately equal in tables. Where three subsamples were created, however, N's will be approximately equal only where three distinct question forms were developed. In some surveys three random subsamples were needed for certain experiments but not for others; in the latter cases one question form was administered to two subsamples and the other

the question provide the categories of a dependent variable. Such a simple bivariate table is tested for statistical significance using the likelihood-ratio χ^2 (chi square) with probabilities evaluated as two-tailed. A probability of less than .10 is ordinarily regarded as borderline, $p < .05$ as significant, and $p < .01$ as highly significant.[3] The term *significant* is always intended in its statistical sense, unless context clearly indicates otherwise.

Since we are also interested in the effect of question form on associations between responses to the question and some other set of responses (either from another attitude question or from a background variable such as education), many of our analyses test whether the associations in two tables differ significantly. In evaluating such three-way interactions (response to one item by response to another item by question form) we use the method of log-linear analysis explicated in Goodman (1978), and employ the computer program ECTA (Fay and Goodman, 1973). Occasionally an analysis requires a four- or even five-way test of interaction; essentially the same procedures are followed in such cases.

Whereas many of the tables analyzed make use of only a nominal level of measurement, in some cases a variable is legitimately and efficiently regarded as ordinal. In particular, we often consider a form difference in the relation of a dichotomous attitude item to education, the latter treated as a three-category (0–11, 12, 13+) or five-category (0–8, 9–11, 12, 13–15, 16+ years of schooling) variable. In such cases, we need an ordinal measure of association to test statistical significance. We have found that the Goodman–Kruskal gamma and the effect parameter (lambda) for linearity produced by ECTA yield very similar probability levels in most cases, though the former tests only for monotonicity and the latter

---

form to one subsample, creating a ratio of N's of approximately 2 to 1. Furthermore, in these instances, and also where panel data involved administering varying question forms to the same respondents at two different points in time, the terms *question form* and *questionnaire form* are not synonymous as they are in all other instances. Where ambiguity would arise, we retain the term *form* to refer to variations in questions, and use *subsample* to refer to random divisions of the total sample.

Missing data are generally omitted from tables *except* where they are important to an experimental comparison, but we have looked at all full tables ourselves so far as possible and comment on any missing data categories that appear meaningful. See also the discussion in Appendix B.4.

[3] We have used tests assuming simple random sampling, since a number of calculations indicated that design effects due to clustering are quite small in these attitude experiments. See Appendix B.1. The likelihood-ratio χ^2 and the more common Pearson χ^2 ordinarily yield quite similar results, but the former has the advantage of allowing exact partitioning of tables. (We use the symbol χ^2 because of its familiarity to most readers, although other notation is now beginning to appear in the statistical literature.)

TABLE 1.1
Sources and Description of Experimental Survey Data

Organization–year	Month-Season	Population	Mode	Final N	Response rate (%)	No. of forms	Experimental items	Notes
DAS-71	May–Aug.	Metr. Detr.	F	1881	80.2	2	19	
NORC–74	Spring	National	F	1484	Not reported	2	2	
SRC–74	Fall	National	F	1519	73.8	3	20	
SRC–75	Feb.	National	T	1374	50.5	3	15	a
SRC–76	Feb.	National	T	1269	46.0	2	13	
SRC–76	Spring	National	T	1688	70.6 ⎫	2	4	b
			F	1548	74.3 ⎭			
DAS–76	May–Aug.	Metr. Detr.	F	896	75.4	2	18	
SRC–77	Feb.	National	T	426/777	72.8/44.0	2	6	
SRC–77	Aug.	National	T	579/635	62.4/36.0	2	5	c
SRC–78	Feb.	National	T	629/647	67.6/44.8	2	2	
SRC–78	Mar.	National	T	390/403	68.4/54.6	2	3	
SRC–78	May	National	T	655/643	67.8/41.7	2	5	
NORC–78	Spring	National	F	1532	73.5	2	3	
SRC–78	Aug.	National	T	365/820	64.7/47.6	2	12	
SRC–78	Oct. ⎫	National	T	356	59.7	3	11	d
SRC–78	Nov. ⎬ Fall	National	T	720	69.6	3	11	d
SRC–78	Dec. ⎭	National	T	521	66.5	3	11	d
SRC–79	Jan.	National	T	598	69.0	2	3	
SRC–79	Mar.	National	T	534	72.9	1	2	
SRC–79	Apr.	National	T	730	72.6	2	6	
SRC–79	June	National	T	651	74.2	2	4	
SRC–79	July	National	T	509	69.8	2	5	
SRC–79	Aug.	National	T	679	66.1	2	8	
SRC–79	Sept.	National	T	523/420	72.1/57.3	3	9	e

SRC-79	Oct.	National	T	392	58.5	1	1	f
SRC-79	Nov.	National	T	759	72.7	2	1	
SRC-80	Feb.	National	T	470/518	68.8/50.4	2	6	
U/M-80	Feb.	Students	F	382	73.9	1	1	g
SRC-80	Mar.	National	T	290	39.6	1	1	h
NORC-80	Spring	National	F	1468	75.9	3	1	
SRC-80	May	National	T	374	68.1	2	2	
SRC-80	June	National	T	369/319	69.8/54.7	2	6	
SRC-80	July	National	T	356	66.9	2	2	
SRC-80	Sept.	National	T	395/273	67.6/51.6	2	4	i

Explanations of terms in Table 1.1. Column Headings:

Organization: *DAS* is the Detroit Area Study conducted by the University of Michigan (U/M). (See also Population.) *NORC* is the National Opinion Research Center, University of Chicago; all recent NORC surveys referred to in this book come from NORCs General Social Survey (GSS), carried out since 1972 (see NORC, 1980). *SRC* is the Survey Research Center of the University of Michigan's Institute for Social Research (ISR); in 1974 and 1976, SRC carried out general-purpose or omnibus surveys, but in later years the SRC surveys we used were primarily aimed at assessing consumer behavior.

Year: The year in which a survey was carried out is abbreviated to the last two digits. It is combined with the organizational prefix (and usually month or season) to provide an abbreviated reference to the surveys discussed throughout the text—e.g., NORC-74 or U/M-80 or SRC-80 March.

Month-Season: If a survey was administered within a single month, the month is ordinarily abbreviated. Otherwise, a span of months or a season is given. (In later text, the month or season is not given if the survey is uniquely identified by organization and year.)

Population: The national population sampled by both SRC and NORC is the noninstitutional population of the 48 coterminous states. The metropolitan Detroit population sampled by DAS included the city and surrounding suburbs in 1971, and the entire Detroit Standard Metropolitan Statistical Area (SMSA) in 1976. All such surveys considered persons 18 years and over as eligible respondents, but there are some small differences among surveys in the ways respondents were chosen within households. (See Bianchi, 1976; NORC, 1980; and Surveys of Consumer Attitudes, 1980, for technical reports.)

Mode: "F" indicates interviews that were obtained on a face-to-face basis; "T" indicates interviews obtained by telephone. In SRC-76 Spring, separate telephone and face-to-face samples were interviewed (see Appendix B.2).

Final *N*: This is the total number of interviews in the survey, although some "missing data" (particularly break-offs in the phone samples) often reduce the analytic samples slightly. Some surveys consisted of two parts, a new random-digit-dial (RDD) sample and a reinterview sample several months later; the *N* for the RDD components is given first, followed by the reinterview *N*. When only a single figure is given, it represents a new probability sample: RDD for the telephone surveys and area probability for the face-to-face surveys (excepting NORC-74, which employed quotas at the block level; SRC-75 Feb. and SRC-76 Feb., which are recontacts of face-to-face surveys; and U/M-80, which drew a systematic random sample from the student directory).

(Continued)

TABLE 1.1—*Continued*

Response rates: Response rates (i.e., interviews actually obtained divided by total number of eligible respondents) are those reported by the organization that conducted the survey. A single figure, unless otherwise noted, represents a response rate for an original RDD or probability sample. For two-part samples, the rates for both the RDD and the reinterview components are given. The reinterview rate is always lower because it is a function of an original RDD response rate times the response rate for the reinterviews. See also Appendix B.3.

Forms: Experimental variations were carried out by using either two (2) or three (3) randomly assigned questionnaire forms. Exceptions occur for within-sample designs using only one form.

Experimental items: This is the total number of items that enter into our analysis from a given survey, excluding background variables such as education or an information measure. An item is counted only once even if it appeared on two or three forms. The count is approximate since some items are ambiguous in status (e.g., a question and its separate filter are here counted as a single item, but might be counted as two).

Table Notes

[a] In SRC–75 February, 1077 of the interviews were with respondents who had originally been interviewed in SRC–74 Fall; hence these data allow panel analysis. (Form of item was deliberately varied between the first and second experiment in most instances.) The remaining 297 cases were reinterviews of respondents from an earlier survey in which we did not have questions, hence these respondents are not included in the panel analysis.

[b] SRC–76 Spring was an experimental comparison of independent samples, part obtained by telephone and part by face-to-face interview. (See Appendix B.2.)

[c] SRC–77 August included reinterviews with a subsample of respondents originally interviewed in SRC–77 February, thus providing a small amount of panel data.

[d] Most experiments in the SRC–78 October, November, and December surveys were identical in order to provide a larger sample for analysis, and are thus designated SRC–78 Fall. However, for certain items only two months are available, and for one item only a single month.

[e] SRC–79 September included reinterviews with a sample of respondents originally interviewed in SRC–78 March for two items dealing with abortion (Chapter 10).

[f] SRC–79 October data are only for reinterviews from SRC–79 April for the standard form of an item on the Monetary Trade Bill (Chapter 5).

[g] This probability sample of students from The University of Michigan's College of Literature, Science, and the Arts was used to replicate a context experiment on student-party preference (see Chapter 2, p. 41). Interviews were carried out by students in a research methods course taught by the senior author. The student directory, checked for accuracy, was used for sampling.

[h] The response rate for SRC–80 March was very low because it was a third-wave reinterview of respondents interviewed first in SRC–79 March and then in SRC–79 September. (See Chapter 10.)

[i] The reinterview portion of this sample came from the SRC–80 June RDD sample. In September the respondents received experimentally varied versions of questions asked originally in the June survey. The full September sample is also used for cross-sectional analysis in Chapter 7.

for linearity. We have ordinarily used gamma for bivariate tables, but for multivariate tables we use lambda, transforming it for simplicity (by squaring its standardized value) into a χ^2. (The term "linear χ^2" is employed for this test in later tables and text.) This introduces an inelegant mixture of different statistics, but it proved the most efficient way to proceed, given the large number of tables we analyzed.

Emphasis on significance testing is sometimes deprecated on the grounds that investigators should be concerned with estimating the magnitude of effects, not merely whether they are different from zero. Moreover, measures of association control for variations in sample size that make direct comparisons among significance levels impossible. We often do provide estimates of magnitude, using gamma for most 2 × 2 tables and for larger bivariate tables with ordinal level variables;[4] odds ratios at points where they are especially enlightening;[5] and of course percentage differences throughout—implicitly or explicitly—since most of our tables are presented in percentage form. (We treat percentage differences with caution where variables are highly skewed, since in such cases they lead to conclusions at variance with measures based on log-linear assumptions, and it is the latter that guide our analysis.)[6] But

[4]Although gamma is ordinarily used below as a simple summary measure for tables involving two different variables, we employ phi (equivalent to the Pearson *r*) for the special case where reliability of a single dichotomous item over time is estimated. In these latter cases, assuming no true change, the marginals do not constrain the association to be less than 1.0 and we prefer to avoid the ambiguities of gamma. The point is seldom of great import, and in one matrix (Table 10.2) where we computed both gammas and phis, their rank order correlation (Spearman's rho) was .88.

[5]For readers unfamiliar with odds ratios, it may be noted that unlike most measures of association, 1.0 represents complete absence of a relation, with deviations in either direction from 1.0 representing an increasing relation. See Duncan and Duncan, 1978, Appendix A, for a discussion of odds ratios and their relation to chi square statistics.

[6]A good example of how an analyst may be led to divergent conclusions depending on whether percentage differences or odds ratios are used occurs for the 1974 Russia no opinion experiment (Chapter 4). Here is a summary table of percentage don't know by education by question form (with base *N*'s shown in parentheses).

	Education		
	0–11	12	13+
Standard DK form	27.2%	12.7%	7.9%
	(151)	(157)	(190)
Filtered DK form	58.5%	37.1%	21.9%
	(147)	(175)	(187)
Percentage differences	31.3	24.4	14.0
Odds ratios	.26	.25	.30

for the contingency tables dealt with in this book, different ways of measuring magnitude can yield different conclusions and therefore no estimated magnitude can be definitive, even apart from sampling error. Equally important, with national samples of the size employed in most of our work, statistically significant results—especially for higher-order interactions—are by no means as easy to obtain as is often assumed by the inexperienced analyst. Indeed, as shown in Appendix A, the establishment of the reliability of effects, in and of itself, is more problematic than many users of survey data realize. Yet demonstrating reliability of results is crucial in an investigation that attempts to chart a largely unexplored area. For this reason significance testing is indispensable to our research, although we attempt throughout to be sensitive to factors such as sample size that are critical to evaluating obtained levels of significance. We also recognize, of course, that the null hypothesis may best be regarded as a heuristic fiction; failure to reject it can be translated into a statement such as "we are uncertain even as to direction of a difference in this case and at any rate it is probably too close to zero to be of importance." (For a similar justification of the use of the null hypothesis, see Kruskal, 1968, especially p. 246.)

Beyond the magnitude and significance level of any given finding, we have placed considerable emphasis in our research on replicating important results. Replication can be carried out at several levels (see Lykken, 1968), but simple success at exact or literal replication would seem to be the sine qua non of trustworthy social research. The pervasiveness of random error, which is heightened by the necessarily exploratory nature of thorough survey analysis, means that all statistics (including those estimating error) are only estimates, and our best assurance for the reliability of a finding is the ability to obtain it again in situations where there is every reason to expect it to occur. This did not always happen in our investigations, and in Appendix A we describe some puzzling in-

---

Examination of the percentage differences suggests a form effect that decreases with education: The difference across forms for the low-educated respondents (31.3%) is more than twice as large as that for the college-educated group (14.0%), and the pattern across the three education groups appears linear. But examination of the odds ratios yields a very different conclusion. The linearity is gone—the pattern is no longer even monotonic—and the differences among the three educational groups are quite small. This impression is confirmed by the χ^2 testing the three-way interaction, which is only .24 for the full $2 \times 3 \times 2$ table ($df = 2$), and only .13 if the linear trend is tested ($df = 1$). (For further discussion of these results, see Schuman and Presser, 1977: footnote 9.) Such marked divergence between conclusions based on percentage differences and conclusions based on odds ratios will occur only where the extreme tails of the percentage distributions are involved (e.g., 7.9% in this table). For a discussion of the difference between percentage scales and log-odds scales, see Goodman, 1975.

stances of non-replication that have persuaded us even more strongly of the crucial role that replication must play in this type of research. Of course, there are certain cases where nonreplication can plausibly be ascribed to real changes in attitudes (Chapter 4 presents an important nonreplication that we believe is best explained in this way), but for the kinds of experiments and time periods we deal with, nonreplication due to real change must be regarded as the exception rather than the rule.

Significance tests, measures of association, and efforts at literal replication are all ways of assuring ourselves and our readers that we are talking about facts of some empirical import. Equally essential is understanding what these facts mean and testing this understanding wherever possible by deriving new hypotheses that lead to further experimental results, including replications that are at the level of construct validation. Each of the succeeding chapters moves in this direction, and our interpretations try to bring into balance both statistical results and the theoretical sense they make. In some places we feel that a satisfactory theoretical interpretation has been arrived at, whereas in other areas not even a tentative sense of closure seems possible at this point. Throughout the book, however, results are reported in sufficient detail to contribute to a larger picture of the effects of question form, wording, and order that survey research must attempt to develop.

2

Question Order and Response Order

Des Moines, Iowa—A criminal trial scheduled for next week has been delayed because of the higher standard of morality that might exist in Des Moines as a result of the Pope's four-hour visit Thursday.

Ronald Arthur Massey of Des Moines had been scheduled to go on trial next week on a charge of keeping a house of prostitution. But his lawyer, Alfredo Parrish, went to court seeking a delay. Mr. Parrish argued that the papal visit "creates the immense possibility that the standard of morality may be magnified 50-fold, causing an adverse effect on the defendant."

—*The New York Times*, Sept. 29, 1979

A major threat to the interpretation of any question form difference—or indeed any survey result at all—is the possible impact of preceding parts of the questionnaire. What looks to be a response due to question form or content may in fact be partly or entirely due to question *order*. Moreover, order effects can conceivably occur within questions, as well as between them, and such unintended response-order effects may be confounded with more deliberate experimental variations in question form.[1]

One aim of this chapter is to assess the seriousness of these problems for our experiments on question form. But the issue of order effects between and within questions is of great importance to survey research more generally and our review and results are therefore presented here for their own sake, as well as being preliminary to later chapters.

---

[1]Terminology for these problems is not uniform in the research literature. In this book, we will use *question order* to refer to relations among questions, and include under it the subsidiary terms *context effects* (for transfers of meaning) and *sequence effects* (for other more mechanical types of artifacts). We use *response order* to refer to the listing of alternatives within a closed question.

QUESTION-ORDER EFFECTS

Apart from sampling error, question-order effects are probably the most frequently offered explanation for an unexpected or unreplicated survey finding. Since individual survey questions are not asked in isolation, but as part of a continuous flow of items, the context in which any question appears, or its position in a sequence of items, may conceivably influence the answers given to it. The problem is a potentially serious one for several reasons. First, any attempt to generalize about survey results is suspect if they might be a function of a particular order of questions. This is true for the methodological generalizations about question form reported in this book, just as it is true for the substantive conclusions that appear in other reports of survey results, whether in brief newspaper columns on polls or in extended analysis in academic monographs. Furthermore, for trend studies, question order effects are important even if they merely shift marginals, since the primary results of such studies are nothing more than changes in marginals. Consequently, unless an entire questionnaire can be repeated, inferences about the relation of any item to time will be compromised if a question-order effect exists. Finally, since question-order effects are usually assumed to arise because items similar in content influence one another, their prevention calls for separating such items in an interview. Yet the smooth organization of a questionnaire ordinarily requires asking similar items together, so as to make the interview seem sensible and coherent to respondents. Thus the design of questionnaires for ease of interviewing is at cross-purposes with the avoidance of order effects.

For all these reasons, one might expect to find a substantial literature on question-order effects. In fact, however, the number of experimental studies is not large, and if restricted to surveys of the general population, there are probably no more than two dozen reports in English over the past 50 years. Most of these describe a single one-shot experiment, with little sign of cumulative knowledge and understanding. Moreover, there are nearly as many reports of no or trivial order effects as there are of important effects. At present, therefore, the frequency, size, and nature of question-order effects in standard surveys of the general population are matters of considerable uncertainty. There is little doubt that they can occur, but whether they are rare or common is unknown, and the forces that produce them are only beginning to be conceptualized.

We will present seven question-order experiments from our more recent research, describe more briefly seven sets of experiments from DAS–71, and review all the trustworthy experimental reports by others that we have been able to locate in the survey literature.[2] Results are grouped under conceptual headings so far as possible, but as will be noted, it is difficult to develop mutually exclusive categories, let alone a dynamic classification that points clearly to causes.

THE FREQUENCY OF QUESTION-ORDER EFFECTS IN AN ATTITUDE SURVEY

Before looking in detail at individual experiments designed in many cases to produce order effects, it is useful to obtain some rough sense of how frequently such effects occur when they are *not* intended. The 1971 Detroit Area Study (DAS-71) was an investigation of social change, and it therefore repeated attitude questions from nine previous surveys covering a wide range of issues and topics.[3] Most of the questions were constant over all respondents, but the hour-long questionnaire had two forms in order to allow a number of split-ballot variations in either question wording or question order. The first departure from constant

[2]We have drawn on bibliographies provided by Bradburn (1978), Kalton *et al.* (1978), and our own searches, with concentration on studies that offer reasonably adequate information based on general population samples. This excludes such reports as Duverger's (1964) mention of an order effect in a French poll on varying degrees of punishment for collaborators after World War II. Although a 6% difference due to order is noted, no measures of significance or sample size are provided, nor any identification or description of the poll itself. Such a result is of uncertain empirical value and since it introduces no new theoretical point, we see little reason to consider it a useful datum. At the same time, there are a number of rather artificial classroom studies by psychologists that involve context and report significant order effects. For example, Nakamura (1959) shows that when a question refers to an ideal norm of behavior it is likely to influence an immediately succeeding question in which an individual is asked to describe his own intended behavior in the same area. Such studies seem worth drawing on when they provide theoretical insight into the nature of order effects, but not as evidence for the likelihood or size of such effects in realistic general population surveys. We also do not refer in detail to reports that seem to us unclear in meaning, such as an experiment described by Rugg and Cantril (1944) on whether the United States was seen to be at war in 1939; or those that are so highly particularized as to have little implication for questionnaires in general, as is true both of another Rugg and Cantril (1944) experiment on draft-age limits and of an experiment dealing with foods reported by Noelle-Neumann (1970–1971). (Other Rugg and Cantril, 1944, order experiments are discussed later in this chapter, and Noelle-Neumann's work is also drawn on at a later point.)

[3]An overview of the substantive parts of the study appears in Duncan, Schuman, and Duncan (1973), and a more intensive analysis of much of the data is reported by Duncan and Duncan (1978). The total number of interviews for this survey was 1881, which is fairly large by usual standards, though some of the questions were asked only of subsamples (e.g., mothers).

questions occurred after the first 17 attitude questions, and there were additional variations at fairly frequent intervals thereafter.

Here our interest is not in the deliberate order experiments themselves, which will be described at appropriate points in this chapter, but in the so-called constant items. These were not intended to be influenced by order, but were perhaps affected nevertheless, for once a single order or other experimental variation is created, *all* subsequent items are placed in different contexts. Thus, question 34, although identical on the two forms of the DAS–71 questionnaire (which were physically separate and even differently colored), could have produced results different by form due to the interaction of its wording with the series of experimental variations that began at question 18 and extended through question 33. This may be even more true of constant items that occur later in the questionnaire, since they appeared on two forms that had, so to speak, quite different historical developments. We can get some sense, therefore, of the vulnerability of ordinary attitude items to accidental context effects by comparing differences in marginals between questionnaire forms for all items preceded by, but not directly involved in, experiments.[4]

For DAS–71 we identified 113 attitude items that were not the intended objects of experiments, but occurred after the experiments began. Assuming independence, one might expect just 1 of these items to show by chance a difference between the two questionnaire forms registering as significant at the .01 level, whereas we find 3. One might expect 6 differences significant at the .05 level, whereas we find 8 (including the 3 that reach the .01 level). We examined carefully the 8 items significant at the .05 level and concluded that 3 of them (including 2 at the .01 level) are reasonably explicable in terms of a preceding variation in the questionnaire, while the remaining 5 seem quite inexplicable and are probably due to sampling error.[5]

[4]Several of the "constant items" were actually parts of an order experiment, serving to separate agree–disagree items from one another on one form, but placed before the same items on the other form. (See page 53 for an account of this experiment.) It was not expected that the "buffer items" would be affected by their placement, and we include them among the constant items in the present analysis. Although two of them are in the group reported below to show meaningful differences between forms, this is probably not due to their involvement as buffer items in the order experiment, but because of experimental variation in the wording of an earlier item (see footnote 5).

[5]Two of the three interpretable effects involve items that are contiguous and follow closely another question that was similar in content but experimentally varied in wording (see Schuman and Duncan, 1974, pp. 240–249, for a discussion of the latter and of its relation to one of the former). The remaining interpretable effect involves an item that immediately follows an order experiment on a series of political efficacy items (discussed on pages 53–55); since it is somewhat related in content, it may have been affected by changes in the order of the political items.

In sum, there are a few more unintended effects attributable to order than would be expected in terms of sampling error in DAS–71, but not a great many more. One hundred and five of the items do not show significant form differences, and this includes most of those near the end of the questionnaire, which means they had followed many previous variations in order. Such results suggest that order effects are not pervasive in a typical attitude survey. This is not to say that they are unimportant, or that they cannot occur unexpectedly, for just the opposite will be demonstrated below; but these summary findings put the problem in some perspective and indicate the need to determine exactly where and how such effects do occur.

TYPES OF RELATIONS AMONG QUESTIONS AND TYPES OF ORDER EFFECTS

Virtually all reported question-order effects involve two or more questions that deal with the same or similar issues. It is useful, however, to distinguish what we will call part–whole combinations of questions from part–part combinations. Part–whole combinations involve two or more questions where one question is more general and is intended to contain, summarize, or imply another in some important sense, but not necessarily the reverse. For example, theoretically, a question on happiness in general should tend to summarize questions on happiness about one's marriage, one's job, etc. Of course, the summary is not absolute, since one could be generally happy (or unhappy) but at the same time report an unhappy (or happy) marriage. In another and even stronger sense—that of Guttman unidimensional scaling—yes to a question about legalizing abortions on demand implies yes to questions about legalizing abortion for more specific reasons (e.g., in case of pregnancy due to rape). These two types of part–whole relations are not precisely the same, but in both examples one question is more general than the other, and we will include them under the same broad heading.

Part–part relations involve questions that are at the same level of specificity. For example, a question about allowing Soviet reporters to travel in the United States and a question about allowing American reporters to travel in the Soviet Union stand in part–part relation. Neither question includes or summarizes the other, though of course they may have implications for each other.

When we turn from types of relations between questions to types of effects, the classification is somewhat tighter. There are two possibilities: consistency and contrast. Consistency effects occur when responses to a later question are brought closer than they would otherwise be to those already given to an earlier question. The assumption is that the respondent needs to feel, or at least to appear, consistent in his or her answers. Contrast effects, on the other hand, lead to greater differences between responses to two or more questions as a result of their ordering. It is less evident why this would occur, but we will present examples below.

Part–Part Consistency Effects

Communist and American Reporters

This type of question-order effect occurs when respondents try to appear consistent and therefore bring a response to a later item into line with a response to an earlier one that is similar in some important respect. Hyman and Sheatsley (1950) report such an order effect from a 1948 NORC experiment on American and Communist reporters, based on the questions shown in Table 2.1. We repeated the experiment exactly in 1980, and when the 1948 and 1980 results are considered together, the comparison across time in Table 2.1 raises issues for attitude surveys that are of profound importance.[6]

Table 2.1 shows, first, a large and highly significant order effect in both years. Respondents are more likely to allow Communist reporters into the United States after having answered a question about allowing American reporters into Communist countries, and they are less likely to want American reporters admitted to Communist countries after answering the question on letting Communist reporters into the United States. The obvious interpretation is that when either question is asked first, many respondents answer in terms of pro-American or anti-Communist sentiments, but when the second question is asked a norm of reciprocity is immediately made salient and a substantial number of respondents feel bound to follow that norm and provide an answer that is consistent with their previous response (cf. Gouldner, 1960). Cross-tabulations (not shown here) of the two items in 1980 suggest that this simple consistency interpretation for the effect is due almost entirely to a shift from approval to both questions (when the American reporter

[6]There were actually two replications in 1980, one in SRC–80 May and a second in SRC–80 July in order to be more certain of the May findings. The two replications produced almost identical results (see Table 2.1 footnote) and are pooled here to save space. We are indebted to Patrick Bova, Herbert Hyman, and Paul Sheatsley for helping us locate the relevant 1948 baseline data and for providing additional useful information on the original experiment.

TABLE 2.1
Order Effects on Communist and American Newspaper Reporter Items in 1948 and 1980[a]

Communist reporter item: *Do you think the United States should let Communist newspaper reporters from other countries come in here and send back to their papers the news as they see it?*
American reporter item: *Do you think a Communist country like Russia should let American newspaper reporters come in and send back to America the news as they see it?*

Year	Order Com/Amer	Amer/Com	Test	χ^2	df	p
Percentage yes to Communist reporter item:						
1948	36.5% (581)	73.1% (635)	Order effect in 1948	168.17	1	.001
1980	54.7% (342)	74.6% (335)	Order effect in 1980	29.76	1	.001
			Year effect for Com./Amer. order	28.97	1	.001
			Year effect for Amer./Com. order	.27	1	n.s.
			Three-way: response × order × year	10.07	1	.01
Percentage yes to American reporter item:						
1948	65.6% (567)	89.8% (635)	Order effect in 1948	101.68	1	.001
1980	63.7% (336)	81.9% (331)	Order effect in 1980	28.23	1	.001
			Year effect for Com./Amer. order	.34	1	n.s.
			Year effect for Amer./Com. order	11.55	1	.001
			Three-way: response × order × year	5.76	1	.02

[a] The 1948 data are from NORC Survey 159 DU-1, with DK responses ranging from 5.6–8.3% omitted. The 1980 data are from SRC–80 May and SRC–80 July combined, with DK responses ranging from 1.5–2.9% omitted. The percentages for the May and July surveys considered separately in no case depart by more than 3% from the corresponding combined figures shown in Table 2.1.

question comes first) to disapproval to both (when the Communist reporter question comes first); the proportion of respondents willing to approve one type of reporting but not the other is essentially unaffected by question order.

Considering now only answers to the Communist reporter question, the table shows that the order effect leads to diametrically different conclusions about the direction of attitude change over the three decades. If we use the Communist–American order from 1948 as the baseline, then replication of that same order (or of the Communist item alone) reveals an 18% increase in willingness to allow Communist reporters into this country, presumably because of a lessened fear of Communists. But if the American–Communist order had provided the baseline data from 1948, then use in 1980 of either the other order or simply the Communist reporter item alone would lead to exactly the opposite conclusion: a drop of 18% ($\chi^2 = 33.25$, $df = 1$, $p < .001$) in willingness to allow Communist reporters into the United States.

The natural solution would seem to be to repeat the exact context when replicating items to study change. But the results for the Communist item in Table 2.1 demonstrate that even this strategy cannot always solve the problem. The two contexts, even when held constant, lead to different conclusions: When the Communist item comes first, there is the rise of 18% already noted; when it comes second there is no significant change. Keeping context constant cannot produce unequivocal conclusions with respect to direction of change for the Communist reporter item. Moreover, this point, along with the preceding ones, holds for the American reporter item as well.

The crux of the matter seems to be that the reporter questions have two meanings, one involving an attitude toward an object and the other an attitude toward a norm. Moreover, this is *not* because the questions are ambiguous in a way that might have been avoided by more careful question construction and pretesting. The ambiguity has to do with the nature of language, the fact that words and sentences take part of their meaning from the context in which they occur (cf. Searle, 1979). The results in Table 2.1 indicate that attitudes toward Communist reporters have changed substantially since 1948, but that the strength of the norm of reciprocity in this application has remained about the same over that period. Having both contexts at both points in time allows us to see the two trends clearly, though it cannot but leave one wondering about other trends that are invisible for this or other items because of the absence of systematic contextual variation.

Analysis of the 1980 reporters experimental data by education reveals a further important finding, as shown in Table 2.2. The effect of order on responses is located mainly among those with less than college experience and tends to disappear among the college educated. The three-way interaction reaches significance only for responses to the American item, but both items show the same trends and we suspect that both are reliable. (Similar trends occur in both the May and July 1980 surveys considered separately, and in the original 1948 data as well.) We believe that the interaction arises mainly from the fact that most college educated respondents are agreeable to allowing Communist reporters into the United States even when that question is asked first, and thus they are not "caught" when the item is asked second and the norm of reciprocity is brought into play. There is thus a kind of ceiling effect operating for the college educated, though it is not exactly an artifactual one. For the noncollege population, however, the disjunction between attitudes toward Communism and the response required by the reciprocity norm is large indeed, and it is therefore these

TABLE 2.2
Percentage Saying Yes to Each Reporters Item by Order and Education in 1980

	Education			gamma	SE
	0–11	12	13+		
Communist reporters					
Order: Com./Amer.	24.3% (70)	43.4% (122)	78.0% (141)	.66	.06
Order: Amer./Com.	53.6% (69)	76.2% (105)	84.3% (153)	.45	.09
Odds ratios	.28	.24	.66		
	Response × order × education: linear χ^2 = 3.32, df = 1, p < .10				
American reporters					
Order: Com./Amer.	34.8% (66)	57.7% (123)	82.6% (138)	.60	.07
Order: Amer./Com.	68.2% (66)	83.7% (104)	87.6% (153)	.36	.11
Odds ratios	.25	.27	.67		
	Response × order × education: linear χ^2 = 3.99, df = 1, p < .05				

people for whom question order becomes of great importance in defining the meaning of the item in a way that changes responses.[7]

Other Examples of Part–Part Consistency Effects

We have located two similar examples of part–part consistency effects. One is reported by Rugg and Cantril (1944):

> *Should the United States permit its citizens to join the French and British armies?*   (Yes: 45%)

[7]In an effort to clarify the reporter results further we included in the SRC–80 July survey an additional item on perceptions of Communism: *When you think of Communism, do you feel extremely negative, somewhat negative, or not very negative?* (The item was placed near the end of the survey, separated from the reporter items by about 25 questions on automobile purchases.) It turns out that the order effect is located primarily among those with the strongest antipathy toward Communism. This seems surprising if we proceed on the assumption that it is people with the least intense feelings on an issue who should be most affected by context, but the explanation is partly similar to that for education. Those who feel most strongly opposed to Communism generally are most likely to want to exclude Communist reporters from the United States, but most likely also (and this differs from the low education result) to want American reporters allowed into the USSR—when *either item is asked first*. Thus they are under more pressure to change when either item is asked second. Moreover, the order effect disappears most completely among persons who are *both* college educated and feel less negative toward Communism: Almost all these people agree to having Communist reporters enter the United States even when the question is asked first, hence there is little room for the reciprocity norm to operate.

Should the United States permit its citizens to join the German army?   (Yes: 31%)

When the order of the items is reversed from that just given, the percentage saying yes to the German question drops by 9% (to 22%) and the percentage saying yes to the French and British question drops by 5% (to 40%). Significance tests and N's are not given, but we assume that at least the change for the German question was reliable, although neither shift is very large. (Cross tabulation is not provided, so it is not possible to tell how the two sets of responses are related.) Since the consistency is in terms of a larger value—should Americans be permitted to join a foreign army—the effect can be further classified as normative.

The other example of apparent normative consistency is reported by Link (1946), using questions on the rights of workers to strike and of businessmen to lock out workers. Support for strikes (which was generally higher than support for lockouts) dropped slightly (4%) when the strike question followed the lockout question, whereas the latter rose slightly (6%) when it followed the strike question, both differences being significant at the .01 level. Presumably a norm of equal rights in a labor dispute came into play. Like the two earlier examples, the consistency effect seems to involve a clear norm of equal treatment of two parties, one of whom may be better liked and therefore given greater preference when the norm is not invoked by context.

Two other part–part order experiments involving consistency depend less on normative principles than on a kind of logical inference in deriving policy conclusions from preceding questions. A 1976 NORC experiment reported by Turner and Krauss (1978) asked on one form about whether spending in each of 11 areas (e.g., space exploration, environment, defense) should be increased, followed by a single question on whether the federal income tax paid by the respondent was too high. On the other form the tax question preceded the spending items. In the latter case 14% more respondents said taxes were too high than did so when the spending questions had been posed first, a difference significant beyond the .001 level of confidence. We carried out a further analysis of these data to determine whether the order effect interacted with education, and obtained negative results: The difference appears equally at all educational levels. Furthermore, there is no evidence that responses to the spending items change as a function of question order; only the single tax item seems to be affected.

Finally, one of the early order effects in the survey literature is a report by Sayre (1939) that respondent estimation of the amount of radio time devoted to commercials decreased significantly when respondents were first asked whether they would be willing to pay a radio tax in lieu of advertisements. This appears to be a kind of dissonance effect, although whether it occurred consciously or not is unknown.

Part–Part Consistency Experiments
Yielding Negative Evidence

We carried out two experiments in 1974 and 1975, respectively, that were intended to test for normative consistency (see Table 2.3). In both cases the items were contiguous in the questionnaire, with their order merely reversed on the two forms. In the first pair of items (in SRC–74 Fall), we expected respondents to have more confidence in the motivations of doctors than of lawyers, as indeed occurred, but also to

TABLE 2.3
Two Order Experiments Involving Normative Consistency[a]

Doctor–lawyer pair (SRC-74 Fall)	Percentage saying interested in public good	Position of items		χ^2	*df*	*p*
		First	Second			
Would you say that most doctors in this country are really interested in the public good, or are most doctors just out to make a lot of money?	To doctor item	47.9% (480)	52.2% (896)	2.32	1	n.s.
Would you say that most lawyers in this country are really interested in the public good, or are most lawyers just out to make a lot of money?	To lawyer item	26.2% (906)	30.0% (450)	2.21	1	n.s.

Women–Jew pair (SRC-75 February)	Percentage saying vote for President	Position of items		χ^2	*df*	*p*
		First	Second			
If your party nominated a woman for President, would you vote for her if she were qualified for the job?	If woman	86.5% (441)	84.0% (895)	1.88	1	n.s.
If your party nominated a Jew for President, would you vote for him if he were qualified for the job?	If Jew	91.4% (897)	89.8% (441)	.92	1	n.s.

[a] Base Ns are shown in parentheses. Although there were only two forms to these two experiments, the surveys in which they appeared were divided into three forms for other purposes. The lawyer first sequence and the Jew first sequence were assigned to two forms, which accounts for their larger N's. Randomization is not affected by this uneven allocation of cases.

try to bring the two beliefs into closer correspondence when one was asked immediately after the other. In the second experiment (in SRC–75 February) we hypothesized that a person who accepted either Jews or women as viable presidential candidates might feel pressure to accept the other group as well; in this case we anticipated that the higher percentage approving Jews would lead to an increase in the percentage of approval for women when the latter came second in the questionnaire. Whatever the merits of either line of reasoning, Table 2.3 shows little sign of order effects for either experiment at the marginal level, nor are there any interactions approaching significance when education, sex, or age are introduced as third variables. There is also no significant difference by form in the way the doctor and lawyer items are intercorrelated, nor for the items about Jewish and women presidential candidates. In retrospect neither pair of items seems particularly well chosen, since the norm for the doctor–lawyer pairing is somewhat speculative, and the women–Jews items have marginals that provide only about 5% room for change toward consistency. Still it is of importance that there is so little sign of a consistency or other order effect in either experiment. Evidently, not all closely related items influence each other to a degree detectable with these fairly large samples.

A nonnormative hypothesis about consistency effects was tested in DAS–71 using a standard item on subjective social class:

> *A large community like the Detroit area is made up of many kinds of groups. If you had to place yourself in one of these groups, would you say that you are in the* **upper** *class,* **middle** *class,* **working** *class, or* **lower** *class?*

In one questionnaire form, the class item appeared after an extended series of inquiries concerning the respondent's educational and occupational history. In the other form, it appeared before the education and occupation questions in order to dissociate it from obvious objective factors (though it was preceded by questions on home ownership and the number of telephones and televisions sets owned, which might be considered style of life indicators). We expected that on the first form respondents would feel more pressure to bring their class identification into line with their education and occupation, producing stronger associations between objective and subjective class measures, as well as possibly a form difference in the marginals for the subjective class question. The hypothesis about association is not confirmed by the data, there being no significant difference or noticeable trend between forms in this respect. There is, however, a trend in Table 2.4 for the forms to show different subjective class marginals, and the trend reaches signifi-

TABLE 2.4
Subjective Social Class by Order[a]

Percentage choosing	Placement relative to education and occupation	
	Before	After
Upper class	2.1%	2.5%
Middle class	43.1	48.1
Working class	50.3	45.2
Lower class	4.5	4.2
	100	100
	(925)	(928)
	$\chi^2 = 5.39$, $df = 3$, n.s.	

[a] Carried out in DAS-71.

cance ($p < .05$) if the upper and middle class and the working and lower class categories are collapsed to eliminate small cells. (See Evers, 1974, for additional analysis.) Given the importance of the subjective social class measure in sociological writings, the possible effect in DAS-71 deserves replication, but at present it must be regarded as small in size, uncertain in reliability, and unclear in source and meaning.

Also falling under part-part consistency is a report by DeLamater and MacCorquodale (1975) regarding the ordering of sets of questions to 18- to 23-year-olds concerning sexual behavior with current partner, partner's sexual ideology, and the nature of the relationship with that person. The authors conclude that order effects were generally absent in their data.

In sum, merely placing two questions with similar content next to each other does not necessarily create an order effect. Only if respondents have a need to make their answers to the second question consistent with their answers to the first will such an order effect be created. Based on the results at hand, the prime way to do this is for the conjunction of questions to make salient a norm of fairness or even-handedness toward the different parties asked about in two similar questions. Such a norm can have considerable power, as the experiment on the American and Communist reporters items demonstrated dramatically. In addition, there is some evidence that consistency can be created in nonnormative ways when question order emphasizes the fact that two preferred answers are contradictory in policy implications, as in the 1976 NORC experiment on spending and taxes.

Part–Whole Contrast Effects

General and Specific Abortion Questions

We turn now to a type of order effect that has not previously been clearly delineated, but that is one of the most reliable we have found and that also is especially challenging from both theoretical and practical standpoints. We first discovered the effect when, for other purposes (see Chapter 9), we employed a relatively general item on abortion from NORC's General Social Survey (GSS). Our results in SRC–79 March showed majority support for legalizing abortion, and were rather different in this respect from the majority opposition reported for the same item by NORC in 1978 (see Table 2.5). Since our telephone survey tended to underrepresent less-educated persons, and education is related to support for abortion, a small part of the difference could be explained in this way. Enough of a difference remained after standardizing for education, however, to suggest a possible context effect, for the general abortion item was the only question we asked on that issue, whereas in the GSS the item was preceded by a more specific question on abortion in the case of a defect in the unborn child. Of course, there also were other possible explanations, such as true change over time or a difference between telephone and face-to-face modes of interviewing, that needed to be ruled out.

We included both the general abortion item and the more specific defective-child item in a split-ballot question order experiment in June, 1979. The questions were adjacent to each other, but with their order reversed on the two questionnaire forms. (The question immediately

Table 2.5
Discrepancy between NORC and SRC Results on General Abortion Question

Do *you* think it should be possible for a pregnant woman to obtain a **legal** abortion if she is married and does not want any more children?	NORC GSS–78	SRC 79–March	Adjusted SRC[a]
Yes	40.3%	58.4%	54.9%
No	59.7	41.6	45.1
	100	100	
	(1483)	(490)	
	$\chi^2 = 48.34$, $df = 1$, $p < .001$		

[a] SRC results standardized on NORC educational distribution.

preceding the abortion items concerned labor unions, and no earlier items dealt in any way with abortion issues.) Table 2.6 presents the cross-tabulations of the two items separately by questionnaire form, so that both the marginal differences and the intercorrelations can be compared for the two orderings. Examination of the marginals at the bottom of the subtables shows that the general abortion item received substantially more support (by 13%) when asked first (which is equivalent to being asked alone) than when asked after the child-defect item. The latter item, on the other hand, was unaffected by its placement. Furthermore, almost all of the effect on the marginals of the general item is due to persons who said yes to the defective-child item, although a trend in the same direction occurs among those who said no to the defective-child item.

Since the specific–general order increases the difference in marginals between the two items over that which would occur if the two items were each asked separately, the effect is one of contrast rather than consistency. Note also that the effect produced experimentally accounts for much of the nonexperimental difference shown in Table 2.5, especially when the original SRC results are adjusted to take account of the NORC–SRC difference in educational distributions.

Because of the importance of the abortion results, we replicated the

TABLE 2.6
Order Effects on Abortion Items[a]

		Order: Specific/General					Order: General/Specific		
		General abortion item					General abortion item		
		Yes	No				Yes	No	
Specific abortion item	Yes	47.1	36.9	84.0	Specific abortion item	Yes	57.4	25.6	83.0
	No	1.0	15.0	16.0		No	3.3	13.8	17.1
		48.1	51.9	100% (293)			60.7	39.4	100% (305)
		Gamma = .90					Gamma = .81		

General abortion marginals × order: $\chi^2 = 9.52$, $df = 1$, $p < .01$
Specific abortion marginals × order: $\chi^2 = .11$, $df = 1$, n.s.

Three-way interaction (general item × specific item × order): $\chi^2 = .99$, $df = 1$, n.s.

[a] Carried out in SRC–79 June. Percentages are based on grand totals. The general item is the one shown in Table 2.5. The specific item was worded as follows: *Do you think it should be possible for a pregnant woman to obtain a legal abortion if there is a strong chance of serious defect in the baby?*

experiment in SRC–79 August, and included in the same survey an item to obtain religious preference and a question on ambivalence toward abortion. The basic order effect appeared even more strongly this second time: agreement with the general abortion item is 17.4% higher when it comes first rather than after the defective-child item ($\chi^2 = 19.66$, $df = 1$, $p < .001$), whereas there is no significant order effect ($\chi^2 = .27$) for the defective-child item itself. (Intercorrelations are also quite similar to those in Table 2.6.) Thus the order effect on the general abortion item seems to be both large and highly reliable. It takes on even greater practical importance because it does not result from an artificially created demonstration, but arose inadvertently from the decision, common in survey research, to move individual items from one questionnaire location to another.

The exact interpretation of the effect is less clear than is its reliability. We call it a part–whole effect because agreement to the more general abortion item would ordinarily imply agreement to the defective-child item, but the reverse is not true. (Compare the bottom left and top right cells in either half of Table 2.6.) One plausible explanation for the effect turns on the fact that there are a number of different reasons for supporting legalized abortion. A possible defect in an unborn child is a specific reason that appeals to a large part of the population, as is shown by the marginals for that item. When the more general item is asked first, some respondents may say yes but mainly with such a specific reason in mind. When the item on abortion because of a defective child is asked first, however, this indicates to respondents that the general item that follows does not refer to such a specific case. Thus respondents who are generally reluctant to favor abortion except within narrow limits should find it easier to oppose the general rationale after favoring (and "subtracting") the more specific rationale about the defective child.

A subtraction process can be conceptualized as a purely cognitive process, a redefinition of what the general abortion item is about. It is also possible that an element of ambivalence is involved, so that a respondent who has favored the defective-child item feels freer to swing to the other side when faced with the general item. Perceptual contrast offers still another line of interpretation, with order influencing the perceived gap between the two items (cf. the Crespi phenomenon, noted in McGuire, 1969, p. 213). None of these interpretations is readily tested directly, and the simple redefinition hypothesis, which appeals most strongly to us, is not entirely consistent with the finding in Table 2.6 that a shift occurs not only among those saying yes to the defective-child item, but among those saying no as well. Although the latter trend is based on too few cases to be at all sure of its reliability, it occurs in the August replication as well.

We attempted to test whether ambivalence is involved in the order effect by including at the end of the SRC-79 August questionnaire a question intended to tap ambivalence about abortion, as shown in Table 2.7. (Between the original abortion items and the question on ambivalence were over 50 questions on automobiles and the energy shortage.) For those who show ambivalence by saying that the abortion issue is one they find difficult to decide on, the order effect is quite large (28%) and highly reliable; for those who are very certain about the issue, only a nonsignificant trend (10%) toward an order effect appears. However, although the ambivalence item does condition the order effect, it may actually measure strength of opinion (see Chapter 9), not ambivalence in the sense of conflicted attitudes, and thus simply reflect a greater resistance to order effects by those who feel strongly about an issue. The two interpretations are not easily distinguished.[8]

We also examined the abortion order effect by religion (Protestant versus Catholic), sex, and education. Only religion shows a possible interaction, but it is not even borderline in significance $(.10 < p < .20)$. For now we conclude that both religious categories, both sexes, and three educational groupings (0-11, 12, 13+) are all susceptible to the order effect shown in Table 2.6. The lack of an interaction trend for education in either the June or August abortion experiment is noteworthy and differs, as we have seen, from what happened when consistency effects occurred for the reporter items.

Other Part–Whole Contrast Effects

In addition to the part–whole abortion experiments we ourselves carried out, two experiments reported by Kalton, Collins, and Brook (1978) can be considered of the same type. In one, respondents in England

---

[8]On the assumption that those who shift their responses to the general item would be especially ambivalent, we expected ambivalence to be higher for proabortion respondents when the general question came first (and included the shifters as pros) than when it came second. This does occur. Similarly, we expected ambivalence to be higher for antiabortion respondents when the general item came second (and included the shifters as antis). Surprisingly, this does not happen. Complicating the interpretation is the fact that the ambivalence item itself, though placed more than 50 items after the main abortion questions, shows a borderline $(p < .10)$ difference in response between forms: There is more ambivalence registered on the form with the general item coming first. Only replication can establish whether this difference points to a remarkable order effect that "jumps" across 50 items, or whether it is a result of chance. (This same survey also included a centrality item immediately after the general and specific abortion items, but we concluded that this was too complicated a compounding of possible order effects and do not consider those data further.)

TABLE 2.7
Attitude on General Abortion Item by Question Order and Ambivalence[a]

The last question is on a different subject. Some people are very certain about their feelings about when legal abortions should be permitted. Other people see this issue as a difficult one to reach a decision on. Would you say that you are more like those who are very certain, or that you are more like those who see this issue as a difficult one to reach a decision on?

General question on abortion	Order:	Very certain		A difficult issue	
		General–Specific	Specific–General	General–Specific	Specific–General
Favor		68.1%	58.0%	67.8%	39.9%
Oppose		31.9	42.0	32.2	60.1
		100	100	100	100
		(135)	(150)	(174)	(143)
		$\chi^2 = 3.15$, $df = 1$, n.s.		$\chi^2 = 25.07$, $df = 1$, $p < .001$	

Three-way interaction: $\chi^2 = 4.42$, $df = 1$, $p < .05$

[a] Carried out in SRC–79 August. The "general" and "specific" abortion terms are those shown in Tables 2.5 and 2.6.

were asked whether driving standards were getting lower for (*a*) people in general, and (*b*) for young drivers specifically. When the general question came second, respondents were significantly less apt to say standards had gone down than when it came first; there was no effect of order on the question about young drivers. This also can be described as a contrast effect: After having been asked about young drivers, respondents' views of drivers in general are moved further away (in the positive direction) from their views of young drivers. Furthermore, the Kalton *et al.* analysis yields a meaningful three-way interaction, since the order effect occurred only for respondents who were themselves classified as older (45 and over), and they are probably the people most likely to perceive young drivers as especially reckless. The authors also suggest a subtraction explanation for the order effect: After answering about young drivers, respondents redefine the general drivers item to exclude young drivers and therefore give a less negative response.

The second part–whole experiment reported by Kalton *et al.* (1978) manipulated an item about the noise of traffic in general and an item specifically about the noise of truck traffic. Again there is a significant order effect that seems to involve contrast, but this time it is only the specific item that is affected, contrary to the other part–whole experiments already discussed or discussed below. No obvious reason for this discrepancy in results is apparent in the nature of the item, nor do Kalton *et al.* offer an explanation.

Part–Part Contrast Effects

The only claimed effect of this type that we have located is a report by Willick and Ashley (1971) that college students at a University of California campus were less apt to report their political party identification to be the same as that of their parents if the questions about parents' party preceded, rather than followed, the question on self. The authors interpret the result as indicating an assertion by the students of independence from their parents, and further suggest that it raises serious problems with findings about intergenerational transmission of party preferences that rely solely on the report of the child. The result would indeed be an important one if generalizable to all young adults, or even to all college students.

We attempted to replicate the Willick and Ashley study in interviews with a probability sample of 380 University of Michigan undergraduates in U/M–80. A random half of the sample was asked for own party preference first, then father's and mother's preference; the other half was asked father's, mother's, and own preference in that order. When students are classified in terms of whether they reported the same or a different party preference from their parents (using only cases where both parents had the same preference), the proportions are almost identical (43.5%) on the two forms of the questionnaire. Other analyses of the data along lines proposed by Willick and Ashley (1971) also fail to show any sign that question order had an effect on self-reported party identification. Thus, the generality of the original result, and perhaps its reliability as well, is left in considerable doubt.

Part–Whole Consistency

General and Marital Happiness

Entries in this category are uncertain both as to classification and nature of effect, but not thereby less important from the standpoint of order effects generally. An intriguing example involves a question on general happiness and a question on marital happiness, as shown in Table 2.8. Smith (1979) compared surveys that had asked the marital item and then the general item with surveys that asked only the general item, and found that for married persons the general happiness question received more positive responses when it was asked after the question on happiness in marriage. Since marital happiness was greater than general happiness, Smith suggested that asking the marital question first tended to increase positive responses to the general question by causing it to be defined in terms of marital happiness. This can obviously be seen as a consistency effect, and one where the general question is influenced by answers to the more specific one.

A split-ballot experiment included in the 1980 General Social Survey supports Smith's nonexperimental findings, for general happiness increases significantly (linear $\chi^2 = 5.68$, $df = 1$, $p < .02$) when the item follows the marital happiness item. However, there are also two contradictory results from other experiments. Turner (personal communication, 1979) included the same two-item experiment in a national telephone survey carried out by the Washington Post in 1979, and found only a very slight and nonsignificant difference in the direction just described. More perplexing still, we carried out an experiment apparently identical to Turner's in SRC–79 August and discovered a significant difference in the opposite direction (as shown in Table 2.8)—that is, an apparent contrast effect much like that reported earlier for the abor-

TABLE 2.8
General and Marital Happiness by Question Order[a]

General happiness

Taken altogether, how would you say things are these days:
would you say that you are very happy, pretty happy, or not too happy?

| | Order | |
	General–Marital	Marital–General
Very happy	52.4%	38.1%
Pretty happy	44.2	52.8
Not too happy	3.4	9.1
	100	100
	(206)	(176)
	linear $\chi^2 = 7.41$, $df = 1$, $p < .01$	

Marital happiness

Taking things all together, how would you describe your marriage: would
you say that your marriage is very happy, pretty happy, or not too happy?

| | Order | |
	General–Marital	Marital–General
Very happy	69.8%	63.1%
Pretty happy	28.3	32.4
Not too happy	2.0	4.5
	100	100
	(205)	(176)
	linear $\chi^2 = 2.29$, $df = 1$, n.s.	

[a] Carried out in SRC–79 August. Married respondents only.

tion items.[9] Since any of the three findings taken alone is easy enough to
interpret, the important point is to establish the facts reliably and to
reconcile the divergent results. One possibility is that the GSS experimental findings involve a still more complex context effect, since in the
1980 GSS (but not in the other two experiments) both happiness items
followed a set of five items on life satisfactions in domains such as
friendships and family. But this would account for only part of the
discrepant results, and at present we are far from solving the problem.

[9] Analysis of our experiment in SRC–79 August by education, sex, and age did not turn
up any significant three-way interactions, and the two happiness items are themselves
intercorrelated to the same degree on the two forms.

One point worth emphasis, however, is that it is the general happiness item that shows shifts traceable to order, *not* the more specific marital item, in both the SRC and NORC experiments; this accords with most other results in this chapter pointing to the vulnerability of general items to context effects.

Religious Interest

An unusual but potentially important example of a consistency effect is reported by Duncan and Schuman (1980) and involves both wording and context operating together. The association between self-reported change in attending religious services and change in general religious interest is significantly stronger when the two questions have similarly worded response alternatives than when somewhat differently worded alternatives are used. The religious interest question, which can be re-garded as the whole in a part–whole combination, always followed the attendance question in this experiment, but the three response categories for both questions used much the same wording on half the questionnaires and slightly different wording on the other half. The interpretation seems to be that although the order of the questions did not vary, respondents were led to be more consistent when the wording of the response categories pointed up the connection between the two items. Thus when questions can be perceived as more or less closely related, mechanical features of phrasing may increase or decrease con-sistency between them. The importance of the example comes from the demonstration that context itself can be altered by a slight change in wording, without an actual change in the order of items.

Salience Effects

The salience hypothesis is that a particular response is made more available or more attractive through a kind of consciousness-raising pro-cess created by preceding questions. The effect is not completely separa-ble from the consistency effects just discussed, but the emphasis here is on the total context in which a later item appears, rather than on its connection to another single question. Moreover, it is assumed that the respondent's internal set is changed, rather than that a merely presen-tational form of consistency is produced, although the two are difficult to distinguish. Finally, although we do not here make a formal distinc-tion between part–whole and part–part, the idea behind the classifica-tion continues to be useful.

Victimization Reports

A striking example of an apparent salience effect on factual items is reported by Gibson, Shapiro, Murphy, and Stanko (1978) and Cowan, Murphy, and Wiener (1978). The National Crime Survey, conducted by the Census Bureau in 26 cities from 1972 through 1975, obtained respondent reports of victimization experience during the preceding 12-months. On a random half of the interviews, these reports followed 16 attitude questions about crime; on the other half the attitude questions were omitted. Victimization reports, especially of less serious crimes, increased significantly and appreciably for the subsample asked the attitude questions. The most plausible interpretation is that the attitude questions stimulated memory for and willingness to report more experiences, although some degree of misreporting cannot be ruled out. It is important to emphasize that this order effect involves survey questions of a factual nature. Indeed, the attitude questions had been placed first in the survey on the common assumption that they, not the factual questions, would be sensitive to context.[10]

Increases in General Interest in Politics

In terms of our distinction between part–whole and part–part relations among questions, the preceding example is closer to the part–part type. McFarland (1981) provides an instance interpretable as salience that is of a part–whole nature, or at least involves a distinction between more specific and more general questions. Single items about interest in politics and interest in religion ("very interested," "somewhat interested," or "not very interested") preceded or followed specific questions on each topic, using a split-ballot design as part of a telephone sample of Kentucky households. The percentage saying "very interested" was significantly higher for the two general interest questions when they followed the specific items, whereas order had no effect on the specific items. There were no significant interactions with education or sex. General–specific experiments were also conducted in the same survey on the topics of energy and the economy, but in these cases the general questions were not about subjective interest but asked for judgments of the seriousness of the problems; in neither case was there an order effect. The overall results fit a salience model fairly well, where a

[10]Gibson *et al.* (1978) also describe three other Census Bureau studies where salience may have changed responses, but other explanations (including variations in interviewer behavior) seem at least as plausible.

series of specific questions tends to heighten general interest in an issue.

We can also classify here, as well as under "rapport effects" (discussed at a later point), an experiment by Sigelman (1981) on a well-known Gallup question: *Do you approve or disapprove of the way that _____ is handling his job as President?* When the question followed a series of 48 items about a wide range of social and political issues, there were significantly fewer "don't know" responses than when it came at the beginning of the questionnaire. All of the differences occurred among less-educated respondents—none among those with college education. There was no effect on the distribution of approval and disapproval responses as such, in line with our general finding in Chapter 4 that changes in DK proportions typically leave substantive marginals unaltered.

Confidence in National Institutions

In accounting for nonexperimental discrepancies between Harris and NORC results for a set of items designed to measure confidence in national institutions, Turner and Krauss (1978) suggest that at least part of the difference may have been due to whether the series was or was not preceded by a set of items on political alienation. Fortunately, this plausible hypothesis was tested in a split-ballot experiment in the 1978 General Social Survey (Smith, 1979b). Only the first item (on "Major Companies") in the confidence set showed a significant decline in confidence (of 7.4%, $p < .01$) when the set was preceded by six political alienation items, indicating that the context effect on marginals was neither as large nor as pervasive as the nonexperimental differences Turner and Krauss (1978) discovered. Nor were the political alienation items themselves affected by context. An unexpected finding appeared, however, when the alienation scale and the confidence scale were intercorrelated, namely, an appreciably higher correlation (.44) on the form where alienation preceded confidence than on the form where their order was reversed (.29). Most of the individual alienation by confidence correlations also increased, the mean increment being .05. Thus even though marginal effects due to question order were small and limited, correlational effects were pervasive—a clear warning that associations must be examined even in the absence of univariate effects. In the present case, it appears that the degree of alienation that people feel, when made salient, influences their answers to the confidence items, creating greater consistency between the two scales even where the overall response proportions on each are unchanged. Thus, the primary effect here may be one of part–part consistency, rather than of salience.

Absence of Salience Effects Where Expected

There are a number of experiments where we or other authors expected salience effects, but where there is little evidence that they occurred. Three come from DAS–71 and involved attempts to determine whether early questions would invoke group or other norms that might then influence responses to later questions. The most striking of these experiments concerned a question that seemed particularly likely to yield an order effect, since the item had already shown vulnerability to external cues. The question asks respondents to *tell me who two or three of your favorite actors or entertainers are;* the names spontaneously mentioned are later coded as to race. In an earlier 1968 race-of-interviewer experiment (Schuman and Converse, 1971), black respondents mentioned a significantly higher proportion of black entertainers when the interviewer was black than when the interviewer was white. In 1971, the race-of-interviewer variation was replicated together with a variation in the context of the question, producing a 2 × 2 factorial design. (Only data for black respondents were obtained.) In one form the entertainer question was located at the end of a long series of racial questions dealing with perceived discrimination, distrust of whites, and "black consciousness." In the other form, the entertainer question appeared earlier in the questionnaire after questions on friends and neighbors and before any explicit racial questions. Our hypothesis was that mention of black entertainers would increase on the first form, and further that it might do so more when the interviewers were black rather than white. However, as shown in Table 2.9, neither context hypothesis is supported: Although the entertainer question again produces a large and highly reliable race-of-interviewer effect ($\chi^2 = 31.52$, $df = 4$, $p < .001$), there is no sign of a significant effect by question order either alone ($\chi^2 = 1.68$, $df = 4$) or in interaction with race-of-interviewer ($\chi^2 = 1.55$, $df = 4$). Apparently an item can be highly sensitive to the interviewing context and yet not be at all sensitive to questionnaire context.

A second experiment in DAS–71 varied the placement of the following two questions:

> *If you were driving in another state and got a ticket for parking just a few minutes overtime while getting your lunch, would you bother to pay the fine? (**If yes**) Would you pay it even if you were in a big hurry and knew that the police in that town would never bother you if you didn't pay the fine?*

In one form the questions follow items on the performance of state and local officials. In the other form the questions follow a long series of items on religion and morality. We hypothesized that respondents

TABLE 2.9
Race of Entertainers by Context and Race of Interviewer[a]

Could you tell me who two or three of your favorite actors or entertainers are?

	Black interviewers		White interviewers	
Race of entertainers	Form A	Form B	Form A	Form B
Blacks only	45.5%	39.1%	14.8%	19.2%
Mainly black	22.8	29.9	22.2	25.0
Black and white equally	8.9	6.9	11.1	7.7
Mainly white	14.9	18.4	29.6	25.0
Whites only	7.9	5.7	22.2	23.1
	100	100	100	100
N	(101)	(87)	(54)	(52)

[a] Carried out in DAS-71. In Form A the entertainer question follows non-racial questions; in Form B it follows a set of racial questions. The sample for this experiment consisted of black respondents only.

would be more likely to say they would pay the fine on the second form than on the first. No such effect occurs, the difference between forms being only 1% for the first question ($\chi^2 = 0.81$, $df = 1$) and 3% for the second ($\chi^2 = 2.52$, $df = 1$).

Another DAS-71 experiment on salience had more mixed results. It dealt with a question on whether the respondent's interest in religion had risen, declined, or remained the same over the past 10 or 15 years. On one form, the question followed more or less objective items about religious behavior, such as church membership and church attendance. On the other form, the religious interest question followed more subjective questions concerning belief in God and belief in life after death. The initial hypothesis was that the second context would lead to more reports of heightened interest in religion. In fact, there is a significant effect of context, but it is different from that hypothesized. Fewer respondents report that their interest remained the same when the interest question followed the subjective belief questions ($\chi^2 = 7.29$, $df = 2$, $p < .05$). The effect is not large, nor do we have a clear interpretation as to what causes it.[11]

There are also several reports in the survey literature of unsuccessful attempts to obtain order effects by making an issue salient. In one of the earliest experiments on salience, Bradburn and Mason (1964)

[11]Actually the wording of the question itself was varied experimentally, so that the full design was a 2 × 2 factorial. However, the wording variation does not appear to be involved in the present effect, so for simplicity we here treat the two wordings as a single one. (Earlier, on page 44, a main effect due to the wording variation in the experiment was discussed.) For a full analysis of the experiment, see Duncan and Schuman, 1980.

hypothesized that the number of types of response to an open question on "worries" would be affected by previous questions on marital and work problems, but found no evidence in support of the hypothesis. Similarly, Hitlin (1976) tested the hypothesis that preceding a question about Richard Nixon's job performance with an item about Nixon's possible impeachment would affect the evaluations of performance, but found no difference by form.

Kalton *et al.* (1978) also included two experiments that might be thought of under the heading of salience. In one case they asked about the dangers to children from traffic, followed or preceded by a question on whether safety should be increased. In the other case, they asked whether truck deliveries presently cause traffic jams, followed or preceded by a question on whether truck deliveries should be encouraged at (i.e., diverted to) night time. Neither experiment seems to have shown a clear marginal effect due to order, though the second shows an ambiguous trend. Other results are not reported.

In summary, the evidence for salience effects is quite mixed. Results reported in the research literature provide evidence that effects can occur both at the marginal level (as with the National Crime Survey victimization reports) and in terms of item intercorrelations (as with the alienation and confidence items) that are most easily understood in terms of salience. Yet several past experiments failed to show such effects where they might have been expected, and our own DAS-71 results were generally negative. Particularly surprising was the absence of a salience effect for race of entertainer on an item that showed large response effects due to race of interviewer. This type of order problem is an especially difficult one because salience is a nebulous concept, and operationally it is difficult to specify exactly what is needed in the way of a context for an item to show an effect. Of the four clearly positive effects we located, one might better be thought of in terms of consistency, but such reclassification for the purposes of parsimony does not fit the other three. Two of the four resemble the part–whole distinction and two the part–part, with both of the latter having been unanticipated, rather than being designed with the outcome clearly in mind.[12]

Other Types of Order Effects

Many of the order effects discussed to this point deal with the way one item (or in the case of salience, a set of items) affects a response to a

---

[12]An interesting salience interpretation is offered by Goldberg, Sharp, and Freedman (1959) for discrepancies in the number of children expected by Catholics in different surveys. Unfortunately, the hypothesis was never tested experimentally.

related item that is asked at a later point. The assumption is that respondents attempt to be "psycho-logical" (cf. Abelson and Rosenberg, 1958), either in the sense of simple consistency—*If I said X to question A, then I should say X to question B*—or in some more complex way—*Having said X to question A, I am now free to say Z to question B.* The hypotheses are fairly straightforward because the relation is one the investigators can perceive easily and one they believe (whether correctly or not) they could have predicted in advance.

We turn now to types of order effects that are more formal in character. Some of these concern the items that open a questionnaire (*rapport effects*); others, the closing items in a long series or at the end of a long questionnaire (*fatigue effects*). Still others involve items that are quite similar in substance or form, but relate not to the transfer of meaning but to changes in frame of reference that come from being first in a sequence rather than later, or involve the accentuation or disruption of response sets through clustering or dispersing of items.

Rapport effects are assumed to occur because respondents become more relaxed, trusting, or committed as an interview proceeds, thus facilitating frank responses. At the extreme, few investigators would think it wise to open an interview with a question on income, infidelity, or illegal drug use. However, we know of no experiment that demonstrates order effects involving these or other threatening subjects. In fact, the only positive experimental report that seems to bear on rapport effects is one by Thumin (1962) based on telephone interviews with 336 St. Louis respondents. In half the interviews, after a brief introduction, respondents were asked: *Have you ever been troubled by insomnia—or had difficulty falling asleep?* In the other half, the same question was preceded by a question on colds and one on allergies. Affirmative responses to the insomnia question were 12% in the first sequence, 23% in the second ($p < .02$). The author assumes that the insomnia question is more personal than the others, that the increase occurs because of greater rapport when it is asked third, and that the higher proportion reflects greater accuracy, though none of these points is tested directly. In contrast to Thumin's report, Clancy and Wachsler (1971) failed to find that a greater number of socially undesirable responses were given to six personally threatening questions when they were asked at the end rather than at the beginning of a 25-minute telephone survey.

Fatigue effects also can hardly be doubted in the sense that after enough questions respondents should begin to tire and perhaps answer with less deliberate thought. How many is "enough," however, and what concrete effects will be produced is hard to say. Clancy and Wachsler's (1971) experiment, noted before under rapport effects, also hypothesized a fatigue effect in the form of an increase in mechanical agreeing responses to the six items when they came late rather than early in their telephone survey. No such general effect occurred, although a single item showed a significant change for unknown reasons. More positive evidence for fatigue effects is reported by Kraut, Wolfson, and Rothenberg (1975) from placement of 46 Likert-type items in early and late parts of a 168-item self-administered questionnaire. Nonresponse rose slightly but significantly for items placed near the end, and there was also a significant decrease in the use of extreme categories on Likert-type item scales. Other more substantive effects are also reported, but they are not very reliable and it is in any case uncertain whether these are due to fatigue or to unspecified contextual influences from earlier items. More generally, except for formal measures like nonresponse and extremity of response, it is difficult to see how fatigue effects can be separated from effects due to the meanings carried by preceding items.

Initial Frame of Reference Effects

When respondents are asked to rate a series of items on numerical scales, they face the problem of establishing an initial reference point.[13] Two sets of experiments suggest that the first item in a series is especially likely to be reacted to differently from later items. Carpenter and Blackwood (1979) varied the starting point in 12 different lists of questions asked in a national telephone survey measuring attitudes toward animals (especially coyotes). The low salience of the topic, together with the numerical length of the scales (0–10 and 0–100 points), may have maximized the likelihood of significant order effects. For example, in one question, respondents were required to rate on 10-point scales the acceptability of each of 6 ways of killing coyotes (traps, slow poisons, etc.). Six random subsamples were used, so that each method of killing appeared once in each of the 6 possible positions in the list. Order effects on mean ratings were pervasive for this and similar lists, with an item usually receiving either its highest or its lowest rating when it was presented first. The authors suggest that the lack of evaluative reference points results in the assignment of extreme values initially, which are then moderated for the following items on the list. However, in most

---

[13]We treat these item sets as a matter of question order because each one is responded to on a separate scale. There are obvious similarities, however, to response order problems within questions, as indicated by the fact that sheer place in a sequence, rather than contextual meaning, appears to be an underlying cause of the effect.

cases, effects on means were not large enough to change ordinal rankings, for example, slow poison always had the least acceptable rating, regardless of when it was asked. Furthermore, there appeared to be no reliable three-way interactions; hence the relations of the ratings to other variables was not significantly affected by position in a list.

A study similar in using ratings, but on a mail questionnaire, was carried out by Ferber (1952). Credit managers were asked to rate each of 42 occupations as good, fair, or poor credit risks, and in addition to define "good," "fair," and "poor" in terms of percentage of defaults expected. Occupations were listed hierarchically from professional to unskilled labor on one form and in reverse order on the other—the two forms constituting a split-ballot experiment. When the higher status occupations came first, they were rated "good" less often than when they came later. Respondents also set stricter standards (defined "good" as referring to a smaller proportion of defaults) when the occupations believed to be more creditworthy were listed first. Thus both these experiments indicate that rating a series of objects is apt to create sequence effects because of shifting frames of reference.

Other Unspecified Sequence Effects

Several investigators have simply changed the sequence of a series of related items in order to determine if *any* effect occurs, without necessarily having an initial hypothesis about the nature of the effect. The most meaningful of these experiments involved a seven-item self-administered Guttman scale designed to measure anxiety (Hayes, 1964). The 2 × 2 design had the items arranged either serially (from "hard" to "easy") or in disarrayed order, and either adjacent or separated by irrelevant items. Adjacency had no effect on total anxiety scores, but the disarrayed form produced significantly higher anxiety scores than the serial form, a finding later replicated with a panel design. Disarray (but not lack of adjacency) also significantly lowered reproducibility coefficients, which the author interprets as implying interference with respondent perception of the underlying dimension. In other words, unidimensional scaling of items is facilitated if the items are presented in a way that emphasizes the underlying scale.

Negative evidence on more miscellaneous sequence effects comes from Kirchner and Uphoff's (1955) study of the attitudes toward union matters held by union members. Half the self-administered questionnaires had 77 items grouped under seven headings, such as Local Union and Local Offices; half had the same items spread at random through the questionnaire and unlabeled. When scales were formed for the item groups, only one of the 7 groups showed a significant difference in means between the 2 forms. A similar design was used by Metzner and Mann (1952), but item intercorrelations were analyzed in this case. In general, grouping made little difference in the sizes of the many correlations examined, although the authors note a few differences that may be real but seem uninterpretable.

The DAS–71 survey included experiments on three sets of agree–disagree items concerned with personal and political alienation, the main goal being simply to see what happened when such sets of items were asked (*a*) adjacently or nonadjacently, or (*b*) were asked in different orders. The first experiment presented the following four Anomia items in an unbroken sequence to a random half of the sample:

> *Most people don't really care what happens to the next fellow.*
> *Children born today have a wonderful future to look forward to.*
> *Nowadays a person has to live pretty much for today and let tomorrow take care of itself.*
> *The chances are very good that someday we'll have another depression as bad as the one in the thirties.*

The other half of the sample received the same four items in this same sequence, but with at least three other questions different in both form and content interposed between each pair of Anomia items. The expectation was that the interposed items might break any existing response set, and therefore that agreement with the later Anomia items would be lower in that sequence than in the adjacent sequence. However, there are no significant differences by form for any of the four items, nor do associations among them vary meaningfully by form (see Martin, 1980, for a complete analysis).

A second experiment dealt with the order among two additional Anomia items (*These days a person doesn't really know whom he can count on*, and *It's hardly fair to bring children into the world the way things look for the future*), and a much more concrete item of a different character (*Every American family should be required by law to own a flag*). The "count on" Anomia item and the flag item appeared in reverse orders in the two forms, with the remaining Anomia item always in the third position. There is no sign that the different ordering of concrete and nebulous items affected agreement, either in item marginals or intercorrelations.

Third, seven agree–disagree items measuring mainly "political efficacy" were asked in one order on one form, and in exactly the reverse order on the other form. Again the hypothesis was that a cumulative agreeing response set would be encouraged such that a given item would elicit more agreement when it appeared near the end of the sequence than near the beginning. The results in Table 2.10 do provide convincing evidence that question order had effects, with five of the seven items showing significant ($p < .05$) form differences in marginals, but the simple "cumulative agreement" hypothesis is not confirmed. Extended analysis of this sequence of items (Duncan and Schuman, 1976) indicated that respondents tend to use less extreme modifiers toward the end of the series (consistent with the fatigue hypothesis), that there are a variety of other order effects involving extremity when the items are cross-tabulated with one another, and that more complex interactions with education are present for one pair of items. Only the first of these, the decrease in extreme categories (strongly agree, strongly disagree), points to a general conclusion that may go beyond this set of items, especially since it is consistent with results noted above from Kraut *et al.* (1975). The other effects seem more plausibly tied to the particular content of the seven items in the DAS-71 political efficacy series, though use of Likert-type extremity scales may well increase the likelihood of order effects of all kinds.

Considering all the experiments reviewed in this section, sequence effects seem to occur most clearly where (*a*) there is an intrinsic logical order to a set of items that is facilitated or disrupted by the order in which the items are asked, and (*b*) lengthy response scales are used that can detect small effects. In either case, it appears that the effects develop from the respondents' need to establish a frame of reference and some evidence suggests that an item is especially likely to receive an extreme response when it comes first in a sequence. For the most part, other manipulations of item sets, whether through reversal or dispersion, do not have significant effects on marginals or associations. The fact that one series of items on political alienation does reveal seemingly reliable effects prevents a blanket statement in this regard. But judging from both our own experiments and past research, the effects are not common.

A Further Puzzle and a Caution

We report one last question-order experiment of our own that points up the need to understand respondent behavior, and not merely make plausible inferences from differences in question marginals. The experiment was originally designed to be a part–whole experiment, and uses questions from an earlier investigation that compared abstract principles and specific situations of racial discrimination (Schuman, 1973). We expected one or both of the questions in Table 2.11 to show consistency effects with the other. As the marginals of the subtables indicate, this seems to happen: The general item produces significantly more support

TABLE 2.10
Sequence Experiment on Political Efficacy Items[a]

People have different ideas about how they think American life should be. I am going to read you some statements which represent some of these ideas. In each case please tell me whether you strongly agree, agree, disagree, or strongly disagree.

		Distribution							
	Form	Strongly agree	Agree	Disagree	Strongly disagree	Total	N	χ^2	p[b]
1. *How about this one? Public officials really care about what people like me think. Do you strongly agree, agree, disagree, or strongly disagree with that?*	A	4.1%	42.3	41.8	11.7	100	(921)	31.16	.001
	B	2.6%	50.8	41.0	5.6	100	(931)		
2. *So many other people vote in elections that it doesn't matter much whether I vote or not.*	A	2.5%	10.2	53.9	33.4	100	(931)	3.97	n.s.
	B	1.9%	10.2	58.0	29.8	100	(939)		
3. *People like me don't have any say about what the government does.*	A	4.3%	26.8	57.0	11.9	100	(928)	33.45	.001
	B	6.4%	33.7	54.3	5.6	100	(934)		
4. *Sometimes politics and government seem so complicated that a person like me can't really understand what's going on.*	A	12.4%	52.5	30.5	4.5	100	(925)	18.05	.001
	B	17.3%	55.8	23.6	3.4	100	(938)		
5. *Voting is the only way that people like me can have any say about how the government runs things.*	A	13.0%	48.3	34.6	4.1	100	(925)	.99	n.s.
	B	12.1%	48.1	34.9	4.9	100	(934)		
6. *Given enough time and money, almost all of man's important problems can be solved by science.*	A	2.5%	27.1	59.3	11.1	100	(919)	11.22	.05
	B	5.3%	28.4	56.7	9.6	100	(924)		
7. *I don't think public officials care much about what people like me think.*	A	6.1%	42.2	48.8	2.9	100	(918)	15.91	.01
	B	10.3%	40.3	44.7	4.7	100	(933)		

[a] Carried out in DAS-71. Items are listed in order given in form A. In form B, the items were given in the reverse order: 7, 6, 5, 4, 3, 2, 1.

[b] Probabilities given are for 3 degrees of freedom. If strongly agree and agree are collapsed and strongly disagree and disagree are collapsed, χ^2 for the 2 × 2 tables for the 7 items are: 8.8, .1, 16.5, 14.2, .2, 3.5, 1.0.

for discrimination when it follows the specific item, whereas the latter is unaffected by order. Noting that discriminatory responses are more frequent to the specific than to the general question, an explanation of the order effect at the marginal level seems straightforward: Some respondents who first give a discriminatory response to the specific item do so also to the general item in order to be consistent, whereas they would have given a nondiscriminatory response to the general item had it appeared first or alone. But this interpretation fails when we examine the cross-tabulations of the two items in Table 2.11: The order effect occurs more strongly among respondents who give nondiscriminatory responses to the specific item, which is just the opposite of our expectation. Indeed, consistency as measured by gamma goes down, not up, on the form that produces more similar marginals. (Further analysis indicates that all these effects occur entirely among noncollege educated respondents.) We have not been able to arrive at a satisfactory explanation of the changes produced by this experimental manipulation of order, but it does seem clear that the type of effect suggested by the marginal change is *not* supported by the shifts within the table. We are thus warned against assuming from marginal differences that we understand the psychological forces at work when order effects occur.

Before attempting to sum up what we have learned from this extensive review of question-order effects, we present much more briefly what is known about response-order effects within questions.

RESPONSE-ORDER EFFECTS

Closed survey questions present two or more alternatives from which respondents are to choose. If the order in which alternatives are read influences choice, we speak of response-order effects. Despite the obvious similarity to the problem of the ordering of questions, the consequences, and probably the nature, of response-order effects are different from those that occur between questions. Since the alternatives to a closed question are ordinarily asked in the same order whenever it is repeated, there is not the problem of different effects appearing from one survey to another. On the contrary, response-order effects may remain completely invisible, so that an investigator never realizes, for example, that the third of three alternatives is chosen not because of its substance, but because it is the last in the list. Furthermore, response-order effects are usually assumed to arise largely from the difficulty respondents face in attending to or keeping in mind all the alternatives presented, whereas question-order effects seem to involve mainly trans-

TABLE 2.11
Order Effects on Job Discrimination Items[a]

*Now I'd like your opinions about a different subject. Suppose that a well-qualified black engineer applied for an executive-level engineering job. The personnel director explained: 'Personally, I'd never give your race a thought, but the two people you would have to work with most closely—the plant manager and the chief engineer—both have strong feelings about blacks. I **can** offer you a job as a regular engineer, but **not** at the executive level, because any serious friction at the top could ruin the organization.'*

[General item] *In general, do you think employers should hire persons for top management without paying attention to whether they are white or black?*
[Specific item] *Was it all right for the personnel director in this case to refuse to hire a black engineer as an executive in order to avoid friction with the other employees?*

Order: Specific/General

	General Discrim.	Nondiscrim.	
Specific Discrim.	3.2	13.8	16.9%
Specific Nondiscrim.	7.9	75.1	83.1
	11.1%	88.9	100 (189)

gamma = .38

Order: General/Specific

	General Discrim.	Nondiscrim.	
Specific Discrim.	2.1	13.8	16.0%
Specific Nondiscrim.	2.7	81.4	84.0
	4.8%	95.2	100 (188)

gamma = .64

General discrimination marginals × order: $\chi^2 = 5.28$, $df = 1$, $p < .05$
Specific discrimination marginals × order: $\chi^2 = .06$, $df = 1$, n.s.

[a] Carried out in SRC–80 February. Data are for white respondents only. Tables have been constructed in terms of discriminatory versus nondiscriminatory responses, since yes has opposite meanings in terms of discrimination for the two questions. Percentages are based on grand totals. Discrepancies are due to rounding error.

fers of meaning from one question to another. Thus the two phenomena are quite different, except that they both arise out of the serial nature of verbal communication. In addition, from the special standpoint of this book, both are preliminary to investigations of fundamental aspects of question form.

The survey literature on response order is even more limited than that on question order. We have located only a handful of studies that deal adequately with typical attitude survey questions, and these mainly concern lists and scales, rather than more typical questions with two or three alternatives. The more general problem of response order has occupied psychologists for many years, and there is a large literature based on experiments using lists of various kinds of traits; we make no attempt to cover this literature since its relevance to survey problems, except in commonsense ways having to do with memory, appears limited. (For a brief review of the problem in the attitude change area, see McGuire, 1969: 214–217.)

Three types of response orders in survey questions have received experimental attention, the first of which will be treated in greatest detail because it is of most relevance to our research in subsequent chapters, as well as to survey questions more generally.

General Closed Survey Questions

Past Research

Payne's (1951) report of a large split-ballot experiment for the American Petroleum Institute provides the most useful past data available, since the 16 dichotomous and trichotomous items he employed are fairly typical in form of many survey questions on public issues, though probably more difficult than average in content and wording. Using an N said to be approximately 3200 for each form, nine of the variations in response order produced neither a significant difference ("significant" is not defined), nor a percentage difference greater than 2%.[14] However, seven questions showed differences ranging from 4.5% to 7.5%, all of which are characterized by Payne as significant. In 6 of the 7 cases, the last mentioned alternative received the higher choice—a recency effect. In the remaining case, a primacy effect appeared, presumably because of

---

[14]The two forms of the split-ballot differed in one way besides order of alternatives: One form "carried a brief description of the oil industry." This could have completely confounded the response order manipulation, but as reported below in Table 2.12, we successfully replicated two of Payne's results without this unwanted addition.

peculiarities unique to that question. The 7 susceptible questions were found to differ overall from the 9 unaffected questions by having one and a half times as many words, with more of these words polysyllabic as well. Payne concludes that question length and difficulty are the factors that create response-order effects, though he does not attempt to explain why these result in a recency bias.

Rugg and Cantril (1944) also claim that when response-order effects occur they involve recency, and they attribute the effects to "complicated" questions and to the fact that issues are asked about on which opinion is "uncrystallized." They quote two dichotomous questions that they say showed recency effects, but give no figures of any kind. They also mention that only the two quoted examples produced such effects, whereas an unspecified number of other cases failed to reveal order effects of any kind. The only other experimental study we have located that deals with typical survey questions administered to a general population sample (in England) is reported by Kalton *et al.* (1978). Four experiments were carried out involving reversals of three- and four-point scales, two concerning attitudes about traffic safety and two attitudes toward the European Common Market. The data are not presented in sufficient detail to allow unequivocal conclusions, but despite some leaning by the authors toward identifying a primacy effect, the order differences are small and it appears unlikely that any is statistically significant.

Replications of the Oil Industry Items

We were initially skeptical of response-order effects with dichotomous survey questions, and therefore decided to replicate experiments from the most compelling report in the literature: Payne's (1951) questions on the oil industry. Most of the questions are even more timely today than in the late 1940s, and our replication could not only test the reliability of the early results but also eliminate a defect in the original experimental design (see footnote 14, p. 58). We chose two of the questions that had shown significant response-order effects, repeating the exact wording of one on competition among oil companies and adapting (by changing the time frame) one about the remaining supply of oil.[15] Both experiments

[15]Payne's original oil supply question used 15 years for one end of the time frame, but 100 years for the other end. We retained 15 years but changed 100 to 25 (see Table 2.12 for exact wording). In administering this question a problem arose that was not mentioned by Payne: A number of respondents asked whether the total world supply or only the U.S. supply was to be considered. We decided to have interviewers answer "world supply" to such inquiries.

were carried out in SRC-79 January, and then repeated (for reasons we will explain) in SRC-79 April. Results are presented in Table 2.12, where the main comparison of interest is between the percentage choosing an alternative when it was listed first and the percentage choosing the same alternative when it was listed last.

For all four comparisons a response is chosen more often when it is read last than when read first, and in three of the four cases the difference is significant. Three of the percentage differences are fairly small

TABLE 2.12
Response Order Experiments on Oil Companies and Oil Supply Questions[a]

Oil companies	Survey	Percentage giving "competition" response by response order in January and April 1979 surveys			
		Response order			
Which of these statements comes		"Competition" first	"Competition" last	χ^2	*p*
closest to your own idea of how					
gasoline and oil prices are decided:					
Each company sets its own prices	SRC-79 Jan.	33.8%	39.5%	1.94	n.s.
to meet the competition, or the oil		(287)	(271)		
companies get together and set					
prices for their products?	SRC-79 April	32.4%	40.2%	3.86	<.05
		(445)	(214)		

Oil supply	Survey	Percentage giving "plenty" response by response order in January and April 1979 surveys			
		Response order			
Some people say that we will still have		"Plenty" first	"Plenty" last	χ^2	*p*
plenty of oil 25 years from now.					
Others say that at the rate we are	SRC-79 Jan.	63.5%	77.3%	13.00	<.001
using our oil, it will all be used up		(293)	(273)		
in about 15 years. Which of these					
ideas would you guess is most	SRC-79 April	60.7%	68.8%	4.17	<.05
nearly right?		(443)	(218)		

[a] The order of the two alternatives within each item was reversed in half the questionnaires. Each χ^2 tests (with $df = 1$) response choice by response order for each item in each survey. Numbers in parentheses are bases on which percentages are calculated. In SRC-79 Jan., the oil companies item preceded the oil supply item. In SRC-79 April, the oil supply item preceded the oil companies item.

(6–8%), but the fourth (14% in January for the oil supply item) is as large as many substantive differences treated as important in surveys. The differences are also generally as large or larger than Payne reports, despite the fact that the issues are probably more meaningful today than three decades ago, although other differences between Payne's and our surveys (e.g., face-to-face versus telephone mode of administration) make exact comparisons risky.

When we noted that the response order effect in the January survey was greater for the second item (oil supply) than for the first (oil companies), it seemed possible that the effect tended to increase over a series of such questions, thus producing a combined question-order and response-order effect. Therefore, in April we reversed the sequence of the questions, placing the oil supply experiment first and the oil companies experiment second. This time, however, results were almost identical for the two items. Moreover, the three-way interaction of response by response order by question sequence does not approach significance ($p > .20$) for either item considered separately. Hence there is not much evidence that question sequence intensifies order effects in these experiments.[16]

The successful replication on two separate occasions of two of the original Payne (1951) experiments makes it clear that even dichotomous items can produce serious response-order problems. Two practical issues immediately arise. First, are the effects shown by the oil items true of many survey questions, or are they limited to unusual topics asked about (as Payne suggests) in a long-winded way? Second, are our own methodological experiments on individual items compromised by uncontrolled response-order effects? Experiments on several types of items, chosen from our later chapters, are reported below in order to address both issues simultaneously.

Open–Closed Question Comparisons

Open questions avoid the possibility of a response-order effect, since no alternatives are read to respondents. But answers to closed questions

---

[16]One may also note an increase from January to April, 1979, in the proportion of respondents on one form who believe that oil supplies will be used up in 15 years ($\chi^2 = 4.26$, $df = 1$, $p < .05$). Since a similar change does not occur on the other form, we doubt that this particular over time difference should be taken seriously. Interpretation is complicated here by the fact that time and sequence are confounded in the January–April comparisons.

can, as we have seen, be affected by the order in which alternatives are read. Thus differences in responses to open and closed questions could be due merely to order effects on the closed version of the question. The problem seems potentially serious for the kinds of items used in our open–closed experiments, since they include a large number of response alternatives (typically five) and either a primacy or a recency effect could easily be hypothesized. We therefore carried out three experiments to determine whether answers to the closed questions used in our open–closed comparisons are influenced by the order in which they are read. (All three experiments were carried out in telephone surveys, hence show cards were not used.)

The results for the first of these experiments are shown in the top panel of Table 2.13. The five closed alternatives of an item on work values, discussed in detail in Chapter 3, were presented in SRC-77 February in five different orders to randomly defined subsamples. Each ordering began with a different alternative and continued sequentially through the other four. Thus, although not every permutation of the five alternatives was tried, each alternative appears first in one subsample, second in another, and so on.

There is no evidence in Table 2.13 that response order influenced choice of a work value. Nor is there evidence for such an order effect when only less-educated respondents (those with less than 12 years of schooling) are considered separately. Furthermore, when a later work values item containing only three closed alternatives was administered in three different orders (see Chapter 3, footnote 16), it too failed to show any sign of an order effect ($\chi^2 = 2.41$, $df = 4$, $p > .50$). Finally, another question in SRC–77 February asked respondents to choose the "most important problem" facing the country from a list of five alternatives; the list was also presented in five different orders. Again, there is no significant relation between order and choice, nor any meaningful trend that might point to a primacy, recency, or other order effect (see Table 2.13, bottom panel).

In sum, when a fairly large set of alternatives is read to respondents, we find no evidence at all of order effects. (It should be noted that in these experiments interviewers were instructed to say at the end of the question: *I'll read those again if it would be helpful.*) This suggests that it is not the sheer number of alternatives or even the total number of words that create response-order effects. From our more immediate research standpoint, the absence of order effects from these questions indicates that the main open–closed experiments discussed in Chapter 3 were not subject to this type of artifact.

TABLE 2.13
Percentage Choosing Particular Alternatives by Order of Alternatives

Work-values order experiment (SRC–77 Feb.)[a]

		Order of Alternatives				
	Alternatives	ABCDE	BCDEA	CDEAB	DEABC	EABCD
A.	Work that pays well	10.0%	11.7%	6.6%	9.6%	10.5%
B.	Work that gives a feeling of accomplishment	30.9	36.7	33.6	28.1	41.1
C.	Work where there is not too much supervision and you make most decisions yourself	13.6	7.5	13.9	15.8	9.7
D.	Work that is pleasant and where the other people are nice to work with	23.6	19.2	22.1	28.1	22.6
E.	Work that is steady with little chance of being laid off	21.8	25.0	23.8	18.4	16.1
		100	100	100	100	100
		(110)	(120)	(122)	(114)	(124)

$\chi^2 = 15.56$, $df = 16$, n.s.

Most-important-problem order experiment (SRC–77 Feb.)[b]

		Order of Alternatives				
	Alternatives	ABCDE	BCDEA	CDEAB	DEABC	EABCD
A.	Crime and violence	16.8%	14.8%	17.8%	21.6%	25.2%
B.	Rising prices	22.1	28.7	21.2	13.8	15.1
C.	Not enough jobs	31.0	29.5	36.4	36.2	31.1
D.	Poor quality of government leaders	15.9	7.4	10.2	8.6	12.6
E.	Breakdown of morality among people in general	14.2	19.7	14.4	19.8	16.0
		100	100	100	100	100
		(113)	(122)	(118)	(116)	(119)

$\chi^2 = 21.07$, $df = 16$, n.s.

[a] The work-value question read: *This next question is on the subject of work. People look for different things in a job. Which one of the following five things would you most prefer in a job?*

[b] The most important problem question read: *Which one of the following five problems do you think is the most important problem facing this country at present?*

The Addition of a Middle Alternative

Another type of experiment that might be susceptible to response-order effects is presented in Chapter 6: the addition of a logical middle alternative to a previously dichotomous item. If the middle alternative is added at the end, choice of it could be caused by a recency effect.[17] We initially carried out two response order experiments in SRC–79 April with items that had originally been used in middle-alternative experiments. In both cases, placement of the middle alternative last rather than second in the response sequence increased the proportion choosing it, as shown in Table 2.14.

In one case (the Vietnam item) the increase seems slight (4%) and does not approach significance when the two alternatives involved in the interchange of order are compared. In the other case (the divorce item) the increase is substantial (12%) and highly significant. This is an instance, however, where an apparent difference in results may be exaggerated by the combination of different sample sizes (there are only 40% as many cases in the interchanged categories for the Vietnam item as for the divorce item) and different item skews in terms of the percentage scale. If odds ratios are used to evaluate magnitudes, the divorce item shows an order effect that is only a little stronger than the Vietnam item (.55 to .68), and if the Vietnam difference had been produced with as many cases as the divorce item, it would reach the .05 level of significance. It is safest, therefore, to conclude that one of the items tested shows a highly reliable recency effect, whereas the other shows a nonsignificant trend difficult to evaluate because of the small number of cases in the strategic cells.

Whatever the conclusion about the Vietnam item, it is striking that the divorce item, which is neither exotic nor verbose, reveals a strong response-order effect. This suggests that almost any item might be susceptible to such order effects, and more urgently for us it raises the issue of whether our study of middle alternatives (Chapter 6) is confounded

[17]Note that "middle alternative" refers to a *logical* middle position, not to a position in a serial listing. Thus a middle alternative may be ordered last in a question, as it ordinarily was in the experiments described in Chapter 6, and this is what gives rise to the problem discussed here. A similar problem occurs when don't know (DK) options are added in the last position in experiments, as described in Chapter 4. However, we have not investigated response order effects on DK items for two reasons. First, many of our DK results are based on DK filter questions that precede a substantive item, and hence response order effects are not a confounding factor. Second, in those cases where the DK is part of a single question, it is difficult to place it anywhere other than at the end. Nevertheless, such an experiment would be of value from a theoretical standpoint.

TABLE 2.14
Response-Order Effects with Middle Alternative Items[a]

Vietnam Aid (SRC–79 April)

| Looking back, do you think our government did too *much* to help the South Vietnamese government in the war, *not enough* to help the South Vietnamese government, or was it about the *right amount*? | 1. Too much
2. Not enough
3. Right amount | 66.3%
13.8
19.8 | Looking back, do you think our government did too *much* to help the South Vietnamese government in the war, about the *right amount*, or *not enough* to help the South Vietnamese government? | 1. Too much
3. Not enough
2. Right amount | 67.7%
16.4
15.9 |
| | | 100
(419) | | | 100
(195) |

$\chi^2 = 1.75, \ df = 1,$ [b] n.s.

Divorce (SRC–79 April)

| Should divorce in this country be *easier* to obtain, more *difficult* to obtain, or *stay as it is now*? | 1. Easier
2. More difficult
3. Stay as is | 22.6%
36.2
41.2 | Should divorce in this country be *easier to obtain, stay as it is now,* or be more *difficult to obtain?* | 1. Easier
3. More difficult
2. Stay as is | 25.6%
45.7
28.8 |
| | | 100
(464) | | | 100
(219) |

$\chi^2 = 10.28, \ df = 1,$ [b] $p < .01$

[a] Numbers preceding alternatives indicate the order in which responses were read.
[b] Chi squares have 1 *df*, since the test employed the second and third positions only.

by adding the alternatives to the ends of items. We pursued these issues by means of several further experiments.

First, given the counterintuitive nature of the order effect for the divorce item, it seemed important to replicate it. The first two sections of Table 2.15 show an almost exact replication in September of the recency effect discovered in April. Second, in the September survey we also included a third questionnaire form that omitted a middle alternative altogether, in order to determine whether the middle-alternative effects described in detail in Chapter 6 could be explained simply as response-order effects. A comparison of the second and third question forms in Table 2.15 shows clearly that this is *not* the case: Even when the middle alternative is placed in the second position, it produces a highly significant increase in choices over the form that allows for such responses only when they are verbalized spontaneously. This point will become clearer in the context of Chapter 6.

Finally, we carried out an order experiment with a two-alternative divorce item, in which only the responses "easier" and "more difficult" were offered, and they were rotated over two forms. The purpose of the experiment (in SRC–79 June) was to determine whether the previously discovered order effect with three alternatives also occurred when only two alternatives were offered. The results are clearly negative: "easier" was chosen by 46% (of 276 persons) when listed first and by 43.9% (of 280 persons) when listed second ($\chi^2 = .24$, $df = 1$).

Thus, the divorce item reveals a highly reliable recency effect when three alternatives are employed, but the effect disappears entirely when the logical middle alternative is omitted and only two alternatives are used. Furthermore, although the recency effect means that the last listed alternative obtains about 10% of the responses merely because of its serial position, this artifact does not account for most of the effect of adding a logical middle alternative to an item, at least not in the one case we tested. Nonetheless, the order effect is worrisome, since it is fairly large (10–12%) and occurs with an item that does not seem exceptionally lengthy or difficult.

Counterargument Additions

In Chapter 7 we consider questions where balance is attempted through addition of a counterargument. In all such cases there is evidence that proportions shift in favor of the negative (counterargument) side of the issue. But since the counterargument is always added at the end of the question, we may have confounded the increment due to the

TABLE 2.15
Separation of Order Effects and Middle Alternative Effects for Divorce Item (SRC–79 Sept.)[a]

A. *Should divorce in this country be easier to obtain, more difficult to obtain, or stay as it is now?*		B. *Should divorce in this country be easier to obtain, stay as it is now, or be more difficult to obtain?*		C. *Should divorce in this country be easier or more difficult to obtain than it is now?*	
1. Easier	21.0%	1. Easier	23.4%	1. Easier	39.5%
2. More difficult	33.7	3. More difficult	41.4	2. More difficult	50.2
3. Stay as is	45.3	2. Stay as is	35.2	Stay as is (volunteered)	10.4
	100		100		100
	(309)		(290)		(299)

Form A versus form B: $\chi^2 = 6.10$, $df = 1$,[b] $p < .05$ Form B versus form C: $\chi^2 = 53.92$, $df = 1$,[c] $p < .001$

[a] Numbers preceding alternatives indicate the order in which alternatives were read.
[b] 1 df, since the test employed the second and third alternatives only.
[c] 1 df, since the test is of the middle alternative versus the two extremes collapsed.

counterargument with that due to a recency order effect. We investigated this possibility by varying the order of the response alternatives in a question on unions taken from Chapter 7. As Table 2.16 shows, there is no evidence that the order in which the responses are read influences their choice. It was not practical to do order experiments on other items from Chapter 7, though this would obviously have been desirable. We doubt, however, that the primary effects of balance in dichotomous items can be reduced to response-order effects.

Forced-Choice Items

A special but important form of balance occurs when agree–disagree items are transformed into forced-choice questions. When we find differences between the two forms, this may not be due to removal of an agreeing response set, but rather to the creation of a response-order effect on the forced-choice form. We tested this possibility with two items that showed large form effects originally presumed to be due to an agreeing set: the individual versus social conditions and the adequate-housing items, discussed in Chapter 8 and Appendix D, respectively. Results for these response-order experiments are shown in Table 2.17.

The individual–social conditions item shows no sign at all of an order effect when the two alternatives are reversed. However, the adequate housing item not only shows a large order effect, but it is a primacy rather than recency effect. This is puzzling, for the question seems to be similar in format and length to the two oil industry items we replicated from Payne (1951). In searching for an explanation for the primacy effect, a suggested hypothesis was that both alternatives of the housing item have very high appeal to respondents, and the one that is heard first may create a favorable commitment to it, which in turn produces a negative reinterpretation of the alternative that follows. This reasoning is similar to Asch's (1946) explanation of primacy effects when subjects make summary impression ratings after hearing a set of personality traits read to them.

In order to test the applicability of the hypothesis to response-order effects, we carried out an experiment on an item on open housing that had been developed some years ago in an effort to create alternatives equally high on social desirability (Brannon et al., 1973). The item and the results are shown in Table 2.17. No evidence for the hypothesis appears. Either this explanation of the adequate-housing order effect is not correct, or the open housing item somehow fails to provide two highly appealing alternatives. The latter seems unlikely, leaving us

TABLE 2.16
Response-Order Effects with Counterargument Addition[a]

Unions (SRC–79 June)

	2. Required 1. Left to individual		1. Required 2. Left to individual	
If there is a union at a particular company or business, do you think that it should be left to the individual to decide whether or not he wants to be in the union, **or** do you think that all workers there should be required to be union members?	17.9% 82.1	If there is a union at a particular company or business, do you think that all the workers there should be required to be union members, **or** do you think it should be left to the individual to decide whether or not he wants to be in the union?	21.0% 79.0	
	100 (307)		100 (329)	
	$\chi^2 = .95$, $df = 1$, n.s.			

[a] Numbers preceding alternatives indicate the order in which alternatives were read.

TABLE 2.17
Response-Order Effects with Forced-Choice Items[a]

Individual/Social conditions (SRC–78 Dec.)

	1. Individuals 2. Social conditions		2. Individuals 1. Social conditions	
Which in your opinion is more to blame for crime and lawlessness in this country—individuals or social conditions?	43.4% 56.6	Which in your opinion is more to blame for crime and lawlessness in this country—social conditions or individuals?	44.7% 55.3	
	100 (309)		100 (159)	
	$\chi^2 = .07$, $df = 1$, n.s.			

(continued)

TABLE 2.17—*Continued*

Adequate Housing
(SRC–79 Aug.)

Some people feel the federal government should see to it that all people have adequate housing, while others feel each person should provide for his own housing. Which comes *closest* to how you feel about this?

1. Government	44.6%	2. Government 29.5%
2. Each person	55.4	1. Each person 70.5
	100	100
	(327)	(329)

Some people feel each person should provide for his own housing, while others feel the federal government should see to it that all people have adequate housing. Which comes *closest* to how you feel about this?

$\chi^2 = 16.26, df = 1, p < .001$

Open Housing
(SRC–79 Nov.)

Suppose there is a community-wide vote on which of the following two laws to put into effect. One law says that a home-owner can decide for himself who to sell his house to, even if he prefers not to sell to someone because of their race or color. The second law says that a home-owner cannot refuse to sell to someone because of their race or color. Which law would you vote for?

1. Owner decide	44.1%	2. Owner decide 46.4%
2. Open housing	55.9	1. Open housing 53.6
	100	100
	(340)	(362)

Suppose there is a community-wide vote on which of the following two laws to put into effect. One law says that a homeowner cannot refuse to sell to someone because of their race or color. The second law says that a home-owner can decide for himself who to sell his house to, even if he prefers not to sell to blacks. Which law would you vote for?

$\chi^2 = .37, df = 1, $ n.s.

[a] Numbers preceding alternatives indicate the order in which alternatives were read.

without a satisfactory explanation for the primacy order effect that occurred with the adequate housing item.[18]

Interactions with Education

As with most of our experimental variations, we hypothesized that response-order effects would be greatest for less-educated respondents. Such respondents should be slower to comprehend the content of a question and therefore more apt to have their choice influenced by an irrelevant cue such as the order of responses. There are some trends in the data that support this hypothesis, but none of the three-way interactions involving education (i.e., response by response order by education) is significant at the .05 level, and there are enough contrary trends to render the conclusion doubtful. At this point, we do not see any consistent evidence that response-order effects vary systematically by educational level.

Conclusions

We carried out a total of 12 experiments (plus 3 replications) in which response order was randomly varied. In 8 of the experiments there is little or no sign of an effect, but in 4 experiments reliable evidence appears that forces us to conclude that such effects are real and can be moderately large. (All of these experiments were successfully replicated by ourselves, as well as replicating in 2 cases results presented originally by Payne in 1951.) For 3 of the positive cases, the effect involves an increase in the last mentioned response—a recency effect—but in one case a primacy effect appears.

[18]The adequate housing experiment was replicated in SRC–79 Sept. and produced results similar in direction to, though not as strong as, those in Table 2.17: 40.3% (of 303 respondents) chose the government alternative when it came first; 33.3% (of 297) when it came second ($\chi^2 = 3.10$, $df = 1$, $p < .10$). The September survey also included a third form of the question: *Do you agree or disagree with the following statement: The federal government should see to it that all people have adequate housing.* The percentage agreeing was 55.1% (of 301), which is significantly higher ($p < .01$) than both of the forced-choice figures. Thus the government response receives its highest acceptance (55%) when it is stated alone in agree–disagree form; its second highest when stated first in forced-choice form (40%); and its least acceptance when stated second in forced-choice form (33%). This at least raises the possibility of a continuum in some cases between acquiescence and order effects, but since most of the latter are of a recency—not a primacy—variety, the continuum would not have much generality.

Exactly what causes these response-order effects is much less clear. Payne's explanation that it is question length and number of syllables per word seems reasonable and it fits the data he had at hand. Yet the divorce item, which shows a highly reliable effect, does not seem unusual in either of these respects. Nor does the number of alternatives per se seem crucial, since the oil items with only two alternatives *do* show effects, whereas the work values and important problem items with five alternatives show *no* effects. An additional mystery is the appearance of a large primacy effect in one experiment, in contrast to recency effects in three others.

At present we are unable to offer a fully adequate way of distinguishing questions that show order effects from questions that do not and we can only note that effects did not occur with very brief dichotomous items. We also have no way of knowing whether the proportion of items showing such effects is similar to the one-third found in our experiments with a nonrandom sample of items. We do feel fairly sure from the data that major findings in later chapters are not due to response-order effects, although such effects may have complicated some of our results. Finally, it is evident that further research, preferably systematically over a range of items, is needed to establish more adequately the frequency and if possible the causes of response-order effects with typical two- and three-alternative forced-choice survey items. Since there is no clear evidence that the effects are tied to educational level, exploratory work may not need to be limited to probability samples of the type we employ.

Long Lists

Evidence for primacy effects appears consistently in choices of five favorite types of radio programs from a cardlist of 16 included at the end of a large household survey ($N = 16,193$) by Becker (1954). The author concludes that "the chances of a program type being chosen as a 'favorite' seems to improve steadily as the program type moves from the sixteenth to the first position on the check-list." An earlier study (Campbell and Mohr, 1950) using the same list had found only a slight trace of such an order effect, but Becker attributes this to the authors' use of brief group administration with college students, rather than lengthy interviews with busy individuals in homes. It seems likely that it was the setting rather than the sample that produced the difference, since Becker reports that education, age, and sex did not interact with the order effect he discovered. Further relevant evidence for a primacy effect when long lists are used comes from studies of voting behavior: candidates whose names appear near the top of a ballot apparently gain votes from position alone, at least in nonpartisan elections where there are many names (Mueller, 1970; Brook and Upton, 1974). We did not ourselves carry out any experiment on long lists, since none of our question-form experiments involve such lists. However, the closed items in the open–closed experiments discussed previously involve lists of five alternatives and they showed no order effects of any type, as already reported. Quite likely, only a much longer list produces effects, and perhaps only when it is to be read by the respondent.

Item Scales

Primacy effects also appear in four investigations using verbal rating scales: for example, agree strongly, agree, disagree, and disagree strongly. Quinn and Belson (1969) included in interviews 38 scales in the traditional order (favorable alternative first) for half of a sample of English adults, and in reversed order (unfavorable alternative first) for the other half. Most, but not all, of the scales showed significant primacy effects: that is, an alternative received more choices when read first than when read last. No interactions with education, age, or sex were discovered. Similar order effects were found in an earlier study by Belson (1966) using self-administration in group settings; in a mail survey reported by Payne (1971); and in an interview survey using show cards by Carp (1974) where evaluative items but not factual items showed consistent primacy effects. Payne's (1971) order effects, although always in the primacy direction and generally consistent with those of Quinn and Belson (1969), were not so large in magnitude, a difference he attributes to the greater time respondents have to look over the alternatives in a self-administered setting, as against an interview.

All three of these studies involved printed scales, since even Quinn and Belson (1969) used show cards. Kalton *et al.* (1978) suggest that this may be a critical factor in producing primacy effects in these cases. However, an experiment by Powers, Morros, Goudy, and Keith (1977) failed to find response-order effects over a variety of similar items and scales, although show cards were used for many of them.[19] Thus we doubt that the presence or absence of show cards is the key factor,

[19]Powers *et al.* (1977) do not indicate whether show cards were used, but Powers responded to a personal inquiry by noting that "for all the scales and about one-third of the item measures the respondent was handed a card with the response categories, appropriately ordered for the two forms of the questionnaire."

although it would be useful for a face-to-face interviewing survey to manipulate this variable experimentally with extended scales of the kind Belson (1966) employed.

If a primacy effect does commonly occur with agree–disagree scales, it could help explain what is usually regarded as acquiescence bias. Virtually all agree–disagree items are presented with the agree end of the scale listed first, even when the original item content is reversed. Thus, agreement with both the original and the reversal could arise not because of a bias toward agree, but because of a bias toward choice of the first listed alternative. This possibility, even if unlikely, is so important that we carried out one experiment to test it using an item that plays a key role in our discussion of acquiescence in Chapter 8:

> *Please tell me whether you agree or disagree with this statement:*
> **Individuals** *are more to blame than* **social conditions** *for crime and lawlessness in this country.*

This standard version provided one form of the question in SRC–80 February; the other form was identical except that the words agree and disagree were interchanged in the introduction. Results show the distribution of agree and disagree to be the same to the percentage point (59% and 41%, respectively) on the two forms. Thus there is no evidence that the order in which agree and disagree alternatives are read to respondents affects their choice at all. Since the item tested has only two scale points (agree and disagree), it does not provide a test of primacy effects with longer scales, but the results are directly relevant to the kinds of items employed in our own work (Chapter 8).

CONCLUDING DISCUSSION

In practice, survey research proceeds as though order effects were nonexistent or at least a trivial matter. Questions are moved from one survey to another with little regard for effects on response, and changes in the order of alternatives are likewise assumed to make no difference. These convenient assumptions must be challenged in the light of both past research and our own experiments. Question-order effects are evidently not pervasive, as our analysis of the 1971 Detroit Area Study questionnaire indicated, but there are enough instances to show that they are not rare either. They, as well as response-order effects, occur with sufficient frequency and are sufficiently large in magnitude to compete with substantive explanations when an item produces different results in different surveys.

With regard to question order, a major problem arises out of the increasing use of attitude questions as indicators of social change. If the meaning of a question is influenced by preceding questions, then replicating a question in different contexts confounds order effects with true change. We saw a number of instances where this would certainly occur: For example, an NORC item intended to measure attitudes toward abortion varied by some 15% depending on whether or not a related item was included. This was not an artificially constructed example, and could easily have misled an investigator who borrowed the item out of context—as is the common practice with attitude surveys. An even more striking instance appeared when we replicated a 1948 experiment by Hyman and Sheatsley in which the order of two items about Communist and American reporters is varied: The direction and even the nature of social change would have been misinterpreted without having *both* contexts at both points in time.

Yet there were also many instances where order effects might well have occurred, but did not. It is clearly not the case that *any* disruption of context or sequence will change responses or relationships, and the majority of survey results are probably not so delicately dependent on surrounding items. Our problem then is to discover what types of questions and what types of contexts are most likely to prove especially sensitive in this respect. This chapter provides some suggestions, though none can be considered to be firmly established.

First, context effects occur when two or more questions deal with aspects of the same issue or with closely related issues. This may seem so obvious as not to be worth stating, but it takes on practical importance because questionnaires are ordinarily constructed by grouping together questions on the same subject matter. Thus our very method of questionnaire design tends to encourage context effects. Of course we do not know—no one seems ever to have tested the point—that separation of items within the same questionnaire will eliminate order effects (see footnote 8 for a clue that it may not). Nor can we always claim that the "true meaning" of an item is manifested only when the question appears in isolation. Certain context effects tell us just the opposite: The meaning of items is not fixed and cannot be detached from placement, so that isolation from related items is itself a kind of context.

Second, general summary-type questions seem to be more sensitive to order than are more specific questions. When we ask people to evaluate a complex topic in an overall way we are probably inviting contextual effects. It may be that a general question has so many facets, or that its frame of reference is so open to alternative definitions, that respondents can provide an answer only by specifying it in some way, and a major aid in this specification is the context or sequence in which the question appears. Thus, investigators should be particularly wary of moving general summary items around, or for that matter of assuming that people are able to answer such questions in the summary way that investigators might like. As individuals our thoughts are probably more concrete and situational than are the questions we can frame as scientists.

Third, two questions considered in conjunction can create or at least emphasize a norm that is not obvious when the questions are considered separately. A norm of evenhanded treatment of two parties to a dispute seems to be particularly powerful in certain context effects. Here again, it is not clear that there is a right or a wrong way to ask a question, but rather that investigators need to decide what it is they are after in order to make an intelligent decision about context.

Fourth, context effects themselves are not all of the same type. Although context usually increases consistency between responses to two or more items, in some instances context seems to sharpen the perceived difference and produce contrast. Furthermore, although most context effects show up in the form of marginal differences, sometimes only correlations among items appear to be affected. These last points emphasize that question-order effects are not easy to predict. We ourselves were usually wrong in thinking that we could create such effects at will, and most of the important effects we did produce were matters of accident or depended upon use of earlier examples. Although this may testify to the limitations of the present authors, it also suggests that knowledge of the nature of question order effects is still slight. One illustration of this was the decision in the National Crime Survey to place attitude items before factual items in order to avoid context effects on the former—only to find that the attitude questions produced important changes in responses to the factual questions.

Finally, we must acknowledge that the implications of order effects for our own question form experiments are serious. When the first such form experiment (e.g., one involving open and closed questions) appears in a questionnaire, any difference discovered could conceivably involve interaction with a preceding set of questions that were common to both halves of the split-ballot. The problem then becomes even more acute for subsequent experiments in that interview, for the first experiment itself creates different contexts for the parts of all later experiments. Thus the problem is compounded when more than one experiment is included in a single survey, as indeed must often be done for reasons of efficiency. All we can do is to be on the alert for possible form differences that may be due partly or entirely to order differences, and, furthermore, to try to replicate form effects whenever possible in order to test their generality beyond any particular context. The inherent difficulty of the enterprise helps us understand why knowledge of question effects of all kinds is likely to be a slow and uphill struggle.

The problem of response order is of a different nature than that of order between questions. Since the ordering of alternatives within a closed question is ordinarily constant from one survey to another, there is not the likely possibility of confounding true change with a response-order effect. But any attempt to interpret absolute response proportions runs into the problem that these can be due in part to recency or perhaps primacy effects—that is, to a tendency by some respondents to choose the last or the first alternative offered regardless of content. Furthermore, any variable correlated with this tendency could lead to spurious conclusions, although we did not in fact discover such sources of correlated error. Response-order effects can be particularly troublesome for research on question form, since certain features of question form (for example, addition of a logical middle alternative) are easily confounded with response order. Fortunately, a series of experiments reported in this chapter seems to show that such confounding did not constitute a serious problem, although the possibility certainly remains a live one.

The exact causes of response-order effects are far from settled. The entirely plausible notion that they occur with long and difficult questions and response categories does not fit all of our data comfortably. There are exceptions on both sides: a relatively short and seemingly straightforward question that shows such effects (the divorce item), and two questions with five alternatives each that do not (e.g., the work values item). Moreover, the fact that the effects are not greater for low-than for high-educated respondents does *not* fit a model stressing poor verbal comprehension or short-term memory as causes of response order effects. Unfortunately we did not include attitude strength as a variable in any of the response order experiments.

Overall, order effects of all kinds seem to us to constitute one of the most important areas for methodological research. They can be very large, are difficult to predict, and are intimately tied up with both substantive research issues and with further work on individual question forms. At this point research needs to be aimed not merely at producing more examples, but at understanding why those already obtained occur. Moreover, we must attempt to find out whether separating two items by several or many others eliminates a known context effect, as is commonly assumed. Greater understanding of these fundamental issues is urgently needed if attitude surveys are to avoid tripping on their own artifacts.

3
Open versus Closed Questions

A free form does not assure freedom. As a form, it is just one
more form.
—Wallace Stevens, *A Note on Poetry*

"Since the beginning of social research," wrote Paul Lazarsfeld (1944),
"students have tried to combine the value of detailed qualitative applica-
tions with the advantages of more formalized techniques which could be
managed on a mass basis." Since Lazarsfeld's often cited paper was
written, the controversy over open as against closed modes of inquiry in
surveys has been largely resolved in practice by the victory of the closed
form—no doubt because of the evident efficiency of such questions for
interviewing, coding, and analysis. Despite a few exceptions, the results
of social surveys today are results based mainly on what are varyingly
called closed, fixed-choice, or precoded questions.[1]

What is most remarkable about the triumph of closed questions is that
it occurred with so little direct confrontation of the two question forms.
Despite the controversies among practitioners and organizations in the
1930s and 1940s, and the endless discussions in textbooks ever after, it is
difficult to locate a single rigorous experiment in which closed and open
versions of essentially the same attitude question were asked of the
same general population in a split-ballot or other experimental design.
Argument for the superiority of one form or the other is based almost
entirely on common sense and anecdotal experience.[2] This chapter

[1]The General Social Survey of the National Opinion Research Center (NORC), for
example, deliberately excludes open attitude questions entirely.

[2]A recent treatment by Bailey (1978: 104–108) is fairly typical. It discusses in a sensible
way a large number of advantages and disadvantages of each form, but cites no empirical
evidence. Moreover, the issue is apparently regarded as settled, since the Instructor's

reports one of the few systematic efforts to compare complex open and closed questions within the framework of the standard large-scale attitude survey.

All our comparisons attempt to keep open and closed questions as alike as possible, varying only the presence of fixed alternatives as against instructions to record answers verbatim in order to allow their later coding by trained coders. We do not deal with the issue of closed questions versus more general unstructured or semistructured inquiries. Although that broader issue preoccupied investigators in the early years of survey research (e.g., Stouffer, 1933), nonstandardized interviews or case histories are rarely employed in contemporary large-scale survey research, though they may be used to gain insights where only small samples are involved (Smith, Bruner, and White, 1956; Lane, 1962) or where validation of previous closed questions is the goal (Schuman and Harding, 1964).

PRESUMED ADVANTAGES
OF OPEN QUESTIONS

When all is said and done, there appear to be two principal arguments for using open questions in attitude surveys despite their greater inefficiency. First, closed questions constructed in an a priori way may fail to provide an appropriate set of alternatives meaningful in substance or wording to respondents. This argument, however, leads straight to the recommendation of Lazarsfeld (1944) and others (e.g., McKennell, 1974, Moser and Kalton, 1971) that survey questionnaire design should *begin* with open questions in pilot or pretest work, then use the resulting responses as a basis for developing a meaningful set of closed alternatives. Such sensible-sounding advice is perhaps more often preached than practiced—and even where practiced is usually compromised by the small, unrepresentative, and hurried nature of much pretesting. In any case, it indicates a preliminary rather than a definitive advantage of open questions.

Manual (Kiecolt, 1978) for the book offers the following multiple-choice item for testing students, with the first alternative keyed as "correct":

Which of the following is the best type of question for gathering information about complex issues? (a) open-ended (b) closed-ended (c) interval-level

In our concluding discussion we will discuss the few empirical open–closed comparisons that we have located in the survey literature.

The second argument is that respondents are apt to be influenced by the specific closed alternatives given, and that therefore a more valid picture of respondent choice is obtained if they must produce an answer themselves. There are several versions of this argument: for example, an interest in measuring what is most salient to respondents; a desire to avoid "social desirability" effects; a concern to prevent mechanical choice or mere guessing. All these have in common the assumption that the superiority of open questions is inherent in the form, and cannot be provided through *any* precoded set of alternatives.

GOALS

Ideally, experiments comparing open and closed questions should test separately *both* advantages of open questions. We succeeded in doing this fully in only one instance, but made two other attempts where the failures are also instructive. As in our other experiments on question form, we attempted to start from items of some demonstrated usefulness—a question on work values, one on child values, and one on the most important problem facing the United States—each of which had appeared in one form or the other in an important past survey. We begin with the experiments on the most-important-problem question, for although they were in a sense abortive, we learned two quite important lessons: one about the advantages of closed questions and the other about the advantages of open questions. We then turn to our most complete series of experiments, dealing with the work-values item. Here it was possible to approximate an ideal model of question development, and the findings are instructive in a number of respects. Finally we present briefly a more puzzling set of results concerning an inquiry into childrearing values.[3]

Two possible kinds of open–closed differences are of interest in these analyses: (*a*) differences in marginal or univariate distributions that purport to say something about the importance of one value or problem as compared with another; and (*b*) differences in bivariate or multivariate relations, which the analyst uses in trying to discover the location and determinants of responses in a general population. Our results will be relatively straightforward where open and closed forms do *not* differ

[3]Experiments on all three items were first carried out in DAS–76. All later experiments were in SRC national telephone surveys. Two of the latter had some respondents in common, which provides panel data.

beyond sampling error in either of these two ways. In such cases, survey investigators are free to use whichever form suits them, though cost considerations will undoubtedly push toward closed questions. The matter is more complex where differences do occur, since the issue of which form is more valid naturally arises at that point. We cannot provide definitive evidence on this issue, but the problem will be posed sharply and some tentative conclusions offered that have important implications for the development of survey questions.

THE MOST IMPORTANT PROBLEM
FACING THE COUNTRY

The "most important problem" question is one of the very few regularly posed in open form in surveys. It is used in both Gallup Polls and ISR Election Studies to determine the relative importance of issues for the general public. We drew on the 1974 ISR Election Study open codes to construct a closed item with eight alternatives. Both it and a parallel open version were administered as part of a split-ballot experiment in the DAS–76 survey. Open codes were constructed to be equivalent to the closed alternatives, with others added (on the basis of preliminary review of 150 cases) to accommodate other types of responses.[4] The questions, codes, and univariate results by form are presented in Table 3.1.[5]

Crime

Of the eight categories common to both forms, only three—Crime, Inflation, and Unemployment—produce appreciable proportions of respondents on the open form, but for these the form comparison is quite interesting. Inflation and Unemployment yield essentially the same proportions on both forms, despite the fact that the open form spreads

[4]These could not be the first questions in the questionnaire, but the preceding questions were all constant across form, and most dealt with irrelevant issues. The one prior mention (crime) that might have affected our analysis was brief and appeared much earlier in the questionnaire. It does not seem to have had an important effect, since it is the closed rather than the open form that produced a high crime percentage.

[5]Checkcoding of 61 of the open responses yielded perfect agreement in 84% of the cases. Other experiments reported in this chapter also had agreement percentages in the 80s, except for one of 76% for work-values Experiment I.

TABLE 3.1
Most Important Problem: Experiment I[a]

Closed Form		Open Form	
*Which of these is the **most** important problem facing this country at present?*		*What do you think is the **most** important problem facing this country at present?*	
1. *Food and energy shortages*	6.0%	1. Food and energy shortages: natural resources problems, e.g., *not enough fuel; ecology; overpopulation.*	1.7%
2. *Crime and violence*	34.9	2. Crime: public order problems, e.g., *courts are too easy on criminals.*	15.7
3. *Inflation*	12.6	3. Inflation: high prices, e.g., *increases in the cost of living.*	13.3
4. *Unemployment*	19.7	4. Unemployment: lack of jobs, e.g., *too many out of work.*	19.1
5. *Decreased trust in government*	9.9	5. Decreased trust in government: lack of confidence in government generally, e.g., *people don't think the government will do what is right; the people aren't behind the government.*	3.0
6. *Busing*	1.1	6. Busing	1.1
7. *Breakdown of morals and religion*	9.2	7. Breakdown of morals and religion: loss of traditional morality, e.g., *family disintegration; alcohol, drugs, and sex; turning away from God.*	5.7
8. *Racial problems*	1.6	8. Racial problems: majority–minority group problems.	2.4
		9. Quality of leaders: dissatisfaction with behavior of officials, e.g., *crooked politicians; government officials who commit crimes.*	7.0
		10. Characteristics of people: faults and desires of individuals, e.g., *people want too much; greed; people don't get along with others.*	4.6

(*continued*)

TABLE 3.1—*Continued*

Closed Form		Open Form	
		11. Characteristics of the system: defects in social structure, e.g., *not enough equality;* *the government is too big,* *inefficient, or unresponsive.*	3.0
		12. Supportive references to welfare: more should be done for the less well-off, e.g., *poverty;* *hunger; medical care.*	1.5
		13. Unsupportive references to welfare: too much is done for the less well-off, e.g., *welfare fraud;* *the welfare mess.*	.9
		14. National defense: military security.	.4
		15. Foreign affairs: relations with other countries.	.9
		16. The 1976 Presidential primaries or election	4.6
		17. Communism: unspecific references.	.7
		18. The economy, money problems: mentions of the economy not codable in 3 or 4.	3.7
		96. More than one codable response with no indication of priority.	5.4
97. Other	1.8	97. Other	3.0
98. DK	.2	98. DK	1.1
99. NA	3.0	99. NA	1.3
	100		100
N	(436)		(460)

[a] Carried out in DAS-76.

responses among more categories. But the Crime-and-violence category attracts more than twice as many respondents when it is offered explicitly on the closed form than when it is coded from spontaneous answers to the open form. Indeed, on the closed question Crime is clearly the leading problem, whereas on the open form it is second to Unemployment.[6]

A quite plausible explanation, although not one we could test directly, is that the reference in the open question to "in this country" discourages respondents from including crime, since crime is perceived by many as a local problem. Although the same constraint appears in the wording of the closed question, provision of Crime-and-violence as an alternative obviously legitimizes it there. Thus, paradoxically, the open form of the question produces the narrower frame of reference in this case, and of course if this explanation is correct, the open question seriously underestimates public concern over crime.[7]

The Winter of 1977: Unforgettable or Easily Forgotten?

After discovering form effects for the most-important-problem question in the DAS-76 Survey, we proceeded to construct a new closed item less susceptible to these effects, though we did not attempt to change the national frame of reference. We picked from DAS-76 the 5 most frequently given categories of open responses: unemployment, crime, inflation, quality of leaders, and breakdown of morals and religion. These were also essentially the five most frequent closed choices, al-

---

[6]A review of the noncommon open codes suggests that some "crime" responses may be going into other categories (9, 10, and 13 in Table 3.1), in which case the open question shows that Crime has a number of different meanings in the minds of respondents, whereas the single closed alternative collects these under a single rubric. However, even lumping together all these possibly relevant open categories does not eliminate the significant open–closed Crime difference. (It must also be noted that part of the difference might be due to the closed label reading "crime and violence," not simply "crime.")

[7]We also examined interactions of question form separately by education and sex, finding them both significant ($p < .05$). For sex, the main source of interaction is that women give disproportionately more Crime responses on the open than on the closed form, whereas men do not. For education, on the closed form more years of schooling is positively related to choosing Inflation and negatively related to choosing Crime, whereas there is no relation on the open form. (We are indebted to Richard Kulka for his suggestions regarding the explanation discussed in the text.)

though not exactly in the same order. The 5 were included as the closed alternatives in a new experiment in February of 1977, with a parallel but more extended list making up the codes for an open form of the question. (The closed question was limited to 5 alternatives because pilot studies indicated that 5 was the maximum number that could be easily absorbed by respondents in a telephone interview where show cards were not available.) Among the possible DAS–76 closed alternatives *not* carried over into the new experiment was "Food and energy shortages," since only 8 people out of 460 had mentioned such a problem spontaneously in the DAS–76 survey.

The best-laid plans of both the country and the present investigators were disrupted when just as our 1977 telephone survey commenced, the eastern half of the United States was struck by the coldest winter in recent history. Buffalo, New York, became a symbol of other hard-hit cities, factories were shut down in a number of areas, and there were fears of widespread shortages of natural gas. During the 35 days our survey was in the field, The New York Times carried 62 stories on the cold spell and its implications, 8 of the stories on the front page. This sudden reemergence of the energy crisis could manifest itself easily on the open version of our question: The Food-and-energy-shortages code recorded these concerns by making that category the second highest (22%) after Unemployment (24%) and ahead of Inflation (16%).

The closed form of the same question, on the other hand, was impervious to the winter events, since only a single person (coded "other") out of 592 respondents mentioned the energy crisis; the 5 fixed alternatives account for over 99% of the substantive answers given. The results bring home an obvious and yet profound point about survey questions: Almost all respondents work within the substantive framework of priorities provided by the investigators, whether or not it fits their own priorities.[8]

(It might be thought that adding an explicit "other" alternative to an otherwise closed question would allow for spontaneous responses that could later be handled through the creation of new categories. However, a comparison of "complete lists" with lists omitting certain alternatives but adding an "other" category showed that the latter procedure produces only a small fraction of the responses elicited by the complete list

---

[8]This is less true of nonsubstantive responses such as don't know (DK). As documented in Chapters 4 and 5, respondents show considerable willingness to say DK when confronted with issues they know nothing about, although presence of an explicit DK raises the number appreciably.

(Lindzey and Guest, 1951). Moreover, a study comparing checklists with parallel open questions indicated that alternatives omitted from the checklist are mentioned much more frequently to the open question than to the explicit "other" category of the check list (Belson and Duncan, 1962). Thus, there is probably no adequate way to obtain a full array of responses by combining closed and open methods in a single question, because the very provision of closed alternatives discourages spontaneous responses that do not fit the listed alternatives. One must use either an open question or a closed question, not a compromise.)

The migration of respondents on the open form of the most-important-problem question into the Food-and-energy code is by no means drawn in equal proportions from the five categories common to the two forms. Inflation and Unemployment retain nearly the same percentages on the open question as on the closed question. Much diminished, however, are the percentages of respondents giving Crime, Poor-leaders, or Breakdown-of-morals responses. Unfortunately, interpretation of these differences is compromised by possible questionnaire-context effects. Both inflation and unemployment were subjects of questions at the beginning of the 1977 interview, and it is conceivable that this accounts for the maintenance of their proportions, compared to the other categories that virtually disappear on the open form. Because of this problem, together with the effects of the unusual winter, we shall not present detailed analysis of these SRC–77 February data. They do provide a dramatic lesson, however, in the differences produced by question form when external events affect answers. A historian searching opinion-poll data for effects of the 1977 severe winter would find them clearly in results based on our open question. The closed form of the same item shows not a trace of the events of that winter. Conceivably an investigator could argue for using either question form depending upon the goals of the research, but it is evident that these goals had better be clear to both writer and reader, for they are not only goals but major constraints as well.

Conclusions from this investigation are therefore double-edged: The open question can allow responses that an investigator does not anticipate, yet at the same time it can subtly prevent responses that the investigator considers legitimate. Both examples reported here involved important constraints that could have gone unrecognized but for the comparison between the two forms. Beyond these simple but important conclusions, we must turn to a more extensive series of experiments on another question (work values) to consider more fully the comparability and differential validity of open and closed question forms.

THE WORK-VALUES EXPERIMENTS

Experiment I: DAS–76

In a study of *The Religious Factor* in American life, Lenski (1963) employed the following closed question about what people value in jobs, asking it of a sample of metropolitan Detroit:

> *This next question is on the subject of work. Would you please look at this card and tell me which thing on this list you would **most** prefer in a job? (Married women: . . . in your husband's job?) Which comes next? (Etc. to obtain Ranking)*
> 1. High income
> 2. No danger of being fired
> 3. Working hours are short, lots of free time
> 4. Chances for advancement
> 5. The work is important, and gives a feeling of accomplishment

In later years this question was occasionally repeated by the Detroit Area Study (see Duncan, Schuman, and Duncan, 1973) and in 1973 it was adapted by NORC for inclusion as a standard item in its General Social Survey (NORC, 1980). The NORC version differs only in that it asks all respondents about their own preferences rather than asking wives about their husbands' jobs.

We first employed the NORC version of the work-values item with a random half of the DAS–76 sample, administering at the same time an open version of the question to the other half of the sample.[9] Table 3.2 presents both forms of the question, the codes for the open form, and the univariate results from this first experiment. The first 5 categories are meant to be comparable across closed and open question forms, al-

---

[9]The closed version of the work-values question asked for a second choice as well, but we do not deal with those results since the open form had no similar follow-up question. Respondents did sometimes give two or more codable responses to the open form, but in these cases interviewers were instructed to ask which one represented their main preference. Occasionally this probe was omitted and such responses are treated as missing data (code 96). An alternative and more common procedure would be to code the first mentioned response. For the child-values experiment (discussed later in this chapter) we examined those multiple-response answers that had been probed, in order to determine whether there is indeed a relation between the order in which responses are given and their importance as judged by respondents. Of 55 persons giving two codable child-value responses, the probe for *most important* led 27 to pick their first and 28 their second response. Thus, order seems unrelated to importance as evaluated by the respondent.

TABLE 3.2
Work Values: Experiment I[a]

Closed Form		Open Form	
*This next question is on the subject of work. Would you please look at this card and tell me which thing on this list you would **most** prefer in a job?*		*This next question is on the subject of work. People look for different things in a job. What would you **most** prefer in a job?*	
1. High income	12.4%	1. Pay	11.5%
		Remuneration, e.g., *The money is what counts.*	
2. No danger of being fired	7.2	2. Security	6.7
		Steady employment and source of income, e.g., *No danger of being fired; a good retirement plan; insurance plan.*	
3. Working hours are short; lots of free time	3.0	3. Short hours/Lots of free time	.9
		Jobs that give time for other things, e.g., *the chance to be with my family.*	
4. Chances for advancement	17.2	4. Opportunity for promotion	1.8
		Chance for advancement, e.g., *the chance to get ahead.*	
5. The work is important and gives a feeling of accomplishment	59.1	5. Stimulating work	21.3
		Work that makes some demand on the worker, e.g., *work that is challenging; varied; creative; work that gives a sense of accomplishment or leads to fulfillment; helping people; interesting work.*	
		6. Pleasant or enjoyable work	15.4
		Usually concerns pleasant social relations, e.g., *congenial people.* Code here mention of happiness and also mention of social situation of work.	
		7. Work conditions	14.9
		Factors affecting how job is done. e.g., *being able to set one's own pace; safety; being free from interference; an understanding boss.*	
		8. Satisfaction/liking the job	17.0
		Unspecific answers not codable in 5 or 6, e.g., *Doing what I like; Being satisfied with the job is most important.*	
		95. Specific job	3.0
		I would want to be an accountant.	
		96. More than one codable response	1.4
		97. Other	2.1
98. DK	.2	98. DK	1.4
99. NA	.9	99. NA	2.7
	100		100
N	(460)		(436)

[a] Carried out in DAS-76.

though in this first experiment we did not maintain exact identity in labels and there are some substantive differences to be discussed below. Additional substantive categories were created (on the basis of preliminary review of 150 cases) to handle open responses that did not fit the 5 main categories well; these will also be discussed below.

Univariate Results by Form

Several conclusions can be drawn from Table 3.2:

1. All but a tiny fraction of the closed responses fall within the five precoded categories, but nearly 60% of the open responses fall *outside* these same five categories. Thus the two questions show gross differences in the answers they elicit. Respondents on the closed form restrict themselves with apparent ease to the five alternatives offered, whereas respondents on the open question produce a much more diversified set of answers.

2. If we confine our attention to the five categories common to both question forms, it will be noted that the first two categories produce almost identical percentages, the third only a little discrepancy, but the fourth (Advancement) and fifth (Accomplishment) lead to major differences between question forms. Evidently, the Advancement and Accomplishment alternatives are much less often stated spontaneously than they are chosen when offered explicitly. (The overall difference in univariate distributions by form for the 5 × 2 table is highly significant: $\chi^2 = 46.8$, $df = 4$, $p < .001$.)

3. It is necessary to keep in mind—and often easy to forget—that even for the five common categories, meanings may be different between the two forms. Thus, open category 2 on Security is probably broader in content than the comparable closed category (No danger of being fired) and therefore even the apparent similarity in percentages may be misleading. One recurrent problem with open categories is that their labels and examples may not tell us enough about what has actually been coded into them. Of course, the same is true in another sense with regard to closed alternatives, since an alternative may carry different meanings to different individuals. Reification of categories is a serious danger in both forms.

4. What of the categories that appear on the open form but not on the closed form? Two new types of responses occurred with enough frequency to justify substantive codes. Fifteen percent of the open sample responded in terms of the job being pleasant or providing enjoyable social relations. We grouped all these responses into a single category

(6), which turns out to be one of the larger ones in the table. A different but almost equally common kind of response is grouped under "Work conditions" (7), referring both to job autonomy and to more concrete job factors such as "safety." Along with these clearly meaningful new responses is an increase on the open form in the "don't know," "other," and related kinds of missing data (categories 95–99). Perhaps better interviewing would reduce these categories, but we believe that open questions tend in general to produce more missing data. Finally, the Satisfaction (8) category seemed to us at first to contain essentially tautological responses and thus to be another form of missing data, but later analysis (reported below) suggests that it represents a meaningful if vague kind of answer.

Background Variables and Work Values: Sex and Education

It has been a traditional, although usually implicit, assumption of survey analysis that the form differences we have been describing do *not* extend to associations between an item and other variables. In order to test this assumption of *form-resistant correlations*, we employed education and sex throughout this analysis because they are two of the most frequently used and important variables in survey research regardless of the content of the study. They are also not redundant with each other (their association in DAS–76 is trivial and nonsignificant); they apply to all respondents (as occupation does not); and they have few missing data (unlike income). In addition, we began this research with a general hypothesis that more-educated respondents would be less affected by question form variations than the less educated, on the assumption that education is associated with somewhat more self-developed and stable concepts.

Sex does show a different relation to work values on the two forms, as indicated by a significant three-way interaction of form, sex, and response ($\chi^2 = 12.18$, $df = 4$, $p < .02$). (In this and later analyses, significance tests are calculated using only categories common to the two forms, but tables show all categories.) Based on the closed form, one would conclude that men are more likely to value Pay and Advancement, whereas on the open form there seems to be little sex difference in these respects (see Table 3.3). On the other hand, on the closed form women are more apt to stress Accomplishment, with if anything the reverse being the case on the open form. Furthermore, women are more likely to give codable open responses that fall outside the five categories common to the two forms, in particular responses coded Pleasant.

When education is the background variable rather than sex, the

TABLE 3.3
Work Values by Sex and Form: Experiment I

	Closed		Open	
	Men	Women	Men	Women
1. Pay	16.3%	9.5%	10.5%	12.2%
2. Security	8.2	6.4	10.5	3.7
3. Free time	2.6	3.4	.0	1.6
4. Advancement	21.9	13.6	2.1	1.6
5. Accomplishment	50.0	65.9	24.2	19.1
6. Pleasant	—	—	12.1	17.9
7. Work conditions	—	—	13.2	16.3
8. Satisfaction	—	—	16.8	17.1
95. Specific job	—	—	2.6	3.2
96. Multiple responses	—	—	2.1	.8
97. Other	—	—	2.6	1.6
98. DK	.0	.4	.0	2.4
99. NA	1.0	.8	3.2	2.4
	100	100	100	100
N	(196)	(264)	(190)	(246)

three-way interaction is also significant ($\chi^2 = 15.50$, $df = 8$, $p < .05$). It is more difficult in this case to pinpoint differences (see Table 3.4), but the form difference in the relation of Security to education is replicated in experiments to be presented below.[10]

Conclusions from Experiment I

Our comparison of open and closed forms of the work-values question indicates that marginals for the two differ in important ways, and that the associations of background variables with work values also differ by form. Thus, it may be unwise to draw conclusions about the character of American work values from the absolute size of the original closed categories, as Lenski did in his 1963 volume, or even from the

[10]We also examined Protestant–Catholic differences by form, since the closed work-values item was used by Lenski (1963) to study such differences. In the DAS–76 sample there is a trend on the open form for Protestants to give what Lenski considered the primary Protestant ethic response—Accomplishment—more often than Catholics, but not on the closed form. However, the interaction is not significant and the results for the closed form differ from those obtained in earlier studies and from a later partial replication (Experiment IIb).

TABLE 3.4
Work Values by Education and Form: Experiment I

	Closed			Open		
	0–11	12	13+	0–11	12	13+
1. Pay	13.3%	11.9%	12.0%	14.4%	13.3%	6.2%
2. Security	11.9	5.0	5.1	5.8	5.4	9.2
3. Free time	2.1	3.8	3.2	.0	1.2	1.5
4. Advancement	22.4	14.5	15.2	1.4	.6	3.8
5. Accomplishment	48.3	64.8	63.3	18.7	15.1	32.2
6. Pleasant	—	—	—	12.2	19.9	13.1
7. Work conditions	—	—	—	20.9	12.0	12.3
8. Satisfaction	—	—	—	6.5	24.7	17.7
95. Specific job	—	—	—	7.2	1.2	.8
96. Multiple responses	—	—	—	1.4	.6	2.3
97. Other	—	—	—	2.2	3.6	.0
98. DK	.7	.0	.0	2.9	.6	.8
99. NA	1.4	.0	1.3	6.5	1.8	.0
	100	100	100	100	100	100
N	(143)	(159)	(158)	(139)	(166)	(130)

relative ranking of the choices, as Duncan, Schuman, and Duncan (1973) did in a later replication. Advancement, to take the most striking example, differs in both percentage and rank in the open as compared with the closed results. Moreover, it is unclear which form provides the more valid representation of respondent values: Proponents of open questions can hold that a value is not really important if it is seldom offered spontaneously, whereas proponents of closed items can argue that that form provides a fairer test by presenting the same frame of reference to all respondents. Both positions seem plausible, and it is difficult on an a priori basis to decide between them.

However, although this form comparison throws some light on the work-values alternatives as they have generally been asked, implications for the open–closed controversy are limited by the fundamental ambiguity discussed at the beginning of the chapter. Discrepancies by form could have come about merely because the closed alternatives fail to capture what many people want to say in answer to the question, either because the five alternatives were not initially developed on the basis of open pretesting, or having been so developed in the 1950s may no longer represent well the responses of the present. Therefore, we decided to use the open data in Table 3.2 as a kind of large-scale pretest to construct a new set of closed categories reflecting more adequately how people spontaneously answer the work-values question in the mid-1970s. We also took this opportunity to clarify or otherwise amend the phrasing of certain closed alternatives, as will be described next. In taking these steps we necessarily gave greater weight to categories constructed from the free answers of respondents than from categories created a priori by an investigator.

Work-Values Experiments IIa and b

In the next experiment (SRC–77 February) we attempted to create a new set of alternatives as representative as possible of the open responses just discussed. This experiment (IIa) produced results that seemed important to test further for reliability and validity, and hence Experiment IIb was carried out as an exact replication 18 months later (SRC–78 August). To conserve space, the two are combined here where possible in tabular presentation and discussion, but analysis was also carried out for each separately and similarities and differences in results will be noted.[11] Both these new experiments used national telephone samples, whereas our earlier data came from a Detroit SMSA sample and employed face-to-face interviewing. It was therefore necessary to assume that the earlier results could be used as a pretest for the later study. This assumption can be tested by comparing the open percentages from Table 3.2 with the new national open percentages in Table 3.5. Although there are some differences, they are not major and none would have led to changes in the decisions we reached on the basis of the earlier DAS results.

---

[11]The 1977 February and 1978 August samples differed somewhat in within-household selection. The former required random selection among all adults, but the latter required selection of head of households in three-quarters of the cases. However, our analysis indicates that none of the results reported in this section is a function of this difference. Comparison of the two surveys within form does·show a highly significant ($\chi^2 = 20.23$, $df = 4$, $p < .001$) change in work-values marginals for the *closed* form between February 1977 and August 1978: Virtually all of the change involves a sharp rise in the Pay choice, with compensating smaller declines in Accomplishment and Pleasantness. Since similar trends appear on the open form, but to a smaller and nonsignificant degree, it seems likely that the difference reflects real changes in value emphasis in the national population, perhaps due to the impact of inflation, rather than to coding or other survey-related problems. (The changes are not due to differences in selection procedures, since they occur to the same extent when only male heads are considered.) Despite these univariate differences between Experiments IIa and b, all bivariate and trivariate results reported in this section hold within the two surveys separately. Therefore tables in this chapter present combined results only, although Appendix B.3 contains one breakdown by survey.

The following changes were made in the alternatives of the closed form for Experiments IIa and b. In certain corresponding instances, labels and definitions of open-code categories were also altered, as noted.

First, two alternatives were *dropped* because they had shown tiny open percentages in Experiment I: Short hours and Advancement (3 and 4 in Table 3.2). This decision is more problematic for Advancement, since it was frequently chosen on the closed form, but the decision follows the logic of starting from open responses. We cannot see the same type of artifact here as occurred with the Crime category in the most-important-problem open question (page 85), and the discrepancy for the Advancement category represents an unresolved puzzle.

TABLE 3.5
Work Values: Experiments II a and b Combined[a]

Closed Form		Open Form	
This next question is on the subject of work. People look for different things in a job. Which one of the following five things would you **most** *prefer in a job?*		*This next question is on the subject of work. People look for different things in a job. What would you* **most** *prefer in a job?*	
1. *Work that pays well*	13.2%	1. Pay (work that pays well) Remuneration, e.g., *the money is what counts; salary; wages; overtime; bonuses; profit-sharing.*	16.7%
2. *Work that gives a feeling of accomplishment*	31.0	2. A feeling of accomplishment Work that makes some demand on the worker, e.g., *work that is challenging; work that leads to fulfillment; creative; helping people.*	14.5
3. *Work where there is not too much supervision and you make most decisions yourself*	11.7	3. Control of work (work where there is not too much supervision and you make most decisions yourself) Factors affecting how job is done, e.g., *being able to set one's own pace; being free from interference.*	4.6
4. *Work that is pleasant and where the other people are nice to work with*	19.8	4. Pleasant work (and where the other people are nice to work with) Usually concerns pleasant social relations, e.g., *congenial people.* Code here unspecific mentions of *happiness* and mentions of the social situation at the workplace.	14.5

(continued)

TABLE 3.5—*Continued*

Closed Form		Open Form	
5. *Work that is steady with little chance of being laid off*		5. Security (work that is steady with little chance of being laid off)	7.6
		Steady employment and source of income, e.g., *no chance of being fired.*	
		6. Opportunity for promotion	1.0
		Chance for advancement, e.g., *the chance to get ahead.*	
		7. Short hours/lots of free time	1.6
		Jobs that give time for other things, e.g., *the chance to be with my family.*	
		8. Working conditions	3.1
		Good lighting; well insulated; safe.	
		9. Benefits	2.3
		Health/life insurance, retirement plan.	
		10. Satisfaction–liking the job	15.6
		Unspecific answers not codable in 2 or 4, e.g., *doing what I like; being satisfied with the job is most important.*	
		95. Code here mentions of specific jobs, e.g., *I'd like to be a teacher,* that are not otherwise codable.	3.7
		96. More than one codable response with no indication of which is most important.	4.0
97. Other	.4	97. Other	3.6
98. DK	.7	98. DK	2.6
99. NA	2.9	99. NA	4.4
	100		100
N	(1194)		(1153)

[a] Carried out in SRC–77 February and SRC–78 August.

Second, two closed alternatives were *added* that had elicited substantial percentages on the open form: Pleasantness and Work conditions (codes 6 and 7 in Table 3.2). Both category labels were changed somewhat in the closed version, with corresponding changes in the open-code labels (see codes 4 and 3 in Table 3.5). Pleasantness was simply spelled out more clearly to include both the sociability and the general enjoyment responses that had been coded on the DAS–76 open form. Work conditions, however, was changed to focus on autonomy (*3. Work where there is not too much supervision and you make most decisions yourself*), which had seemed to us the main content of the previous open code; a new corresponding open code on autonomy, labeled 3. *Control of work,* was created. (The label *Work conditions,* however, was retained as an open code [8] for purely physical conditions of the environment, and should not be confused with the more omnibus label used in Table 3.2.)

Third, three alternatives retained from the Table 3.2 closed form were each relabeled in order to correspond more closely and clearly to the content of the Table 3.2 open categories. Specifically:

(a) *Work that gives a feeling of accomplishment* is a shortening of the alternative *The work is important and gives a feeling of accomplishment.* The latter seemed at once redundant and loaded in a socially desirable fashion by stressing *importance.* We expected this change to decrease the closed percentage, bringing it closer to the percentage that spontaneously gives the Accomplishment response to the open question. (A test of this reasonable, but as it turns out incorrect, assumption is reported below.)

(b) *Work that is steady with little chance of being laid off* is an expansion of *No danger of being fired.* The latter seemed to us unduly limited and not to capture the real concern over job security that appears important to respondents. (However, open responses dealing entirely with fringe benefits were separated out into a new "Benefits" category.) The reason for this change was entirely conceptual, since the change might be expected to increase rather than decrease the open–closed difference.

(c) *Work that pays well* is the new name for what Lenski called *High income.* The new label was intended to apply more easily to all job levels, though we expected at most a slight effect on responses.

Thus all five closed alternatives are either newly developed or reworded to fit our experience with open responses in the previous survey as closely as we could manage. (The five will be referred to below as: Pay, Accomplishment, Autonomy, Pleasantness, and Security.) Furthermore, in Experiments IIa and b we were careful to use essentially the same labels for the parallel closed alternatives and open categories, and open coders were trained to think in terms of these labels.

One further refinement was added in Experiment IIa in order to check for a possible order effect on responses to the closed form. The closed version of the question actually consisted of five randomly administered subforms—each of which began with a different alternative and continued sequentially through the other four. Thus although not every possible permutation of the five alternatives was tried, each alternative appears first in one subsample, second in another, and so on. Cross-tabulation of the five orders by the five choices yields no sign of a primacy, recency, or other systematic type of order effect, and the over-all table shows no relationship between order and response choice: $\chi^2 = 15.56$, $df = 16$, $p > .30$. (See Chapter 2, Table 2.13, for detailed results.)

Form Differences in Marginals

Given a method of construction designed to maximize similar results from open and closed forms, how successful was the effort? The answer appears to be: Somewhat successful, but not by any means completely so. Examination of Table 3.5 yields the following results:

Spread of Responses

Open responses still spread substantially beyond the five categories common to both forms, but these categories on the open form now contain 58% of all open responses as against 42% in the first experiment ($\chi^2 = 31.49$, $df = 1$, $p < .001$). All but one of these open common categories (and all of the closed alternatives) produce more than trivial percentages, and no other large open category (with the exception of the vague Satisfaction category) appears outside the common set of five.[12] In sum, our five focal work values seem to have captured more adequately the spontaneous answers of respondents, though there are still a variety of small substantive and missing data categories.[13]

Effects of Relabeling on Closed Alternatives

Three alternatives were carried over from Experiment I, but relabeled, and two of these show marked shifts in size from the first experiment. Security goes *up* from 7% in the first experiment to 20% in the second,

---

[12]The one failure here is the Autonomy category (*control of work*), which draws only 4.6% on the open form. If the Working-conditions category is joined to it, the percentage rises to 7.7%. We were incorrect in believing that Autonomy alone would be an adequate size category.

[13]In Experiments IIa and b (but not Experiment I) we instructed coders to give priority in ambiguous cases to the first 5 categories. However, a later recording of 50 randomly drawn cases from Experiment IIa by a new coder not using the priority system produced only a single response where the priority instruction might have changed the assigned category, and even this one was equivocal.

in line with its expansion in meaning from *No danger of being fired* to *Work that is steady with little chance of being laid off*. At the same time, the Accomplishment category goes *down* from 59% in the first experiment to 31% in the second, as might have been expected from omission of the loaded phrase *the work is important*.

However, these shifts in percentage could have been due to the change in the total set of alternatives offered respondents, rather than to the rewording of individual alternatives. Since the possible effect of social desirability is an important issue in using closed questions, we tested the change in the Accomplishment alternative in a later experiment (SRC–79 January). The closed work-values question from Table 3.5 was asked to half this sample, whereas the other half received a question identical in all respects except that the phrase *The work is important* was added back into the Accomplishment alternative. Contrary to prediction, this change did not produce a significant difference ($\chi^2 = 2.38$, $df = 1$), and in fact the shorter version elicited more choice (38% of 278) than the longer version (32% of 300). Thus we find no evidence, even in the case where we most expected it, for social desirability of wording to play a role in respondent choice of an alternative. The percentage shift in this case, and perhaps for the Security alternatives also, is evidently due to the change in the set of alternatives offered—rather than to the exact wording of any one alternative.

Overall Form Differences

If we confine our attention to the five categories in Table 3.5 that are common to both question forms, there is a noticeable difference for each category, with Pay yielding a higher percentage on the open form and the four others a higher percentage on the closed form. The latter might occur simply because open responses are spread over more categories, hence on each form we repercentaged the five common categories on their own base. However, the mean repercentaged form difference is only slightly smaller (7.8%) than the mean difference using the original percentages (9.0%), and the overall difference between forms is highly significant: $\chi^2 = 82.95$, $df = 4$, $p < .001$. Pay and Pleasantness are given relatively more often on the open form, whereas Accomplishment, Autonomy, and Security are given more often when a precoded list is presented. Moreover, the rankings of the five values, which are unaffected by repercentaging, also differ between the two forms, as indicated most strikingly by the fact that Pay ranks first in frequency of response to the open question and close to last to the closed question.

Were it not for one important exception, a more general post factum interpretation of these findings would be persuasive: Most respondents think in terms of material benefits, social pleasures, or absence of demands when required to provide their own work values, but are strongly attracted to "higher" aspects of work (especially the opportunity for a sense of accomplishment) when these are suggested to them. The latter would then be due more to a type of social desirability response than to genuine desire for more challenging work. However, the pattern for Security does not fit this interpretation, since security is hardly a challenging characteristic of a job, yet it shows one of the larger increases when we move from an open to a closed format.[14] Evidently the process is not entirely—or possibly not at all—one involving social desirability of response, but has something to do with the frame of reference that a respondent brings to questions about work. The plausibility of this interpretation is increased when we consider the relation of open–closed form effects to background variables.

Relation of Form Differences to Education, Sex, and Unemployment Experience

Education

Although education is significantly related ($p < .001$) to work values on both open and closed form, these relations (shown in Table 3.6) differ significantly between the two forms ($\chi^2 = 27.49$, $df = 8$, $p < .001$). Most strikingly, the Security category on the closed form reveals a sharp negative association with education, while on the open form Security shows no clear relation to education. (The interaction of form, education, and Security versus other common categories combined yields: $\chi^2 = 24.52$, $df = 2$, $p < .001$.) This difference for the Security alternative is equally strong in Experiments IIa and b taken separately; it is even more striking when five educational levels are used instead of three; and the same trend appeared in Experment I.

Careful examination of Table 3.6 suggests a partial interpretation for the different relations of Security to education, an interpretation that takes account of the somewhat opposite trends for the Pay category (Pay shows a negative association with education on the open but not on the closed form). We believe that the *open* Pay category fails to distinguish

[14]See Appendix B.3 for further discussion and some qualification of this result for the Security response.

TABLE 3.6
Work Values by Education and Form: Experiments II a and b

	Closed			Open		
	0–11	12	13+	0–11	12	13+
1. Pay	13.8%	15.9%	11.0%	20.0%	20.0%	12.8%
2. Accomplishment	11.1	28.4	44.4	6.2	8.0	24.3
3. Autonomy	8.4	8.9	15.9	3.1	3.4	6.5
4. Pleasant	24.5	23.9	14.1	14.8	15.7	13.2
5. Security	36.0	20.0	12.4	4.8	11.1	6.9
6. Advancement	—	—	—	.0	.9	1.8
7. Free time	—	—	—	1.0	2.3	1.6
8. Work conditions	—	—	—	3.8	4.0	2.2
9. Benefits	—	—	—	2.8	3.1	1.6
10. Satisfaction	—	—	—	10.0	14.6	19.5
95. Specific jobs	—	—	—	8.3	3.7	1.2
96. Multiple responses	—	—	—	3.1	4.6	4.1
97. Other	.4	.5	.4	6.9	2.9	1.8
98. DK	1.9	.5	.2	7.2	2.3	.2
99. NA	3.8	1.9	1.6	7.9	3.4	2.2
	100	100	100	100	100	100
N	(261)	(415)	(498)	(290)	(350)	(493)

two different types of responses: those referring to high income and those referring to steady income, and that this is especially true for less-educated respondents who may simply verbalize something ambiguous such as "It's the money that counts." The closed form of the question allows these respondents to clarify their views, since it makes the Pay–Security distinction explicit. We thus learn from the closed form that high Pay is valued about equally at all educational levels, but that Security is stressed much more often by the least educated. Such a finding makes good intuitive sense, and leads us to hypothesize that the closed form produces more valid information than the open form about the relation of work values to education. This interpretation also accounts for part of the unexpected overall increase in Security responses on the closed form.[15]

Furthermore, there is another piece of evidence suggesting that the

---

[15]Results using a four-category occupation variable (professional and managerial, clerical and sales, skilled workers, operatives and unskilled) are similar in nature and strength to the tables that employ education, leaving unsettled the extent to which the results depend on cognitive as against positional factors.

closed form may be superior to the open. "Satisfaction" is the one category that appears with high frequency on the open form but which we did not include on the closed form because it seemed an inferior type of response, almost a tautology (e.g., "I would prefer work that is satisfying"). However, if that were the case one might expect Satisfaction to relate negatively to education, as does inappropriate mention of a Specific job (category 95). Instead, Satisfaction shows a clear positive relation to education—in fact one that parallels the relation of the Accomplishment category to education on both forms. Later examination of 100 open responses from Experiment IIa revealed that a number of those coded into Accomplishment had begun by mentioning "satisfying work," which was then elaborated to spell out the Accomplishment emphasis when probed. We now think that the open Satisfaction category consists primarily of vague and inadequately probed responses representing mainly the Accomplishment value, although occasionally some other value such as Pleasantness, and that this is clarified on the closed form when specific categories are offered to respondents.

There is indeed some direct evidence that most respondents in the open Satisfaction category would choose Accomplishment on the closed form. A small subsample of respondents to the open version of the work-values question in Experiment IIa were reinterviewed 6-months later and asked a 3-category closed work-values item (as described in footnote 16). Of the 26 persons who originally were coded in the open Satisfaction category and later reinterviewed, 69% chose Accomplishment on the reinterview closed question. This is a much higher figure than for any other group of reinterviewed respondents except those who initially gave Accomplishment itself (for whom the figure is 83%). Thus people who are coded into the Satisfaction category on the open form tend to choose Accomplishment on the closed form, and it is reasonable to think that this is what they intended to imply by their open response.

Sex

Unlike education, sex produces very similar patterns on the open and closed work-values form in Experiment IIa and b combined. Men are more likely to choose Autonomy and women to choose Pleasantness on each form. There is a trend for men to choose both Security and Pay to a greater extent on the open form, but the overall three-way interaction reaches only borderline significance ($\chi^2 = 9.06$, $df = 4$, $p < .10$) and is not replicated in data from other experiments.

Unemployment

One further variable was introduced into Experiment IIb in an effort to provide a critical test of whether the open or closed results for the Security category were more valid. At the end of the interview, we asked respondents whether they had been unemployed and looking for work at any point in the past 5 years. We assumed such an experience would be an important stimulus to giving the Security response, and that therefore the form showing a higher association between Security and unemployment could be viewed as having greater claim to validity. For example, if the open question reflects salience in the sense of personal importance, then its Security category should show the stronger relation to experience with unemployment. To our surprise, the test itself failed, for actual unemployment experience (reported by one-fifth of the sample) is not related to the Security category (or to any other category) on either form.[16]

Conclusions from Work-Values Experiments

We believe the initial discrepancies between the open and closed work-values questions were partly due to the fact that the closed

---

[16]Two further special analyses will be noted briefly. First, the reinterview data mentioned in footnote 3 on p. 81 were used to study the large number of inadequate responses (DK, NA, mentions of particular jobs only) on the open form. Of the 23 missing data cases from the original open question in SRC-77 Feb. who were reinterviewed in August of the same year, over 60% chose Pleasantness on the reinterview 3-category closed item and only 4% chose Pay. This is significantly different from an expected random distribution of one-third in each category ($\chi^2 = 7.7$, $df = 2$, $p < .05$), and thus it does not appear that respondents who provide missing data on the open form contribute mainly random error on the closed form, though we are not sure why they choose the Pleasantness alternative.

The three-category work-values closed question (SRC–77 August) was itself part of a further experiment to determine what happened when only the three most frequently used categories from Experiment II (Pay, Accomplishment, and Pleasantness) were included in the closed form. Detailed results are not presented here because we now think that the attempt to reduce the closed work-values item to three categories was a mistake, since it lost the important distinction between Pay and Security. However, it is worth noting that the Pay category in this experiment is negatively associated with education on the closed as well as on the open form, as would be expected once the Security alternative is eliminated and such respondents move into the Pay alternative—a demonstration that relationships to these choices are partly a function of the exact set of alternatives offered. This experiment had one other useful feature, a further test for order effects among the closed alternatives; again the results were negative ($\chi^2 = 2.41$, $df = 4$, n.s.).

categories were not sufficiently developed from open responses. Alternatives were included that were not within most respondents' frame of reference for the question, whereas other alternatives were omitted that were important to many respondents. The revised set of closed alternatives developed for Experiments IIa and b retain quite well Lenski's original theoretical goals, yet at the same time serve to represent more adequately and for more general purposes the work values that respondents offer spontaneously.[17]

Once so developed, however, we think the closed form of the question is superior because it separates types of responses that were often indistinguishable in the open coding (those emphasizing high income and those stressing steady income), while at the same time it merges responses (Accomplishment and Satisfaction) that the open coding tends to separate because of nonsubstantive verbal differences in expression. Whatever the advantages of the open question for assessing salience and for avoiding social desirability effects—and we have been unable to discover firm evidence that either of these advantages actually occurs—there seem to be even greater disadvantages arising from vagueness of expression by respondents, frequent failures to probe adequately by interviewers, and occasional misunderstanding by coders. All this is avoided in closed questions, where respondents are in essence asked to code themselves, with minimal intervention by third parties. In sum, although open questions seem essential for obtaining the frame of reference of respondents and for wording alternatives appropriately, once this is done we are unable to find any compelling reason to keep the open form for the work-values question. Finally, it will be recognized that these conclusions are suggested, rather than rigorously demonstrated, by the previous results, and are stated here in a forthright fashion for heuristic purposes.

VALUES FOR CHILDREN

A question on preferred values for children provided the basis for our third attempt at open–closed experimentation. But in this case we did not move beyond the initial comparison in DAS–76 because the spread

[17]At a late stage in this research, we discovered that the closed work-values question employed by Lenski (1963) was almost identical to one used in a 1954 Consumer Behavior study by the Survey Research Center (see Boulding, 1960) except that the earlier version included as a sixth alternative, *Income is steady!* Moreover, unpublished pretests for that study suggest that an alternative referring to liking *the people one works with* was also

of open responses appeared too great to allow reconstruction of an adequate closed question for use in a telephone survey. As Table 3.7 shows, 98% of the closed responses fall into categories of the original closed question (taken from Lenski, 1963), but only 9% of the open responses are accommodated by these same categories. Moreover, the closed response *To think for themselves* attracts over 60% of the respondents on that form, but only 5% are coded into the comparable category on the open form. Yet it is also interesting to note that the five common categories are ranked almost identically on the two forms, and thus the discrepancy may not be as ineluctable as at first appears.

Eleven additional open categories were used to handle the spontaneous open responses, not counting a relatively large (9%) residual category of miscellaneous "other" responses. The new categories are of three kinds. At one extreme, a number of legitimate responses involving religious and moral qualities appear that are not readily covered in any way by the closed question. At the other extreme, it is easy to see how certain open categories (e.g., *To be self-reliant*) could be assimilated into existing closed alternatives (*To work hard* or *to think for themselves*), though with some loss of the original meaning. Finally, the largest category of the open codes, *To get an education*, seems to involve a misinterpretation of the purpose of the question by respondents; it thus illustrates the point occasionally noted (e.g., by Campbell, 1945) that open questions, lacking the additional cues of fixed alternatives, may need to be more clearly focused than closed questions.

The General Social Survey (NORC, 1980) regularly asks respondents to provide a partial ranking of 13 qualities desirable in children. The list we constructed from open responses overlaps the GSS list to a fair extent, but some of the qualities that we obtained most often on the open form (e.g., *to be religious*) are not provided by NORC, and some on NORC's list (e.g., *that he is interested in how and why things happen*) seemed not to occur to our respondents. Since the GSS initial question is slightly different from the Lenski question we used, and the national population may produce frequencies different from those based on metropolitan Detroit, a precise comparison is not possible. However, it is conceivable that a closed set of alternatives could be developed that more closely parallels spontaneous open response categories, provided

---

considered for inclusion at one point, possibly on the basis of earlier open interviewing. Thus in a sense our experiments have led to restoration of alternatives dropped by previous investigators without sufficient documentation (or perhaps full awareness) of why these decisions were made. Other survey inquiries into work values also occurred during the 1940s and 1950s (see Hyman, 1953), but they differ in wording too greatly from the Lenski item to be directly relevant to our experiments.

TABLE 3.7
Child Values[a]

Closed Form		Open Form	
*While we're talking about children, would you please look at this card. If you had to choose, which thing on this list would you pick as **the most important** thing for children to learn to prepare them for life?*		*While we're talking about children, would you please say what you think is **the most important** thing for children to learn to prepare them for life?*	
1. *To obey*	19.0%	1. To obey	2.4%
2. *To be well-liked or popular*	.2	2. To be well-liked or popular	.0
3. *To think for themselves*	61.5	3. To think for themselves	4.6
4. *To work hard*	4.8	4. To work hard	1.3
5. *To help others when they need help*	12.6	5. To help others when they need help	.9
		6. To be self-reliant: independence, e.g., *providing for oneself*	6.1
		7. To be responsible: fulfillment of one's obligations, e.g., *to be a responsible citizen; to be a good father*	5.2
		8. To have self-respect: self-esteem or confidence, e.g., *to like oneself*	4.1
		9. To have respect for others: acceptance of rights of others, e.g., *to be tolerant of others*	6.7
		10. To have self-discipline: self control	3.5
		11. To be honest: truthfulness	7.4
		12. To have other moral qualities: general mentions of morality	3.0
		13. To be religious: mentions of God or religion, e.g., *to be a good Christian*	5.4
		14. To love others: mentions of love	2.0
		15. To get an education	12.8
		16. To learn a trade or job skill	.9
		17. To get along with others: e.g., *to live and work with others*	5.0
		96. Multiple responses: no indication of most important	16.1
97. Other	.0	97. Other	9.3
98. DK	.0	98. DK	1.3
99. NA	1.8	99. NA	2.0
	100		100
	(436)		(460)

[a] Carried out in DAS-76.

that the number of alternatives can go beyond the limit imposed by use of the telephone.[18]

CONCLUSIONS

Not every existing closed attitude question can be asked in a parallel open form. In fact, in searching for questions useful for experimentation, we found most closed items unsuitable for transformation into open form. Of course, respondents can always be asked to discuss a general topic, and likewise it is almost always possible and useful to ask an open follow-up to a closed item, but neither of these provides a truly parallel form. Although we did not fully realize it at the time, it is probably no accident that the questions we settled on involved multiple nominal responses to broad inquiries about values and problems. This is the type of question that one initially thinks of in open form, then closes largely for practical reasons having to do with ease of administration, coding, and analysis. By the same token though, this is the type of question where a comparison of forms is most urgent, since the transformation typically assumes that the two forms yield essentially identical results.

Our data show that this is certainly not true in any simple way as far as univariate findings go. Every comparison we made revealed statistically significant and substantively important differences in marginal distributions between open and closed forms. Likewise, most previous experimental comparisons, although rather specialized in type of question tested, also show important differences by form: Belson and Duncan (1962); Bradburn, Sudman, and Associates (1979); Dohrenwend (1965); Marquis, Marshall, and Oskamp (1972); Rugg and Cantril (1944). Our own investigation adds to this previous research three instances of complex questions more typical of current attitude surveys—in one case investigating the differences through repeated reconstruction of the

[18]The NORC list is apparently an adaptation of a measure developed by Kohn (1969), which in turn was partly stimulated by a list of categories provided by Duvall (1946). Kohn notes that his own "list was compiled from the suggestions made by parents interviewed during the development and pretesting of the interview schedule [1969: 19]," but no pretest results are given to explain the selection or wording of alternatives. Duvall's work is especially relevant to ours because it was based on an open question (*What are five things a good child does?*). Given the difference in the exact question, plus differences in date and in sample composition, there is a fair degree of overlap between Duvall's categories and ours. (Our understanding of the development of research on values for children has benefitted from discussion with Duane Alwin.)

closed categories. We also demonstrate that the assumption of form-resistant correlations is not a good one with respect to open–closed comparisons. The differences in results extended to associations with important background variables as well as affecting marginals; in particular, the relation of education to a distinction between *high pay* and *steady pay* in work values differs meaningfully depending on which form of the question—open or closed—is used.[19]

It is not possible at this point to draw definitive conclusions about when open–closed differences will occur or whether one form will always be more valid than the other. But our findings do suggest several propositions that are at once tentative conclusions and hypotheses for future research.

1. Form differences will be minimized if investigators begin with open questions on large samples of the target population and use these responses to construct closed alternatives that reflect the substance and wording of what people say spontaneously. This point is so obvious as to be embarrassing to state, yet it is probably violated in survey research more often than it is practiced. Of course, there may be times when an investigator deliberately wishes to exclude frequently given alternatives or add others, but this should be stated and justified explicitly. Otherwise we risk having respondents confirm our own frame of reference without even being aware of it. The "energy shortage" result is a simple and dramatic example of this phenomenon, but omission of "Pleasantness" as a possible closed work-value alternative from the original Lenski (1963) question is perhaps a more important and typical instance.

2. At the same time, investigators must be sensitive to the fact that open questions are not always as open as they seem. Inadvertent phrasing of the open question itself can constrain responses in unintended and unrecognized ways. We believe that this accounts for the discrepancy between the number of mentions of "crime" to open and closed versions of the most-important-problem question in our DAS–76 experiment, and moreover that the Crime category may be generally underestimated in standard use of the open form of this question in national surveys. We can see no way to discover subtle constraints of this kind except by including systematic open-closed comparisons when an investigator begins development of a new question on values or problems.

3. Where *properly constructed* closed and open forms of questions do

---

[19]The one previous report of such interactions that we have located is by Robinson and Rohde (1946). However, when their tables are reanalyzed using recently developed statistical techniques (Goodman, 1978), none of the reported three-way interactions approaches significance.

differ, it appears that at least in some cases the former may be more valid—where valid means correctly classifying respondents *and* correctly describing relationships. For the work-values question, the reconstructed closed form allows an important distinction to emerge that is obscured on the open form, and shows the distinction to have construct validity in terms of other relationships. In addition, the closed form eliminates a large open category that seems in retrospect to have been due more to vagueness of response than to substantive distinctiveness. In the most-important-problem question, the open form probably limits some respondents to a frame of reference not intended by investigators, as noted previously, whereas just the opposite happens in the open form of the child-value question, where the largest open category (*To get an education*) is outside the desired frame of reference. Closed forms of the two questions avoided both these problems. And of course there is much missing data (e.g., multiple responses) to open questions that are eliminated entirely by adequate closed versions. Yet it will not do to say at this point that closed forms, even where carefully constructed on the basis of open responses, are generally superior. Certain important form differences for the child-values question have not been successfully interpreted, and the issue of whether well-built closed questions are always more valid cannot be considered settled on the basis of experiments with only three questions.

What little evidence on the issue of validity appears in past literature is mixed, and most of it deals with types of items different from those used here or in most attitude surveys. Belson and Duncan (1962) show that checklists yield more mentions than do open questions of magazines and newspapers read "yesterday" and of television programs seen "yesterday." Although validity data were not available, the investigators deliberately included several items about nonexistent TV programs on the checklists, and found only a tiny number of false reports concerning these, which suggests that invalidity in the sense of overreporting may not have been a serious problem on the closed form. Marquis, Marshall, and Oskamp (1972) also present evidence in favor of closed questions, but their results are based on a special factual situation remote from most surveys. Dohrenwend (1965) too offers results indicating that closed questions are superior in certain respects, but her investigation involved a rather special experimental situation, and in addition the investigators do not seem to have standardized the questions employed. Sudman and Bradburn (1974), in their review of research on response error, conclude that open questions are generally preferable to closed questions on especially threatening topics. Based on their later research, Bradburn, Sudman, and Associates (1979) report that open questions yielded higher rates of drinking and sexual behavior than did closed questions. They assume that the higher rates are more accurate, but do not have direct evidence for this assumption, and in addition it is not clear that their closed alternatives were developed from pilot open questions. Some other studies occasionally cited as bearing on open-closed comparisons (e.g., Metzner and Mann, 1952) have too many features that vary between comparison groups to allow useful inferences regarding the problems treated in this chapter. In sum, the previous evidence on the open-closed controversy after almost 50 years of survey research is meager, usually quite specialized in form or setting, often problematic in important respects, and almost always lacking in validity data.

4. It is often assumed that closed questions bias respondents by presenting attractive alternatives that they would not have thought of themselves—the problem of social desirability. Wherever we were able to test this assumption the evidence was negative, and although we do not doubt that social desirability bias may occur under certain circumstances, it seems a less serious hazard than we had initially assumed. Likewise, response-order bias did not appear even slightly in three experiments on closed-question alternative orderings, though we know from experiments in other areas (see Chapter 2) that it is a real danger. Thus the failures of closed questions do not seem to be due primarily to misrepresentation of beliefs and attitudes by respondents, but (as noted under the first point) to unrepresentativeness of the categories of thought and values provided by investigators. Geertz's (e.g., 1976) concern for meaning should be at least as much of a reference point when we construct questions as Goffman's (1959) emphasis on self-presentation.

5. Some important findings do remain constant across form in our investigations. For example, Accomplishment as a work value is positively related to education in all of our experiments, despite differences in form, in wording, and in the number and nature of the other alternatives present. There is thus a robustness to the relationship that simply does not hold for other associations equally interesting and equally significant statistically in particular analyses. An investigator should probably feel more confidence in the meaningfulness of such a stable finding.

6. Open-closed differences appear to be smaller for some parts of the population than for others, in particular for more-educated as against less-educated respondents (see Table 3.8). This is largely due to the fact that the least educated bulk disproportionately large in open missing-data categories, and it is these responses that must, in a sense, be redistributed when the closed question is asked. Nevertheless the effect is real in terms of creating a greater gap between open and closed results for less-educated respondents than for the more educated.

TABLE 3.8
Mean Percentage Differences for Common Categories
by Education[a]

	Education		
Experiment	0–11	12	13+
Work values I	9.7	14.2	4.9
Work values II	12.5	8.1	6.0
Work values III[b]	12.7	12.5	8.0
Important problem I[c]	14.4	6.8	7.2
Child values	16.1	10.0	4.7

[a] Using common categories only, absolute percentage differences between the two forms were calculated for each category and averaged to give the figures in this table.

[b] This experiment is described in footnote 16 (p. 103).

[c] The second important-problem experiment was not included in this analysis because of the likelihood of strong context effects, as noted in the text.

7. Finally, since our results fail to provide strong support for the superiority of open questions, the implication may seem to be that after sufficient pilot work an investigator can rely exclusively on closed items. But we think that total elimination of open questions from survey research would be a serious mistake. For one thing, open questions may be needed to document the *absence* of a type of response, as in Stouffer (1955) and Converse (1964), though as we have seen, considerable care must be taken that the wording of the open question does not subtly prevent the emergence of relevant types of responses. Open "why" questions can also be especially valuable as follow-ups to important closed questions, providing insight into why people answer the way they do (see an example in Chapter 8, and also examples in Crutchfield and Gordon, 1947, and Schuman, 1966 and 1969). They are needed as well where rapidly shifting events can affect answers, or indeed over longer stretches of time to avoid missing newly emergent categories. And of course in some situations the set of meaningful alternatives is too large or complex to present to respondents—a serious problem with telephone surveys where cards are not possible.

Furthermore, as survey data come to provide the material for history, open interview responses take on increasing value because they allow future social scientists to create in retrospect new categories undreamt of by the original investigators—to put, in effect, new questions to one's predecessor's respondents. Consider that remote ancestor of present-day research, the Domesday Survey, carried out in 1086 with William the Conqueror the Principal Investigator. The new king was less interested in the attitudes of his subjects than in their holdings; but supposing he had obtained a representative sample of public opinion in the late eleventh century, we would find its value considerably greater if what were preserved were the spontaneous thoughts and language of men and women of those days, rather than simply choices among alternatives a, b, and c. The same will not be less true in our own time, and investigators with a concern for the future should make certain that more than numerical codes are transmitted to social scientists of the next decade, century, or millenium.[20]

[20]This assumes that responses are recorded with substantial accuracy, of course, and that these raw responses are available for later recoding. As Duncan, Schuman, and Duncan (1973:36) discovered, use of earlier open-coding categories and results can be quite misleading. Where the goal is to study social change via exact replication, it is important that all sets of responses be coded by the same set of coders (if possible blind to the sources of the responses), lest changes in coding practices be mistaken for changes in respondent attitudes. New methods of electronic recording of verbal responses should make storage much easier in the future.

4
The Assessment of
No Opinion

I was gratified to be able to answer promptly, and I did.
I said I didn't know.
—Mark Twain, *Life on the Mississippi*

To virtually any attitude, opinion, or belief question in a survey, a possible reply is "I don't know." Whether the question deals with the performance of the president or the possibility of life after death, some respondents may prefer to give what survey investigators commonly call a *DK response.*

But survey questions differ in the extent to which they facilitate such responses. The typical practice—what we shall call the *standard question form*—is not to include a DK alternative as part of a question. Interviewers are instructed to record DK only when a respondent gives it spontaneously rather than choosing one of the fixed alternatives provided in the question.[1] Indeed, some survey units take additional steps to reduce the number of DK responses. The current Survey Research Center *Interviewer's Manual* (1976: 17) points out that the answer "I have no opinion on that" can mean merely, "Wait a minute, I'm thinking," and advises that "it is a good idea to probe all of the 'don't know' responses that occur during the first few pages of a questionnaire." It seems likely that such interviewer behavior will communicate to most respondents the undesirability of saying DK and thus minimize the frequency of DK responses. (See Cannell, Oksenberg, and Converse, 1977, on the effects of interviewer feedback.) This is probably not objectionable to most survey analysts, who typically regard DK responses as a

---

[1]This discussion assumes the use of closed questions, although it would apply with little change where open questions are used.

form of "missing data" and therefore a reduction in effective sample size.[2]

The practice of discouraging DK responses makes most sense if such responses are regarded as momentary hesitancies, evasions, or signs of ambivalence. But some theoretical discussions give the DK response a more important meaning. Bogart (1967: 337), for example, writes that "what people think about public issues is really secondary to ... whether they think about them at all. . . . The first question to ask is: ' . . . Do you have an opinion?' " This emphasis fits the repeated finding that the strongest background correlate of DK responses is low education (Francis and Busch, 1975; J. Converse, 1976–1977). An obvious interpretation of this correlation is that DK often reflects lack of knowledge or opinion about the issue contained in the question, in which case urging the respondent to make a substantive choice would not seem a useful way to proceed. In fact, Philip Converse's (1970) analysis of a three-wave panel study suggests that much error in survey data flows from random responses by persons who really have no views on the issues under inquiry and simply flip mental coins in order to satisfy the interviewer's expectation of an answer. It also seems quite possible that respondents who lack opinions on an issue will be especially susceptible to various response sets, thus contributing systematic as well as random error to survey data.

The reasoning just outlined suggests that respondents should be allowed, perhaps even encouraged, to see DK as a legitimate response in attitude surveys. Items designed to accomplish this goal will be called *filter questions*, since they attempt to screen out respondents from substantive categories by making it explicit that DK or no opinion is a perfectly acceptable response. Thus, the biennial Election Studies carried out through the Institute for Social Research (ISR) include some questions that first ask: *Have you been interested in this enough to favor one side over the other?* before requesting a choice among alternatives; and other questions offer *haven't thought much about this* as one of the alternatives read to respondents.[3] Gallup (1947) long ago recommended such a

[2]The National Opinion Research Center (NORC) interviewer instructions ("A Brush-up on Interviewing Techniques," 1972, p. 7) are very similar to those of the Survey Research Center. Practices of the commercial polls are less clear, but from what we have been able to learn, several of the commercial organizations do not discourage DK responses in this way, and it is interesting to note that their DK levels tend to be higher than those of SRC and NORC (Converse and Schuman, 1981, and Smith, 1978). DKs are less of a problem in simple reporting of item marginals than in multivariate analysis, and this may account for the difference in procedure.

[3]Strictly speaking, the first kind of preliminary question will be called a *full filter*, and the second a *quasi-filter*. Where the distinction is not needed, as in this general discussion, *filter* refers to both kinds.

procedure, and examples are found occasionally in Gallup and other surveys. But use of filters is not common, which is why we refer to unfiltered questions as the *standard form*.

There exist, then, two different approaches to the treatment of DK or no opinion responses in surveys, each represented by a distinct way of asking questions. Under these circumstances it would obviously be useful to know whether the difference in question form leads to important differences in results, and if so what implications this has for conclusions drawn from survey data.[4] But though both forms of questions, standard and filtered, have existed for many years, albeit in different proportions, systematic comparison of the two seems never to have been undertaken prior to our first experiments in 1974. In this chapter we report and analyze a number of such experimental comparisons.

DESIGN

In the standard form of our experiments the DK alternative is not mentioned as part of the question, but it is printed in the questionnaire under the notation *If volunteered*. Interviewers are instructed to accept such responses when offered spontaneously, but otherwise not to encourage them.[5] Filtered forms differ somewhat among the several experiments, but each of them includes as some part of the question an explicit DK or no opinion option.

There are several issues one may usefully address when comparing standard and filtered versions of the same question.

1. *DK Proportions:* Does the addition of a DK filter regularly increase the number of persons saying DK, and does the increase depend on the nature of the item, on the initial (unfiltered) level of DK responses, or on the wording of the filter itself?
2. *Substantive Proportions:* When DK responses are increased as a result of filtering, are the proportions giving the various substantive positions also changed vis-à-vis one another?

[4]Filtering would not solve the problem Philip Converse (1970) identified, since his analysis was in fact based on filtered items. But lack of filtering would presumably increase the problem.

[5]We purposely avoided the more extreme step of having interviewers actively discourage DK responses on the standard form. It seemed wiser at this point to make the comparison between question forms only, rather than include other interviewer behavior as an additional source of variation.

3. *Relationships:* Does filtering change the relation of attitude items to other attitudinal or background variables?

The rest of this chapter addresses in turn these three major issues.

EFFECTS OF FILTERING ON DK PROPORTIONS

Graded Foreign Affairs Items

Three of the items employed in these experiments were especially constructed by us to form a scale of decreasing salience for the general public. That is, we chose topics where knowledge, and therefore the existence of opinions, could be expected a priori to vary in a predictable way. Using the area of foreign affairs, one item dealt with "Russia" (assumed to be best known to the public), one with "Arab nations" (assumed to be somewhat less familiar), and one with the 1974 Portuguese revolution (assumed to be relatively unfamiliar to most Americans even when it was asked in 1974). Results on the standard form of the three questions bear out these assumptions (see Table 4.1, based on

TABLE 4.1
Filter Experiments on Foreign Affairs Items (SRC–74 Fall)[a]

Standard form		Filtered form	
1. Russia			
Here are some questions about other countries. Do you agree or disagree with this statement? The Russian leaders are basically trying to get along with America.		*Here are some questions about other countries. Not everyone has opinions on these questions. If you do not have an opinion, just say so. The Russian leaders are basically trying to get along with America. Do you have an opinion on that? (If yes) Do you agree or disagree? (Repeat original statement if necessary)*	
Agree	49.9%	Agree	39.2%
Disagree	34.9	Disagree	23.1
DK (volunteered)	15.2	No opinion	37.6
	100		100
	(499)		(510)

(*continued*)

TABLE 4.1—*Continued*

Standard form		Filtered form	
2. Arabs			
The Arab nations are trying to work for a real peace with Israel. Do you agree or disagree?		The Arab nations are trying to work for a real peace with Israel. Do you have an opinion on that? (If yes) Do you agree or disagree?	
Agree	16.7%	Agree	10.1%
Disagree	60.0	Disagree	44.8
DK (volunteered)	23.4	No opinion	45.0
	100		100
	(492)		(513)
3. Portugal			
How about this statement: The new Portuguese military government is trying to maintain its own control without concern for democracy in Portugal. Do you agree or disagree?		How about this statement: The new Portuguese military government is trying to maintain its own control without concern for democracy in Portugal. Do you have an opinion on that? (If yes) Do you agree or disagree?	
Agree	21.9%	Agree	6.8%
Disagree	14.9	Disagree	5.3
DK (volunteered)	63.2	No opinion	87.9
	100		100
	(498)		(511)

[a] The original order of items in the questionnaire was Russia, Portugal, Arabs; the three experiments are rearranged here in order of expected size of DK or no opinion category.

SRC–74 Fall). The DK percentage is lowest for the Russia item (15%), somewhat higher for the Arabs item (23%), and much higher for the Portugal item (63%). The finding that over three-fifths of the sample spontaneously volunteered DK to the Portugal item is worth special note, since it tends to contradict the assertion sometimes made that most respondents are unwilling to admit ignorance in survey interviews. We will return to this issue in Chapter 5.

Yet Table 4.1 also demonstrates that addition of a filter raises no opinion or DK percentages significantly and substantially: by 22 to 25 percentage points for the 3 foreign affairs questions. It is remarkable that the effect is almost identical for the 3 items despite the difference in their

DK base rates on the standard forms. For the Russia item only 15% say DK on the standard form, and this is increased by 22 percentage points on the filtered form. For the Portugal item, 63% say DK on the standard form, and this is increased by 25 percentage points on the filtered form.

We shall use the term *floaters* to refer to respondents who would give a substantive response to a standard version but a DK response to a filtered version of the same question. In these split-ballot experiments we have no direct way of identifying individual floaters, since we have simply the total DK percentage on a standard form for one subsample and the total DK percentage on a filtered form for a comparable subsample. The difference in percentage DK between two forms of a question allows us to estimate how many floaters there are, subject to sampling error for the two subsamples, but this is a constructed percentage and does not represent a single set of individuals responding to both forms.

It is possible, however, to characterize floaters indirectly. Thus, the mean education (years of schooling) of respondents who say DK on the standard form of the Russia item is 10.5, whereas on the filtered form it is 10.9. This implies, again subject to sampling error, that the mean education of the floaters on this item must have been 11.2.[6] On the Portugal item the same type of calculation yields a mean educational level for the floaters of 12.8 years of schooling. Thus the average educational level is estimated to be appreciably higher for the floaters on the Portugal item than for the floaters on the Russia item, suggesting that it is largely a different set of individuals who float on these two items. If different individuals at different educational levels are involved, however, this makes it even more remarkable that the proportion of floaters is approximately the same for the two items. Floating may be a behavior that many or perhaps even most respondents can engage in under certain circumstances. (For the Russia and Arab items, however, where floaters have very similar estimated educational levels, 11.2 and 11.3, respectively, it is possible that many of the same individuals are involved.) We will return at a later point to the issue of who floaters are.

Additional Experiments

We created DK filter experiments for six other questions, different from the foreign policy items in origin, subject matter, and wording. The questions, shown in Table 4.2, are from the following sources:

[6]The calculation is based on the assumption that DK respondents on the filtered form consist of persons who would have said DK on the standard form, plus the floaters. Using the known proportion and mean education of each type, an estimate of the mean education of the floaters is provided by solving for x in the following equation: $(.152)(10.5) + (.376 - .152)x = (.376)(10.9)$.

Courts

The standard form of this item is a regular NORC General Social Survey question. We were permitted to pair it in NORC–74 with a new form having a DK alternative. The latter is not a DK filter in the strict sense of preceding the substantive question; rather it provides an additional alternative to the question. We refer to such DK alternatives as *quasi-filters*.

Government

The filtered form of this item has been used for a number of years as part of the ISR Election Studies. We created a standard form of the item by omitting the filter about interest. It will be noted that the filter in this case refers to having an interest rather than to having an opinion, but lacking evidence initially as to whether this made a difference, we included the item in our experiments because of the desire to work whenever possible with questions used in previous important surveys. The first experiment with this item appeared in SRC–76 February.

Communist Book

The standard form of this item is part of the classic survey carried out by Stouffer and included in his *Communism, Conformity, and Civil Liberties* (1955). The first experiment with this item appeared in SRC–77 February.

Leaders

The standard versions of these questions—one about the "crookedness" of government officials, the other about their "smartness"—were taken from the ISR Election Studies. Our initial experiments with them were in SRC–78 May.

Liberal–Conservative

The standard form of this item appears regularly in the NORC General Social Survey. We wrote a filtered version that is similar to the one asked in ISR Election Studies. Our only DK experiment with the ques-

TABLE 4.2
Six Additional DK Filter Experiments

Standard form	Filtered form

1. Courts (NORC-74)

In general, do you think the courts in this area deal too harshly or not harshly enough with criminals?

In general, do you think the courts in this area deal too harshly or not harshly enough with criminals, or don't you have enough information about the courts to say?

Standard form		Filtered form	
Too harshly	5.6%	Too harshly	4.6%
Not harshly enough	77.8	Not harshly enough	60.3
About right (volunteered)	9.7	About right (volunteered)	6.1
DK (volunteered)	6.8	Not enough information to say	29.0
	100		100
	(745)		(723)

2. Government (SRC-76 February)

Some people are afraid the government in Washington is getting too powerful for the good of the country and the individual person. Others feel that the government in Washington is not getting too strong. What is your feeling, do you think the government is getting too powerful or do you think the government is not getting too strong?

Some people are afraid the government in Washington is getting too powerful for the good of the country and the individual person. Others feel that the government in Washington is not getting too strong. Have you been interested enough in this to favor one side over the other? (If yes) What is your feeling, do you think the government is getting too powerful or do you think the government is not getting too strong?

Standard form		Filtered form	
Too powerful	55.0%	Too powerful	45.0%
Not too strong	35.1	Not too strong	21.6
DK (volunteered)	10.0	Not interested enough	33.3
	100		100
	(613)		(606)

3. Communist Book (SRC-77 February)

This next question is about a man who admits he is a communist. Suppose he wrote a book, which is in your public library. Somebody your community suggests the book should be removed from the library. Would you favor removing the book or oppose removing the book?

This next question is about a man who admits he is a communist. Suppose he wrote a book which is in your public library. Somebody in your community suggests the book should be removed from the library. Would you favor removing the book, oppose removing the book, or do you not have an opinion on that?

Standard form		Filtered form	
Favor removing	29.1%	Favor removing	17.2%
Oppose removing	67.9	Oppose removing	56.6
DK (volunteered)	3.0	No opinion	26.2
	100		100
	(563)		(533)

(continued)

TABLE 4.2—*Continued*

Standard form	Filtered form

4. Leaders smart (SRC–78 May) *Do you feel that almost all of the people running the government are smart people, or do you think that quite a few of them don't seem to know what they are doing?*

*Do you feel that almost all of the people running the government are smart people, **or** that quite a few of them don't seem to know what they are doing, **or** do you not have an opinion on that?*

Standard form		Filtered form	
Are smart	37.0%	Are smart	28.9%
Don't know what they're doing	58.1	Don't know what they're doing	49.7
DK (volunteered)	4.8	No opinion	21.4
	100		100
	(597)		(594)

5. Leaders crooked (SRC–78 May)
*Do you think that **quite a few** of the people running the government are crooked, **not very many** are, or do you think **hardly any** of them are crooked?*

*Do you think that **quite a few** of the people running the government are crooked, **not very many** are, **hardly any** of them are crooked, or do you not have an opinion on that?*

Standard form		Filtered form	
Quite a few	14.2%	Quite a few	11.2%
Not very many	42.1	Not very many	37.2
Hardly any	39.5	Hardly any	32.2
DK (volunteered)	4.2	No opinion	19.4
	100		100
	(625)		(608)

6. Liberal–conservative (NORC–78)
*We hear a lot of talk these days about liberals and conservatives. I'm going to show you a seven-point scale on which the **political** views that people might hold are arranged from extremely liberal—point 1—to extremely conservative—point 7. Where would you place yourself on this scale?*

*We hear a lot of talk these days about liberals and conservatives. I'm going to show you a seven-point scale on which the **political** views that people might hold are arranged from extremely liberal—point 1—to extremely conservative—point 7. Where would you place yourself on this scale, or haven't you thought much about it?*

Standard form		Filtered form	
Extremely liberal	1.3%	Extremely liberal	1.6%
Liberal	9.1	Liberal	8.6
Slightly liberal	16.0	Slightly liberal	14.2
Moderate, middle-of-the-road	34.2	Moderate, middle-of-the-road	31.1
Slightly conservative	18.6	Slightly conservative	15.1
Conservative	13.9	Conservative	9.6
Extremely conservative	2.5	Extremely conservative	1.4
DK (volunteered)	4.4	Haven't thought much about it	18.4
	100		100
	(757)		(768)

tion was in NORC–78, though we also use a similar item in middle alternative experiments (Chapter 6).

Distributions on these six items, presented in Table 4.2, show DK differences between standard and filtered forms in the range of 14 to 23 percentage points—not too different from those for the foreign affairs items. This finding is noteworthy when one realizes that the present items appear in 5 different surveys, so that the actual samples, as well as item content, nature of filter, and base rates, are different from one another and from the foreign affairs experiments. Later replications of most of these items, shown in Table 4.3, provide a broader range of increments due to DK filters, but the overall average (both mean and median) for the total of 19 experiments that we carried out is 22%, and two-thirds of the increments fall within the range of 13 to 23 percentage points.[7]

Varying the Nature of the Filter

There is more than one way to construct an explicit DK alternative, as we have already noted. If a single set of people exists who are unwilling to voice DK when it is not offered explicitly, but ready to give it when invited, then the exact form of the filter should make no difference. If willingness to voice DK is a matter of response to encouragement, however, we might expect the DK level to vary by degree of encouragement. We tested these opposing hypotheses by repeating the Russia item in a split-ballot experiment using two types of filters: a replication of the full filter employed in Table 4.1 (with minor grammatical changes) as one

[7]The replications in the Detroit Area Study (DAS–76) of the courts item and of a somewhat altered version of the government item show results somewhat different from the original ones. For the courts item, the DK difference drops to 10%, and for the government item to 15%, although both remain highly significant ($p > .001$). (In both cases, the drop is almost entirely due to a decrease in DK% on the filtered form. Further analysis does not reveal any obvious factor such as race or size of place that can account for the decrease.) Later replication of the government item (in SRC–78 March) restores the 23% difference of Table 4.2 exactly; replications of the book item lead to similar figures (22% and 20% in SRC–78 March and SRC–78 May); those for the Russia and Arabs items to higher figures (34% and 29% for the former in SRC–78 May and SRC–78 Fall; 31% for the latter in SRC–78 May); and a replication of the crooks item to a lower figure (13% in SRC–78 Fall). It seems possible that the smaller effect on the crooks and liberal–conservative items is due to their offering a middle-response category. There is also some evidence that DK level is affected by mode of interviewing, based on a special experiment with the Arabs item in SRC–76 Spring as part of a large-scale comparison of face-to-face and telephone interviewing. See Table 4.3, No. 3, and the further discussion in Appendix B.2.

TABLE 4.3
Filter Experiment Replications

Standard form		Filtered form	
1. Russia (SRC–78 May)			
(Questions are identical to Table 4.1, item 1)			
Agree	54.5%	Agree	30.7%
Disagree	33.7	Disagree	23.7
DK (volunteered)	11.8	No opinion	45.6
	100		100
	(627)		(616)
2. Russia (SRC–78 Fall)			
(Questions are identical to Table 4.1, item 1)			
Agree	48.2%	Agree	31.4%
Disagree	38.2	Disagree	26.1
DK (volunteered)	13.6	No opinion	42.5
	100		100
	(508)		(1020)
3. Arabs (SRC–76 Spring)			
(Questions are identical to Table 4.1, item 2)			
Telephone			
Agree	31.0%	Agree	10.9%
Disagree	37.4	Disagree	21.7
DK (volunteered)	31.5	No opinion	67.4
	100		100
	(802)		(825)
Face-to-face			
Agree	20.1%	Agree	12.0%
Disagree	43.5	Disagree	24.0
DK (volunteered)	36.4	No opinion	64.0
	100		100
	(711)		(803)
4. Arabs (SRC–78 May)			
(Questions are identical to Table 4.1, item 2)			
Agree	39.7%	Agree	28.1%
Disagree	46.3	Disagree	26.6
DK (volunteered)	14.0	No opinion	45.4
	100		100
	(620)		(595)
5. Courts (DAS–76)			
(Questions are identical to Table 4.2, item 1)			
Too harshly	3.9%	Too harshly	3.2%
Not harshly enough	84.0	Not harshly enough	76.6

(*continued*)

TABLE 4.3—*Continued*

Standard form		Filtered form	
About right (volunteered)	5.0	About right (volunteered)	2.6
DK (volunteered)	7.2	No opinion	17.6
	100		100
	(545)		(568)

6. Government (DAS-76)
(Questions are identical to Table 4.2, item 2, except the filter is changed to:
Do you have an opinion on this issue?)

Too powerful	58.2%	Too powerful	51.9%
Not too strong	31.4	Not too strong	22.6
DK (volunteered)	10.5	No opinion	25.4
	100		100
	(545)		(570)

7. Government (SRC-78 March)
(Questions are identical to No. 6 above)

Too powerful	40.8%	Too powerful	41.0%
Not too strong	48.2	Not too strong	25.1
DK (volunteered)	11.0	No opinion	33.9
	100		100
	(363)		(363)

8. Communist book (SRC-78 March)
(Questions are identical to Table 4.2, item 3)

Favor removing	29.5%	Favor removing	18.9%
Oppose removing	62.3	Oppose removing	50.6
DK (volunteered)	8.3	No opinion	30.6
	100		100
	(363)		(360)

9. Communist book (SRC-78 May)
(Questions are identical to Table 4.2, item 3)

Favor removing	24.5%	Favor removing	14.1%
Oppose removing	69.5	Oppose removing	59.6
DK (volunteered)	6.0	No opinion	26.3
	100		100
	(616)		(601)

10. Leaders crooked (SRC-78 Fall)
(Questions are identical to Table 4.3, item 5)

Quite a few	12.5%	Quite a few	8.3%
Not very many	27.4	Not very many	26.0
Hardly any	55.3	Hardly any	47.9
DK (volunteered)	4.8	No opinion	17.7
	100		100
	(497)		(1010)

version; and a simple addition of a DK alternative (a quasi-filter) following substantive choices as the other version. (A standard version was not included in this SRC–77 February experiment.) The two forms and marginal results are shown in Table 4.4.

As can be seen from the marginals presented with each item, the DK percentage is nearly 14 points higher on the full filter version than on the quasi-filter version ($\chi^2 = 20.86$, 1 *df*, $p < .001$). On replication in SRC–78 March, the difference is 10% ($\chi^2 = 7.48$, 1 *df*, $p < .01$). Thus a full filter that precedes an item and emphasizes the frequency of no opinion is more effective in encouraging DK responses than is a quasi-filter.

Another possibly important variation in type of filter is that between questions asking whether the respondent has an opinion (e.g., the foreign policy items in Table 4.1) and those asking whether the respondent is interested or informed (e.g., courts and government items in Table 4.2). Claiming an opinion is probably easier than claiming information or interest, and thus one might expect DK to be higher with the latter type of filter. Our own experiments do not permit such comparisons, but in an analysis of seven NORC split-ballot experiments, Bishop, Oldendick, and Tuchfarber, (1978) report significantly more DKs with the use of an *interest* compared to an *opinion* filter. Thus here, as in the case of quasi-filters versus full filters, it evidently makes a difference how a DK option is constructed. Both results indicate that floaters are not a fixed set of people, but rather vary in number depending upon the wording of the filter.

TABLE 4.4
Comparison of Two Types of Filters[a]

Full filtered version				Quasi-filtered version		
*Here is a statements about another country. Not everyone has an opinion on this. If you do **not** have an opinion, just say so. Here's the statement: The Russian leaders are basically trying to get along with America. Do you have an opinion on that?*				*Here is a statement about another country: The Russian leaders are basically trying to get along with America. Do you agree, disagree, or do you not have an opinion on that?*		
No opinion	Yes, have opinion			Agree	Disagree	No opinion
	↓					
56.3%	*Do you agree or disagree?* (Repeat statement if necessary.)			27.7%	29.5	42.8
	Agree	Disagree	Total			Total
	22.9	20.9	100 (551)			100 (596)

[a] Carried out in SRC–77 February.

THE EFFECTS OF DK FILTERS ON
SUBSTANTIVE PROPORTIONS

We have demonstrated that the addition of a DK filter to an opinion question will typically induce more than a fifth of the sample to shift from substantive positions into the DK category. We call these people floaters, since they move between substantive and DK categories depending upon the form of the question. An important practical issue that results from this demonstration is whether or not such movement affects the percentage distribution for the substantive alternatives to a question. Of course, in most cases the percentage giving any one substantive alternative will shrink when a DK filter is added to an item. But this problem is handled by calculating substantive percentages with DK responses omitted. This is often done on standard versions of questions and by performing the same operation on both forms we can determine whether the filtering process alters substantive distributions. Alteration will occur if floaters come disproportionately from a single substantive response category.

The simple step needed for this analysis is illustrated here with the Russian leaders item from Table 4.1:

	Standard*	Filtered**
Agree	58.9%	62.9%
Disagree	41.1	37.1
	100	100
	(423)	(318)
	$\chi^2 = 1.24$, $df = 1$, n.s.	

*Omits 76 DKs
**Omits 192 DKs

For this item, the agree–disagree response distributions do *not* differ significantly once DKs are omitted. Even though an estimated 22% floaters are giving substantive positions on the standard form but drop out entirely from the filtered form, this appears not to affect the substantive comparison.

Including the Russia item just presented, we have 9 original experiments and 10 replications on which it is possible to compare substantive distributions omitting DKs. On 14 of these 19 comparisons, the distributions of substantive positions do not differ significantly between standard and filtered versions, once DK responses are removed. (There is also no significant difference on the variant of the Russia experiment that compared 2 different types of filters, nor on its replication a year later.) Of the 5 significant differences, 4 are small: On the original government experiment the *too powerful* response is slightly greater (6.6%, p < .05) on the filtered form; on 2 of the book experiments the *favor removing* response is slightly larger on the standard form (6.7%, p < .02 in SRC–77 February and 6.9%, p < .01 in SRC–78 May); and on the SRC–76 Spring replication of the Arabs experiment the standard form shows more agreement (5.9%, p < .05).[8] Only the SRC–78 March replication of the government item produces a large univariate difference as shown below:

	Standard	Filtered	Diff.
Too powerful	45.8%	62.1%	16.3%
Not too powerful	54.2	27.9	
	100	100	
	(323)	(240)	
	$\chi^2 = 14.71,\ df = 1,\ p < .001$		

This was one of three administrations of the Government experiment, however, and our best estimate of the univariate shift is probably the weighted average of the 3, which is 8.0%. In sum, our conclusion based on all 19 comparisons is that filtering can on occasion significantly alter the division of substantive opinion, but that it typically does not; when it does, its effect is usually small.[9]

It might seem from these findings that the opinions of floaters tend to be like those of nonfloaters, since the movement of floaters usually has little effect on substantive proportions. The failure to discover strong univariate effects of filtering, however, has limited implications. For one thing, it is also difficult to reject other theoretical models of how floaters behave. Thus if one postulates that floaters act in a purely random way, choosing substantive alternatives on the standard form of the Russia item by mentally flipping a coin, this leads to expected values of 59.5% and 40.5% for the agree and disagree categories, which cannot be dis-

[8]This last effect occurs only for the interviews conducted by phone; the face-to-face part of the sample shows no agree–disagree difference by form. For a discussion of this interaction see Appendix B.2.

[9]Bishop *et al.* (1980) found significant filtering effects on substantive marginals for three of their eight experiments. Two were 6% differences, one 10%.

tinguished statistically from the observed standard distribution.[10] Furthermore, it is possible for floaters to behave exactly like other respondents, but for somewhat different reasons, as we see in the following section.

EFFECTS OF DK FILTERING ON RELATIONSHIPS

The most fundamental issue about DK filtering is whether it affects substantive conclusions about the relation of one variable to another—whether the variables be individual items, indexes constructed from items, or background factors such as education or age. In other words, will social scientists doing bivariate or multivariate analysis come to different conclusions about their data depending upon whether or not DK filters are used?

There are three possibilities, at least two of which have some sanction in traditional survey assumptions:

1. No important form effects on relationships will occur. That correlations are form-resistent is the implicit assumption of most survey investigators, as indicated by the lack of consideration usually given to the filtering problem in survey reports and survey textbooks.
2. The magnitude of associations involving filtered forms will be greater than for standard forms. If floaters tend to answer standard-form questions by guessing, then associations ought to be increased when such random error is removed. Presumably those investigators who use filters do so on this ground.
3. Associations will be greater on standard than on filtered forms. This would seem to be the least likely possibility, but it might occur when floaters are susceptible to some type of systematic error (for example, acquiescence).

These three hypotheses are not mutually exclusive, and we must allow for the possibility that different ones may apply in different circumstances.

---

[10]Expected values for the random model are obtained by adding half the estimated number of floaters to each of the two substantive categories on the filtered form. (The number of floaters is derived by subtracting the DK proportion on the two forms and multiplying the result by the *total* N on the filtered form.) Thus for the Russia example there are (37.6%–15.2%) × 510 = 114 floaters. On the filtered form, 57 of these are added to the 200 agree responses and 57 to the 118 disagree responses, yielding 257 and 175 or 59.5% and 40.5%. These expected values are not significantly different from the observed values on the standard form (58.9% and 41.1%).

Interattitude Relationships

We begin by relating substantive responses for the Russia and Arabs items, two experimental questions that were included in the same survey (SRC–74). (Although the Portugal item is also in that survey, its DK proportion is so atypical that we have not made use of it for analysis of this type of interrelationship.) One subsample of the survey was asked the standard form of both items; a second subsample was asked the filtered form of both items. Table 4.5 presents the cross-tabulation of the two items within each subsample after omitting all DK responses.

It is immediately apparent that the two associations are dramatically different and that the three-way interaction involving form is highly significant. On the standard form, respondents who agree that the Russians are trying to get along with the Americans also tend to agree that the Arabs are working for peace with the Israelis. On the filtered form,

TABLE 4.5
Response to Russia by Response to Arabs by Form[a]

Standard form

Arabs	Russia	
	Agree	Disagree
Agree	60	13
Disagree	146	129

$$\chi^2 = 22.01, df = 1, p < .001$$
$$gamma = .61$$

Filtered form

Arabs	Russia	
	Agree	Disagree
Agree	23	14
Disagree	121	69

$$\chi^2 = .03, df = 1, \text{n.s.}$$
$$gamma = -.03$$

Russia response × Arab response × Form:
$$\chi^2 = 8.78, df = 1, p < .01$$

[a] Data from SRC–74 Fall. Entries are frequencies, and DK responses are omitted. If agree and disagree responses are combined into "opinions," then opinions versus DK on Russia is related to opinion versus DK on Arabs for each form ($p < .001$), but the magnitude of the associations do not differ significantly by form ($\chi^2 = .81, df = 1$, n.s.)

however, there is no association whatever between response to the Russia item and response to the Arab item. Therefore, if only one form of the items were used in a survey, conclusions would be qualitatively different than if the other form were used.

What causes this difference by form? Our attempt to answer that question led to an unusual set of interlocking results. Since the Russia and Arabs items were not originally designed to be associated, our first hypothesis was that the positive correlation on the standard form was artifactual. A likely artifact, moreover, was close at hand, for both items are in an agree–disagree format and therefore presumably susceptible to acquiescence bias, which has long been recognized as a possible source of correlated error in surveys (see Chapter 8). The hypothesis assumes that there is no true correlation between substantive opinions on the two items, as indicated for the filtered forms. Floaters are of course excluded from the calculation for these filtered forms, since they have opted out by saying DK, presumably because they feel ignorant about the subject matter of one or both items. On the standard form, however, floaters feel pressured into giving an opinion, and lacking any substantive attitudes on these issues they succumb (so the hypothesis goes) to acquiescence cues and agree to both items.

This line of reasoning is consistent with the data in Table 4.5, but it is inconsistent with two other findings. First, the assumption that floaters tend to agree with the Arab and Russia statements should lead to higher agreement on the standard than on the filtered form of each item, once DKs are excluded from the percentage base. As shown earlier (p. 126), this does not happen at all on the Russia item, and it happens to only a small (3.4%) and nonsignificant ($\chi^2 = 1.10$, $df = 1$) extent on the Arab item. Although these results are not completely irreconcilable with an acquiescence interpretation (some floaters could be chronic yea-sayers, others chronic naysayers), they are not favorable to it.

A second set of findings is more decisive in forcing rejection of the agreeing response set line of reasoning. The 1974 survey that included the foreign affairs items was actually divided into three random subsamples. The standard forms of items were administered to one of these subsamples and the filtered forms to another; the third subsample received a forced-choice form of the same items. For the two items discussed here, the forced-choice forms read as follows:

> *Would you say that the Russian leaders are basically trying to get along with America, **or** that they are basically trying to dominate America?*

> *Do you think the Arab nations are trying to defeat Israel, **or** are they trying to work for a real peace with Israel?*

TABLE 4.6
Response to Russia by Response to Arabs for the
Forced-Choice Form[a]

	Russia	
Arabs	Trying to get along	Trying to dominate
Working for peace	32	13
Trying to defeat	120	148
	$\chi^2 = 10.95$, $df = 1$, $p < .001$	
	gamma $= .50$	

[a] Data from SRC-74 Fall.

No DK filter is included with the items, but DK was accepted if volunteered exactly as on the standard forms.[11]

If the hypothesis about acquiescence is correct, then there should be no relation between opinions on these forced-choice versions because they are not in agree–disagree form and therefore do not allow an acquiescence response. Table 4.6 shows, however, that there is in fact a highly significant association between the Arab and Russia forced-choice items. Apparently, the observed relation on the standard agree–disagree form is not mainly due to an acquiescence bias, since a similar relation is obtained on the forced-choice form where such a bias could not be operating.[12]

It still seems likely that respondents who would say DK on the filtered form but give substantive responses on both the standard and forced-choice forms are responsible for the positive associations on the latter two forms. We cannot directly identify these floaters in the cross-section data, but we can make an estimate of their behavior by using reinterview data obtained on the Arabs item in SRC-75 February several months after the original survey. Respondents asked the standard version of the Arabs item in the original survey were asked the filtered version in the

[11]The DK percentage is 15.3 on the Russia item and 27.4 on the Arab item, both of which are close to the DK percentages on the standard forms in Table 4-1.

[12]The forced-choice form does result in lower selection on each item of the alternative that had been represented by agreement on the standard form. This provides evidence that some mild acquiescence may occur on the standard form, but it appears to be independent of the interaction we are discussing, since the interaction does not disappear when acquiescence is eliminated. It should also be noted that the correlation between the Arabs and Russia forced-choice items cannot be explained by a response-order effect, that is, by assuming a propensity to choose the last (or the first) alternative offered. The correlation in Table 4.6 is produced by a disproportionate number of those choosing the first stated alternative on the Russia item and the second stated alternative on the Arabs item, and vice versa.

reinterview. Individuals who initially gave an opinion on the standard form but then said DK when reinterviewed with the filtered form are, by definition, floaters. They only approximate floaters in the original cross-section because factors such as true attitude change, recollection of initial response, mode of administration (the original interview was face-to-face, the reinterview by telephone), and panel attrition all could make respondents who are inconsistent over time different from our hypothetical group of floaters in the cross-section. To keep in mind these possible differences, we will call them *panel-floaters*. [13]

Based on results thus far, we expect panel-floaters to show a strong relationship between their positions on the Russia and Arab issues for the original standard form, and expect all other respondents to show no relation. As the reader can see in Table 4.7, the results fit these expectations almost perfectly. There is a large correlation between the Russia and Arabs responses for the panel-floaters, but no association at all among other respondents. Thus, the original observed relation on the standard agree–disagree form seems entirely due to individuals who gave an opinion to that form but would not have done so had an explicit DK alternative been easily available. The results also strongly suggest that panel-floaters correspond closely to floaters as defined originally by comparisons between standard and filtered forms in the SRC–74 Fall cross section.

The puzzle we now face is why the opinions of floaters on these two topics are related, whereas the opinions of other respondents are not. We believe that the floaters are answering on the basis of a general underlying orientation that is tapped vaguely by both items, whereas others are responding on the basis of the specific situations referred to in the separate items. Notice that both the Russia and the Arabs items ask about peaceful intentions of leaders of other countries: Are the Russians trying to get along with the Americans? Are the Arabs trying to get along with the Israelis? Floaters in this case appear to be persons who have no detailed opinions about these matters based on the particulars of Soviet–American or Arab–Israeli relations (and thus say DK on a filtered form); but when faced with a standard form that discourages DK, they draw on general positive or negative (or perhaps optimistic or pessimistic) feelings about political leaders. Thus they respond consistently by attributing good intentions to both Russians and Arabs *or* bad intentions to both. (Note that some floaters must lean toward positive attributions and some toward negative attributions. If most floaters leaned in only

[13]It should be noted that nonfloaters as defined by the panel need not be consistent in the *substantive* responses they give. In fact, however, 72% of these panel nonfloaters are consistent in saying agree both times or disagree both times to the Arabs item.

TABLE 4.7
Response to Russia by Response to Arabs on
Standard Form for Panel-Floaters and
Nonfloaters[a]

a. Floaters

Arabs	Russia	
	Agree	Disagree
Agree	24	1
Disagree	41	46

$$\chi^2 = 23.64, \ df = 1,$$
$$p < .001$$
$$gamma = .93$$

b. Nonfloaters

Arabs	Russia	
	Agree	Disagree
Agree	16	8
Disagree	73	43

$$\chi^2 = .12, \ df = 1, \ n.s.$$
$$gamma = .08$$

Russia response × Arabs response ×
Floater versus nonfloater:
$$\chi^2 = 11.54, \ df = 1, \ p < .001$$

[a] SRC–74 Fall and SRC–75 February panel data.

one direction, this would show up in the marginals of the standard forms.) In a sense this consistency in response to the two items might also be considered a response set, but it is not an artifactual one like agreeing irrespective of item content: It reflects a genuine attitudinal disposition. As Allport (1954) pointed out, one of the early and basic meanings of the word "attitude" was that of "set." (For a demonstration of the generality of the optimistic–pessimistic dimension, see Mueller, 1979).

If this interpretation is correct, then opinion on the Arab or Russia questions and opinion on other seemingly unrelated attitude items tapping the same underlying positive–negative dimension should be associated in samples including floaters, but not in filtered samples. The most suitable attitude items to be found for this purpose are a set of five trust-in-government questions in standard form, which were included by other investigators in SRC–74 Fall. (See Robinson and Shaver, 1968:633, for a discussion of these frequently used items; two of them were also employed experimentally at a later point in our research, as shown in Table 4.2, items 4 and 5, but this was unconnected with the use of the items here.) We summed the five items to create a simple trust-in-government index, and related the mean score on the index to response to the Arabs item, separately for panel-floaters and nonfloaters. When this is done, the relation is highly significant for panel-floaters ($F = 8.30$, $df = 1,106$, $p < .005$), with those trusting the Arab nations also trusting American politicans. The relation for panel-nonfloaters, on the other hand, does not approach significance ($F = 1.41$, $df = 1,119$).[14]

The intricate pattern of confirming crosschecks in the preceding analysis would seem to justify considerable confidence in the initial Arab-Russia difference by form, and we do indeed believe that the relations were highly reliable at that point in time. However, when we repeated the Russia and Arabs experiments four years later in SRC–78 May, the 1974 interaction was no longer apparent and there was simply a small but nonsignificant relation on *both* forms between responses to the Arabs and Russia items. (The same survey included two trust-in-government items and these showed only nonsignificant trends to be related more strongly to the Arabs and Russia question on their standard forms than on their filtered forms.) We believe that the explanation for the disappearance of the 1974 interactions lay in the impact on public opinion of events between 1974 and 1978—a period which saw a strong Arab diplomatic offensive. Indeed, although the DK level does not differ much between the 1974 and 1978 surveys (not at all on the filtered form and by about 9% on the standard), there is a sharp shift on both forms in the distribution of those who give an opinion. Whereas about a fifth of the opinion-givers in 1974 were favorable to the Arabs, this was true of about one-half of those giving opinions in 1978 ($\chi^2 = 129.6$, $df = 1$, $p < .001$). Compared to the magnitude of change on other issues during the same time period (Davis, 1978) this was a massive shift.

Moreover, if changing events caused some people to move from disagreeing with the item to uncertainty (and thus to DK) and others from DK to agreeing—instead of directly shifting people from disagree to agree—then the group of people who floated was probably quite different in the two surveys. (In fact, at an intermediate measurement point

---

[14]A more extensive analysis of the trust-in-government index in relation to floating is reported in Schuman and Presser (1978).

in SRC–76 Spring, the DK level was much greater than in either 1974 or 1978; see Table 4.3, No. 3.) Whereas in 1974 floaters were likely to have been uninformed about the Middle East, in 1978 floaters may have been informed but ambivalent. We cannot be certain, of course, but in 1978 floaters may no longer have needed to fall back on general orientations to construct an opinion, and so their responses were no longer linked to the separate Russia issue.[15]

The analysis thus far has presented evidence that in some circumstances a standard question form can produce a meaningful attitudinal association where a filtered form shows no association. It has also led to conceptualization of that part of the sample responsible for the difference: the floaters. Moreover, the finding that floaters can be carriers of certain correlations between attitudes is quite opposite in spirit to the traditional assumption that filtering will remove respondents without meaningful opinions and will therefore increase correlations between variables.

However, there is one other significant interaction in our set of experiments that is much more consistent with traditional notions. The SRC–74 Fall study included for other purposes (see Chapter 6) an item about marijuana laws that was constant in wording across the two subsamples that received standard and filtered DK question forms. Responses to this marijuana law item are related to responses to the question about Russian leaders, as shown in Table 4.8. The direction of the association appears interpretable in terms of a broadly conceived liberal–conservative dimension: Persons least willing to trust the Russian leaders (i.e., more "conservative" in foreign affairs) are also more inclined to favor harsher penalties for use of marijuana. But the association is noticeably and significantly larger on the filtered form, from which floaters have been removed. On exact replication of the two items (one constant and one varied in DK form) in SRC–78 Fall, a similar three-way interaction is obtained ($\chi^2 = 3.32$, $df = 1$, $p < .10$), although the bivariate relations are lower on both forms than in Table 4.8 (on the standard

---

[15]In addition to the striking change in marginals, there is one other important difference between the 1974 and 1978 results that may be related to the Arab–Russia lack of replication. In 1974 education did not affect the relation shown in Table 4.5 between the Arab and Russia items: None of the educational groups showed a relation on the filtered form; all of them showed a positive relation on the standard form. In 1978, in contrast, high school graduates and those who had been to college show no relation on either form, but respondents who did not graduate from high school show a positive relation between items on both forms. The three way interaction, Arabs opinion by Russia opinion by education, controlling for form, is highly significant ($\chi^2 = 15.35$, $df = 2$).

TABLE 4.8
Response to Russia by Response to
Marijuana Laws by Form[a]

	Russia: Standard	
Marijuana	Agree	Disagree
More strict	138	118
Less strict	81	32

$$\chi^2 = 10.56, df = 1,$$
$$p < .002$$
$$gamma = .37$$

	Russia: Filtered	
Marijuana	Agree	Disagree
More strict	84	84
Less strict	89	16

$$\chi^2 = 36.17, df = 1,$$
$$p < .001$$
$$gamma = .70$$

Russia response
× Marijuana response × Form:
$$\chi^2 = 5.85, df = 1, p < .02$$

[a] Data from SRC–74 Fall. The marijuana item is constant in wording across these two forms and reads: *In your opinion, should the penalties for using marijuana be more strict or less strict than they are now?*

form, gamma = .08, n.s.; on the filtered form, gamma = .32, $p < .05$).

We therefore have evidence that floaters can reduce meaningful associations, in addition to creating them. The reduction, however, does not seem to be due simply to the introduction of random error by floaters. It is possible to estimate the bivariate Russia-marijuana distribution for floaters by subtracting each cell frequency in the filtered subtable from each cell frequency in the standard subtable. If the resulting subtable for floaters in SRC–74 Fall is treated as though arising from random sampling of a population, it shows a highly significant association ($\chi^2 = 26.61$, $df = 1$, $p < .001$) in the direction opposite to that shown for nonfloaters (Table 4.8 filtered form). (This procedure is subject to sampling error from both the original subtables and it also requires minor adjustments such as treating one small negative difference as zero; but the resulting χ^2 appears too large to be threatened by problems due to these assumptions. In addition, the near-zero relation on the standard form of the replication also indicates the relation is in the reverse direction for floaters.) If this estimate is correct, it indicates that floaters perceive in the two items something that links them in a way opposite to that for nonfloaters. What that something is we do not know, and perhaps it is best conceptualized as artifactual since it interferes with what appears to be the main substantive relationship in Table 4.8. However treated, the connecting of the two items in a distinctive way by floaters is consistent in a larger sense with what happened earlier for the Arabs–Russia association. In fact, what is a meaningful substantive association and what is an artifactual one is not entirely clear from the totality of these results: It would seem to depend on what the investigator is attempting to measure.

Taken together, the two sets of results discussed in this section indicate that there are cases in which DK form effects can influence substantive interpretation of data in important ways. At the same time, it must be emphasized that floating does not usually seem to affect associations between items. In addition to the Arab–Russia–trust and Russia–marijuana interactions, we examined about 20 possible form effects on relationships and only those already reported reveal clearly significant interactions.[16] Although this might suggest that the Arab–Russia and Russia–marijuana interactions themselves are due to sampling error, we believe that the set of interlocking results for the former and the replication of the latter make this unlikely. It does appear, however, that filtering for DK does not typically change interitem associations to a detectable extent.

Possible Background Correlates

In some instances, standard and filtered forms of attitude questions appear to yield different correlations with other attitude questions. Do they also produce different correlations with background variables such as education? This question actually breaks into two questions: One is

[16]We looked at all correlations between opinions on DK experimental items that were in the same survey, as well as at relations between the DK items and non-experimental items in two surveys (SRC–74 Fall and NORC–78). Although there are some intriguing trends, at present they are probably best regarded as chance findings. (For example in DAS–76, the courts and government experiments show a significant association between opinions on the standard forms ($p < .03$) but not on the filtered forms ($p > .30$); however, the three-way interaction does not approach significance.)

concerned with DK responses versus all substantive responses combined, whereas the other focuses on substantive alternatives vis-á-vis one another. We need to consider each and the link between them.

We began this research with the general hypothesis that education and other indicators of cognitive sophistication would help account for form effects. The basic notion was that those low in cognitive sophistication would be more tightly bound to the exact options presented by the interviewers and less aware that such unspoken alternatives as DK are legitimate. Thus on the standard form these respondents would feel forced to choose a substantive alternative, no matter the lack of commitment to it, whereas on the filtered form they would be quick to accept the explicit DK option. We used education as the main measure of cognitive sophistication throughout, primarily because of its general importance as an explanatory variable in attitude surveys, but in SRC–74 Fall we also included a single question on interest in the news and a three-item measure of information about public figures (see Appendix C).

Even if our hypothesis were confirmed, it speaks only to the issue of whether form influences the relation of education to DK. It does not address the more practically important issue of whether form influences the relation of education to substantive categories. The link between these two problems seems to us to be a plausible but not a necessary one. For example, if a disproportionate number of floaters are found to be low-educated, and if when given the standard form these low-educated floaters choose substantive responses on some basis (e.g., chance) different from that used by nonfloaters, then a form effect involving the relation of education and substantive responses is likely to appear. In any case, it is useful to analyze both these problems separately as well as jointly.

Results for the 1974 Arab experiment by education and form are given in Table 4.9, with percentages, raw numbers, and odds ratios provided.[17] A study of this table, with appropriate calculations, yields the following conclusions:

1. (a) On each form, there is a strong and quite reliable tendency ($p < .001$) for less-educated respondents to say DK regardless of how the table is partitioned. (b) There is also a somewhat weaker tendency on each form, once DK is omitted, for high-educated respondents to disagree with the statement about the Arab nations working for peace with Israel ($p < .05$).

---

[17]Identical analysis using education as a five-category variable (0–8, 9–11, 12, 13–15, 16+) has been carried out with essentially the same results.

TABLE 4.9
Arab Item: Response by Education and Form[a]

		Standard		
Education:		0–11	12	13+
Agree		20.7% (31)	17.2% (27)	13.0% (24)
Disagree		40.7 (61)	63.7 (100)	72.8 (134)
DK		38.7 (58)	19.1 (30)	14.1 (26)
		100 (150)	100 (157)	100 (184)
		Filtered		
Education:		0–11	12	13+
Agree		9.4% (14)	10.3% (18)	10.6% (20)
Disagree		20.3 (30)	44.0 (77)	64.5 (122)
DK		70.3 (104)	45.7 (80)	24.9 (47)
		100 (148)	100 (175)	100 (189)
		Odds ratios		
Education:		0–11	12	13+
Opinion versus DK		.26	.28	.50
Agree versus disagree		.92	.85	.89

[a] Data are from SRC–74 Fall.

2. There are only weak signs, however, that question form affects these relations, and then only for DK versus opinion. (*a*) There is no evidence of three-way interaction for the entire table ($\chi^2 = 3.24$, $df = 4$, n.s.); (*b*) there is no sign at all that the relation of education to substantive responses (agree versus disagree) is affected by form ($\chi^2 = .02$, $df = 2$); and (*c*) there is a nonsignificant trend for DK versus opinion (combined substantive responses) to be more strongly related to education on the filtered form (gamma $=.56$) than on the standard form (.43) ($\chi^2 = 3.39$, $df = 2$, n.s.). The linear component of this trend is borderline in significance ($\chi^2 = 2.90$, $df = 1$, $p < .10$), with less-educated respondents being more affected by question form, as indicated by the odds ratios for opinion versus DK.

Thus, we find only a trace of evidence for statistical interaction involving education and form for the Arab item in 1974, although there are quite reliable relations between education and response at the bivariate level. The same is true if interest or information measures are substituted for education in the three variable analysis, and it is also true when other background variables such as age and sex are used instead. Similar conclusions also emerge from analysis of the other experiments, despite a few significant interactions. In three cases, the relation between DK and education is significantly different on the two forms; stronger on the filtered version in two instances (Arabs in SRC–78 May and in the phone part of SRC–76 Spring, although not—as noted in Appendix B.2—in the face-to-face part); and stronger on the standard form in the third case (courts in NORC–74). These three cases are alike in that it is less-educated respondents who are disproportionately responsible for the form effect. In none of these instances, however, does form affect the education by response relations once all DKs are excluded. Moreover, most of the other experiments do not show even borderline trends for education to interact significantly with the DK difference by form.[18] (Analyses with a variety of background variables for the early experiments are reported in Presser, 1977).

Thus most of our experiments fail to confirm the original hypothesis that higher educated respondents will be more resistant, and lower educated respondents more susceptible, to form effects involving DK filters. Yet in the next chapter, we demonstrate that when items are so obscure that a large proportion of respondents say DK even on standard forms, floating is indeed more common among the low than among the high educated. Why then does this evidence appear only weakly, at best, for the more ordinary items discussed in the present chapter? We are inclined to believe that although there is a basic process that tends to produce more floating by less-educated respondents on all items, it is usually counterbalanced by other forces, so that only in certain special situations is it clearly visible. In the concluding discussion, we speculate on what these other forces are, but one point can be noted here. If one thinks in terms of "resistance" to form effects, then the original hypothesis focused on only one source of resistance, namely, the tendency of higher educated respondents to give substantive opinions regardess of form. The original hypothesis failed, however, to take account of another source of consis-

---

[18]The strongest positive result can be found if the three foreign affairs items, which appeared in the same survey, are dichotomized into DK versus substantive responses and added to form a *DK index*. This index has a correlation with education of $-.39$ on the filtered version and $-.26$ on the standard version. The difference between the two correlations (and also between the corresponding regression coefficients) is significant at the .05 level.

tency across forms: DK-saying by the least-educated parts of the population regardless of form. Since for items such as those on foreign affairs, DK is given spontaneously by the least educated, and since there is good reason for these same persons to give DK to a filtered form, low education can contribute to consistency just as high education does.[19]

FURTHER EVIDENCE ON THE IDENTITY OF FLOATERS

To What Extent Are Floaters a Distinct Group?

Near the end of the research for this book, we carried out one pair of over-time experiments that provides some direct evidence on the extent to which floaters on one item are the same people as floaters on another item. Standard DK forms of abortion and divorce items were asked in SRC-80 June, and then each question was repeated in filtered form in reinterviews of the same sample in SRC-80 September. Thus floaters can be identified separately for each question and their degree of overlap examined for this one pair of items. Table 4.10 presents both the questions and the results from these special panel data.

[19]The Arab panel data allow us to test the hypothesis that persons giving a DK response on a standard form (where it is harder to give) will also give it on a filtered form. Likewise, those giving a substantive opinion on the filtered form (despite the presence of an easy DK alternative) should give a substantive opinion on a standard form (where DK is not available). These hypotheses lead to the prediction of a single empty cell in each of the two cross-tabulations below:

	Standard (Time 1)				Filtered (Time 1)		
		DK	Opinion			DK	Opinion
Filtered	DK	61	124	Standard	DK	54	21
(Time 2)	Opinion	8	145	(Time 2)	Opinion	84	194
		gamma = .80				gamma = .71	

Although there are some "errors" in the cells predicted to be empty, they are very few and gamma is quite high for both tables. The hypothesis that filtered DKs "include" standard DKs, and that opinions on the standard form "include" opinions on the filtered form, is strongly supported.

TABLE 4.10
Floaters on Abortion and Divorce Items[a]

	Abortion item	
Divorce item	Opinion–opinion	Float
Opinion–opinion	139	14
Float	39	13

[a] Frequencies are from interviews in SRC–80 June and reinterviews in SRC–80 September. The abortion question varied slightly in wording (see Chapter 11), but this did not appear to affect results and the two questionnaire subsamples are pooled here. The actual questions asked were as follows:

SRC–80 June: *Do you think it should be possible for a pregnant woman to go to a doctor to (end her pregnancy/have an abortion) if she is married and does not want any more children?*

Should divorce in this country be easier or more difficult to obtain than it is now?

SRC–80 September: (The above items were asked, but in each case preceded by a full filter modeled after those shown in Table 4.1.)

Qualified by both high sample attrition (half the sample was not successfully reinterviewed) and the uniqueness of the two items, the data suggest that floaters overlap somewhat but not greatly between the two items. On the one hand, of the total of 66 persons who float on either item, only 13 (20%) float on both items. This certainly argues against there being a single, largely unchanging set of floaters. On the other hand, persons who float on the one item are somewhat more likely than nonfloaters on that item to float on the other item: starting from the abortion item, almost half (48%) of the floaters, as contrasted with only 22% of the opinion–opinion respondents, float on the divorce item; starting from the divorce item, the parallel figures are 25% and 9%. The association shown in Table 4.10 is also highly significant: $\chi^2 = 7.62$, $df = 1$, $p < .01$.

Can Floating Be Predicted from Low Attitude Strength?

It is possible that the people who float on an item are those whose attitudes on that item are weakly held. When pressed by a standard question to give a substantive response, such people are willing to do so, but provided the opportunity to say don't know, they are eager to take that option. If a substantial correlation between floating and self-reported attitude strength does exist, it would be possible to employ a standard DK question form in order to obtain answers from as many respondents as possible, and then use a measure of degree of attitude strength to separate responses in a way equivalent to what a DK filter does.

We attempted to assess this possibility with the panel data on the abortion and divorce items described in the previous section. The questions were in standard form in SRC-80 June, followed in each case by an attitude strength measure—the centrality measure described in Chapter 10. In SRC-80 September, as many as possible of the same respondents were reinterviewed using filtered versions of the abortion and divorce items. In the case of the divorce item, those who in June gave an opinion but reported low strength were in September significantly more likely than those who reported high strength to say DK to the filtered version (linear $\chi^2 = 4.68$, $df = 1$, $p < .05$). A similar but nonsignificant trend (linear $\chi^2 = 1.30$, $df = 1$) occurs for the abortion item. However, in neither case is the association between reporting low attitude strength and saying DK on a filtered form very great. In particular, the majority of respondents who reported low attitude strength in June nevertheless gave opinions to the filtered forms in September. Thus, low strength is not, in practice, interchangeable with DK to a filter item.

CONCLUDING DISCUSSION

We have shown that DK filters can substantially increase the proportion of respondents who give DK responses, and that this increase itself is a function of the nature of the filter used. For the nine items analyzed here, the increase does not seem to be related to question content, or to the DK level that prevails on the standard (unfiltered) form. The most typical DK increment found in our experiments is in the range of 13–23 percentage points, with the overall average (both mean and median) being 22%. Thus DK filters affect about a fifth of the original sample for most items.

We have introduced the term *floaters* to refer to persons who give a substantive response to an item in standard form and a DK response to a filtered version of the same item. The phenomenon of floating turns out to produce consequences that are by no means those one would have predicted in advance. Once DK responses are excluded from both forms, univariate proportions are usually unaffected by form, hence floating is not often an important source of instability in item marginals. And there seems to be little effect of floating on the relations between attitude items and a number of standard background factors. Contrary to our initial hypothesis, education is not visibly involved in any simple way in these form effects.

However, the relations among attitudinal variables themselves can be importantly altered as a function of use of filters. In one instance, the change fits traditional expectations that filtered forms of items will show stronger associations than standard (unfiltered) forms. Thus floaters can be seen as diminishing true correlations, although our evidence suggests that they do so less by adding random error than by introducing correlations in the opposite direction to that of the larger nonfloating part of the population.

In another case, our results appear to challenge traditional notions, for filtered forms indicate no association between the two items, whereas standard forms reveal a highly reliable association. Floaters in this instance seem to see in the items a dimension of trust or distrust in leaders that is not perceived by nonfloaters. The results suggest that important attitudinal dispositions may at times be "carried" almost entirely by a group of respondents who say DK when it is offered, but make a substantive choice when it is not.

Several other form comparisons show nonsignificant trends along one or the other of these two lines, but they are probably best regarded as instances where DK form makes little or no difference in associations. Indeed, our conclusion at present must be that filtering does not in most cases alter correlations, though the number and nature of substantively important interactions attributable to floating remains open.

The major theoretical problem raised by the research reported in this chapter concerns the nature of floating and the identity of floaters. Two quite different models can be delineated. One is a trait model, and conceives of floaters as a distinct group of people who are eager to say DK when it is offered on filtered question forms, but who do not volunteer such responses on standard question forms. The researcher's task becomes that of discovering the trait or traits that lead to their unusual behavior. However, we have not been successful in discovering any general personality or social characteristics that distinguish floaters from other respondents. In fact, there are several findings that argue against there being a single, fixed group of floaters (e.g., initial evidence of near constancy turned out to have numerous exceptions). Nevertheless, in the next chapter we show that in a limiting case where questions concern extremely obscure issues, floaters do come disproportionately from the least-educated ranks. This accords with our original hypothesis that the least educated are more constrained by question form than the high educated, and further suggests that willingness to challenge constraint may be a trait worth trying to measure directly. Yet this cannot be the whole story, since the same interactions with education are not generally found for the questions discussed in the present chapter.

A quite different model of floating, which can be called a threshold or process model, also seems plausible. According to the threshold model there is no special set of people who float on most items, but simply a process of floating created by question form for any given item. In order to understand the process, one must focus on the correlates of DK responses, regardless of form, rather than on the construct "floaters." We saw in Table 4.9 that low education is strongly related to giving DK responses on both standard and filtered question forms, and this relation also holds for most other attitude items in general population surveys. The same is true for a more proximate set of psychological indicators, such as lack of political information and low general attitude strength, which can be seen as mediating the relation between education and DK responses. (In analysis not shown here, the addition of education to such psychological variables adds little explanatory power when predicting DK responses, whereas these psychological variables add considerable predictive power above that of education.) In addition, there is evidence that even on questions dealing with remote foreign affairs issues, ambivalence also plays a role in creating DK responses; this is the only way we can account for the sharp rise and fall of DK proportions for the Arabs item between 1974, 1976, and 1978 (compare relevant entries in Tables 4.1 and 4.3).[20] Let us assume then that all these psychological variables contribute to an underlying propensity to give a DK response to an attitude question, though their relative contributions may vary from one item to another.

The threshold model postulates that the frequency of DK responses depends in part on the respondent's position on the DK-propensity dimension and in part on the height of the barrier created by question form. Where the question form strongly discourages DK responses, only those very high on the dimension will insist on giving a DK response. Where the question form facilitates or even encourages DK responses

---

[20]DK responses to certain items with strong moral content may be due largely to ambivalence, as Converse (1976–1977) noted in pointing out the lack of DK–education relation in some cases. (By our later count, using Converse's data, 14% of 312 Gallup and Harris items do not show a significant or noticeable DK–education association.) Coombs and Coombs (1976–1977) also present evidence that ambivalence is an important component of DK responses for a set of items concerning abortion, an issue in the moral domain. (For one recent but not very successful attempt to stress the role of ambivalence in DK responses, see Faulkenberry and Mason, 1978. For a quite different approach to locating the meaning of DK responses, see Clogg, 1980.)

(e.g., by providing a full DK filter preliminary to the opinion question), those with both high and moderate positions on the dimension will choose the DK option. In both instances, the underlying dimension is the same, but the question form creates different cutting points on it. Moreover, the difficulty of the question content (remote versus familiar issues) will also greatly affect cutting points on the dimension, though, according to the model, equally for both standard and filtered question forms. Thus the DK propensity dimension influences the giving of DK responses on both forms, but there is no special trait that distinguishes floaters as such, nor is there a special group of people to be set apart and described by this term.

Whether DK question form will also affect relationships (as occurred for the Arabs–Russia association in 1974) will depend on whether persons occupying particular locations on the DK-propensity dimension differ in between-attitude correlations from persons at other locations. This can be expected to vary not only by item, but probably also even over time for the same item, since the salience of news events can change cutting points on the dimension for one or both question forms.

As ideal types, the trait and threshold models are mutually exclusive, the one telling us to search for a unique constellation of traits to characterize floaters, the other suggesting that such a unique constellation may not exist and that floaters on any item have simply a different amount of the same trait or traits that characterize other respondents. In practice we suspect that both models have some truth, and that floating has more than a single cause.[21]

---

[21]Two other complicating factors should be noted. One is variation in interviewer behavior, which can be expected to be less on a filtered than on a standard question form, since the former includes a DK alternative as part of the question, whereas the latter requires the interviewer not to mention DK but to accept it when volunteered. Anecdotal evidence noted at the end of Chapter 5 suggests that interviewers varied more than we intended in their handling of volunteered DK responses on standard forms. The SRC–76 Spring telephone survey provided approximate random assignment of interviewers for a replication of the Arabs experiment, and we do find that variance accounted for by interviewers in opinion versus DK responses is slightly greater on the standard form (rho = 2.0%) than on the filtered form (rho = 0.8%), but the difference seems too small to be of crucial importance—even if generally replicable. A second complication is that of possible context effects on DK responses, especially the fact that filtered questions may legitimize DK responses to subsequent questions even though the latter are in standard form. We tried to minimize this possibility by using one questionnaire subsample for all standard questions and one for all filtered questions. Moreover, items that preceded DK experiments did not offer DK alternatives (i.e., were in standard form).

5
The Fine Line between Attitudes and Nonattitudes

> In every object there is inexhaustible meaning; the eye sees
> in it what the eye brings means of seeing.
> —Carlyle, *The French Revolution*

We saw in the previous chapter that almost two-thirds of a national sample volunteered "don't know" to a question about the 1974 Portuguese revolution, even though it was relatively easy to pretend to offer an opinion on the issue by simply agreeing or disagreeing. Such a result appears to contradict the often heard claim that most people are unwilling to admit ignorance in survey interviews. One figure sometimes cited to support the claim is Gill's (1947) report that 70% of a sample gave opinions about a fictitious Metallic Metals Act. Payne's widely read book on question construction (1951) discusses the Gill finding twice, and others (e.g., Weissberg, 1976) have continued to refer to it. Examination of the original report reveals, however, that it is hardly more than an anecdote: The population sampled is identified only as "a group of people" and the size of the sample is never given.

More solid but indirect evidence on this issue comes from Philip Converse's (1970) discussion of nonattitudes. Converse shows that inconsistencies in a set of panel data fit a model assuming mostly random responses, and he argues that such meaningless responses are given in order to avoid saying "don't know," which is regarded by respondents as a confession of "mental incapacity" (1970: 177). Still a third basis for the claim that respondents will offer answers to questions not meaningful to them comes from Hartley's (1946) finding that large majorities of college students willingly provided attitudes about three nonexistent nationality groups, "Danireans," "Pireneans," and "Wallonians."

All three of these frequently cited sources suggest that there are appreciable amounts of uninformed answering, but only Converse used survey data from the national population. In this chapter we report evidence on the nonattitude issue in the context of further experiments on how the don't know (DK) option is presented to respondents. Standard and filtered don't know question forms were employed (as described in Chapter 4) to ask about issues that the general public was assumed to know nothing about.

THE AGRICULTURAL TRADE ACT

Two forms of a question about the Agricultural Trade Act of 1978 were included at the end of November and December 1978 Survey Research Center telephone surveys.[1] The Agricultural Trade Act (ATA) was not fictional, since we did not wish to lie to respondents, but it was so little known (as confirmed by inquires to generally well-informed colleagues) that we presume virtually no respondents were familiar with its nature or contents. Of course, they could make some unsupported inference from the wording of the question, and we had interviewers record all comments that respondents offered when giving their answers. But assuming that respondents had never heard of the act, "don't know" was the most sensible answer to give to our survey question.

Univariate Effects

The percentage of respondents saying DK to each form of the ATA question is presented in Table 5.1. To the standard form, which allows DK only when offered spontaneously by respondents, 31% of the sam-

---

[1]Unexpectedly, the DK percentage was significantly higher in November than in December for the filtered question form (92.3% versus 86.9%; $\chi^2 = 6.33$, $df = 1$, $p < .02$), although the difference for the standard form was nonsignificant and trivial (69.1% versus 69.5%). The November questionnaire was considerably longer than the December one, and a possible interpretation is that respondents were more eager to end the task by saying DK in November, but that this appears only where the filtered form makes a DK response easy to give (see Appendix B.2 on the effects on DK of impatience with telephone survey length). Since the DK difference just described is small and does not interact significantly with other variables discussed in this chapter, we present the November–December data as a single merged sample.

TABLE 5.1
Response to Agricultural Trade Act Question by Form[a]

Standard		Filtered	
The last question is about a different subject. Congress has been considering the Agricultural Trade Act of 1978. Do you favor or oppose the passage of this act?		*The last question is about a different subject. Congress has been considering the Agricultural Trade Act of 1978. Do you favor or oppose the passage of this act or do you not have an opinion on that issue?*	
Favor	19.4% } 30.8	Favor	6.4% } 10.1
Oppose	11.4	Oppose	3.7
DK (if volunteered)	69.2	No opinion	90.0
	100		100
N	(387)	N	(787)
Full table: $\chi^2 = 74.78$, $df = 2$, $p < .001$			
Favor versus oppose: $\chi^2 = .00$, $df = 1$, n.s.			

[a] Carried out in SRC-78 November and December (combined). Selection of which respondents received the standard or filtered form was done on a systematic random basis, but a 1/3 to 2/3 ratio was used for reasons unconnected with this particular experiment.

ple gave an opinion about the Agricultural Trade Act and 69% volunteered DK. Thus it is incorrect—for this question at least—to claim that the majority of Americans will offer an opinion on an issue unknown to them. Nevertheless, the proportion that does so is quite substantial: nearly a third of the population.

A filtered form of the question increases considerably the willingness of respondents to say DK or its equivalent (no opinion). In this case only 10% of the population felt called upon to offer an opinion. This is still not a trivial percentage, but it is much more congenial to the assumption of a public willing to indicate its ignorance when that is appropriate. The tenability of the assumption evidently depends on the form of the question, as well as on the respondent: If ignorance is to be revealed, it should be legitimized. What is particularly impressive is that the 21% difference in DK percentages produced by the two forms is almost exactly the increment that would be predicted on the basis of the average value found in our previous comparisons of standard and filtered questions in Chapter 4.

Finally, the large difference between forms in DK percentages does not seem to affect the distribution of substantive (favor or oppose) choices. The ratio of favoring the act to opposing it is a little less than 2 : 1 on each form. Thus here, as in most of our previous DK experiments, provision of a filter does not appreciably alter the division of opinion once DK reponses are removed.

Education and the DK Response

Education is the variable most strongly associated with the DK response across a wide range of issues (J. Converse, 1976–1977). Particularly where knowledge of public affairs is needed, less-educated persons are more apt to give DK or "no opinion" answers. The results in Table 5.2 are therefore surprising, as we move to this limiting case where none of the respondents is assumed to possess the requisite knowledge to express an opinion. On the standard form, willingness to say DK *rises* with education, that is, it is the most educated who most readily admit ignorance (gamma $= .24$, s.e. $= .09$, $p < .01$). Results for the filtered form also differ from most past findings, since on this form there is no

TABLE 5.2
Agricultural Trade Act Response by Education and Form[a]

| | Standard form | | |
| | Education | | |
	0–11	12	13+
Favor	28.4%	19.9%	15.0%
Oppose	14.8	10.3	10.2
DK	56.8	69.9	74.9
	100	100	100
	(81)	(136)	(167)
	Filtered form		
	Education		
	0–11	12	13+
Favor	7.1%	7.2%	5.4%
Oppose	1.8	5.0	3.6
DK	91.1	87.8	91.0
	100	100	100
	(169)	(279)	(333)

[a] Data from SRC–78 Nov. and Dec. (combined).

relation of no opinion to education (gamma = .04, s.e. = .09), with all the educational categories producing a quite high DK percentage. The linear component of the three-way interaction for education, form (standard versus filtered), and opinion versus DK does not quite reach conventional levels of significance ($\chi^2 = 3.52$, $df = 1$, $p < .10$), but identical patterns occur in the November and December surveys taken separately, giving us some confidence in their reliability.[2]

When all DK responses are omitted and the relation of education to substantive responses is examined, neither form shows a reliable relation between education and pro–con position on the issue, nor is there any evidence of three-way interaction.

It is instructive to compare the results for the Agricultural Trade Act with those from the item on the 1974 Portuguese revolution discussed in Chapter 4.[3] The latter might seem to be almost equally esoteric, but the vicissitudes of the revolution occupied newspaper headlines for a period in 1974 in a way that the ATA never did. Thus, we might expect those persons with a considerable interest in serious news to have known about Portugal in 1974 when the question was asked, but even a devoted reader of the daily *New York Times* in 1978 would have been unlikely to know anything about the Trade Act. In fact, the proportions giving an opinion on Portugal (see Table 4.1) are quite similar to those on the Agricultural Trade Act, but it turns out that this conceals an important difference in the relation of education to who gives an opinion on the two items.

Unlike the Trade Act, the Portugal item shows on all forms the usually found relation of education to DK responses: more DK with less education. Moreover, a higher proportion of college-educated Americans (13+

[2]When a five-category education variable is employed, the results for grade school and some high school respondents are virtually identical, and likewise results for the some college and the college graduate groups are essentially the same. Hence the relation on the standard form is stepwise, rather than strictly monotonic. We also looked at the effects of three other widely used background variables: age, sex, and race. Controlling for education, younger people are more likely than older respondents, men more than women, and blacks more than whites to give an opinion, but this occurs mainly on the standard form. Finally, given the content of the question, we looked at the responses of farmers in the November survey (occupation was not asked in the December survey) and found them to be little different than those of others. Of the 17 farmers in the sample, only 4 gave an opinion, 3 in favor and 1 opposed.

[3]In addition to the forms of the Portugal item shown in Table 4.1, there was a standard forced-choice form, which asked: *In your opinion, is the new Portuguese military government trying to move toward democracy, or is it trying to maintain its own control without concern for democracy in Portugal?* Results for this form are given in footnote 4.

years of school) offer an opinion on the Portugal item than on the Trade
Act, whereas among the least educated (0–11 years of school) the Trade
Act produces an opinion more often than does Portugal.[4] The former
trend is easily explained by the greater knowledge that the high educated presumably had of the Portugal issue than of the ATA. But what
explains the tendency of low-educated respondents to offer an opinion
on the ATA more frequently than on Portugal? We assume that the low
educated know little about either issue, and suspect that two other factors produce the surprising results. First, the Trade Act item deals with
the United States (*Congress has been considering*...) and therefore may
appear to require an opinion more urgently than do the remote affairs of
Portugal. Second, the question about the Trade Act allows a fairly simple
(even if inaccurate) guess as to the subject matter of the question,
whereas the Portugal item may be more difficult to comprehend and to
figure out a conceivable position on. Of course, linked to both these
factors is the possibility that low-educated respondents are especially
susceptible to pressures in the interview to give an opinion even where
they have none.

Sources of Favor and Oppose Responses

Opinions on the Agricultural Trade Act cannot be "real" in the conventional sense assumed in attitude surveys, since respondents have
never heard of the act before being asked. Yet the favor to oppose ratio
of nearly 2 : 1 also departs quite significantly from the 50–50 coin-flipping
model that generally has been assumed for "nonattitudes" ($\chi^2 = 13.66$,
$df = 1$, $p < .001$). This suggests that respondents who offer opinions on

[4]For comparison with Table 5.2, the percentages giving an opinion on Portugal in 1974
by education were as follows:

	0–11	12	13+
Standard (agree–disagree)	30%	32%	46%
	(153)	(156)	(188)
Standard (forced–choice)	17%	24%	34%
	(161)	(167)	(155)
Filtered (agree–disagree)	5%	10%	19%
	(147)	(175)	(188)

All the relevant response by education by item (Portugal versus ATA) interactions are
significant ($p < .01$). Data are from SRC–74 Fall. Ns are in parentheses.

the ATA do not simply guess mindlessly, but are able to construct some meaning from the question. We have interviewer recordings of some 35 spontaneous asides by respondents, and in most of these cases it does appear that individuals made interpretations of the ATA that facilitated or were at least consistent with their substantive choice, for example, "We need more trade" (favor), and "Shipments from Japan are killing our products here" (oppose).

Although this interpretive process might seem narrowly limited to the words of the ATA item, it is likely that respondents call on more general attitudes to help with their specific evaluations. Indeed, general attitudes can be conceptualized in just this way—as broad orientations that provide guidance about how to respond in novel situations (Allport, 1935). If this is the case, then we ought to find associations between substantive responses to proposed Congressional action on the ATA and responses to other items that are similar to it in some way. As Table 5.3 indicates, this is indeed the case for an item on confidence in the economic policy of the government: Those favoring the act show more confidence in the government's management of the economy than those opposed to the act. (No difference approaching significance occurs between filtered and standard forms in this or other relations discussed below, although the samples are small for detecting such three-way interactions.) On another item concerning the honesty of government officials, there is a nonsignificant trend for those opposing the ATA to perceive more "crookedness." These two results, plus a replication re-

TABLE 5.3
Evaluation of Government Economic Policy by Response to Agricultural Trade Act[a]

As to the economic policy of the government— I mean steps taken to fight inflation and unemployment—would you say the government is doing a good job, only fair, or a poor job?	Position on the Agricultural Trade Act	
	Favor	Oppose
Good job	20.0%	11.0%
Only fair	57.5	41.1
Poor job	22.5	47.9
	100	100
	(120)	(73)
	$\chi^2 = 13.63$, $df = 2$, $p < .001$	
	gamma $= .43$	

[a] Data from SRC-78 Nov. and Dec. combined. Standard and filtered forms combined, with all DK and no opinion responses omitted.

ported below, suggest that one basis for arriving at an opinion about the ATA is confidence in government economic action, or perhaps in government more generally.[5]

Our clearest conclusions therefore are, first, that some people favor or oppose Congressional passage of the ATA on the basis of their general confidence in government, regardless of the specific content of the act, and second, that some people reach an opinion based on what the words "Agricultural Trade" suggest to them. How much these two bases for constructing an opinion overlap cannot be determined from the present data. But it does appear that the distinction between meaningful and meaningless responses to attitude survey questions is not as simple as is sometimes assumed.

REPLICATION: THE MONETARY CONTROL BILL

In an April 1979 SRC survey we attempted a partial replication of the Trade Act results by asking a national telephone sample about the Monetary Control Bill of 1979, employing in all other respects the same wording as for the ATA. (The Monetary Control Bill was then a real issue before the House of Representatives but also one not at all likely to be known by respondents. Its actual content concerned banking practices.)[6] As Table 5.4 shows, basic results for both overall marginals and relations to respondent education are quite similar to those for the ATA shown in Tables 5.1 and 5.2. The overall DK proportions are slightly higher for both forms of the new question, but the difference in DK percentage between forms is again about 20%. Moreover, on the standard form, the proportion of DK responses rises significantly with education (gamma $= .19$, s.e. $= .08$, $p < .05$), whereas on the filtered form there is no sign of a relation, just as had occurred with the Agricultural Trade Act.[7]

[5]This kind of interpretation also fits Hartley's (1946) finding that attitudes about his three nonexistent nationality groups were related to, and could be thought of as part of, prejudice against real groups. (We also examined the relations between opinions on the Trade Act and several other attitude items that were available in the survey; although one other item showed a significant association ($p < .05$) we are uncertain of its meaning—those favoring the act were more likely to favor liberalizing marijuana laws.)

[6]Subsequently, in 1980, the Monetary Control Bill was combined in Congress with other measures and enacted into law as the Depository Institutions Deregulation and Monetary Control Bill (*The New York Times*, March 31, 1980), but we are convinced that in 1979 virtually none of our respondents had heard of it.

[7]The effects of race and sex are similar to those for the ATA (see footnote 2) in that men

TABLE 5.4
Monetary Control Bill Response by Education and Form[a]

	Standard form				
	Education				
	0–11	12	13+	Total	
Favor	15.8%	12.9%	12.2%	13.2% ⎫	26.4%
Oppose	16.8	15.7	9.2	13.2 ⎬	
DK	67.4	71.3	78.6	73.6 ⎭	
	100	100	100	100	
	(95)	(178)	(196)	(469)	
	Filtered form				
	Education				
	0–11	12	13+	Total	
Favor	5.0%	3.3%	2.2%	3.1% ⎫	6.7%
Oppose	0.0	4.3	4.4	3.6 ⎬	
DK	95.0	92.4	93.4	93.3 ⎭	
	100	100	100	100	
	(40)	(92)	(91)	(223)	

[a] Carried out in SRC-79 April.

Substantive attitudes (favor and oppose) toward the Monetary Control Bill approximate a 50–50 split on both question forms, but our experience with the ATA advises against assuming that this indicates mere guessing. (The 50–50 split here also argues against an interpretation of the earlier ATA 63–37 split as due to either a positivity or an acquiescence effect.) Since there is no sign of a relation of the favor–oppose division to education (as was also true for the ATA), we again turn to other attitude questions for evidence that substantive choices involved interpretations of the question, rather than a purely random process of responding.

---

and blacks are more likely to offer an opinion (controlling for education), but unlike the earlier results this is more the case on the filtered than on the standard form. The age results are similar to those for the ATA—younger people are more apt to give an opinion—except that an earlier hint of a reversal among the college educated is more pronounced (the older, well educated give an opinion more than expected).

Only two directly relevant attitude items are available from the April survey, but these two have readily interpretable associations with substantive responses to the Monetary Control Bill (MCB). A direct replication was hypothesized for the question on evaluation of government economic policy, since the Monetary Control Bill, like the ATA, was presented as an economic issue before Congress. Results parallel those reported earlier in Table 5.3: Of respondents favoring the bill, the percentages saying the government is doing a good job, fair job, and poor job respectively, are 19%, 48%, and 33%; of those opposing the bill, the corresponding percentages are 7%, 46%, and 46%. (Gamma for the relation of the two items is: .30, SE = .14, $p < .05$.) This finding provides further evidence that general confidence in government is a source for answers to both the Agricultural Trade Act and the Monetary Control Bill.

At the same time, opinion on the Monetary Control Bill in April was also significantly related to a question on whether the respondent believed *unemployment or inflation [would] cause the more serious economic hardship for people during the next year or so.* Of those who favored the bill, 86% chose inflation; of those who opposed the bill, 70% chose inflation ($\chi^2 = 5.04$, $df = 1$, $p < .05$). This suggests that some of the people favoring the Monetary Control Bill did so because—not unreasonably—they believed it to be intended to reduce inflation, a hypothesis supported by some recorded respondent comments: for example, "That's a bill that has to do with controlling inflation" (favor). However, a wide range of other plausible interpretations were also offered: for example, "Well, it must be about a balanced budget" (favor); "Bill has to do with controlling pay raises" (oppose). We should also note that not all respondent comments suggest such an effort at rational interpretation: for example: "I don't know what it is, so I'll oppose it" (oppose) and "It has a bad ring to it" (oppose). One thing does seem clear: The association with the unemployment–inflation question is specific to the Monetary Control Bill, since the same question showed no significant relation to the ATA and in fact a trend in the opposite direction (fearing inflation went with opposing the ATA).

However, when we replicated the Monetary Control Bill question in July, 1980 (standard form only), it showed only a weak relation to the confidence-in-government item (gamma = .09, SE = .16), and no trend at all for an association to the inflation–unemployment item ($\chi^2 = .03$, $df = 1$). The MCB itself showed marginals in July almost identical to the percentage point to those seen earlier in Table 5.4 for April, hence the virtual disappearance of the relations cannot readily be attributed to rapid change in the MCB item. There were, however, highly significant

($p < .001$) changes in both of the economic questions between April and July, with an increase of about 8% in concern over unemployment relative to inflation and a decline of nearly the same amount in confidence in government economic policies. When cross-tabulations of each of the economic items with the MCB is examined at the two points in time, it appears that the changes in the economic items occur entirely among those who favor the MCB (and equally among those who said "don't know" to the MCB question), but not at all among those who oppose the MCB. It is this differential shift that can be said to have eliminated the original correlations. The reason for the differential shift itself is not clear, but the analysis suggests that the original results were conditional on certain levels of economic concern. Nonreplication in this instance qualifies the generality of results and links more tightly to "time" the relations discovered earlier, although this might not be the case for other equally obscure issues. As we see below, however, responses to the MCB question itself continue to carry some meaning later in 1980 in terms of over-time reliability.

CONSISTENCY OVER TIME

In October, 1980, SRC interviewers reinterviewed 344 respondents from the April survey, and the standard form of the Monetary Control Bill question was asked again. (Interviews were attempted only with those who had been given the standard form in April, since we wished to maximize the proportion answering favor or oppose, rather than don't know.) Table 5.5 presents the over-time correlations. Respondents are shown to be moderately consistent in giving either an opinion or a don't know answer at both points in time (Panel A). If the table is percentaged as a whole, 75% of the respondents give the same type of answer on both occasions. The more important result in Table 5.5 appears in Panel B for those respondents who gave a substantive response in both April and October: Despite an N of only 45, consistency in favoring or opposing the MCB approaches significance (or indeed is significant at the .03 level using a one-tailed test, as seems appropriate in this instance where the prediction was clearly directional). Moreover, the phi coefficient of .29 is within the range of the "continuity correlations" presented by Converse and Markus (1979) for a number of domestic issues that would ordinarily be assumed to be familiar to the general public, although our period of time (6 months) was shorter than theirs (4 years). Thus, opinion on the Monetary Trade Bill is not merely the result

TABLE 5.5
Reliability Over Time of Responses to Monetary Control Bill

A. Reliability of opinion giving

		Time 1: SRC–79 April		
		Opinion	DK	
Time 2:	Opinion	46.9%	14.5%	
SRC–79 October	DK	53.1	85.5	phi = .34
		100	100	$\chi^2 = 37.34$, $df = 1$, $p < .001$
		(96)	(248)	

B. Reliability of pro–con position

		Time 1: SRC–79 April		
		Favor	Oppose	
Time 2:	Favor	61.9%	33.3%	
SRC–79 October	Oppose	38.1	66.7	phi = .29
		100	100	$\chi^2 = 3.72$, $df = 1$, $p < .10$
		(21)	(24)	

of a momentary attempt to handle an interviewer's unfamiliar question, but shows a degree of consistency over time that forces us to consider these responses to be much like true attitudes.[8]

CONCLUDING DISCUSSION

Our analysis of questions about two issues unknown to the American public leads to several important conclusions. First, a substantial minority of the public—in the neighborhood of 30%—will provide an opinion on a proposed law that they know nothing about *if* the question is asked without an explicit DK option. This figure is certainly lower than the "majority" sometimes bruited about, but it is obviously large enough to trouble those assessing attitudes or beliefs concerning public issues.

[8]For respondents who gave an opinion in October as well as in April, the associations between MCB responses and responses to the inflation–unemployment question are of the same magnitude on the two occasions. However, these respondents do not show any sign of a relation between the MCB and the confidence in government economic policy item in October, despite having shown such a relation in April, presumably for the reasons discussed earlier in the text.

Second, it is interesting to note that in some of these cases interviewers recorded comments indicating considerable respondent uncertainty (e.g., "Favor—though I really don't know what it is," "You caught me on that. I don't know, but from the sound of it I favor it"). Moreover, we can tell from other cases where marginal comments are available that some respondents initially confessed ignorance, and then chose favor or oppose only after the interviewer inappropriately repeated the question, contrary to our instructions to accept DK responses when they were volunteered. Thus, it is not true that all those who give an opinion do so in order to avoid confessing ignorance. Indeed, this evidence of respondent willingness to admit ignorance may account in good part for the finding that the DK level rises dramatically to 90% or more when that option is fully legitimized for *both* interviewers and respondents by being read as part of the question.[9]

Third, although we clearly cannot rule out the possibility that many of those who offer opinions do so on a random basis, it is equally evident that a fair number do not respond by merely flipping mental coins, as the original concept of non-attitude suggests. In the last chapter, we argued that respondents lacking opinions about the particular issue referred to in a question may construct answers by drawing on an underlying disposition not specific to the issue but vaguely relevant to it. A similar process appears to apply here in a number of cases. Respondents make an educated (though often wrong) guess as to what the obscure acts represent, then answer reasonably in their own terms about the constructed object. Such responses fit Converse's notion of nonattitudes in the sense that there was no thought about the attitude object prior to the interview, but our evidence on the way the responses are consistent over time and linked to other issues suggests that the attitudes themselves are often quite real. Thus it is probably a mistake to attempt to add to attitudes and non-attitudes a third concept such as quasi-attitudes or pseudo-attitudes, as we were tempted to do initially.

Indeed, opinions on the Agricultural Trade Act and the Monetary Trade Bill bear more than a slight resemblance to opinions on many other more known but almost equally complex and remote subjects, like the safety of nuclear power plants or strategic arms limitation agreements. Whether in opinion polls, referenda, or issue-related elections, many respondents may make inferences about such issues that are only a little more firmly based than was true for the Agriculture Trade Act or Monetary Control Bill. The evidence in this chapter nar-

[9]Similar results were obtained in a recent Cincinnati survey that asked about a fictitious Public Affairs Act. To a standard form, about a third volunteered an opinion; to a filtered form about 7% (see Bishop, Oldendick, Tuchfarber, and Bennett, 1980).

rows, if indeed it does not eliminate, the conceptual distinction between attitudes and non-attitudes. Whereas Converse showed that real objects could elicit non-attitudes, the present results indicate that what are essentially nonobjects can elicit real attitudes.

Looked at subjectively, the meaningfulness of attitude objects for respondents must be considered to be a product of both knowledge about the specific object and more general dispositions evoked by other aspects of the question. Thus, whether filtered or standard questions should be used in a questionnaire would seem to depend on whether an investigator is interested mainly in "informed opinion" on an issue or mainly in underlying dispositions. Since both goals are pursued through survey research, there may be no general solution to the problem of which form of question is better.

Finally, there is one noteworthy finding in the present experiments that does distinguish them from most other attitude data. Ordinarily, DK responses are given most frequently by the least educated, but for the two issues dealt with here, DK is volunteered on standard form questions more often by those with more education. Apparently higher-educated respondents can more readily tell the difference between questions that are difficult and questions that are impossible, and perhaps even more important, they are more willing with the latter to assert ignorance. The least educated, on the other hand, are more apt to offer an attitude when pressed. (The distinction should not be overdrawn, since even the most educated include some 20–25% willing to offer opinions about specific attitude objects that are unknown to them.) This difference by education, together with the lack of difference by education when DK filters are added to the questions, creates exactly the interaction we had hypothesized early in our research: Those persons most influenced by question form (termed *floaters* in Chapter 4) are the least educated. [10] Since the same basic process presumably operates with less extreme issues, we can only speculate about why we did not obtain similar evidence when dealing with more ordinary issues in Chapter 4. A complete theory will have to reconcile the finding that low-educated respondents are disproportionately constrained to give an opinion on the standard form of obscure questions with the more general finding that low-educated respondents are more likely to say don't know on most other standard form questions.

[10]The Portugal item shows a similar interaction, despite the differences from the ATA in its bivariate relation to education. Using the data for standard and filtered agree–disagree forms in footnote 4, less-educated respondents show a nonsignificant trend to float more than the more educated. Thus all three items having an extreme DK level provide evidence in support of the initial hypothesis about education, though items with more typical DK levels failed to show the same interactions in Chapter 4.

6
Measuring a Middle
Position

> In everything that is continuous and divisible it is possible to
> take more, less, or an equal amount.
> —Aristotle, *Nichomachean Ethics*

Many survey questions require respondents to choose between two
contrasting alternatives. Frequently there is a logical middle position
that some respondents might prefer to either end of the implicit attitude
dimension. For instance, whether one is liberal or conservative could be
answered by "middle-of-the-road"; whether laws on marijuana should
be more strict or less strict implies the possibility of "same as now";
whether the U.S. government provides too much or too little aid to
another country can lead to the answer "right amount." Survey investigators must decide whether such a middle alternative should be built
explicitly into a question, as against merely accepted when offered spontaneously or even discouraged altogether.

Our primary concern in the present chapter is whether this decision
has consequences for the conclusions drawn from attitude surveys.
After documenting the fact that the presence or absence of an explicit
middle alternative generally affects the proportion of such responses,
we consider two types of possible consequences: (*a*) Is the univariate
distribution of the other alternatives altered significantly by the movement of respondents into or out of a middle position? (*b*) Does the
relation of an item to other variables change importantly depending
upon whether a middle alternative is offered?

Related to these practical questions are theoretical issues having to do
with the nature of the middle position in a set of attitudinal alternatives.
Three hypotheses are implied by the way the middle position is handled
in the wording of questions. First, when survey investigators decide

161

against offering an explicit middle alternative, they are usually assuming that the middle category consists largely of responses from those who lean toward one or the other polar alternatives, although perhaps with little intensity. Thus it is legitimate to press respondents to choose one of these alternatives, rather than allowing refuge to be taken in a middle position. Second, some investigators omit the middle alternative in the belief that it tends to attract people who have no opinion on the issue and find it easier to choose a seemingly noncommittal position than to say "don't know." Third, investigators who do offer a middle alternative are probably assuming that respondents who opt for it really do favor the middle position, and if forced to choose a polar alternative will contribute some form of random or systematic error.

To address these issues, two forms of an item, administered to random subsamples of the same survey, are compared in each experiment: on the *Offered form*, a middle alternative is explicitly read to respondents; on the *Omitted form*, no middle alternative is presented, although it is accepted if given spontaneously by the respondent.[1] Chart 6.1 presents the exact wording for the five items used in these experiments. The marijuana item was adapted from a 1972 Gallup survey, the local education item comes from the Institute for Social Research (ISR) Election Studies, and the divorce item appears regularly in the National Opinion Research Center (NORC) General Social Survey. The other two questions (Vietnam and liberal–conservative) were modeled on frequently asked questions about those subjects (e.g., Mueller, 1973; and Roper Center, 1975).

EFFECTS OF THE MIDDLE ALTERNATIVE ON MIDDLE RESPONSES

Prior to our work, the only middle alternative split-ballot experiments that we were able to locate were carried out in the 1940s. Rugg and Cantril (1944: 33–34) provide the marginals for two such comparisons: In one, offering the middle category increases its choice by about 30%; in the other, by only 3%. Tamulonis (1947:68–73) presents four additional

---

[1]An "if volunteered" middle-alternative response box was included on Omitted forms and interviewers were instructed to accept that answer if given spontaneously. This almost certainly reduces the size of the form differences we report in Table 6.1, as compared with what would be found if instructions were employed that encouraged interviewers to try to force respondents into one of the polar alternatives, accepting another response only as a last resort. The practice we followed deliberately attempts to confine the experiments to question-form differences, since variations in interviewer practice would involve other factors difficult to standardize.

CHART 6.1
Middle Alternative Split Ballots

Omitted forms	Offered forms
*In your opinion, should the penalties for using marijuana be **more** strict or **less** strict than they are now?*	*In your opinion, should the penalties for using marijuana be **more** strict, **less** strict, or **about the same** as they are now?*
1. More strict 5. Less strict 3. (If volunteered) About same as now	1. More strict 5. Less strict 3. About same as now
*Looking back, do you think our government did **too much** to help the South Vietnamese government in the war, or **not enough** to help the South Vietnamese government?*	*Looking back, do you think our government did **too much** to help the South Vietnamese government in the war, **not enough** to help the South Vietnamese government, or was it about the **right amount**?*
1. Too much 5. Not enough 3. (If volunteered) Right amount	1. Too much 5. Not enough 3. Right amount
*On most political issues, would you say you are on the **liberal** side or on the **conservative** side?*	*On most political issues, would you say you are on the **liberal** side, on the **conservative** side, or **middle-of-the-road**?*
1. Liberal 5. Conservative 3. (If volunteered) Middle of road, half-way between	1. Liberal 5. Conservative 3. Middle-of-road
Do you feel that the federal government has too much or too little control over local education?	*Do you feel that the federal government has too much, too little, or the right amount of control over local education?*
1. Too much 5. Too little 3. (If volunteered) Right amount	1. Too much 5. Too little 3. Right amount
Should divorce in this country be easier or more difficult to obtain than it is now?	*Should divorce in this country be easier to obtain, more difficult to obtain, or stay as it is now?*[a]
1. Easier 2. More difficult 3. (If volunteered) Stay as it is	1. Easier 2. More difficult 3. Stay as is

[a] In SRC-79 Sept., the divorce item alternatives "more difficult" and "stay as is" were listed on one Offered form in reverse order to that shown here.

examples, all of which show substantial shifts in the middle position, ranging from 16 to 52%. Finally, Stember and Hyman (1949–1950) report a middle alternative split-ballot experiment that shows an increase in the middle position of 16%.

The results of our own 16 experiments (5 original experiments and 11 variations and replications) are presented in Table 6.1.[2] Each one shows a highly significant increase ($p < .001$) in the middle category when it is offered explicitly, with the increases ranging from 11 to 20 percentage points in 9 of the cases. All but 2 of the remaining cases involve the question on liberal–conservative self-identification, which reveals a much larger increase of 22 to 39 percentage points, probably because on this issue the Offered "middle-of-the-road" response is not merely a logical middle position, but a politically well-crystallized position as well. If this last explanation is correct, then the fact that the middle response on the Omitted form of the liberal–conservative item is not volunteered very much more than the middle response on other omitted items demonstrates how readily most respondents accept the constraint imposed by the Omitted form. Finally, the relatively large difference produced by the divorce replication and variant in September, 1979, is puzzling to us. (The reason for there being two parts to this experiment is discussed in the next section.)

Response-Order Effects: Location of the Middle Alternative

In a recent analysis of their own middle-alternative experiments, Kalton, Roberts, and Holt (1980) suggest that one factor contributing to the increase in the size of the middle category on Offered forms like those used here may be that the middle option comes at the end of the question, though they did not have experimental data to test the point. To determine whether respondents are affected by such a "recency" bias, we administered two experiments (in SRC–79 April) varying the order of the options in the Offered form of the Vietnam and divorce items, with further experiments on the divorce item carried out in June and September 1979. The most relevant of these experiments included an Omitted form as well (for divorce), and is presented at the end of Table 6.1; the other results are discussed as part of the general problem of response order in Chapter 2. On the one hand, there is compelling evidence that some of the increment due to addition of a middle alternative at the end

[2]Table 6.1 and all succeeding tables omit responses coded "other" and N.A.; in no case is the difference by form in this missing data component greater than 2.5%, and it averages less than 1%.

TABLE 6.1
Response by Question Form in Middle-Alternative Experiments

	Omitted	Offered
Marijuana		
(SRC–1974 Fall)		
More strict	61.0%	55.8%
Less strict	27.0	19.8
About same as now	7.9	19.6
Don't know	4.0	4.7
	100	100
	(1014)	(489)
Marijuana		
(SRC–1976 Feb.)		
More strict	54.6%	43.5%
Less strict	31.6	30.9
About same as now	9.3	22.4
Don't know	4.6	3.3
	100	100
	(637)	(612)
Marijuana		
(SRC–1977 Aug.)		
More strict	49.1%	41.8%
Less strict	41.8	30.6
About same as now	6.1	25.8
Don't know	2.9	1.8
	100	100
	(603)	(562)
Vietnam		
(SRC–1974 Fall)		
Too much	64.1%	56.2%
Not enough	9.9	8.4
Right amount	15.4	26.1
Don't know	10.5	9.4
	100	100
	(986)	(479)
Vietnam		
(SRC–1978 Feb.)		
Too much	68.4%	57.8%
Not enough	13.0	10.9
Right amount	8.4	22.5
Don't know	10.1	8.7
	100	100
	(621)	(550)

(*continued*)

TABLE 6.1—*Continued*

	Omitted	Offered
Vietnam		
(SRC-1978 Aug.)		
Too much	66.7%	57.7%
Not enough	14.9	12.1
Right amount	10.2	22.3
Don't know	8.1	7.9
	100	100
	(529)	(529)
Vietnam		
(SRC-1978 Fall)		
Too much	60.8%	52.8%
Not enough	12.9	11.5
Right amount	10.6	23.5
Don't know	15.8	12.2
	100	100
	(482)	(972)
Liberal-conservative		
(SRC-1974 Fall)		
Liberal	33.1%	16.9%
Conservative	44.4	24.5
Middle of road	16.2	53.7
Don't know	6.3	4.8
	100	100
	(507)	(497)
Liberal-conservative		
(SRC-1976 Spring)		
Liberal	29.2%	15.8%
Conservative	50.4	27.3
Middle of road	12.0	50.8
Don't know	8.3	6.0
	100	100
	(1562)	(1489)
Liberal-conservative		
(SRC-1978 Feb.)		
Liberal	28.9%	27.1%
Conservative	59.5	40.8
Middle of road	5.4	27.5
Don't know	6.2	4.6
	100	100
	(627)	(564)

(continued)

TABLE 6.1—*Continued*

	Omitted	Offered	
Liberal–conservative (SRC–1978 Aug.)			
Liberal	31.9%	23.7%	
Conservative	58.7	41.6	
Middle of road	5.9	30.7	
Don't know	3.5	4.0	
	100	100	
	(542)	(553)	
Liberal–conservative (SRC–1978 Fall)			
Liberal	29.5%	20.0%	
Conservative	57.9	33.3	
Middle of road	6.6	41.8	
Don't know	6.0	4.9	
	100	100	
	(499)	(1006)	
Local education (SRC–1976 Feb.)			
Too much	53.6%	44.7%	
Too little	18.2	15.6	
Right amount	13.7	28.8	
Don't know	14.5	10.8	
	100	100	
	(627)	(617)	
Divorce (NORC–1978)			
Easier	28.9%	22.7%	
More difficult	44.5	32.7	
Stay as is	21.7	40.2	
Don't know	4.9	4.3	
	100	100	
	(760)	(770)	
			Reordered[a]
Divorce (SRC–79 Sept.)			
Easier	38.8%	20.8%	22.6%
More difficult	49.3	33.2	39.9
Stay as is	10.2	44.7	33.9
Don't know	1.6	1.2	3.6
	100	100	100
	(304)	(313)	(301)

[a] In SRC–79 Sept., the Divorce item alternatives "more difficult" and "stay as is" were listed on one Offered form in reverse order. Thus, there were three forms in this experiment.

of an item is attributable to ordinal rather than logical position. On the other hand, the major part is *not* due to an order effect, but can be attributed to the addition of a middle alternative regardless of its location in the question. These results obviously could complicate, though probably not change radically, inferences from analyses presented in this chapter.

Effects of Other Categories on Middle Responses

Do respondents who move into the middle position when it is offered actually lean toward one of the polar alternatives? If so, then we should be able to decrease the size of the Offered middle category (and therefore the size of the form effect) by providing alternatives between the polar positions and the middle point. However, if respondents affected by form truly subscribe to the middle ground, then offering intermediate categories should have no impact on the size of the Offered middle category.

We were able to address this question with data from two of our experiments. In SRC–74 Fall and SRC–78 Fall, in addition to asking the two forms of the liberal–conservative item already presented, we included a third form with a five-point scale: *On most political issues would you say you are liberal, somewhat liberal, middle-of-the-road, somewhat conservative, or conservative?* Although the size of the middle category on this five-point Offered form (41% in 1974, 32% in 1978) is still much larger than on the Omitted form (16% and 7%), it is noticeably smaller than on the three-point Offered form (54% and 51%). Offering the "somewhat liberal" and "somewhat conservative" categories reduces the number of respondents who move into the middle position, though it also draws significantly from the "liberal" and "conservative" categories.[3] It is

[3]The entire five-point response distributions are:

	1974 Fall	1978 Fall
1. Liberal	9.6%	10.8%
2. Somewhat liberal	11.1	13.1
3. Middle of road	41.4	32.4
4. Somewhat conservative	18.8	21.2
5. Conservative	12.9	17.3
6. DK	6.1	5.1
	100	100
	(488)	(490)

The liberal–conservative Offered form in SRC–78 Feb. also contained these same five categories, which have been collapsed in Tables 6.1 and 6.4. The 1978 Feb. uncollapsed

probable that the provision of even more intermediate categories around the midpoint (say, a seven-point scale) would further reduce the size of the middle category, and such experiments would be useful. For the present it appears that at least some respondents who choose the middle category on our three-point Offered forms do lean toward one of the polar positions, but most continue to choose the middle position even when intermediate categories are offered.

THE EFFECTS OF MIDDLE ALTERNATIVES ON OTHER CATEGORIES

Substantive Marginals

Depending on the item, between 11 and 39% of the total sample would take the middle position on our Offered form but move into other categories on the Omitted form. How do these individuals respond on the Omitted form? One hypothesis is that they give responses on the Omitted form much like other respondents. If this happens, the marginals for the Omitted and Offered forms, *excluding all middle responses,* will not differ beyond sampling error.

Data in Table 6.1 allow one to test this null hypothesis for all the experiments, and in only one case can it be rejected. In 15 of the 16 cases the χ^2 (with two degrees of freedom) produced by comparing each pair of Offered and Omitted forms excluding all middle responses is not significant.[4] Thus, apart from the size of the middle category itself, one would generally draw the same conclusions from the marginals for one form as from the marginals for the other form. Moreover, the same holds for the experiments presented three decades ago by Rugg and Cantril (1944), Tamulonis (1947), and Stember and Hyman (1949–1950): Not one of their comparisons reveals a significant change in univariate distributions once middle responses are excluded. The recent experiments of Kalton *et al.* (1980), however, do show some form effects on the polar

---

frequencies, using the category numbers above, are 1) 66; 2) 87; 3) 155; 4) 137; 5) 93; and 6) 26. In SRC–76 Spring the liberal–conservative offered form contained only three positions.

[4]The exception occurs with the reordered offered form of the divorce item (SRC–79 Sept., $\chi^2 = 7.60$, $df = 2$, $p < .05$), in part because the recency effect inflates choice of the alternative "more difficult" when it is read last. If all DKs are also excluded, then, again with one exception, the comparisons continue to be nonsignificant. The exception is the 1978 Feb. liberal–conservative experiment in which $\chi^2 = 5.20$, $df = 1$, $p < .05$, comparing the liberal–conservative ratio by form. Since none of the other liberal–conservative experiments shows this difference (and combining all of them yields no difference by form) we regard it as a chance finding.

ratio with items about health. Thus our findings here can probably be generalized to most but not all survey questions.[5]

Don't Know Responses

The overall comparisons between forms may obscure one finer implication of the middle option—its effect on the don't know (DK) category. It is sometimes claimed that the middle category will attract persons who might otherwise say DK but prefer to give a more substantive sounding response. One implication of this hypothesis is that the proportion of DK responses should go down on the form that includes an explicit middle category. A review of Table 6.1 shows that a decrease in DK does occur for 13 of the 16 comparisons, which would have happened on a chance basis less than two times out of a hundred. At the same time, all of the decreases are quite small, the only two that are significant being about 4% and the average for all 16 less than 2%.[6] Thus there is evidence that offering the middle position is linked to frequency of DK, but also that the connection is quite weak. Moreover, the correct interpretation of the DK difference by form is not necessarily that explicit middle alternatives attract DK respondents. It is equally possible that question forms omitting a middle alternative increase DK levels by forcing persons who hold the middle position to say DK when they find it impossible to choose one of the specified alternatives. Distinguishing between these two possibilities would be theoretically interesting, but the tiny number of respondents involved means that neither process is an important factor in producing the form differences in the size of the middle alternative itself.

[5]The reader may wonder how people who select the middle category on the Offered form would choose between polar categories if asked the follow-up: *If you had to choose, which way would you lean . . . ?* The absence of a form difference in the polar ratio that was just reported might lead one to expect such follow-up choices to be distributed in the same way as those of respondents who made an initial choice. But respondents in the Offered middle category (to whom the follow-up would be asked) *also* include many individuals who would volunteer the middle position on the Omitted form and are thus not involved in the form effect. The expectation of no difference applies only to those who would be shifted by form, and there appears to be no way to identify these particular respondents in a cross-section design.

[6]A comparison of the two Offered forms of the divorce item that are involved in the order experiment also shows a near-significant difference for DK responses ($\chi^2 = 3.76$, $df = 1$).

THE EFFECTS OF MIDDLE ALTERNATIVES
ON ASSOCIATIONS

Although form differences in marginals are of some importance, the more critical issue for survey research is whether associations of variables differ significantly in nature or magnitude depending upon omission or inclusion of a middle alternative. For example, is education related differently to the "same" item when it *omits* rather than *offers* a middle alternative? This type of issue has not been thoroughly studied before: Rugg and Cantril (1944) do not proceed beyond the examination of marginals referred to previously; Tamulonis (1947) does raise the issue but summarizes her results in a generalized fashion that makes their evaluation difficult; and the Stember and Hyman (1949–1950) analysis is limited to a single item and its relation to the special problem of interviewer effects.

Relations to Background Variables

We investigated several ways in which Omitted and Offered forms might produce different results in associations with other variables. Our first hypothesis about form differences in response was that they should be related to education. We expected less-educated respondents to be more influenced by whether or not a middle alternative was offered, on the assumption that a middle position among the better educated would be more crystallized and thus insisted upon regardless of question wording. If this were true, then the shift of a disproportionate number of the less educated from the polar positions to the middle position on the Offered form would also alter the correlation between education and middle versus polar positions on that form.

In fact, there is little evidence for this hypothesis. Conclusions about the relation of education to the middle category of a particular item are generally unaffected by whether or not that category is explicitly offered. A representative example is presented in Table 6.2. As may be observed there, the less educated are more apt to be middle-of-the-roaders but this is equally true on both forms of the liberal–conservative question.

On other items, the simple bivariate relation between education and the middle response is reversed (e.g., on marijuana it is the more educated who are apt to be in the middle) but the reversal is obtained on both question forms. In sum, the important point is that findings about the association between education and the middle position typically do not vary by question form.

TABLE 6.2
Liberal–Conservative by Education by Form (SRC–1974 Fall)

Education:	Omitted form		
	0–11	12	13+
Liberal	25.0%	31.1%	45.7%
Middle of road	23.4	20.1	10.8
Conservative	51.6	48.8	43.5
	100	100	100
	(124)	(164)	(186)

$\chi^2 = 19.77,\ df = 4,\ p < .001$

Education:	Offered form		
	0–11	12	13+
Liberal	10.4%	14.5%	25.8%
Middle of road	64.9	63.8	44.6
Conservative	24.6	21.7	29.6
	100	100	100
	(134)	(152)	(186)

$\chi^2 = 21.75,\ df = 4,\ p < .001$

Three-way interaction: $\chi^2 = .44, df = 4,$ n.s.

We were also able to test variants of the education hypothesis by measuring information about, and interest in, the general kinds of political issues that served as the content of these experiments. The measure of information consisted of three items asking for identification of political figures and the indicator of interest was a single question asking how much attention the respondent paid to national and international news (see Appendix C). Although these tests were restricted to the three experiments in SRC–74 Fall, they showed little evidence of an interaction between form, response, and information or interest. Similar negative evidence for a measure of interest also appears in Stember and Hyman's (1949–1950) analysis of a middle-alternative experiment.[7]

Holding aside the middle category, the relations of polar categories to these variables also do not typically differ by form. For example, if one

[7]We also examined three other background variables (sex, age, and race) widely used in survey analysis and generally found them to be related to response in the same way on the two question forms.

repercentages the figures in Table 6.2, excluding all middle responses, then the better educated are more likely to identify as liberal and the less educated as conservative—irrespective of item form. Thus, in general, the middle alternative form does not seem to affect inferences about the relation between attitude items and a number of different background variables.[8]

Intensity and Choice of the Middle Alternative

Our second hypothesis about form differences in response was that persons feeling less strongly about an issue should be attracted to the middle alternative, hence the Offered form should more completely remove such respondents from polar categories. An implication of this reasoning is that intensity of opinion should be more sharply related to middle versus polar positions on the Offered form than on the Omitted form.

We tested this hypothesis by including intensity measures with three of our experiments—the two marijuana replications and the initial Vietnam experiment. After each of these questions was answered, respondents were asked either, *How strongly do you feel about this issue: quite strongly or not so strongly?* or, for the second marijuana replication, *How important is a candidate's position on penalties for marijuana use when you decide how to vote in an election—is it one of the most important factors you would consider, a very important factor, somewhat important, or not too important?* As can be seen in Table 6.3, in each case the difference in the relation to intensity is as expected: stronger on the Offered form. Although the size of these form differences is not great (in no single case is it clearly significant), the results are consistent in direction in three independent surveys.

The tendency for low intensity to be somewhat more strongly related to the middle position on the Offered form than on the Omitted can be stated in another way: The form effect is larger among less intense respondents than among more intense individuals. We interpret this to mean that people who have more crystallized opinions on an issue are less likely to be influenced by variations in the categories offered (see

---

[8]This conclusion is consistent with that reached by Kalton *et al.* (1980). They report their evidence for interactions with background variables as "predominantly negative," with the few exceptions being either small in magnitude or difficult to interpret.

TABLE 6.3
Response (Polar Alternatives versus Middle) by Form and Item Intensity

	Omitted form		Offered form	
Attitude strength	Polar alternatives	Middle alternative	Polar alternatives	Middle alternative
Marijuana (SRC–1976 Feb.):				
Very strongly	410	34	356	74
Not so strongly	137	24	99	61
	$\chi^2 = 6.61$, $df = 1$, $p < .02$, gamma $= .36$		$\chi^2 = 27.05$, $df = 1$, $p < .001$, gamma $= .50$	
	Three-way interaction: $\chi^2 = .93$, $df = 1$, n.s.			
Marijuana (SRC–1977 Aug.):				
One of most important + very important[a]	163	7	159	17
Somewhat important + not too important[a]	369	29	241	124
	$\chi^2 = 2.18$, $df = 1$, n.s., gamma $= .29$		$\chi^2 = 41.16$, $df = 1$, $p < .001$, gamma $= .66$	
	Three-way interaction: $\chi^2 = 3.24$, $df = 1$, $p < .10$			
Vietnam (SRC–1974 Fall):				
Very strongly	515	70	234	51
Not so strongly	206	77	69	69
	$\chi^2 = 29.84$, $df = 1$, $p < .001$, gamma $= .47$		$\chi^2 = 46.46$, $df = 1$, $p < .001$, gamma $= .64$	
	Three-way interaction: $\chi^2 = 3.03$, $df = 1$, $p < .10$			

[a] The third and fourth strength categories were collapsed because they showed no difference in the way they affected the response–form relation; the first and second categories were collapsed partly for the same reason and partly because of the small number of cases in the first category.

Chapter 10).[9] But although our original hypothesis is supported, it should be noted that even respondents who say they feel strongly show a significant form effect in each of the experiments presented in Table 6.3. Moreover, differentiating the attitude strength dimension more

[9]The argument of Sherif and Sherif (1969) that attitudes are usefully seen as configurations of latitudes of acceptance and rejection applies here. Their finding that the more ego involved (i.e., intense) have smaller latitudes of acceptance and larger latitudes of rejection leads to the same conclusion that the less intense should be more affected by the presence of a middle category.

finely (see footnote a, Table 6.3) did not seem to reduce further the variation due to question form.

Associations between Attitudes

Our final hypothesis involved the issue of whether form affects conclusions about the nature of relations between attitudes themselves. If correlations between attitudes are generally larger for those who feel more intensely (see Chapter 10), then our finding that the average intensity of those in the polar categories is higher on the Offered form than on the Omitted implies that correlations between *polar* opinions should be larger for Offered forms than for Omitted forms.[10] We tested this notion for the three instances where there was a relation between experiments on at least one form.[11] In all three cases the difference is in the expected direction: The association between polar positions is stronger on the Offered form. In only one of these instances does the response by response by form interaction reach significance, but it is an important case since an investigator would draw quite different conclusions from the two forms about the relation of liberal–conservative self-identification to judgment of whether the United States gave too much or too little aid to the South Vietnamese government.

To test further the reliability of this finding, the Vietnam and liberal–conservative experiments were repeated in SRC–78 February. The results shown in Table 6.4 replicate those found in 1974. On the Omitted versions there is no difference in opinion on Vietnam between liberals and conservatives, but on the Offered forms liberals are more likely to say "too much aid," whereas conservatives say "not enough."[12] Thus the relation that might be expected on some ideological grounds occurs on only one form. What seems to be happening is that among liberals the switch to the middle position on Vietnam comes disproportionately

---

[10]We also investigated whether correlations between *middle* versus combined *polar* positions on different items are affected by form. In a preliminary analysis of our first set of experiments, we reported that a generalized set might be implicated in the form effect because choosing the middle position on the Offered Vietnam item was more strongly related to choosing the middle position on another Offered item than on the corresponding Omitted forms (see Presser and Schuman 1975: 21). Analysis of the other experiments failed to generalize this finding.

[11]In the only other case where two experimental items can be intercorrelated (marijuana and local education) there is no relation on either form. Since none of the items were originally designed to be associated, this case does not seem an appropriate test.

[12]In both years, the liberal–conservative offered form had five points, which have been collapsed to three in these analyses.

TABLE 6.4
Vietnam Response by Liberal–Conservative Response by Form[a]

	Omitted forms		
	Liberal	Middle	Conservative
Too much aid	76.7%	71.4%	76.9%
About right	7.0	21.4	9.0
Not enough	16.3	7.1	14.0
	100	100	100
	(172)	(28)	(321)

$\chi^2 = 6.10$, $df = 4$, n.s.
Due to association between polar positions: $\chi^2 = .33$, $df = 1$, n.s.

	Offered forms		
	Liberal	Middle	Conservative
Too much aid	72.0%	59.4%	58.9%
About right	22.0	28.0	24.2
Not enough	6.1	12.6	16.8
	100	100	100
	(132)	(143)	(202)

$\chi^2 = 11.62$, $df = 4$, $p < .03$
Due to association between polar positions: $\chi^2 = 10.19$, $df = 1$, $p < .001$
Three-way interaction: $\chi^2 = 11.81$, $df = 4$, $p < .02$

[a] Data from SRC–78 February.

from the "not enough aid" category, whereas among conservatives it comes disproportionately from the "too much aid" response. It may be that respondents are somewhat uncomfortable holding these combinations of attitudes (liberal with "not enough aid" and conservative with "too much aid"), which are in some sense counter to conventional expectations, and thus are more likely to opt for the middle position on the Offered form as a way to resolve the "inconsistency." However, two more recent attempts to replicate this form difference (in SRC–78 August and SRC–78 Fall) were not successful, for reasons that, even after much investigation, remain unclear (see Appendix A). These failures of replication leave uncertain the original findings, as well as the more general issue of whether middle alternative forms affect associations between attitude items.[13]

[13]We also examined interitem associations between the experimental items and a number of other nonexperimental opinion questions and found none that varied significantly by form.

CONCLUDING DISCUSSION

Offering an explicit middle alternative in a forced-choice attitude item increases the proportion of respondents in that category. On most issues the increase is in the neighborhood of 10 to 20%, but it may be considerably larger. Although there is a very slight decrease in the proportion of spontaneous don't know responses when the middle alternative is offered, almost all the change in the middle position comes from a decline in the polar positions. The decline tends to affect the polar positions proportionately, so that item form is usually unrelated to the univariate distribution of opinion when middle responses are excluded from analysis.

Intensity appears to be one factor that partly distinguishes those affected by form from those not affected. Form effects are greater among respondents reporting low intensity of feeling on an issue than among those reporting high intensity. A number of other respondent characteristics, by contrast, are generally unrelated to the form effect, and conclusions about the link between such variables and attitude items are unaffected by form. Finally, one inference about the association between the polar opinion categories of two different items was significantly affected by question form in two independent surveys. The lack of replications in two additional surveys, however, indicates a need for further work with other items to discover whether such interactions occur on a reliable basis.

Until late in our investigation, our experiments always added middle alternatives as the last response to an item, thus unknowingly confounding logical position with response order. The discovery that recency effects occur in at least one of these experiments indicates that our main findings should be replicated using different orderings of alternatives. We doubt that any major conclusions will change, but it is important to separate logical position from ordinal position in the study of the effects of question form.

Susceptibility to constraint by question form has sometimes been seen in terms of cognitive limitations or passivity in the interview situation (see, for example, Schuman and Duncan 1974: 240). This interpretation, however, appears inconsistent with our finding that the form effect is essentially unrelated to measures of cognitive sophistication such as education and information. An alternative interpretation focuses on what is communicated by question form. There are investigators who purposely omit a middle alternative in order to force respondents into one of the polar positions, and it is not unreasonable to assume that the respondents who feel constrained by question form are in some sense aware of this intention. Question form probably structures these respondents' decision making. Particularly for a respondent with a weak opinion leaning in one direction, the answer to the question *Which of the offered alternatives am I closest to?* will differ depending on whether an investigator presents only the two polar options, or those two plus a middle position. Thus some respondents, admittedly not yet well identified, may simply make different assumptions about the information being requested, depending on which question form is asked.

The identification of the kinds of people or processes involved in responses to the presence or absence of a middle alternative is an important task for the future. There is a parallel here to the DK floaters described in Chapters 4 and 5. In fact, we might well use the term *middle-alternative floaters* to bring out both the parallel and the difference. Except for some evidence that intensity is implicated in the middle-alternative case, we again do not have much evidence as to the distinguishing characteristics of such floaters.

A second related direction for research is to specify further what it is about the middle alternative that attracts people. The phrasing of middle alternatives in most survey questions is quite general, and could cover several distinguishable phenomena. In addition to low intensity and the absence of opinion, both of which we have investigated, phenomena such as ambivalence are obvious possibilities (cf. Klopfer and Madden, 1980). It would be useful to experiment with rewording the middle alternative with more precision in order to define conceptually more homogenous groups.

7
Balance and Imbalance in Questions

There are two sides to every question.
—Protagoras (Diogenes Laertius, *Lives and Opinions of Eminent Philosophers*)

No attitude question can be completely neutral, since the mere act of inquiring about a subject may sharpen the definition of it as an "issue." Yet questions can be more or less neutral in the way they are posed. Some involve little more than brief statement of an issue:

Are you in favor of the death penalty for persons convicted of murder?

Other questions add arguments for one side or the other, as in this example from Harris (1976: 168):

Do you think the Watergate investigation should continue under the supervision of Henry Petersen of the Department of Justice, or should a new special prosecutor, freely independent of President Nixon, be appointed by the courts or by Congress?

This item can be said to contain both a question and an influence attempt. Both intuitively and theoretically (McGuire, 1969) one might expect additions of the latter kind to affect responses, and there is some support for this in early split-ballot experiments in surveys (Rugg and Cantril, 1944). However, the reliability, frequency, and magnitude of these effects are not well established. More important, the crucial issue of whether the effects extend from marginals to relationships has not been adequately explored.

This chapter reports a series of experiments with five attitude items intended to determine the effects of varying the balance of arguments contained in a question. One form of each item was either taken from or modeled on questions already used in large-scale surveys. We then attempted to construct additional forms of the question without changing the basic issue placed before respondents.

The experiments can be divided into two main types:

1. Minor formal changes in a question that make a clearly implicit pro–con choice more explicit.
2. Additions to the negative side of an issue of an explicit substantive alternative or counterargument, which may or may not have been implicit for most respondents.

FORMAL BALANCE OF QUESTIONS

The simplest way to ask questions in attitude surveys is to pose them much as one might in ordinary life. If interested in someone's opinions about capital punishment, for example, one might ask the question posed earlier in our opening paragraph. Just such question forms appeared frequently in surveys until the mid-1940s, but were occasionally criticized (e.g., Kornhauser, 1946–1947: 493) as unbalancing the issue in favor of the "yes" response, since no other possibility was clearly mentioned.

It turns out upon reflection that there is no simple way to provide balance to most survey items, but one elementary step is to make formally explicit the fact that a negative response is as legitimate as an affirmative one. Thus:

> *Do you favor or oppose the death penalty for persons convicted of murder?*

Most recent survey questions provide "formal balance" of this kind. That the distinction is still taken seriously today is indicated by the fact that *both* versions of the capital punishment question quoted above appear in NORC's General Social Survey (GSS)—the first version in 1972 and 1973, the second from 1974 to the present (NORC, 1980). The change from the first to the second form was made precisely because the GSS staff was concerned to provide better balance to the question.

In order to determine whether or not changes of this kind affect respondents in surveys, we began our investigation with the first four experiments shown in Table 7.1.[1] In each experiment, the item on the

---

[1]Table 7.1 and subsequent tables omit DK, NA, and other responses. There appear to be no significant differences by form in these missing data categories taken singly or as a total set.

left side of the table is in unbalanced form, whereas on the right side a word or phrase is added to provide formal balance. Since the change is slight and merely makes explicit what is already clearly implied by the question, it did not seem to us likely that effects would occur, but the point was worth testing as a kind of limiting case.

In fact, of these initial four experiments, three showed no sign of a univariate difference, but counter to our expectation, one (fuel shortage) revealed a highly significant difference, with a 9% increase in the negative response where that was made explicit. It is not at all obvious why

TABLE 7.1
Formal Balance of Items[a]

Unbalanced form		Formally balanced form	
1. Fuel shortage (SRC–74 Fall)			
If there is a serious fuel shortage this winter, do you think there should be a law requiring people to lower the heat in their homes?		*If there is a serious fuel shortage this winter, do you think there should be a law requiring people to lower the heat in their homes, or do you oppose such a law?*	
Yes, should be a law	38.3%	Should be a law	29.4%
No, not a law	61.7	Oppose such a law	70.6
	100		100
	(507)		(494)
	$\chi^2 = 8.90$, $df = 1$, $p < .01$		
2. Unions (SRC–74 Fall)			
If there is a union at a particular company or business, do you think that all workers there should be required to be union members?		*If there is a union at a particular company or business, do you think that all workers there should be required to be union members, or are you opposed to this?*	
Yes	34.0%	Yes, all in union	32.1%
No	66.0	No, oppose	67.9
	100		100
	(497)		(480)
	$\chi^2 = .41$, $df = 1$, n.s.		
3. Abortion (SRC–75 Feb.)			
Do you feel a woman should be allowed to have an abortion in the early months of pregnancy if she wants one?		*Do you feel a woman should be allowed to have an abortion in the early months of pregnancy if she wants one, or do you feel this should not be allowed?*	
Yes	68.0%	Should be allowed	65.5%
No	32.0	Should not be allowed	34.5
	100		100
	(440)		(429)
	$\chi^2 = .59$, $df = 1$, n.s.		

(continued)

TABLE 7.1—*Continued*

Unbalanced form		Formally balanced form	
4. Gun permits (SRC-75 Feb.)			
Would you favor a law which would require a person to obtain a police permit before he could buy a gun?		*Would you favor or oppose a law which would require a person to obtain a police permit before he could buy a gun?*	
Yes	71.0%	Favor	71.7%
No	29.0	Oppose	28.3
	100		100
	(455)		(445)
	$\chi^2 = .05$, $df = 1$, n.s.		
5. Gun permits (SRC-78 Fall)			
(See No. 4 for wording)			
Yes	70.4%	Favor	70.3%
No	29.6	Oppose	29.7
	100		100
	(503)		(485)
	$\chi^2 = .00$, $df = 1$, n.s.		
6. Merged replications of fuel shortage[b]			
(See No. 1 for wording)			
1. Yes should be a law	46.3%	Should be a law	43.5%
2. No, not a law	53.7	Oppose such a law	56.5
	100		100
	(1,368)		(1,300)
	$\chi^2 = 2.24$, $df = 1$, n.s.		

[a] Origin of Questions: Fuel shortage, original; unions, adapted from Noelle-Neumann (1970–1971); abortion, original; gun permits, adapted from NORC (1978).

[b] These data have been merged from three surveys: SRC-77 February, SRC-78 August, SRC-78 Fall (itself a merging of 3 months). Examination of the separate samples yields similar results and the merging is for economy of presentation only. The percentage of negative responses for unbalanced and formally balanced forms are: 47.5% and 48.3% in 1977 February; 57.8% and 62.3% in 1978 August; 58.3% and 62.5% in 1978 Fall.

the fuel-shortage experiment should show such an effect when the others do not, and since the 1974 survey that included the fuel item provided some 20 other experimental comparisons, it seemed possible that this particular "significant" difference was due to chance.[2] In order to test this possibility we replicated the experiment in a 1977 survey, and found

[2]The fuel experiment was the first experiment administered in SRC-74 Fall, that is, there were no preceding variations between questionnaire forms in that survey. Therefore, the anomalous result for the fuel experiment cannot be explained as a main effect of variations in context, though the different forms of the Fuel item could conceivably have interacted with previous questions that were constant in form.

no evidence of the earlier difference. To check the point further, we carried out 2 more replications in 1978, again finding no significant difference between the 2 forms on either occasion. All 3 replications are presented in merged form in Table 7.1 and although there is a slight trend in the direction recorded in 1974, it does not approach significance even with this large number of cases. Although we cannot rule out the possibility of change over time, nor the possibility of an enduring effect that is simply very small, chance does seem to be the best explanation of the 1974 difference. (See Appendix A for further discussion of this puzzling result.) A later replication of the gun permit item in 1978 also showed no form difference.

One other variant of formal balancing was tested: a formally balanced version that might seem to make the two sides of the issue appear more closely parallel in expression. This experiment was first carried out in NORC-78 and consisted of two forms of an item on legalization of marijuana, one form similar to those in Table 7.1, the other attempting a more exact kind of balance by saying that each side of the issue is held by some people. The 1978 results and those from a later replication in 1980 are presented in Table 7.2. The difference in 1978 was in the direction of the affirmative rather than the negative position, a finding that could be explained on grounds that it is the minority or deviant position that needs bolstering by a phrasing which implies equal social support to both sides. But the small size and lack of significance $(.20 > p > .10)$ left

TABLE 7.2
Alternative Types of Formal Balance

1. Marijuana (NORC-78)			
Do you think the use of marijuana should be made legal, or not?		*Some people think the use of marijuana should be made legal. Other people think marijuana use should not be made legal. Which do you favor?*	
Should	28.9%	Make use legal	32.6%
Should not	71.1	Don't make use legal	67.4
	100		100
	(738)		(743)
	$\chi^2 = 2.39$, $df = 1$, n.s.		
2. Marijuana (SRC-80 Feb.)			
(See No. 1 for wording)			
Should	29.1%	Make use legal	30.9%
Should not	70.9	Don't make use legal	69.1
	100		100
	(478)		(489)
	$\chi^2 = .37$, $df = 1$, n.s.		

us uncertain about the reliability of the difference, hence we replicated the experiment in February, 1980. As Table 7.2 shows, although the direction of the difference is maintained, the magnitude became even smaller and more clearly nonsignificant. Our inclination is to regard both differences as due to chance, and to conclude that the "some people, other people" variation in wording formally balanced items does not change marginals. It would be useful, however, to carry out similar experiments on other issues, particularly ones that are even more skewed in distribution than the marijuana issue.

In sum, based on this set of experiments, it does not appear that purely *formal* balance of attitude items makes a detectable difference in their univariate distributions.[3] We also tested for three-way interactions using the form and response categories shown in Table 7.1, cross-classified in turn by education, information, interest, sex, race, and age: There is little evidence that form affects the relationship between response and any of these variables.[4] Since every survey question is to some degree unique, it is foolhardy to rule out entirely the possibility that some replicable instance of a difference due to formal balance can be produced with samples of the size normally used in attitude surveys. But given the intuitive unlikelihood of an important effect of this kind, together with the generally negative results from our experiments with five items, it seems reasonable at this point to place the burden of proof on those whose intuition or experience tells them otherwise.

BALANCE THROUGH SUBSTANTIVE
COUNTERARGUMENTS

Even when formally balanced, some of the questions in Table 7.1 might be said to be biased toward the positive side by their very nature. The fuel item speaks of a possible *serious fuel shortage this winter.* The

---

[3]Rugg and Cantril (1944) report certain experiments where formal balance seems to have a small effect. These experiments, however, almost always involve other types of changes in the items as well, and in addition significance levels, Ns, and replications are not provided. Thus we regard the present set of experiments as providing a sounder base for drawing conclusions about the issue of formal balance.

[4]Of the 4 original items by 6 background variables, only one of the 24 interactions reaches significance at the .05 level: gun permits (SRC–75 Feb.) by race (blacks move more toward the counterargument). This isolated result is not supported by trends for race on any of the other items from Table 7.1 and seems best regarded as due to chance. To be quite certain, we replicated it in SRC–78 Fall, and indeed found no trend by race ($\chi^2 = .01$).

abortion item notes that the woman *wants one* and is *in the early months of pregnancy*. In a sense, such items state only the positive side of the issue, and it may be harder for respondents to say no than to say yes.[5] In order to balance more substantively this presumed tendency, investigators sometimes add an explicit counterargument to a question (Payne, 1951:71–72), essentially a reason for taking the negative side, as in the Harris example quoted at the beginning of this chapter.

There are serious problems with this form of balancing, for there is usually more than one way of expressing or justifying a negative answer to a question. Thus for the gun-permit question in Table 7.1, one common counterargument is in terms of Constitutional rights, whereas another is in terms of the ineffectiveness of such a law. Furthermore, although we think of substantive alternatives as a way of balancing a question, it is impossible to say when true balance is achieved and it is certainly possible for the added alternative to tilt the item too far in the opposite direction from the original unbalanced form. Despite these problems it is usually possible to identify one or two major counterarguments that are likely to be implicit in a formal "no" response, and our attempt here is simply to see what happens to responses and associations when these are made explicit. At a later point, we will also compare different arguments on the same issue.

The hypothesis that there will be effects of counterarguments can be put in rational terms. Respondents who have not previously thought much about an issue are suddenly given a plausible reason for taking the negative side of the issue. The counterargument thus provides a genuine degree of cognitive persuasion, and is not merely a matter of social pressure. Thus, some respondents should be convinced to switch sides when a counterargument is added to a question. (A somewhat similar interpretation has been given to the "risky-shift" and related phenomena in group decision-making; see Burnstein and Vinokur, 1977.) There are also other possible reasons for expecting effects from a counterargument and these will be discussed at a later point.

Our 1974 and 1975 surveys included versions of the four items in Table 7.1 with counterarguments added. (Each of these two surveys was divided into three random subsamples, with one receiving the unbalanced form, one the formally balanced form, and one the form with the counterargument.) Table 7.3 presents results for the counterargument forms for the original four items, plus later replications of three of these. In

---

[5]The effects of stating only one side of an issue might be expected to be even more pronounced when in the form of an assertion with which respondents are to agree or disagree, as in traditional Likert-type items. We consider this issue in detail in Chapter 8.

TABLE 7.3
Effects of Using Counterarguments for Balance

Formal Balance	Substantive Counterargument

1. Fuel shortage (SRC–74 Fall)

If there is a serious fuel shortage this winter, do you think there should be a law requiring people to lower the heat in their homes, or do you oppose such a law?		*If there is a serious fuel shortage this winter, do you think there should be a law requiring people to lower the heat in their homes, or do you think this should be left to individual families to decide?*	
Should be	29.4%	Should be	25.9%
Oppose	70.6	Left to families	74.1
	100		100
	(494)		(482)

$$\chi^2 = 1.43, \ df = 1, \text{ n.s.}$$

2. Unions (SRC–74 Fall)

If there is a union at a particular company or business, do you think that all the workers there should be required to be union members, or are you opposed to this?		*If there is a union at a particular company or business, do you think that all the workers there should be required to be union members, or should it be left to the individual to decide whether or not he wants to be in the union?*	
Yes	32.1%	Required	23.0%
Oppose	67.9	Left to individuals	77.0
	100		100
	(480)		(473)

$$\chi^2 = 9.78, \ df = 1, \ p < .01$$

3. Abortion (SRC–75 Feb.)

Do you feel a woman should be allowed to have an abortion in the early months of pregnancy if she wants one, or do you feel this should not be allowed?		*Do you feel a woman should be allowed to have an abortion in the early months of pregnancy if she wants one, or do you feel a woman should not be allowed to end the life of an unborn child?*	
Should	65.5%	Should	61.4%
Should not	34.5	Should not	38.6
	100		100
	(429)		(422)

$$\chi^2 = 1.56, \ df = 1, \text{ n.s.}$$

4. Gun permits (SRC–75 Feb.)

Would you favor or oppose a law which would require a person to obtain a police permit before he could buy a gun?		*Would you favor a law which would require a person to obtain a police permit before he could buy a gun, or do you think such a law would interfere too much with the right of citizens to own guns?*	
Favor	71.7%	Favor	67.3%
Oppose	28.3	Interfere too much	32.7
	100		100
	(445)		(431)

$$\chi^2 = 2.00, \ df = 1, \text{ n.s.}$$

(continued)

TABLE 7.3—*Continued*

Formal Balance		Substantive Counterargument	

5. Fuel shortage (SRC–78 Fall)
(see No. 1 for wording)

Should be	37.5%	Should be	24.7%
Oppose	62.5	Left to families	75.3
	100		100
	(491)		(490)

$\chi^2 = 18.80$, $df = 1$, $p < .001$

6. Fuel shortage (SRC–80 Sept.)
(Formally balanced version has
same wording as No. 1 but note difference in counterargument.)

If there is a serious fuel shortage this winter, do you think there should be a law requiring people to lower the heat in their homes, or do you oppose such a law because it would be too difficult to enforce?

Should be	39.4%	Should be	26.0%
Oppose	60.6	Oppose a law	74.0[a]
	100		100
	(312)		(339)

$\chi^2 = 13.48$, $df = 1$, $p < .001$

7. Unions (SRC–80 Sept.)
(See No. 2 for wording)

Yes	31.5%	Required	20.4%
Oppose	68.5	Left to Individuals	79.6
	100		100
	(298)		(329)

$\chi^2 = 10.25$, $df = 1$, $p < .01$

8. Gun permits (SRC–76 February)
(See No. 4 for wording)

Favor	75.3%	Favor	68.9%
Oppose	24.7	Interfere too much	31.1
	100		100
	(615)		(585)

$\chi^2 = 6.11$, $df = 1$, $p < .02$

9. Gun permits (SRC–78 Fall)
(See No. 4 for wording)

Favor	70.3%	Favor	62.0%
Oppose	29.7	Interfere too much	38.0
	100		100
	(485)		(471)

$\chi^2 = 7.39$, $df = 1$, $p < .01$

[a] Includes 8.1% who opposed a fuel law but volunteered a different reason.

each case results for the formally balanced version of the same item are included to provide a bench mark for estimating the effect of the added substantive counterargument.

The nine experiments in Table 7.3 all show shifts in the direction of the counterargument, with a median shift of 8% and six of the nine differences significant beyond the .02 level. Five separate surveys are involved here, and the general consistency in results strongly suggests that the effect of a counterargument is reliable and can occur over many types of items. At the same time, some of the differences are quite small (3–4%), as well as nonsignificant, and even the largest difference in the table (13%) is less than effects regularly reported in earlier chapters (e.g., for don't know (DK) filters in Chapter 4).[6] How sizable the differences appear will depend on one's prior expectations, but what does seem evident is that the effects of adding counterarguments are too pervasive and too large to allow the question forms compared in Table 7.3 to be treated as interchangeable, for example, in studies of trends over time.

Several of the more specific results in the table deserve note. First, where exact replications are available (for the fuel-shortage and gun-permit experiments) the size of the effect ranges from the smallest to the largest in the table. Although some of this variation may be due to real changes over time, chance provides a more likely explanation for most of the variation.[7] Second, in the case of the fuel-shortage item, two separate counterarguments are used, and each produces a significant difference. (We compare the two variations more directly below.) Third, one of the smallest effects occurs for the abortion item, where the counterargument is so strong in emotional terms that several of our interviewers objected to asking such a "loaded question." The lack of much effect here is consistent with the assumption that what counts is not crude emotional loading so much as the provision of an argument that respondents may not have thought of before, or thought of in quite the way shown. One cannot place too much weight on this single datum, of

[6]We should note that our experiment on the union item shows a much smaller effect than Noelle-Neumann (1970–1971) reports for a somewhat differently worded item used with a West German sample. Furthermore, whereas the 9% difference for the Union experiment in 1974 is based entirely on a new sample, the 11% difference in 1980 is based on a combined new and reinterview sample (as indicated in Table 1.1) and the new sample taken alone produces only a 4.3% difference.

[7]The small difference reported in Table 7.3 for the fuel-shortage experiment in SRC–74 Fall is directly related to the unexpectedly large difference reported earlier in Table 7.1, since the same 1974 distribution for the formally balanced version appears in both tables and can account for both sets of unexpected results. See Appendix A for further discussion of the 1974 fuel-shortage experiment.

course, given the variation already noted in the table, but a similar lack of effect of obvious "loading" is reported in Chapter 11.

One other general point about counterarguments deserves emphasis. As noted earlier, a difficulty with adding counterarguments to questions is that respondents might want to take the negative side of an issue but not for the reason offered. We did not allow for this possibility in our early experiments, but did do so for the fuel-shortage and union experiments in SRC–80 Sept.—that is, a printed box on the questionnaire instructed interviewers to accept volunteered responses where the negative side of the issue was chosen but for a reason different than the one in the counterargument. The union item yielded only one such respondent out of 346, presumably because the counterargument we offered is almost the only reason for opposing the closed union shop. However, the fuel-shortage item produced 28 such people (about 8%), approximately half of whom mentioned the special heating needs of infants, the aged or the ill, with the rest mentioning individual rights or some other more miscellaneous response. Thus in the case of the fuel-shortage counterargument form, lack of exhaustiveness causes a noticeable problem. Investigators have no way of determining exactly how interviewers handle such responses when a code is not provided, though we assume that they are categorized as negative and treat them that way in Table 7.3. (There is no evidence in earlier experiments that such responses were coded as missing data.) It seems desirable in future use of counterarguments to add regularly such a questionnaire instruction.

Comparing the Content of Counterarguments

We carried out two experiments to determine whether plausible variations in the *content* of the counterargument would affect responses. Using the gun-permit item, we developed in 1977 a counterargument different, and we assumed stronger, than the one about rights of citizens constructed in 1975. Table 7.4 reports an experimental comparison of this new counterargument concerning criminals with the earlier one. It can be seen that there is no evidence that one argument has more impact than the other.

We also compared (in SRC–79 August) the two different counterarguments for the fuel-shortage item that was presented earlier in Table 7.3. In this case one argument does prove significantly stronger than the other: More respondents were persuaded in this 1979 experiment to take the negative side of the issue when the emphasis was on difficulties of enforcement than when it was on individual rights. (The difference be-

TABLE 7.4
Different Counterarguments for the Same Issue

1. Gun permits (SRC-77 February)

Some people favor a law which would re-
quire a person to obtain a police permit before
he could buy a gun. Others oppose such a
law on the grounds that it would interfere
too much with the right of citizens to own
guns. Do you favor or oppose a law that
would require a police permit to buy a gun?

Favor a law	61.6%
Oppose a law	38.4
	100
	(584)

Some people favor a law which would re-
quire a person to obtain a police permit before
he could buy a gun. Others oppose such a
law on the grounds that it would make it
more difficult for honest people to get guns,
*but criminals would **still** manage to get*
them. Do you favor or oppose a law that
would require a police permit to buy a gun?

Favor a law	63.3%
Oppose a law	36.7
	100
	(545)

$$\chi^2 = .33, \ df = 1, \ \text{n.s.}$$

2. Fuel shortage (SRC-79 August)

If there is a serious fuel shortage this winter,
do you think there should be a law requiring
*people to lower the heat in their homes, **or***
do you think this should be left to individual
families to decide?

Should be a law	35.2%
Oppose law	64.8
	100
	(315)

If there is a serious fuel shortage this winter,
do you think there should be a law requiring
*people to lower the heat in their homes, **or***
do you oppose such a law because it would be
too difficult to enforce?

Should be a law	25.5%
Oppose law	74.5
	100
	(329)

$$\chi^2 = 7.20, \ df = 1, \ p < .01$$

tween the two fuel-shortage counterarguments here is greater than the expected differences based on results in Table 7.3, but it is necessary to give more weight to an experimental comparison within a single survey than to a nonexperimental comparison between two surveys taken a year apart.) The finding provides evidence that respondents are influenced by more than explicit mention of a negative side to an issue: The potency of some counterarguments is greater than others, even though all of them are in a sense implicit in the unbalanced or merely formally balanced versions of the item.

Varying the Form of the Counterargument

In one nonexperimental comparison over time (noted in Schuman and Presser, 1977–1978), we found evidence suggesting that a counterargument might produce a stronger effect when presented in the form of *Some people... Other people....* This variant of the earlier counterargument form was therefore tested in a split-ballot experiment in 1977, as shown in Table 7.5A, yielding results of borderline significance ($p < .10$) in the predicted direction. The experiment was repeated in 1978, but this time produced results of borderline significance ($p < .10$) in the opposite direction (Table 7.5B). We are not certain whether these oddly contrary trends are due to chance or to some unidentified context effect, and believe that further experimentation is desirable on the *Some people... Other people* form of presentation in attempts at balancing.

We also explored the possibility that the addition of a counterargument produces a difference not because of its content, but simply because it is added at the end of the question—that what occurs is a recency order effect (as discussed in Chapter 2). This possibility was tested in an experiment in SRC–79 June. The experimental comparison involved the substantively balanced Union item shown in Table 7.3 and a revised version of the same item with the alternatives presented in

TABLE 7.5
Different Forms of the Same Counterargument

A. Gun permits (SRC–77 August)

Would you favor a law which would require a person to obtain a police permit before he could buy a gun, or do you think such a law would interfere too much with the right of citizens to own guns?		*Some people favor a law which would require a person to obtain a police permit before he could buy a gun. Others oppose such a law on the grounds that it would interfere too much with the right of citizens to own guns. Do you favor or oppose a law which would require a police permit to buy a gun?*	
Favor a law	66.5%	Favor a law	61.6%
Law would interfere too much	33.5	Oppose a law	38.4
	100		100
	(588)		(558)

$$\chi^2 = 2.93, \ df = 1, \ p < .10$$

B. Gun permits (SRC–78 August)
   (See above for wording)

Favor a law	58.3%	Favor a law	63.5%
Law would interfere too much	41.7	Oppose a law	36.5
	100		100
	(533)		(543)

$$\chi^2 = 3.04, \ df = 1, \ p < .10$$

Three-way interaction (response × form × survey): $\chi^2 = 5.97, \ df = 1, \ p < .02$

reversed order. The marginal difference does not approach significance and in fact is in the direction opposite to that predicted in terms of a recency hypothesis (see Table 2-16). Thus there is no indication that the effect of a substantive counterargument is due to its placement in the question. Evidence for recency order effects presented in Chapter 2 is strong enough to require that the issue be left somewhat open, but we doubt that such order effects play an important role in the kinds of balance experiments described here.[8]

THE SEARCH FOR THOSE AFFECTED
BY COUNTERARGUMENTS

Education, Information, and Other
Background Variables

We saw in Table 7.3 a set of small but quite likely real effects of counterarguments on univariate distributions. Our expectation was that the effects would be greatest on individuals for whom such counterarguments were not already clearly implicit in the original question. Such people we assumed to be disproportionately less educated and less informed about public issues. Since education is the variable ordinarily available in surveys, we employ it in Table 7.6, but generally similar conclusions are drawn if an information measure (see Appendix C) is substituted.

The evidence for an interaction between question form, education, and response is strongest for the gun-permit experiments. For the formally balanced version of this item, education is essentially unrelated to response in each of the three surveys. (This conclusion is further supported by separate analysis of essentially the same formally balanced gun item in NORC General Social Survey data pooled from 1975, 1976, and 1977: gamma is .04 and nonsignificant, based on 4391 cases.) However, for two of our three parallel versions containing a counter-

---

[8]One further variation in wording that we considered was to state the substantive alternative more clearly as a cause for saying no. The gun-permit item on the right side of Table 7.3 was included in one form of a split-ballot in SRC–80 Feb., and in the other form the wording of the second alternative was altered to read: *or would you oppose such a law because you think it would interfere too much.* . . . The change made no difference, with 36.2% opposing gun permits on the originally worded form and 36.9% in opposition on the modified form.

argument, education is positively and significantly related to an affirmative response and the third shows a similar trend. The three-way interaction of form, education, and response reaches significance in only one survey (SRC–78 Fall), but the results are consistent over the three experiments. An interpretation of the interaction emerges most clearly if one notes that the less-educated respondents move in the direction of the counterargument, whereas the college educated are virtually unaffected by the addition of the argument.

The fuel-shortage item in 1974 also produced some evidence of an

TABLE 7.6
Percentage Giving Negative Response by Education and Form[a]

	Formal Balance			Substantive Counterargument		
	Education			Education		
	0–11	12	13+	0–11	12	13+
1. Fuel shortage (SRC–74 Fall)	61.1% (149)	74.4% (156)	75.4% (187)	71.6% (155)	77.8% (167)	72.3% (155)
	gamma = −.22, SE = .08, p < .01			gamma = −.01, SE = .08, n.s.		
	Three-way interaction: $\chi^2 = 3.36$, $df = 1$, $p < .10$					
2. Fuel shortage (SRC–78 Fall)	59.4% (101)	60.0% (170)	66.7% (210)	71.2% (111)	73.3% (176)	79.3% (198)
	gamma = −.12, SE = .08, n.s.			gamma = −.15, SE = .08, p < .10		
	Three-way interaction: $\chi^2 = .12$, $df = 1$, n.s.					
3. Fuel shortage (SRC–80 Sept.)	60.7% (61)	62.9% (97)	60.3% (146)	66.7% (66)	76.9% (117)	76.4% (144)
	gamma = −.02, SE = .10, n.s.			gamma = .12, SE = .11, n.s.		
	Three-way interaction: $\chi^2 = 1.21$, $df = 1$, n.s.					
4. Unions (SRC–74 Fall)	47.9% (140)	69.2% (156)	83.0% (182)	67.3% (150)	74.5% (165)	88.2% (153)
	gamma = −.50, SE = .06, p < .001			gamma = −.38, SE = .08, p < .001		
	Three-way interaction: $\chi^2 = .89$, $df = 1$, n.s.					
5. Unions (SRC–80 Sept.)	58.3% (60)	59.8% (92)	79.0% (138)	71.0% (62)	77.6% (116)	86.2% (138)
	gamma = −.35, SE = .09, p < .001			gamma = −.30, SE = .11, p < .01		
	Three-way interaction: $\chi^2 = .01$, $df = 1$, n.s.					

(continued)

TABLE 7.6—*Continued*

	Formal Balance			Substantive Counterargument		
	Education			Education		
	0–11	12	13+	0–11	12	13+
6. Abortion	56.3%	30.1%	23.3%	55.6%	39.6%	25.4%
(SRC–75 Feb.)	(103)	(163)	(172)	(99)	(164)	(169)
	gamma = .42, SE = .07,			gamma = .39, SE = .07,		
		$p < .001$			$p < .001$	
	Three-way interaction: χ^2 = .16, df = 1, n.s.					
7. Gun permits	30.1%	28.4%	27.4%	37.5%	36.1%	26.6%
(SRC–75 Feb.)	(103)	(162)	(179)	(96)	(166)	(169)
	gamma = .04, SE = .09,			gamma = .17, SE = .08,		
		n.s.			$p < .05$	
	Three-way interaction: χ^2 = .92, df = 1, n.s.					
8. Gun permits	27.3%	22.5%	24.7%	34.3%	32.4%	28.2%
(SRC–76 Feb.)	(172)	(204)	(239)	(137)	(210)	(238)
	gamma = .04, SE = .08, n.s.			gamma = .10, SE = .07, n.s.		
	Three-way interaction: χ^2 = .21, df = 1, n.s.					
9. Gun permits	28.0%	33.9%	28.2%	47.6%	41.3%	29.6%
(SRC–78 Fall)	(100)	(168)	(209)	(105)	(172)	(189)
	gamma = .03, SE = .08,			gamma = .25, SE = .07,		
		n.s.			$p < .001$	
	Three-way interaction: χ^2 = 4.46, df = 1, $p < .05$					

[a] All χ^2 results in this table test the three-way interaction of response, form, and education, with the latter treated as a linear variable. Df = 1 in all cases.

education–response difference by form. Although in this case a negative relation to education on the formal version disappeared when a counterargument was introduced, the interpretation could be essentially the same as for the gun-permit experiments, since the difference is produced by the movement of the less educated. But on replication in 1978 and 1980, this interaction for the fuel-shortage item was not obtained, leaving the 1974 result uncertain—perhaps unique to that point in time or perhaps due to sampling error.

Education is not implicated in form differences for the union or abortion experiments. In the case of abortion, there was only a small and nonsignificant effect of the counterargument on marginals (Table 7.3), and the inclusion of education as a third variable similarly fails to reveal an effect for the least educated (Table 7.6). In the case of the union item, the relatively large overall effect in Table 7.3 turns out to occur equally for both high- and low-educated persons in Table 7.6. Thus, low education cannot be considered a factor that invariably creates susceptibility to influence by counterarguments.

In addition to these hypothesized interactions involving education, we also examined possible interactions involving age, sex, and race for the four items, but found none reliable or consistent enough to bear reporting.[9] The experimental comparison of two different counterarguments on the fuel question in Table 7.4, however, does show interesting interactions with sex, age, and education, though in this case no unbalanced or formally balanced form is available for contrast. The difference in Table 7.4 turns out to be due almost entirely to a much higher proportion of men accepting the "enforcement" counterargument (79.7%) than accept the "families decide" counterargument (62.6%); for women the difference is slight (69.7% to 67.8%) and the three-way interaction of sex, form, and response is significant ($\chi^2 = 4.72$, $df = 1$, $p < .05$).[10] The appeal of the enforcement counterargument for the fuel item is also significantly greater for our middle-age category (31–50 years) than for either younger or older persons, and it appears to be stronger for the more- than the less-educated. The latter trend, though not quite borderline (for the linear trend, $p = .11$), suggests that the *content* of a counterargument may be a factor in determining which educational level is affected; thus our original hypothesis that less-educated persons would *always* be influenced by counterarguments was incorrect. This, of course, fits the varying findings for different items in Table 7.6, since education is sometimes implicated and sometimes not.

Interitem Correlations

Next we considered the possibility that associations between two attitude items might be stronger on one question form than another, on the hypothesis that the tendency to be affected by counterarguments, whatever its source, should operate across items. But no such three-way

---

[9]A further hypothesis was investigated for the union item, namely that union members would be less affected by form variations than nonmembers, but the evidence does not support this proposition.

[10]A similar borderline trend occurs for the gun-permit item, with men affected more by the counterargument dealing with enforcement than by the counterargument concerned with constitutional rights. The three-way interaction in this case is borderline ($p < .10$). Perhaps the pragmatic emphasis on enforcement in both experiments has particular appeal to men.

interactions occur in the four surveys that included pairs of experiments available for testing.

There is, however, one suggestive piece of evidence along these lines. In SRC-78 November and December, we asked respondents whether they favored or opposed congressional passage of the Agriculture Trade Act of 1978—an issue deliberately selected for its obscurity to all respondents (see Chapter 5). For those persons who claimed to have an opinion on the Trade Act (about 20% of the total sample), favoring the act is positively associated with favoring the fuel law on the combined *unbalanced and formally balanced* forms of the fuel question (χ^2 = 10.66, *df* = 1, *p* < .01). The association can be interpreted as reflecting a more general attitude of confidence or lack of confidence in government actions (for which we presented other evidence in our analysis of Trade Act responses in Chapter 5). However, there is a nonsignificant association in the opposite direction between Trade Act responses and the fuel question when the counterargument form of the latter is used (χ^2 = 1.60, *df* = 1), suggesting that the people who created the original positive association are exactly those who are influenced to switch sides by the counterargument. (The three-way interaction of Trade Act response by fuel response by fuel form is χ^2 = 7.46, *df* = 1, *p* < .01.) Thus, in this special instance, the degree of balance in the fuel item appears to affect critically the correlation of the item with another attitude question.[11]

Counterarguments and Attitude Strength

Who are the people who are influenced when a counterargument is added to a question? We have seen that in some cases it is the least educated, in other cases men, and so forth. The specificity of each of these interactions leaves us still searching for some general characteristic that produces the shifts toward counterarguments shown to some degree for all the items in Table 7.3.

One other hypothesis that seemed plausible was that persons reporting little strength of feeling on a specific issue would shift most readily when confronted with a counterargument, since they had little prior commitment to a position and would be most open to persuasion. It might be argued, however, that such persons would not pay enough attention to a question to be influenced by the counterargument, and

[11]Since most of those giving an opinion on the Agricultural Trade Act were floaters, as described in Chapters 4 and 5, it seemed at first as though floaters might be the specific source of shifting in balance experiments. Further analysis indicates, however, that the association described in the text is due primarily to the small set of persons who give an opinion on the Trade Act on *both* filtered and standard question forms.

that it is persons with enough interest to have an opinion who would be subject to persuasion by a sensible counterargument. These two points of view can be put together to generate still a third, curvilinear hypothesis: Those expected to change will be a middle group that is just interested enough to pay attention to the counterargument, but not so intensely involved in the issue as to resist persuasion.[12]

In three different experiments with the gun-permit item there is no clear support for any of these hypotheses. None of the relevant interactions is significant, and trends are contradictory. Only in these cases did our attitude strength measures have three or more categories and thus allow a test of the curvilinear hypothesis, but at least for the Gun-Permit item there is no evidence at all for it. Using a more behavioral dichotomous measure of strength (described in Chapter 9), there is a trend for those showing more involvement in the issue to reveal least change, but it does not approach significance. The union item also produces a similar trend in relation to a specific strength measure in both 1974 and 1980, but it does not approach significance in either year separately, nor in both years combined ($\chi^2 = 1.40$, $df = 1$, n.s.).

In sum, the slight trends we noted above may indicate that strength of conviction on an issue has a very small effect on susceptibility to influence by a counterargument—indeed, it is hard to believe that the most highly committed persons on an issue are as easily swayed as others—but if so, it is too tiny to be readily detected here. Yet we will see in Chapter 10 that attitude strength on specific issues is significantly related to the reduction of random response error. Thus it is random shifts, but not systematic shifts, that are a function of attitude strength about specific issues. This is a striking conclusion, but it fits a number of results in this book.

The strength measures dealt with thus far have all concerned conviction about particular issues. However, the SRC 1974–75 panel data also included three questions intended as indicators of generalized attitude strength: interest in the news, liking to argue about public issues, and self-reported general strength of opinion. When these are used both singly and as a set to specify counterargument effects there are some trends for those reporting weaker generalized attitude strength to reveal greater evidence of change. Although we at first created an index of the three indicators combined, both initial analysis and later replications showed that the Arguing question alone was as successful in specifying the effects of counterarguments as the more complex index, and we use

---

[12]All the indicators of specific and general attitude strength noted in the following paragraphs are discussed more fully in Chapters 9 and 10, with exact wordings given in Table 10.2.

TABLE 7.7
Percentage Giving Negative Response by Arguing and Form[a]

	Formal balance		Substantive counterargument	
	Like to argue	Dislike arguing	Like to argue	Dislike arguing
Unions	78.3%	64.8%	73.4%	81.9%
	(106)	(182)	(94)	(226)
	gamma = − .32, SE = .13,		gamma = .24, SE = .14,	
	p < .01		p < .10	
	Three-way interaction: $\chi^2 = 8.27$, $df = 1$, $p < .01$			
Fuel shortage	60.0%	62.1%	76.3%	73.9%
	(110)	(190)	(97)	(234)
	gamma = .04, SE = .12, n.s.		gamma = .06, SE = .14, n.s.	
	Three-way interaction: $\chi^2 = .33$, $df = 1$, n.s.			

[a] From SRC–80 Sept.

it to present the remaining results in this chapter. The item is also intuitively meaningful since it deals directly with willingness to resist arguments:

> Some people like to argue about public issues. Other people dislike arguing about public issues. In general, which kind of person would you say you're closer to?

Over the three surveys in which we have used the question, about a third of the respondents say they like to argue about public issues.

Of the four main balance experimental items we have been dealing with in this chapter, only unions showed a statistically significant effect in 1974 due to the Arguing indicator (the three-way interaction of union response by question form by Arguing was: $\chi^2 = 4.32$, $df = 1$, $p < .05$); the trends for the other experiments were too small and unreliable to be of importance taken alone. In SRC–80 September we repeated the union experiment and the Arguing indicator to test the replicability of the 1974 result, and included also a fuel-shortage experiment to test further the generality of the result. Both sets of 1980 data are presented in Table 7.7.

The earlier finding for the union item replicates nicely: All of the effect of the counterargument occurs among those who dislike arguing; those who like to argue show a slight boomerang tendency.[13] However, the

[13]This result is further specified when education is introduced, with arguing having its largest effect among high-educated respondents. The four-way interaction of union response by form by Arguing by education is significant (linear $\chi^2 = 4.71$, $df = 1$, $p < .05$).

fuel-shortage item does not reproduce this specification at all, which indicates that the effect of Arguing for the union question is not a general one. (Arguing had also been included with a gun-permit balance experiment in SRC–76 February, and also failed to specify that counterargument effect.) Together with the other uncertain or negative results in earlier years, the 1980 data suggest that the effect of Arguing, and of general attitude strength indicators more broadly, is tied to some particular content of the union item and does not provide a more general answer to the question of who it is that counterarguments influence. In this sense, the effect of arguing, like that of education, turns out to be much less general in implication than we expected initially on the grounds of theory or of first results.

CONCLUDING DISCUSSION

On the basis of almost 20 experiments with 5 survey items, we can draw several conclusions about the effects of balance and imbalance in the wording of attitude questions. First, it appears to make little, if any, difference whether an item is formally balanced or imbalanced in the sense of adding "oppose" or similar terms to questions that already clearly imply the possibility of a negative alternative. Although this conclusion has limited practical significance for current question construction—it is easy enough and probably sensible to provide formal balance to most new questions—it does have import for analysis of past data. Analysts have sometimes been uncertain about comparing results from questions that are alike except for differences in formal balance. Our evidence suggests that such comparisons can be made safely. Equally important is the theoretical point that not every variation in question form affects results. Such effects certainly do occur, but they are not inevitable each time a word is altered in a question.

Second, when substantive counterarguments are added in support of one side of a question, there is a shift of some respondents in the direction of the argument. The shift is not massive—it ranges from 4 to 13 percentage points in our experiments—but it is not trivial either. One needs to take it into account in comparing univariate responses from such an item with responses from a form that does not include the accompanying counterargument.

Third, there is evidence that particular counterarguments appeal to particular types of persons defined demographically. A counterargument on the gun-permit issue seemed to be especially attractive to less-educated respondents; and among two counterarguments on the fuel-shortage issue, one showed greater appeal than the other to men, but not to women. These specific interactions would lead an investigator to draw different conclusions about relationships depending on which form of a question is employed. It is important to note, however, that such interactions are not pervasive, and in most of the instances we examined, the counterargument form of a question does not yield significantly different relations with other variables than does a formally balanced version of the question.

Fourth, it seems plausible to expect persons having no strong feelings on an issue to be especially susceptible to arguments and counterarguments that are built into the wording of the question. Chapter 10 shows that attitude strength increases consistency of response when an unbalanced or formally balanced form of a question is given at time 1 and a counterargument form is given to the same respondents several months later at time 2. But the increase in consistency is due largely or entirely to reduction in random error, *not* to reduction in the question-form effect. Moreover, although there is evidence that a more generalized attitude strength trait affects susceptibility to a counterargument for one particular item (unions), the effect does not generalize to other items. Attitude strength, like education and information, is not a general explanatory variable for systematic effects due to addition of a counterargument.

These conclusions leave unsettled the issue of whether to add counterarguments to questions, even though they do seem to resolve the simpler issue of lack of balance versus formal balance. The advice sometimes given to add counterarguments appears to arise partly from a belief that the usual unbalanced or merely formally balanced item leans too much in the affirmative direction and thereby invites an affirmative response. In addition, proponents of balance through counterarguments believe that such questions are more complete, reflecting the controversy that goes on around most issues, and that therefore responses are apt to be more meaningful and more stable (Noelle-Neumann, 1970–1971; Roll and Cantril, 1980). On the other side, Hedges (1979) has recently suggested that many questions have no appropriate counterarguments and that attempts to create counterarguments often lead to bias or confusion in the question. Although we do not entirely agree with Hedges, it is true that most questions do not have a *single* counterargument, and therefore when one is introduced the respondent's attention is usually focused in a more specific way than when the negative side is indicated only by an expression creating formal balance. In this sense, counterarguments tend to create new questions, not simply more balanced versions of previous questions.

There is a larger issue that deserves more explicit treatment at this point. Some researchers believe that almost all unbalanced or even formally balanced questions are susceptible to an acquiescence bias, so that there is some general tendency toward agreement apart from content. The evidence in this chapter seemed to us not to support such a view, since neither formal balancing nor shifting to a *Some people.... Other people...* format had systematic effects in reducing agreement. Moreover, the finding that the content of a counterargument influences its effectiveness indicates that counterarguments do more than merely break an acquiescence set—they create definite influence toward the negative side. Yet this latter evidence is based largely on a single experiment, which needs to be replicated and extended across a range of items, and the other evidence is also far from decisive. At this point the issue must be regarded as unresolved.

The point is more than narrowly methodological, for it concerns a fundamental uncertainty about responses to survey questions: Do mechanical sets such as acquiescence play an important role, or are people mainly influenced by the content of words and arguments? Agree–disagree statements provide a special case of unbalanced question forms, and one that raises this larger issue in a different way. The next chapter is devoted to this problem, and toward the end of it we return briefly to the possible link between such statements and more general survey questions. The results, though quite tentative, are surprising.

8

The Acquiescence Quagmire

> Hamlet: Do you see yonder cloud that's almost in shape
> of a camel?
> Polonius: By th' mass, and tis like a camel indeed.
> Hamlet: Methinks it is like a weasel.
> Polonius: It is back'd like a weasel.
> Hamlet: Or like a whale.
> Polonius: Very like a whale.
>   —*Hamlet* (III, ii)

Acquiescence, or *agreeing-response bias,* refers to a presumed tendency for respondents to agree with attitude statements presented to them.[1] Some investigators assume acquiescence also extends to yes/no attitude questions (e.g., Jackman, 1973), but virtually all of the research in this area deals only with assertions that the respondent is asked to agree or disagree with. We concentrate on the latter, but the distinction or lack of distinction is important, and we consider it at a later point.

Unlike most of the issues dealt with in this book, the study of acquiescence has produced a large research literature, mainly within psychology where scales composed of attitude statements are much more common than in general population surveys. The possibility of an agreeing-response bias was anticipated by Likert as early as 1932, but the major outflow of social psychological research grew from criticism that the F scale (Adorno, Frenkel-Brunswik, Levinson, and Sanford, 1950) confounded content with acquiescence. The present chapter can neither review this large literature nor resolve the controversies, but will con-

[1]The terms acquiescence, agreeing-response bias, and yeasaying are sometimes given different meanings, but the differences are not widely accepted and are not distinguished here. We use "bias" rather than "set" or "style" because it is the most descriptive term in the context of this book and also because it does not raise other problems that Rorer (1965) discusses. We also accept in principle Rorer's sharp distinction of acquiescence from social desirability, the latter involving respondent–interviewer interaction not specifically related to question form, but there are aspects of the deference hypothesis (discussed later) where the two overlap.

sider conceptions of acquiescence that are especially relevant to national surveys and provide new evidence bearing on them. We will see that the evidence is not simple and must warn the reader that this is an especially difficult chapter.

THEORETICAL EXPLANATIONS
OF ACQUIESCENCE

There are three different interpretations of the nature of agreeing-response bias—all of which of course assume that it exists. Most psychologists who emphasize the importance of the phenomenon regard acquiescence as a personality trait. As such, it can be studied like any other personality trait, and some psychologists have indeed claimed that it reflects "a central personality syndrome [Couch and Keniston, 1960]." This view has been challenged forcefully by Rorer (1965) and others, and the dominant view in psychology today is probably represented by Nunnally's (1978) statement that:

> The overwhelming weight of the evidence now points to the fact that the agreement tendency is of very little importance either as a measure of personality or as a source of systematic invalidity in measures of personality and sentiments [p. 669].

A less extreme view is the conclusion by Campbell, Siegman, and Rees (1967) that acquiescence is of some importance, but that it contributes much less to covariation between items than does content.

The other two interpretations of acquiescence come more directly out of survey research, and one or the other or some combination has gained wide acceptance among attitude survey investigators, especially sociologists. Both interpretations arise from the fact that national surveys entail personal interviewing of samples heterogeneous in education and social status, as against psychological studies that apply self-administered questionnaires to samples of college students. For psychologists, neither education nor interviewer–respondent interaction is ordinarily a meaningful variable, but for survey investigators both loom large as possible sources of response.

One of the survey-based interpretations, first advanced by Lenski and Leggett (1960) and later developed by Carr (1971), characterizes acquiescence as a form of deference shown by low-status respondents, especially black respondents, toward a largely white middle-class interviewing staff. The other interpretation is described by Campbell, Converse,

Miller, and Stokes (1960: 513) as the "tendency for poorly educated people to be uncritical of sweeping statements and to be 'suggestible' where inadequate frames of reference are available. . . ." This latter reasoning fits Hyman and Sheatsley's (1954) early criticism of F-scale scores as heavily influenced by education (although they did not put their criticism in terms of acquiescence), and it also informs Jackman's (1973) critique of Lipset's (1960) thesis of "working class authoritarianism."

Although both of these interpretations hypothesize an inverse association between education and acquiescence, they imply different dynamics: The Campbell *et al.* line of thought points to limited cognitive abilities, which should probably operate in self-administered as well as interview situations; the Lenski and Leggett explanation focuses specifically on interviewer–respondent interaction and regards education as simply one indicator of social status. We are not aware of any attempt to put the two interpretations in direct competition, nor are they of course mutually exclusive. Deference to interviewers, for example, could heighten the tendency to be uncritical of statements they read.

Often implicit in hypotheses about the susceptibility of low-educated respondents to acquiescence is the assumption that such persons are more apt to lack true attitudes on issues presented to them. This point is also related to two further assumptions in the psychological literature (Peabody, 1961). First, acquiescence is frequently assumed to be a way for a respondent to handle a question to which he or she has no real answer; that is, the agreeing form is perceived to provide a cue to an appropriate answer where one would otherwise simply respond on a chance basis. This is only an assumption, of course, and it is certainly possible that acquiescence sometimes involves the replacement of a real (and disagreeing) response by an agreeing one. The second assumption is that acquiescence will be greatest on items that are vague, ambiguous, or otherwise difficult to answer (as with Hamlet's cloud) and will therefore decrease or even disappear entirely as questions are seen by respondents to be clear and meaningful in terms of previously crystallized attitudes (see Chapter 10 for a discussion of crystallization). This is a difficult assumption to test, since we lack ready measures of question clarity and ambiguity. Moreover, what seems clear to less sophisticated respondents may seem hopelessly unclear to those who are more sophisticated, and vice versa. The difficulty of testing this assumption, and the uncertainty of the previous one, gives some indication of why acquiescence is a more complicated concept than casual use of the term might suggest.

What needs to be emphasized, however, is that Nunnally's (1978) dismissal of the importance of acquiescence in psychological investigations is not incompatible with the assumption of survey researchers that acquiescence is quite important in survey data. The phenomenon could play a dominant role in interviewing educationally heterogeneous populations, yet disappear entirely when student samples and self-administered questionnaires are employed.

MEASUREMENT PROBLEMS

All interpretations of acquiescence are based on the assumption that the phenomenon itself can be clearly demonstrated. Such demonstrations require presenting the same content in different question forms that are not susceptible to the same kind of acquiescence. When this is attempted, however, as by "reversing" items, a skeptical reader can usually argue with some persuasiveness that the two forms are not really complete reversals (that is, it is logically possible to agree to both or else to disagree to both), or indeed that the content itself has been changed substantially in the newly created items (see Rorer, 1965, for examples and further discussion). Thus the failure of the two forms to correlate substantially in the direction expected in terms of content may not unequivocally demonstrate a type of inconsistency attributable to acquiescence.

Consider the "pair of mutually contradictory statements" used by Lenski and Leggett (1960):

1. It is hardly fair to bring children into the world, the way things look for the future.
2. Children born today have a wonderful future to look forward to.

It is apparent that these items are not completely contradictory, since it is quite reasonable to disagree with both of them. So it is only double agreement that can be argued to be inconsistent. Lenski and Leggett report that such double agreement was not common (8% for their sample of 624), but that it increased with lower education and for blacks relative to whites. However, some of the 8% was doubtless due to unreliability of response, which also might increase with lower education, and the authors offer no way to distinguish systematic error such as acquiescence from random error due to "guessing." Thus the entire 8% of double agreement could conceivably represent unreliability—not acquiescence.

It turns out to be extraordinarily difficult to construct items that avoid the problems just discussed, and our own attempts have failed time and again when looked at critically. We shall present in some detail the one effort that seems to hold up best and on which we have unusually rich data, one other that is interesting and in which we have some but lesser confidence, and then note briefly a number of others that are suggestive of the difficulties this whole area presents.

INDIVIDUALS VERSUS SOCIAL CONDITIONS

Our key item, adapted slightly from Gallup (October, 1970), is:

Which in your opinion is more to blame for crime and lawlessness in this country—individuals or social conditions? [2]

In this form the item precludes acquiescence, since the two alternatives (individuals or social conditions) are presented in a balanced forced-choice format. Nevertheless, it might be subject to a response-order effect: One alternative might be chosen more frequently because it is read first (a primacy effect) or last (a recency effect). We tested this possibility in a split-ballot experiment in SRC-78 December, with the order of the choices reversed on one form (social conditions or individuals) from that given above. The difference due to order does not approach significance: *individuals* was selected by 43.4% of the sample ($N = 309$) when it came first and by 44.7% (of $N = 159$) when it came second, with complementary percentages for *social conditions* ($\chi^2 = .07$, $df = 1$). Thus we assume that the item is essentially balanced, and that although choices may be made either on substantive grounds or on a chance basis, in neither case should they reflect either an acquiescence or a response-order effect.

It is possible to convert this forced-choice item directly into two agree–disagree statements that are essentially contradictories, as shown in Table 8.1. This provides three forms of the question, which should logically produce identical results in terms of content. (The one qualification is that a person might want to consider individuals and social conditions as exactly equal causes of crime and lawlessness, and therefore reject either of the agree–disagree forms without implying acceptance of the other. Not much evidence for this coin-on-edge possibility appeared in our experiments with the item, including results from an open-ended

[2] The Gallup item uses the word "society" rather than "social conditions." We made the change because the latter seemed to us somewhat simpler.

TABLE 8.1
Individuals versus Social Conditions Item by Question Form

Form A[a] (agree I's version):   *Individuals are more to blame than social conditions for crime and lawlessness in this country.*
Form B[a] (agree SCs version):   *Social conditions are more to blame than individuals for crime and lawlessness in this country.*
Form C (forced-choice version):   *Which in your opinion is more to blame for crime and lawlessness in this country—individuals or social conditions?*

	Form A (Agree I's)	Form B (Agree SCs)	Form C (Forced-choice)		Comparison[b]	χ^2	p
SRC–74 Fall	Agree (I): 59.6% Disagree (SC): 40.4 ———— 100 (473)	Agree (SC): 56.8% Disagree (I): 43.2 ———— 100 (472)	I: 46.4% SC: 53.6 ———— 100 (448)		A versus B A versus C B versus C	25.55 16.12 .96	.001 .001 n.s.
SRC–76 Feb.	(Form A not included in SRC–76 Feb.)	Agree (SC): 56.7% Disagree (I): 43.3 ———— 100 (591)	I: 45.6% SC: 54.4 ———— 100 (568)		B versus C	.61	n.s.
SRC–78 Oct.–Nov.	Agree (I): 59.4% Disagree (SC): 40.6 ———— 100 (527)	Agree (SC): 50.9% Disagree (I): 49.1 ———— 100 (226)	(Form C not included in SRC– 78 Oct.–Nov.)		A versus B	6.76	.01

[a] Forms A and B each began with the following introduction: *Please tell me whether you agree or disagree with this statement:*
[b] All significance levels reported in this table test the hypothesis that the proportion choosing the individuals response on one form is the same as the proportion choosing the individuals response on a different form. All tests have $df = 1$.

follow-up "why" question to be discussed below.)[3] In later references we shall refer to the three versions, in the order given in Table 8.1, as the *agree I's, agree SCs,* and *forced-choice* forms. Two of the forms should be susceptible to acquiescence, but in opposite directions, and the third should be immune to this bias.

It is possible of course that the individuals versus social conditions (I–SC) item is not one that in content or tone of wording elicits acquiescence. F-scale items tend to be emotionally more loaded and multifaceted, but the I–SC item nevertheless contains the kind of broad generalization that investigators ordinarily worry about as susceptible to agreeing-response bias. A distinction can be drawn between concrete issues (e.g., gun permits, legalization of abortion) and generalizations of the individuals versus social conditions kind. The former, no matter how difficult, are real issues that often must be resolved in legislative terms. The latter, on the other hand, are in reality impossible questions, which fortunately do not ever have to be answered in a simple sense in the real world. Such questions are certainly important—in this case dealing with a basic problem of attribution theory, whether blame for social problems is directed toward individuals or society—but in surveys they are usually intended as measures of ideology or personality, rather than of issue positions.

Results

All three versions of the I–SC item were included in a tripartite split-ballot experiment in 1974, and two of the forms were replicated in 1976 and two in 1978. All these comparisons are presented in Table 8.1.

Cross-Sectional Results

If only the two agree–disagree forms (A and B) in 1974 were available, the evidence for acquiescence at the univariate level would be straightforward. In both cases a clear majority chooses the agree response, although logically if a majority agrees on one form the same proportion (allowing for sampling error) should *dis*agree on the other

[3]Across the three forms (A, B, C) of the question shown in Table 8.1, 2.7%, 1.0%, and 3.5% were coded as having spontaneously said "both" or some similar middle position in 1974. Based on the experiments reported in Chapter 6, these figures could almost certainly be raised by making such an alternative explicit; the evidence in that chapter does not suggest that such an increase would make a difference in our analysis here, but the point would be well worth testing. "Don't know" responses ranged from 3.7–4.6% on the three items in Table 8.1. "Both" and DK responses have been omitted from all tables in this chapter.

form. But this acquiescence interpretation, at least at a simple level, suggests that responses to the forced-choice form should fall between the other two forms. This is not the case, however, for form C is statistically indistinguishable in univariate distribution from form B, although it is significantly distinguishable from form A. If we assume that form C provides the most valid picture of the true response distribution for the item—since acquiescence is removed, leaving only some mixture of substantive choice and chance answering—then form B, which produces essentially the same distribution, can also be said to be unaffected by acquiescence.

Thus acquiescence is clearly visible in one instance but not in another when the two agree–disagree forms are compared with the forced-choice form. Moreover, the replication data in Table 8.1 for 1976 and 1978 are on the whole quite consistent with the 1974 results and provide further evidence that forms B and C produce similar distributions in terms of content, but that form A differs significantly from both. (The apparent difference for form B in 1978 from form B in the earlier years does not reach $p = .10$.)[4]

Panel Results

Approximately 5 months after the SRC–74 Fall survey, all possible respondents were reinterviewed in SRC–75 February (see Table 1.1 for sample details). The panel design for the individuals–social conditions question was as follows, using three random subsamples:[5]

	Original form (1974)	Reinterview form (1975)
Subsample A:	Agree I's version	Agree SCs version
Subsample B:	Agree SCs version	Agree I's version
Subsample C:	Forced-choice version	Forced-choice version

[4]In one attempt to resolve these disparate results, we considered the possibility of a response order effect involving the agree and disagree alternatives themselves. A split-ballot in SRC–80 Feb. included the usual Agree I's version (Table 8.1) and another version identical except that respondents were asked: *Please tell me whether you disagree or agree with this statement* ... The percentage choosing "disagree" was exactly the same (41%) regardless of whether it was read first or last.

[5]Ordinarily we apply the term "form" to both a question version and the part of the questionnaire on which it appears. This is not possible with these panel data, since the same subsample received different question forms at different times. In these cases, form or version continues to refer to questions, and we use "subsample" to refer to the random subsample to which one or more question forms were administered.

Thus, the original forms of the A and B questions were simply switched on reinterview, whereas form C was repeated as an exact replication. The results are shown in Table 8.2.

All three subtables reveal significant consistency according to content, although the consistency is only moderate in degree. The forced-choice form shows higher consistency than the other two forms, but since the forced-choice was an exact replication, whereas the other two involved switched agree–disagree forms, one should not conclude that the forced-choice version shows greater consistency over time than would an exactly repeated agree–disagree form. Indeed, there is reason to expect acquiescence bias to increase response reliability over time if form is held constant, though we are unable to test this point.

Of primary interest are the cells that are inconsistent in terms of content. In subsample C these two cells are approximately equal in size (McNemar's χ^2_m does not approach significance), and they are best viewed as providing an estimate of unreliability of response when the item is repeated several months later.[6] (We assume that any true change is trivial, a plausible assumption that is supported by the nearly identical marginals at the two time points.) The average of these two cells is 14.2% and provides our best estimate of the amount of random measurement error occurring in each of the four cells in this subtable.

The inconsistent cells for the other two subsamples (A and B) offer evidence that acquiescence occurred for these cases. The agree–agree (AA) cell in each of the two subtables is more than twice the size of the disagree–disagree (DD) cell, and McNemar's χ^2_m is highly significant in each case. Our estimate of the proportion of acquiescent respondents depends in part on how we interpret the DD cell. If this cell is assumed to represent random error, then we should probably assume that about the same amount of random error (9.9%, the average of the two DD cells) occurs in all cells in samples A and B, and subtract that amount from the average of the two agree–agree cells (25.6%) in order to arrive at an estimate of acquiescence of 15.7% of the sample. However, if we assume that DD responses represent real choices, either because of genuine disagreement with both forms or because of a naysaying bias, then we might likewise assume that all or most of the 25.6% in the AA cells is also non-random and represents acquiescence. Having no basis for deciding between these two extremes, we will simply estimate that the percentage of acquiescent responses to the agree–disagree versions

[6]McNemar's (1969, p. 261) calculation using χ^2 can be regarded here as a test of the null hypothesis that the cells inconsistent in terms of content are equal in size, or, equivalently, that the time one and the time two marginals are the same. For sample C, the corresponding ratio (I–SC cell to SC–I cell) should not (and does not) differ significantly from 1.0, since acquiescence has been eliminated.

TABLE 8.2
Individuals–Social Conditions Panel Data[a]

Subsample A: Response to agree SCs form (1975) by response to agree I's form (1974)

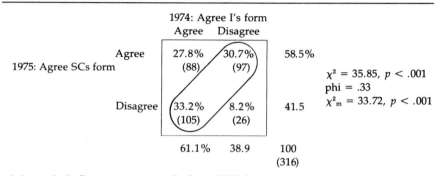

		1974: Agree I's form		
		Agree	Disagree	
1975: Agree SCs form	Agree	27.8% (88)	30.7% (97)	58.5%
	Disagree	33.2% (105)	8.2% (26)	41.5
		61.1%	38.9	100 (316)

$\chi^2 = 35.85, p < .001$
phi $= .33$
$\chi^2_m = 33.72, p < .001$

Subsample B: Response to agree I's form (1975) by response to agree SCs form (1974)

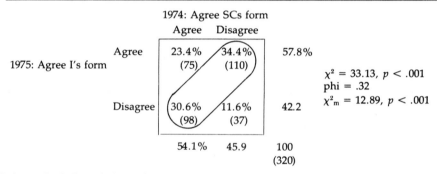

		1974: Agree SCs form		
		Agree	Disagree	
1975: Agree I's form	Agree	23.4% (75)	34.4% (110)	57.8%
	Disagree	30.6% (98)	11.6% (37)	42.2
		54.1%	45.9	100 (320)

$\chi^2 = 33.13, p < .001$
phi $= .32$
$\chi^2_m = 12.89, p < .001$

Subsample C: Forced-choice (I–SC) by forced-choice (I–SC)

		1974		
		I	SC	
1975	I	29.9% (93)	12.9% (40)	42.8%
	SC	15.4% (48)	41.8% (130)	57.2
		45.3%	54.7	100 (311)

$\chi^2 = 58.25, p < .001$
phi $= .43$
$\chi^2_m = .72, n.s.$

[a] Data are from interviews in SRC–74 Fall and reinterviews in SRC–75 Feb. In 1975, subsample A and B respondents were administered the opposite agree–disagree version from the one that they received in 1974. Subsample C respondents were administered exactly the same version as they received in 1974. Percentages within tables are based on grand totals, with actual frequencies in parentheses. The diagonal consistent *in terms of content* has been circled, and the degree of consistency is described by phi coefficients and tested for statistical significance by likelihood ratio χ^2s. McNemar's χ^2_m is employed to test whether the two cells of the content *in*consistent diagonal differ significantly (see footnote 6). For subsamples A and B, these cells are double agree (AA) and double disagree (DD). All χ^2 calculations in Table 8.2 are based on $df = 1$. Totals may be off due to rounding.

of the item lies somewhere between 16 and 26% of the sample.[7] In sum, we have discovered strong evidence for acquiescence in the panel data, although the evidence does not resolve the problem of form differences in marginals confronted earlier in Table 8.1.

One further point of interest can be gleaned from Table 8.2. Form C in that table yielded an estimate of random error of 14.2%. The disagree–disagree cells in the other two subtables (A and B) average 9.9%. If the latter figure is also assumed to reflect random error, rather than substantive double-disagreement, then more than two-thirds of the random error in the forced-choice form also appears in the agree–disagree forms. This would imply that acquiescence does not involve the conversion of virtually all guessing-type responses into agreement. It is still possible, however, that the increment due to acquiescence (the agree–agree cells of the top two subtables) comes from those persons who would have given random responses, since the increment equals approximately the difference between 14.2% and 9.9%, multiplied by four (the number of cells in the table). Whether in fact acquiescent persons come mainly from the pool of those who would otherwise give random responses or mainly from those who would otherwise give consistent answers over time is an important theoretical issue that we are unable to resolve.

Open-Ended Explanations of Response

The individuals versus social conditions item in SRC–74 Fall was followed by the question: *Would you tell me why you feel that way?* Answers were recorded verbatim so far as practical and later coded into empirically derived categories, oriented where possible (but not rigidly) so as to provide explanations that would fit either an individuals or a social conditions response to the original closed item. Of course, open responses to a why follow-up question cannot demonstrate that people answered the original question for the reason they subsequently gave. But the responses can show what proportion of respondents were unable to give *any* reasonable justification for their earlier answer. And it also instructs us about explanations that may not have been within the investigator's or the reader's frame of reference for the closed item and indicates to what closed response the explanations are most relevant. (For further discussion and examples, see Schuman, 1966.)

Table 8.3 presents a summary of the codes and coded responses cross-classified by the respondent's original closed I–SC response and ques-

---

[7]This discussion assumes that acquiescence is equally strong in the panel data for subsamples A and B, as should logically be true, since the same pairing of questions is involved in each case, with only the order of administration different. However, we saw in Table 8.1 that clear evidence for this assumption is lacking.

TABLE 8.3
Open-Ended Explanations of Responses on the I-SC Question (SRC-74 Fall)

	Responses to I-SC Closed Questions[a]					
	Form A (Agree I's)		Form B (Agree SCs)		Form C (Forced-choice)	
Code[b] Explanations to open follow-up	A: I's	D: SCs	A: SCs	D: I's	I's	SCs
Individuals-type explanations						
20 People are responsible for their own behaviors	44.0%	2.7%	.8%	47.7%	48.0%	.0%
90 Individuals make up a society	10.5	1.1	.4	11.7	6.0	.0
10,22 Other individual explanations	4.2	.0	2.8	2.5	3.5	.8
Social-conditions type explanations						
70 Economic problems cause crime	1.5	33.7	18.9	2.0	.5	40.0
80 Environment controls individuals	.4	15.5	8.4	.5	.0	7.6
60 System is unjust	.8	7.5	9.2	1.5	.0	5.8
Ambiguous or tangential explanations						
40 Family socialization	14.3	6.4	11.6	10.7	16.0	11.6
50 Moral decay generally	3.8	8.0	12.9	4.6	1.5	10.7
30 Law enforcement is lax	3.0	5.3	10.0	2.5	6.0	7.6
21 The powerful break the law	3.8	.5	3.2	3.6	4.5	1.8
25,97 Other	4.9	6.4	12.0	2.0	6.0	7.6
98 DK	4.5	3.2	8.0	4.6	2.5	4.4
91 No reason given: R repeats responses	4.5	9.6	1.6	6.1	5.5	2.2
	100	100	100	100	100	100
	(266)	(187)	(249)	(197)	(200)	(225)

[a] In column headings, A = agree and D = disagree. (N.A. responses are not included in the table, but ranged in frequency from 25-30 cases across the 3 forms.)
[b] Original code numbers. See Appendix D for more detailed codes.

tion form. Codes are grouped here according to whether they initially seemed to us to fit the choice of individuals, the choice of social conditions, to be ambiguous or tangential, to be legitimate but rare and miscellaneous ("other"), or to be inadequate justifications for any response (DK or rote repetition of closed response). For example, of the 266 persons on form A of the I–SC question who agreed (individuals), 44.0% explained their answer in a way that was coded into category 20.

Several conclusions can be drawn from the table. First, the majority of respondents on all forms of the questionnaire gave reasonable explanations for their original response. The I–SC item is one that most people can understand to at least some degree. Second, about 30% of the responses fall into categories that were apparently meaningful to respondents but that we had not clearly envisaged as directly related to either the individuals or the social conditions alternative. Most of these explanations were not in fact concentrated in one of the original closed choices; for example, more than 10% of the respondents blamed family upbringing (category 40) for crime and lawlessness in the society, but these respondents come from both the individual and the social conditions sides of the original question, although a little more from the former than the latter. (However, the category "moral decay generally" seems on the forced-choice form to be tied to social-conditions responses, contrary to our expectation, and probably should not be classified as tangential.) Finally, although there are not large differences in type or quality of explanations attributable to the form of the original I–SC question, those who had received the forced-choice version of the question were a little less likely to be unable to answer the why follow-up (DK or rote repetition of the closed response). Given theoretical reasons to prefer form C as barring acquiescence, it is reassuring that it does not do so at the expense of ease of answering.

The distinction between explanations that fit the closed alternatives and those that do not is an important one. Suppose we assume that most respondents have in mind at least vague personal explanations for "crime and lawlessness" before being asked any questions on the subject, as is surely possible with a social issue of this kind. Those whose personal explanations fit clearly either the individuals or the social conditions alternative should have less trouble responding to the closed question, should be less distracted by acquiescence on forms A and B, and should be better able to be consistent over time when we reverse agreeing direction in the 1975 reinterviews. But for those who have in mind explanations tangential to the two alternatives posed, the choice presented by the closed question is not as meaningful and they might be expected to be less reliable in their response to it and perhaps more easily affected by such cues as an agreeing format. This leads to the hypothesis that those giving tangential explanations to the open follow-up will be less consistent over time than those who give explanations of a clearly individual or social conditions type.

Table 8.4 provides some support for this hypothesis. For all three subsamples, those giving clear and appropriate explanations for their closed response were more likely to be consistent over time than were those giving tangential responses.[8] However, this difference is higher and reaches significance only for the two subsamples where content consistency involves the additional capacity to resist acquiescence. This suggests that respondents giving tangential answers are not only generally less consistent over time but also especially susceptible to pressures toward acquiescence.

Although the interpretation of these findings must be somewhat speculative, we believe that respondents who provide tangential explanations are not necessarily less concerned with the issue of "crime and lawlessness," but may simply be less given to explanations that fit the dichotomy posed in the closed question. Thus they are less reliable and more easily shifted by format on this closed question, but when an opportunity to explain their attitude in their own words arises, they are able to do so. In terms of the concept of "crystallization" to be discussed in Chapter 10, these tangential respondents do have crystallized attitudes, but their attitudes do not fit the closed categories offered to them and therefore they cannot be expected to be very consistent in response to such categories. The fault lies not in themselves, but in our question for not providing an adequate range of choices that fits their frame of reference (as argued in Chapter 3). Other interpretations of tangential responses are certainly possible; for example, respondents who acquiesce could also, when forced to explain their answers, tend to come up with less adequate explanations because they have not really thought through their response. Research aimed at deciding between

[8]We considered the first six categories listed in Table 8.3 to be "clear and appropriate explanations," provided they matched the respondent's closed choice. To these we added category 50, *Moral decay generally,* since in the forced-choice sample (where acquiescence is ruled out) it appears clearly to go with social-conditions responses, even though it was not part of the social liberalism set we had in mind. We also omitted entirely from this analysis category 21, *The powerful break the law,* since it leans in the individuals direction, though not so clearly as to be considered appropriate to that response. Thus "tangential explanations" are restricted to categories 40 and 30 from Table 8.3, both of which do seem to accompany both individual and social conditions responses about equally. In Table 8.4 consistent "content" refers to responses consistent in content between time one and time two. For samples A and B we have restricted inconsistent responses to those involving double agreement (acquiescence). If double disagreement were also included, the results in Table 8.4 would be a little weaker (more so for sample B than A), but not basically altered. For sample C, all inconsistent responses are included.

TABLE 8.4
I–SC Consistency over Time by Clarity of Open-Ended Explanation[a]

	Type of Explanation		
	Tangential	Clear and appropriate	
Subsample A:			
Content consistent	54.8%	74.6%	$\chi^2 = 6.11$, $df = 1$, $p < .02$
Double agree	45.2	25.4	gamma = .42
	100	100	
	(42)	(181)	
Subsample B:			
Content consistent	52.2%	83.6%	$\chi^2 = 17.45$, $df = 1$, $p < .001$
Double agree	47.3	16.4	gamma = .65
	100	100	
	(46)	(152)	
Subsample C:			
Content consistent	62.7%	73.3%	$\chi^2 = 2.45$, $df = 1$, n.s.
Inconsistent	37.3	26.7	gamma = .24
	100	100	
	(67)	(176)	

Three-way interactions:
consistency × explanation × A versus B: $\chi^2 = 1.64$, $df = 1$, n.s.
consistency × explanation × (A+B) versus C: $\chi^2 = 2.95$, $df = 1$, $p < .10$

[a] From SRC–74 Fall and SRC–75 February panel. See footnote 8 (p. 216) for definitions of the column headings.

our interpretation and one that sees tangential respondents as merely having nonattitudes would be quite useful in tackling what is a fundamental disagreement over the nature of mass opinion.[9]

Other Possible Sources of Acquiescence

Low Education

The forced-choice form (C) of the I–SC item shows a highly significant relation to education: Less-educated respondents tend to blame individuals for crime and lawlessness (see Table 8.5). We assume that this represents the "true" direction of the relation of item content to education. If one further assumes that less-educated respondents are more

[9] We are indebted to Elizabeth Martin for suggestions that stimulated this analysis.

TABLE 8.5[a]

Individuals–Social Conditions Item by Education and Form

	Education					
	0–11	12	13+	gamma	SE	p
SRC–74 Fall						
Form A (percentage agree I's)	67.7	62.0	51.7	.22	.07	.01
	(133)	(163)	(176)			
Form B (percentage agree SCs)	58.1	58.2	54.7	.05	.08	n.s.
	(136)	(153)	(181)			
Form C (percentage I's)	55.3	44.5	40.5	.19	.08	.02
	(141)	(155)	(148)			
SRC–76 Feb.						
Form B (percentage agree SCs)	51.3	60.2	57.4	.07	.07	n.s.
	(160)	(201)	(230)			
Form C (percentage I's)	52.9	51.7	35.6	.25	.07	.001
	(136)	(207)	(225)			
SRC–78 Oct.–Nov.						
Form A (percentage agree I's)	74.6	68.4	63.0	.16	.07	.05
	(114)	(231)	(276)			
Form B (percentage agree SCs)	51.8	61.1	55.9	.00	.10	n.s.
	(56)	(113)	(145)			

[a] See Table 8.1 for the wording of forms A (agree I's), B (agree SCs), and C (forced-choice). The base N for each percentage is shown in parentheses.

prone to acquiescence, then the relation of form B (Agree SCs) to education should be small, since opposing forces are at work. This hypothesis is confirmed for all three replications of form B: In no case is there a significant association of response to education.

The relation of form A to education, however, does not fit this line of reasoning. On this form, both acquiescence and direction of content (choice of individuals) should propel low-educated respondents toward agreement with the item. Hence the association to education should be quite strong—and noticeably stronger than for form C. But, in fact, the magnitude of the relation for form A is essentially the same as that for form C. A theoretical model that fits all three relations of the item to education in Table 8.5 will have to be more complex than is implied by the usual assumptions about acquiescence.[10] (Analysis using odds ratios (not shown) reveals a trend for the effects of form differences to be less at higher educational levels.)

[10] Age shows much the same patterns of relation as education to the I–SC item on the three forms, with older people choosing the individuals response. When both variables are used jointly, they appear to be about equal in strength.

Strength of Feeling

The I–SC item in the 1975 reinterview was followed by a specific intensity question:

How strongly do you feel about that: quite strongly, or not so strongly?

We hypothesized that those claiming greater intensity would show more immunity to the acquiescence effects, since their position on the question had more internal meaning to them. Although there is a trend in this direction when the two agree–disagree forms (A and B) are compared, it does not approach significance, and there is not even a trend when the agree–disagree forms are compared with the forced-choice form (C).

The 1975 survey also contained a question on Arguing intended as a generalized measure of attitude strength (see Chapter 7, p. 198). All three forms show similar responses in terms of content for those who like to argue ("individuals" is chosen by 48%, 41%, and 47% on forms A, B, and C, respectively), whereas the distributions are further apart for those who dislike arguing (66%, 46%, and 44%). Since liking to argue seems exactly the opposite of acquiescence, this result makes fine intuitive sense and suggests that personality may play a role in agreeing response bias. Any conclusions must be considered quite tentative, however, for the interaction does not reach borderline significance ($.20 > p > .10$).

Race of Interviewer and Race of Respondent

Lenski and Leggett's (1960) explanation of acquiescence in terms of deference to the interviewer placed particular emphasis on the tendency of blacks to give double agree responses to white interviewers. But since there were no black interviewers in their survey, the assumption of a uniquely cross-racial deference could not be tested. Carr's (1971) study did include both black and white interviewers (though with only approximately matched, not randomized, subsamples of black respondents), and he found only a nonsignificant trend for greater double agreement to white than to black interviewers. Fischer (1974) analyzed data from a race-of-interviewer experiment in the 1971 Detroit Area Study, and reports that certain agree–disagree items revealed more agreement by blacks to white than to black interviewers, but that others showed trends in the opposite direction. She concluded from this and other analyses that the "evidence generally casts doubt on the Lenski and Leggett interpretation of agreement as a form of social deference [p. 155]."

None of our surveys manipulated the race of the interviewer, nor do we even have data allowing use of this as a variable. In addition, our black subsamples are too small to permit much in the way of controls. But neither in 1974 nor in 1976 are there significant response differences between blacks and whites on any of the forms of the I–SC item. The deference hypothesis is not, to be sure, being tested directly here (although especially in the 1976 telephone survey blacks were, and probably perceived themselves to be, interviewed mainly by middle-class whites), but we simply do not find a general black–white difference in levels of agreement that would need explanation. It is possible, of course, that times have changed and blacks no longer show the same generalized deference to white interviewers assumed to occur in earlier years.

WOMEN IN POLITICS

A second set of experiments on acquiescence employed an item that we label "women in politics" and that appears in NORC's General Social Survey (GSS). There are only two experimental forms to the item, as shown in Table 8.6, the regular NORC agree–disagree form and a forced-choice form that we constructed in 1974. The forced-choice version actually includes three alternatives, but the alternative *women are better suited than men* obtains only a small number of choices and is combined for analytic purposes with the alternative *men and women are equally suited,* since both should lead to the disagree response on the original GSS item.

Marginal Distributions by Form

Results from four different experiments with the women in politics item are presented in Table 8.6. Compared to the forced-choice form, the agree–disagree form yields significantly higher endorsement of the male superiority option in all four cases.[11] Unless one questions the equivalence of the two forms, it appears that acquiescence adds about 10% above and beyond content to choice of that alternative. Of course, it is

[11]However, the replication in SRC–74 Fall produces a difference noticeably smaller than that on the first experiment in the 1974 NORC General Social Survey. The three-way interaction of response by form by survey is significant ($\chi^2 = 4.37$, $df = 1$, $p < .05$), a difference for which we have no explanation. We are also able to test the effects of mode of administration, since the SRC–76 Spring survey consisted of an experimental comparison of telephone and face-to-face interviewing. The two different types of administration produced estimates of response that are within one percentage point on each form. Therefore, the two modes of administration are combined in Table 8.6.

TABLE 8.6
Women in Politics Item by Form

Form A: *Do you agree or disagree with this statement:*
         Most men are better suited emotionally for politics than are most women.
Form C: *Would you say that most men are better suited emotionally for politics than are most*
         women, that men and women are equally suited, or that women are better suited than
         men in this area? [a]

		Form A		Form C[b]
NORC-74	Agree	47.0%	Men better	33.1%
	Disagree	53.0	Equal	66.9
		100		100
		(698)		(719)
		$\chi^2 = 25.58$, $df = 1$, $p < .001$		
SRC-74 Fall	Agree	45.5%	Men better	39.4%
	Disagree	54.5	Equal	60.6
		100		100
		(966)		(480)
		$\chi^2 = 5.00$, $df = 1$, $p < .05$		
SRC-76 Feb.	Agree	44.3%	Men better	32.5%
	Disagree	55.7	Equal	67.5
		100		100
		(614)		(609)
		$\chi^2 = 18.01$, $df = 1$, $p < .001$		
SRC-76 Spring	Agree	48.2%	Men better	38.3%
	Disagree	51.8	Equal	61.7
		100		100
		(1416)		(1563)
		$\chi^2 = 29.83$, $df f= 1$, $p < .001$		

[a] "Equally suited" and "women better" have been combined under the heading equal. In the four surveys, the "women better suited" alternative was chosen, respectively, by 4.3%, 4.6%, 2.8%, 3.4% of the total Ns shown in the table. DK responses are omitted.
[b] There were actually three questionnaire forms in SRC-74 Fall, but what we here call form A was identical on two of the forms and these are therefore combined for that survey. For consistency with the I-SC item in Table 8.1, the forced-choice version is labeled form C, since we will later consider the two items together.

well to remember that two of the individual versus social conditions forms also yielded unambiguous evidence of acquiescence, yet a third showed the problem to be more complicated. Moreover, the forced-choice form of the women in politics item could be susceptible to a response-order effect (see Chapter 2), although the third alternative garnered too few responses for a recency effect to have been of much importance.

Education and Acquiescence

The data in Table 8.7 test the hypothesis that the acquiescence inferred from the marginal results is located disproportionately among the least educated. The first two surveys, both from 1974, provide some tentative evidence for the hypothesis. The agree–disagree version of the item shows in each case a highly significant relation to education, with low-educated respondents tending disproportionately to accept the proposition that men are better suited than women to politics; but the forced-choice version reveals only a slight and nonsignificant trend in this direction. However, neither of the three-way interactions reaches significance, and the two 1976 surveys show much less of a difference by form, with both versions of the item producing a clear negative relation to education, though the agree–disagree relations remain slightly stronger. (The four-way interaction of response by form by education by combined 1974 versus combined 1976 data yields a linear $\chi^2 = 2.32$, $df = 1$, n.s.)

Even if one were to regard the change from 1974 to 1976 as real, a plausible theoretical interpretation is not available. Therefore, we treat the overall table as showing that both forms of the women in politics item are negatively related to education, but the agree–disagree form more strongly so, presumably because of the additional factor of acquiescence. Pooling all four surveys, the response by education by form interaction is indeed highly significant (linear $\chi^2 = 8.27$, $df = 1$, $p < .01$). (Examination of the odds ratios in Table 8.7 shows fairly consistent trends for question form to have a greater effect at the lower end of the educational scale.)

Women in Politics and Individuals
versus Social Conditions

Both of the items we have been discussing in this chapter appeared in SRC–74 Fall, and thus it is possible to examine their intercorrelations within each subsample. The design was as follows (using the form letters from Table 8.1 but referring to them as subsamples):

	Women in politics	I–SC
Subsample A:	Agree men better	Agree individuals
Subsample B:	Agree men better	Agree social conditions
Subsample C:	Forced-choice	Forced-choice

TABLE 8.7
Women in Politics Item by Form and Education[a]

	Education			gamma	SE	p
	0–11	12	13+			
NORC-74						
Form A (percentage agree)	56.6	44.5	38.7	.24	.06	.001
	(244)	(236)	(217)			
Form C (percentage men more suited)	33.3	37.5	28.1	.08	.06	n.s.
	(243)	(232)	(242)			
Odds ratios	.38	.75	.62			
Three-way interaction (response × form × education): linear χ^2 = 3.03, df = 1, $p < .10$						
SRC-74 Fall						
Form A (percentage agree)	54.3	43.0	41.3	.17	.05	.001
	(276)	(321)	(366)			
Form C (percentage men)	39.1	41.8	36.8	.03	.08	n.s.
	(156)	(165)	(155)			
Odds ratios	.54	.95	.83			
Three-way interaction: linear χ^2 = 2.28, df = 1, n.s.						
SRC-76 Feb.						
Form A (percentage agree)	55.7	44.3	36.0	.26	.06	.001
	(174)	(201)	(239)			
Form C (percentage men)	40.9	33.0	26.9	.20	.07	.005
	(149)	(218)	(242)			
Odds ratios	.55	.63	.65			
Three-way interaction: linear χ^2 = .33, df = 1, n.s.						
SRC-76 Spring						
Form A (percentage agree)	57.9	50.8	38.3	.25	.04	.001
	(363)	(490)	(534)			
Form C (percentage men)	45.0	40.1	31.8	.18	.04	.001
	(407)	(538)	(581)			
Odds ratio	.60	.65	.74			
Three-way interaction: linear χ^2 = 1.25, df = 1, n.s.						

[a] See Table 8.6 (p. 221) for the wording of the women in politics item. Base Ns are given in parentheses.

The two forced-choice versions (C) in Table 8.8 are significantly related: Those who believe men are better suited to politics also believe that individuals are more responsible than social conditions for crime and lawlessness. The direction is intuitively meaningful either as part of a general conservative–liberal dimension or as involving a focus on individualistic versus environmental explanations of social differences.

In the other two 1974 subsamples, the agreeing version of the women in politics item was constant, whereas the I–SC item varied the direction

TABLE 8.8
Women in Politics by Individuals–Social Conditions by Form[a]

A. Agree: men better suited form × agree: individuals form

	Agree: (individuals)	Disagree: (social conditions)	
Agree: (men better suited)	49.3%	40.6%	$\chi^2 = 3.32$, $df = 1$
			$p < .07$
Disagree	50.7	59.4	gamma = .17
	100	100	
	(272)	(180)	

B. Agree: men better suited form × agree: social conditions form

	Disagree: (individuals)	Agree: (social conditions)	
Agree: (men better suited)	42.8%	44.9%	$\chi^2 = .20$, $df = 1$
			n.s.
Disagree	57.2	55.1	gamma = −.04
	100	100	
	(194)	(256)	

C. Forced-choice × forced-choiced

	Individuals	Social conditions	
Men better suited	45.1%	33.5%	$\chi^2 = 6.22$, $df = 1$
			$p < .02$
Equally suited and women better	54.9	66.5	gamma = .24
	100	100	
	(204)	(236)	

[a] Data from SRC–74 Fall.

of agreement. Given the relation on the forced-choice forms, one might expect that sample A (where agreeing direction corresponds with content direction) would show an even higher association, whereas sample B (where agreeing and content directions are opposed) would show a lower or even reversed association. The latter hypothesis is confirmed in Table 8.8B, for there is no relation at all when the two items are worded so that agreement to both leads in opposite content directions (in terms of the forced-choice association previously reported). But the two agree versions that are worded in the same content direction in Table 8.8A produce an association that is slightly weaker, rather than stronger, than that found for the forced-choice form. Although this might be explained in terms of sampling error, it is a puzzling finding and hardly accords with the notion that acquiescence can elevate or create positive associations. (Compare the analysis of the relation between the Arabs and the Russia items in Chapter 4, where a correlation at first attributed to acquiescence also turned out to occur on forced-choice forms of the two items.) Thus, acquiescence seems not to enhance a substantive association where it might be expected to, although it appears to eliminate an association where that is the theoretical expectation.

We take a further step in Table 8.9 and examine the relation of the two items by whether or not 1974 responses to the I–SC item were repeated consistently (in terms of content) in the 1975 reinterviews (as discussed earlier with respect to Table 8.2.) Consistent respondents have demonstrated that they tend to answer the I–SC item in terms of content even where (in subsamples A and B) this requires agreeing on one occasion and disagreeing on another. Inconsistent respondents not only lack content consistency, but (in subsamples A and B) either double agree (acquiescence) or double disagree.

With these meanings in mind, most of the gammas in Table 8.9 make good sense. Row B is the easiest to interpret: The negative association of −.21 shows that those able to maintain content consistency for the I–SC item over time, even though this requires agreeing on one occasion and disagreeing on the other, are able to do the same thing in producing an ideologically consistent (i.e., negative) association between the I–SC item and the women in politics item. The inconsistents, however, are caught between content and acquiescent tendencies, and these cancel out to produce a near-zero (.05) association. Row A, where both content and acquiescence lead in the same direction in 1974, suggests that content is somewhat more important (gamma = .25) than acquiescence (.15) in producing a positive relation between the I–SC item and the women in politics item. Finally, row C suggests that when acquiescence is eliminated as a possible factor in responses, those who have been consistent over time on the I–SC item account for most of the positive association between this item and the women in politics item that was shown earlier in Table 8.8: that association of .24 results largely from an association of .29 for the large group of consistents and −.21 for the smaller group of inconsistents.[12] Only the last-mentioned negative association of −.21 is puzzling, since one might have expected these inconsistent people to

[12]Table 8.8 is based on all SRC-74 Fall cases, whereas Table 8.9 is based only on those cases that could be reinterviewed. Hence the correlations for the two tables do not correspond exactly.

TABLE 8.9
Associations between I–SC and Women in Politics Items by I–SC Consistency[a]

	Content Consistency[b]	
	Consistent	Inconsistent
A. Agree (men) form × agree (Is) form	.25*	.15
	(.14)	(.23)
B. Agree (men) form × agree (SCs) form	−.21	.05
	(.14)	(.21)
C. Forced-choice (I-SC) × forced-choice	.29**	−.21
(men better–equal)	(.13)	(.22)

* = <.10.
** = <.05.
[a] Gammas, with standard errors in parentheses. Ns for the six cells are as follows:

$$107 \quad 192$$
$$106 \quad 198$$
$$220 \quad 86$$

[b] In terms of tendency to agree (or to disagree) those labeled content inconsistents are the respondents who double agree (or double disagree) in subsamples A and B.

show a zero or slightly positive association. (It will be noted that these interpretations take all the associations at roughly face value, rather than treating simply as zero those that are not significant.)

ASSERTIONS VERSUS QUESTIONS

As noted at the beginning of this chapter, most research and theorizing about acquiescence deal with propositions or assertions to which respondents are asked to agree or disagree. Yet sometimes acquiescence is assumed to extend to items that also present an issue in terms of one side, but do so in interrogative form. The distinction is of both theoretical and practical importance: theoretical because it may help us understand the dynamics of acquiescence and practical because it indicates whether the problem can be avoided simply by eschewing agree–disagree item forms.

We took advantage of our experience with the two items discussed thus far by including an agree–disagree version of each in one form of a split-ballot experiment in SRC–80 June, and in the other form a rewording to provide yes–no questions, as shown in Table 8.10. If the interrogative rewording shows the same acquiescence effect found for the assertions, then there should not be significant form differences in the marginal distributions for either item. If, however, the interrogative form

eliminates the acquiescence effect, its marginal distributions should be
closer to those obtained with forced-choice forms of the two items in
previous experiments. (It would have been preferable to have included a
third forced-choice form in the present experiments, but limited sample
size precluded this.)

As Table 8.10 shows, we certainly do not find evidence for an acquiescence effect unique to the agree–disagree versions of these items. The
1–SC item does not produce a significant difference between agree–
disagree and interrogative forms, while on the women in politics item
there are more affirmative responses to the interrogative form than to
the agree–disagree version! The fact that the two experiments have different outcomes argues against any attempt at generalization from these
two items, but clearly the hypothesis of reduction in acquiescence by use
of a purely interrogative form finds little support here.

Two further comparisons by form were possible with the two items in
SRC–80 June, one employing education and the other the cross-
tabulation of the items themselves. Results for both forms are the same
in direction and similar in magnitude to each other, and also in line with
results reported in earlier tables for the two items. Thus, the relation of

TABLE 8.10
Assertions versus Questions[a]

Individuals–social conditions item

Form A: agree–disagree		Form B: interrogative	
1. *Please tell me whether you agree or disagree with this statement:* **Individuals** *are more to blame than* **social conditions** *for crime and lawlessness in this country.* (*Do you agree or disagree?*)		*Do you believe that* **individuals** *are more to blame than* **social conditions** *for crime and lawlessness in this country?*	
Agree (individuals)	59.4%	Yes (individuals)	57.9%
Disagree (social conditions)	40.6	No (social conditions)	42.1
	100		100
	(330)		(309)
	$\chi^2 = .14$, $df = 1$, n.s.		
2. *Do you agree or disagree with this statement: Most men are better suited emotionally for politics than are most women.* (*Do you agree or disagree?*)		*Do you think most men are better suited emotionally for politics than are most women?*	
Agree (men better)	36.3%	Yes (men better)	44.1%
Disagree (equal)	63.7	No (equal)	55.9
	100		100
	(342)		(311)
	$\chi^2 = 4.12$, $df = 1$, $p < .05$		

[a] Administered in this sequence in SRC–80 June.

the I–SC item to education is .35 for the agree–disagree form and .26 for the interrogative forms (cf. Table 8.5). The corresponding relations of the women in politics item to education are .28 and .43 (cf. Table 8.7). The four gammas are all highly significant ($p < .01$), and the figures do not differ significantly by form. Cross-tabulations of the two items themselves do show a bit more of a difference, since gamma for the agree–disagree versions is .34 ($p < .01$), while gamma for the interrogative forms is only .14 (SE = .12, n.s.). However, the two subtables do not differ significantly from each other ($\chi^2 = 1.74$, $df = 1$), and the figure for the interrogative version is actually closer to the gamma of .17 that we reported in Table 8.8 for the cross-tabulation of the two agree–disagree forms in 1974.

Obviously experiments with a wider set of items are needed, but our hypothesis now must be that there is nothing special about agree–disagree assertions (as distinct from interrogative forms) that produces acquiescence. Whatever acquiescence occurs evidently comes from the one-sided nature of a question or statement, as against a deliberate attempt to offer respondents two or more choices that are equally balanced in the way they are presented.

OTHER EXPERIMENTS

In addition to the two experimental items discussed in this chapter, we carried out experiments with seven items from the ISR Election Studies (four political efficacy items and three government social policy items), three original items dealing with foreign affairs (all of which are employed in our analysis of floaters in Chapter 4), and one other specially created comparison. Ten of these experiments involved comparing agree–disagree forms with forced-choice forms, but in almost every case the forced-choice form can be criticized as providing a wording that differs substantively from the agree–disagree item. The eleventh experiment, modeled after the I–SC experiment, and a twelfth involving a political efficacy item, used agree–disagree reversals, but these also have problems with content. Thus in retrospect we do not believe the similarities and differences by form can be treated with the same seriousness as those for the two items already discussed.

All 12 experiments are presented with marginals in Appendix D, and interested readers may make of them what they will. Our own belief is that it is better to concentrate on the I–SC and women in politics items where logical objections seem minimal and a wealth of data are already available.

CONCLUDING DISCUSSION

The results in this chapter provide some answers and sharpen some issues concerning acquiescence, though they also leave important problems unsolved and raise new ones. It is useful to list our conclusions in order of decreasing certainty.

First, the form of the two items discussed at length in this chapter had substantial impact on the results obtained. This is so not only for marginal distributions, which vary by about 10 to 15%, but even more importantly for associations with education and for interitem correlations. Form definitely does influence the conclusions one would draw from use of these items.

Second, unless our reasoning about the contradictory nature of the item forms is faulty, then a large part of the form differences discovered can be attributed to acquiescence. Whether there is a type of naysaying involved as well, we cannot tell. It is possible that, despite our attempt to construct logical contradictories, there is still a tendency for some respondents to reject (disagree with) the agreeing form of the items.

Third, it does not seem possible to tie acquiescence solely to assertions with which respondents are asked to agree or disagree, since such statements do not produce significantly more affirmative responses (and for one item they produced significantly fewer) than interrogative forms. Further comparisons, especially split-ballots including agree–disagree, interrogative, and balanced forced-choice forms, are needed on this issue. It is an issue of great importance, since it defines the problem of acquiescence as either very broad (applying to a large proportion of survey questions) or quite narrow (applying only to agree–disagree statements).

Fourth, it appears that acquiescence—if we have correctly identified it—occurs somewhat more among less educated than among more-educated respondents, but also that it is a continuing force even among those with a college education. Of course, even our college-educated category is more heterogeneous—certainly in age and probably in exact education as well—than most college-student samples used in previous work on acquiescence. There is also some evidence that acquiescence is diminished for persons who report feeling more strongly about the issue under inquiry, and also for individuals who report that they like to argue about political issues generally, but the evidence in these cases is too slight to suggest more than the desirability of further research on one or the other possibility.

Fifth, our understanding of how acquiescence works is far from satisfactory. Simple assumptions do not hold up well, in particular the idea that acquiescence generally creates or adds to associations by means of correlated error, although it does seem able to detract from relations that would otherwise exist on the basis of content.

Sixth, explanations of agreeing-response bias must also account for the kind of responses that acquiescent persons would give in situations where an agreeing-response bias is not possible. Our results are not inconsistent with the assumption that acquiescent persons are primarily those who would otherwise answer in an essentially random manner, but by no means demonstrate the point. In fact, the model of where acquiescers "come from" is probably going to need to be a good deal more complex than is often assumed. Formulating and testing such a model is an important challenge to investigators interested in the phenomenon of agreeing-response bias.

Seventh, given initial theoretical reasons for preferring forced-choice to agree–disagree versions of items, there is some further support for such a preference in the adequacy of open explanations that respondents offer for their answers. Furthermore, forced-choice versions of items seem to show meaningful relations to other variables. Unless counterevidence can be produced, there seems good reason to prefer forced-choice over agree–disagree versions of items where possible.

Finally, it is very important to note that in the case of the individuals–social conditions item, our results for form comparisons in marginals would have been quite misleading if taken to inform us about form differences in relations to education. Forms B and C do not differ significantly or noticeably in marginal distributions (Table 8.1), yet they do differ significantly and decisively in their respective relations to education (Table 8.5). Thus, the absence of a form difference at the marginal level cannot be taken as assurance that there is no form difference in more complex relations involving an item. The latter must be examined in their own terms, not inferred from a study of marginals.

These conclusions are based on extensive data for two survey items. This is fewer items than we use as a basis for conclusions in our other chapters, and we are aware of the limitations this places on generalizations. Moreover, each of the items has some problems and each produces patterns of response difficult to interpret in terms of the simple presence or absence of acquiescence. Our attempts to create experiments based on other items were unsuccessful, as explained above and in Appendix D, but such further experimentation is much needed, since whatever the term acquiescence covers has serious effects on survey data.

9

Passionate Attitudes: Intensity, Centrality, and Committed Action

What if the minority prefers its alternative much more
passionately than the majority prefers a contrary alternative?
—Dahl (1956)

Many attitude questions simply divide respondents on the basis of pro and con direction. Yet it has long been recognized that attitudes vary in other ways, most notably the strength with which they are held. Two people can have the same view, but to one the issue may be of major consequence, while to the other it is only a minor matter. The importance of an attitude for the rest of life, and even the meaningfulness of the attitude in its own terms, would seem to hinge on a distinction of this sort.

Although strength, or something very much like it, is everyone's favorite choice as a second property of attitudes, little theoretical use is made of such measures in survey research. It is true that intensity scales are often created as intrinsic parts of items, and larger indexes with an extremity dimension are regularly constructed from sets of questions. But these steps are usually refinements of the dichotomous pro–con question, and although they may provide practical advantages, intensity and kindred concepts are not thereby used to illuminate the functioning of attitudes either personally or socially. Indeed, there is some evidence that even the practical gain from building intensity scales into individual items may be exaggerated (Peabody, 1962).

A complicating factor in discussions of attitude strength has been the large number of related concepts suggested, each different from the others in ways that are intuitively intriguing but empirically untested: intensity, centrality, salience, certainty, ego-involvement, importance, confidence, crystallization, ambivalence.[1] Apart from a pioneering investigation by Katz (1944), there have been few attempts to see what differences, if any, these distinctions make. In early writings on attitude surveys, *crystallization* was frequently the key word, but it seems never to have been clearly defined or operationalized. At a later point, emphasis was also put on the term *centrality* by Converse and others (1964; 1970; 1975; Newcomb, Turner, and Converse, 1965), but often applied to the classification of issues in relation to respondents, rather than to the development of standard measures of individual differences. And both early and late, *intensity* has probably been the most commonly used term in this area, though seldom with an exact definition. In this chapter we will explore the relative merits and implications of several different ways of assessing attitude strength in large-scale surveys. Moreover, we do so by studying the contribution that measures of attitude strength can make to our understanding of public opinion and public action on important social issues.

Past Research Using Attitude Strength as a Theoretical Construct

One early major attempt to use attitude strength in a more theoretical way has had a curious history. Guttman and Suchman (1947) proposed that by crossing an intensity scale with a unidimensional content scale one could arrive at a zero point to divide a "population into two groups which can be meaningfully labeled as 'positive' or 'negative' [Suchman, 1950, p. 216]." The demonstrations these authors provided won some early support from experts (e.g., Green, 1954) and are still cited in texts. Yet the approach has rarely been applied beyond its original exposition and it is unclear whether specialists in attitude measurement today accept the Guttman and Suchman proposal or not. In part this disregard in practice is probably due to the difficulty of creating the necessary unidimensional scales, but in part to the failure of anyone to show how such a zero point is useful beyond demonstrating its own existence.[2]

---

[1]For discussions of some of these concepts, see Scott (1968), Lemon (1973), and Peterson and Dutton (1975).

[2]What does it mean to divide a population into those having a positive and those a negative attitude in an area? Presumably the division should help predict important behavior, such as how a population would vote on a relevant referendum. But a better predictor to a referendum would almost certainly be a single question modeled after the referendum question, regardless of where it fell in relation to the zero point. Thus the zero

What did come out of the research was a wider recognition that extremity of position and intensity of opinion are related, such that persons at either end of a content dimension tend to feel more intensely than those in the middle. That basic finding, however, had been reported by Cantril (1944) using single Thurstone-type items, and indeed had been discovered much earlier by Allport and Hartman (1925). It is generally assumed that the finding holds universally, although there are some partial dissenters (Sherif and Sherif, 1969) and the point has never been tested systematically over a wide range of issues.

A second and more fertile way of considering attitude strength has been pursued by political scientists. Dahl (1956) posed hypothetically the antithesis between an intense minority and an apathetic majority, and considered (also hypothetically) the political consequences of the disparity between numbers and intensity. A decade later, Converse, Clausen, and Miller (1965) related attitude data on presidential preferences to self-reported letter writing, and presented a picture of the 1964 election that resembled Dahl's model. A somewhat similar approach was taken by Verba and Brody (1970) in an analysis of attitudes and self-reported actions toward the Vietnam War, while Key (1961) used intensity to compare political issues with one another. All these studies actually followed by some years a similar concern for linking attitude strength to pro–anti positions by Cantril (1942); his work attracted less notice, probably because he focused on a case where the majority side (support for England by Americans in the early days of World War II) was also the side showing greater intensity of opinion, thus precluding the kind of paradox posed by Dahl. Our own experiments are in part an application to current issues of Cantril's and Dahl's basic approach, but with an extension to behavior similar to that used by Converse, Clausen, and Miller. The juxtaposition of subjective and behavioral measures turns out to be illuminating.

ISSUES AND MEASURES

We began by choosing two social issues, abortion and gun control, where there was some reason to think public attitudes play a significant

---

point appears to have little meaning outside the scaling technique itself. One suggested use is to compare the zero points of two different populations, or of a single population at two points in time (Dotson and Summers, 1970); we do not know of any attempts to make either of these comparisons. For one early critique of the Guttman and Suchman claims, see Peak (1953), and for some negative empirical evidence, see McDill (1959).

role in political outcomes in a way they might not with more esoteric or technical issues, and where the distribution of attitude strength could well be as important as the distribution of pro and con positions. As we investigated this general problem, we attempted to determine whether different ways of measuring the strength dimension led to different conclusions. The three different measures employed will be called *intensity, centrality,* and *committed action;* in their development, we deliberately separated them from questions measuring attitude direction, so that the two properties of direction and strength could vary independently.

GUN PERMITS

A standard question on requiring police permits for purchase of guns has been asked regularly in polls since 1959. Responses to the question show that a clear and nearly constant majority of about three quarters of the population favors such a law (see Smith, 1980). Yet Congress has thus far failed to pass legislation for a gun-permit (GP) system. There are various explanations for this discrepancy between public opinion, as measured by surveys, and public action (or inaction) as indexed by legislation. One hypothesis is that the anti-GP minority includes a disproportionately large number of fervent individuals who are ready on short notice to translate their sentiments into votes, letters to Congress, or money-raising efforts. We used this hypothesis to guide development and comparison of attitude strength measures.

Intensity and Centrality

Our first test of the hypothesis in 1975 employed a three-point intensity scale, shown in Table 9.1, as a follow-up to the question: *Would you favor a law which would require a person to obtain a police permit before he could buy a gun, or do you think such a law would interfere too much with the right of citizens to own guns?*[3] We use the term "intensity" to refer to subjective

---

[3]For a more general treatment of the gun-permit issue, see Schuman and Presser, 1977–1978. One of the hypotheses tested there (and largely disconfirmed) concerns the possible loading of gun-permit questions toward one side or the other. (The main results of this test are also presented in a different context in Chapter 7.) The fact that changes in question wording never convert the majority position into a minority provides justification for our treatment of the questions as indexing the approximate absolute division of opinion

TABLE 9.1
Intensity and Centrality of Opinion by Gun Permit Response[a]

Intensity (SRC–75 Feb.)	Pro-GP	Anti-GP	Centrality (SRC–76 Feb.)	Pro-GP	Anti-GP
Compared with how you feel on other public issues, are your feelings on this issue extremely strong, fairly strong, or not very strong?			*How important is a candidate's position on permits for guns when you decide how to vote in a Congressional election—is it one of the **most** important factors you would consider, a very important factor, somewhat important, or not too important?*		
1. Extremely strong	49.1%	32.1%	1. One of the most important	3.1%	7.3%
2. Fairly strong	39.1	42.9	2. Very important	25.4	16.3
3. Not very strong	11.8	25.0	3. Somewhat important	41.0	44.4
			4. Not too important	30.5	32.0
	100	100		100	100
	(289)	(140)		(393)	(178)
	$\chi^2 = 16.51$			$\chi^2 = 9.91$	
	$df = 2$			$df = 3$	
	$p < .001$			$p < .02$	

[a] Gun-permit responses were answers to the following question: Would you favor a law which would require a person to obtain a police permit before he could buy a gun, or do you think such a law would interfere too much with the right of citizens to own guns?

strength of feeling, as reported by the respondent, and in this sense the first measure in Table 9.1 is very close to the general term attitude strength itself.

Surprisingly, *pro*-GP people showed significantly greater strength of feeling on the intensity measure than those with anti-GP views—exactly the opposite of the hypothesis. However, such a large proportion of the population (nearly half) claimed to feel intensely about the issue that we doubted the measure's power of discrimination. A four-point scale of centrality of opinion was therefore developed in 1976. We take "centrality" to mean subjective importance and again rely on self-report by the respondent, although we attempted to make the self-evaluation more serious by putting it in terms of an actual choice situation, as shown in the item wording in Table 9.1.[4]

This time the results were more complex. On the one hand, considering the category "one of the *most* important" issues, we detected the originally hypothesized tendency for gun-permit opponents to manifest greater strength than gun-permit proponents. However, once the small (about 5%) group of strongest opinion-givers was set aside, the earlier finding that pro-gun permit people showed greater strength of opinion was repeated.[5]

The fact that the centrality measure identified an extreme group in which anti-GP opinions are disproportionately represented could be

---

on this issue for the country as a whole. The division in this case differs from that proposed by Guttman and Suchman (1947) in that it claims to deal only with a single issue, not with a broader attitude operationalized by a scale of items each of which is about a specific issue (for example, a unidimensional scale measuring attitudes toward gun control generally, with items ranging from no control at all to banning of all guns).

[4]Converse (1970:182) defined centrality rather differently, in terms of the "proportion of 'mental time' which is occupied by attention to the attitude–object over substantial periods." Although that definition certainly captures something important about, for example, the difference between the intense preoccupations called love and hate and a slight positive or negative affect toward a political object, it is not clear that among the latter the time spent thinking varies greatly or that it could ever be measured. We prefer to equate centrality to subjective importance, on the assumption that the two are so closely connected as to be virtually indistinguishable, but with importance much more readily operationalized. Converse's definition is more relevant to his general concern to separate those with a considerable interest in political affairs from those with little such interest. Bem (1970) also uses the term centrality in a way that is difficult to operationalize; however, his usage should also come to much the same thing as importance.

[5]In both the 1975 intensity and the 1976 centrality studies, a formally balanced GP item (p. 182) was also used on other questionnaire forms, and in 1975 a third unbalanced form as well. These all show patterns similar to those that are reported for intensity and centrality, respectively, in Table 9.1. See Schuman and Presser (1977–1978) for more detailed cross-tabulations of the various GP forms by intensity and centrality.

attributed to any of the three ways in which the centrality item differs from the earlier intensity item. First, the centrality item has four ordered categories, whereas the original intensity item had only three. We therefore revised the intensity item to comprise four categories. Second, the centrality measure has a behavioral reference (*when you decide how to vote*), whereas the intensity question refers only to feelings. This suggests the value of asking even more directly about actions relevant to the issue, as discussed below. Finally, the meaning of the words in the intensity and centrality items is different: in one case intensity of feeling; in the other the importance of the issue when reaching a decision. Whether this distinction is meaningful could not be tested directly, but would become plausible if the preceding two differences were shown not to matter.

The four-category centrality measure and a new four-category intensity measure were used as follow-ups to gun-permit questions in a split-ballot comparison in August 1978, as shown in Table 9.2.[6] First, comparing simply the marginals for the four-category intensity and centrality measures, it continues to be true that the centrality item isolates a much smaller group of persons at the high (strong) end of the scale, although there is some compensating effectiveness by the intensity question at the low end. Evidently intensity and centrality items, at least as we have been able to construct them, do divide the population in different ways ($\chi^2 = 55.9$, $df = 3$, $p < .001$, for intensity versus centrality marginals). People apparently find it easier to report feeling extremely strongly about an issue than to say that it is one of the most important issues they would consider in an election, and an investigator who wishes to focus on the most passionate supporters and opponents of an issue would do better to ask about centrality.

Our three-category intensity measure in 1975 had shown anti-GP

---

[6]The actual experiment in SRC–78 August was somewhat more complex. A 2 × 2 factorial design was used, with the intensity and centrality measures comprising one factor and two versions of the GP question the other factor. One GP version was that shown in Table 9.1, footnote (p. 235); the other version used the "Some people. . . . Other people. . ." format presented on p. 191. The two GP versions yield essentially the same results as far as the centrality measure goes, including its relations to behavior. However, respondents show significantly ($p < .05$) greater intensity for both pro and anti positions on the "Some people. . . . Other people. . ." form than on the more standard GP versions employed in Table 9.1 and elsewhere. Possibly this is due to the influence of the social-pressure feature of the "Some people. . . . Other people" form on the rather vague intensity measure; if so, it supports the conclusion that the centrality measure is the better one, in this instance because it is less affected by nonsubstantive features of the preceding question. The effect is not large, however, and does not change the basic relation of intensity to GP position, hence the two GP forms are collapsed in Table 9.2.

TABLE 9.2
Intensity and Centrality Results for Gun-Permit Questions in 1978[a]

	Intensity				Centrality			
		GP Question					GP Question	
Compared with how you feel on other public issues, are your feelings about permits for guns:	Marginal total	Pro	Anti		*How important is a candidate's position on permits for guns when you decide how to vote in a Congressional election. Is it . . .*	Marginal total	Pro	Anti
1. Extremely strong	17.5%	18.2%	16.6%		1. One of the most important	6.3%	5.4%	7.7%
2. Very strong	23.6	23.4	23.9		2. Very important	23.6	22.4	25.5
3. Fairly strong	39.1	41.2	35.6		3. Somewhat important	34.5	38.7	28.4
4. Not strong at all	19.8	17.2	23.9		4. Not too important	35.5	33.5	38.5
	100	100	100			100	100	100
		(325)	(205)				(313)	(208)

Intensity: $\chi^2 = 4.0$, $df = 3$, $p > .25$

Centrality: $\chi^2 = 6.3$, $df = 3$, $p < .10$

[a] Carried out in SRC-78 August. (See footnote 6, p. 237 for a description of the GP question forms used in this experiment.)

people to have weaker feelings than pro-GP people. Only a trace of this finding reappears in Table 9.2 for the intensity measure in 1978. It is possible that the decrease in association occurs because of the addition of a category to the scale, and also possible that changes over time occurred. We are inclined to believe that a weak relation does exist between intensity and GP position, but this conclusion must be regarded as uncertain.

The 1976 results using centrality also showed anti-GP people to have generally weaker views on the issue, but this difference was reversed among the small set of individuals who regarded gun-permit legislation as one of the most important of all issues. Both these trends reappear in August 1978 (see Table 9.2), although not with the degree of reliability that occurred in the 1976 survey. When the August 1978 results are considered along with the 1976 tables and with other data to be noted, the overall evidence is reasonably persuasive that the gun-permit issue produces an unusual distribution of opinion in terms of strength. The pro-GP part of the population is not only in the majority but regards the issue as of at least as great importance overall as does the anti-GP part of the population. Among the tiny group of persons who rate the issue tops in importance, however, the anti-GP side is disproportionately represented. This begins to fit the picture conveyed from more impressionistic reports that the movement against stronger gun control laws relies on mobilization of a relatively small set of people, presumably people who will contribute the letters, money, and votes that can swing a close election, or at least impress politicians that they might do so. Yet even if the advantage at "the most important end" lies with the antis over the pros in percentage terms, these percentages must be multiplied by the numbers in their respective bases; when this is done, the actual number of most-committed partisans turns out to be about equal among pros and antis. Thus even the centrality results cannot fully explain the legislative stalemates.[7]

[7]Two further partial replications are available. In SRC–78 Fall and again in SRC–79 September, an unbalanced, a formally balanced, and a counterargument form of the GP question were repeated, each followed by the standard centrality measure. In all cases, anti-GP respondents are more apt than pro-GPs to say the issue is unimportant. At the high (important) end of the centrality scale, however, the counterargument form—but only the counterargument form—shows antis to be disproportionately represented. On the other two GP forms, the two sides are about equally represented at the high end. The fact that the exact proportions of pro and anti GP respondents may shift slightly depending on the exact form of the GP question reenforces our general conclusion that subjective strength alone cannot explain the effectiveness of the anti-GP minority.

Committed Action

The relative success of the centrality measure in 1976, with its behavioral orientation, led us in the August 1978 survey to ask all respondents (immediately after they had answered either the intensity or the centrality question):

> *Have you ever written a letter to a public official expressing your views on gun permits or given money to an organization concerned with this issue?*

Interviewers coded the replies to this direct behavioral question into categories representing letters, money, both, or neither. The results, when cross-classified against pro versus anti GP opinions, are striking, as shown in Table 9.3.[8]

About 12% of the total sample in Table 9.3 report having written a letter, contributed money, or done both with regard to the gun-permit issue. The percentage of GP opponents who do any of these things, however, is nearly three times as large as the percentage of GP proponents who are active in these ways. Even when one allows for the fact that the number of pros in the sample (and in the country) considerably exceeds the number of antis, almost two thirds of all letter writers and financial contributors on this issue come from the anti side. If we trust these self-reports as approximately accurate, then politicans, editors, and others who take stands on the gun-permit issue will hear from GP opponents noticeably more often than from GP proponents, even though it is the latter who clearly predominate in the country. Moreover, beyond their willingness to write letters, GP opponents are even more conspicuous in donating money to their cause. This no doubt multiplies the effectiveness of their communication system, and it also doubtless plays an important role in election campaigns when financial support is given to one candidate rather than another. Even these results may underestimate the activity of antis, since we did not obtain frequency of letter writing or amounts of contributions.

Social Action and Social Organization

The difference between gun permit pros and antis in committed action is much more impressive than was their difference in subjective

---

[8]As noted in footnote 6 (p. 237), there were two forms of the GP question in SRC-78 August. However, they do not differ significantly in their relation to the behavioral item, and the results are combined here.

TABLE 9.3
Self-Reported Behavior on the Gun-Permit Issue (SRC–78 August)

Behavior reported	Position on gun permits			
	Pro-GP		Anti-GP	
Written a letter	3.7%		6.5%	
Given money	1.7	} 7.1%	7.7	} 20.4%
Both letter and money	1.7		6.2	
Neither	92.9		79.6	
	100		100	
	(653)		(417)	
		$\chi^2 = 46.4$, $df = 3$, $p < .001$		

strength. The overt behavioral difference is clear-cut and decisive, whereas the variation at the subjective level was slighter, more uncertain, and insufficient to account for the political potency of anti-GP partisans. How is it that GP antis are a great deal more active than pros in terms of writing letters and giving money, yet show up as only a little more likely to regard the issue as more important when subjective measures are employed? The answer may lie in the remarkable interaction presented in Figure 9.1, where the association between the centrality and behavior measures is examined separately for GP proponents and GP opponents.

Among opponents of gun-permit legislation, there is a strong monotonic relation (gamma = .61, SE = .09), which can be interpreted to mean that opponents who consider the issue important are quite likely to translate their convictions into political actions (letter writing, fund raising). Among GP proponents, on the other hand, there is little if any relation between centrality of opinion and behavior (gamma = .12, SE = .19), so that conviction about the importance of the issue apparently does not lead to instrumental political behavior. (The linear component of the three-way interaction of behavior by centrality by pro–anti position is significant: linear $\chi^2 = 4.18$, $df = 1$, $p < .05$.)[9] Because of the fundamental importance of this interaction, we replicated it in SRC–79 September. The spread between the centrality–behavior correlations for

[9]The corresponding interaction for behavior, intensity, and pro–anti position shows the same general pattern, but the gammas are not as far apart and they vary systematically by the form of the GP question (described in footnote 6, p. 237). We believe that the latter variation is due to the more labile nature of the intensity measure, as documented in footnote 6, and this may account for its less clear-cut relation to behavior generally.

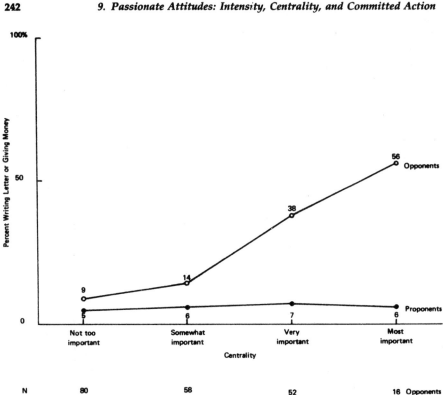

FIGURE 9.1 The Relation of Behavior to Centrality for Gun-Permit Proponents and Opponents (SRC-78 August). The behavioral measure (the vertical axis) is dichotomized into those showing any behavior (letters, money, or both) and those showing none.

opponents and proponents is not quite so extreme (the gammas are .70 and .30 respectively), but with more cases ($N = 867$) the three-way interaction is more significant (linear $\chi^2 = 5.59$, $df = 1$, $p < .02$).[10]

What these findings seem to point to—albeit without direct evidence—is an efficient lobby against gun-control legislation, which is able to *activate* adherents whenever necessary, whereas those on the other side remain unable to come together for effective action. The acti-

[10]As indicated in footnote 7 (p. 239), the SRC-79 September survey included three GP question forms, each followed by the centrality measure. The behavior item followed the centrality measure on each form. The interaction of behavior, centrality, and pro-anti position is replicated over each form of the GP question, and the three forms were pooled to provide the gammas and χ^2 shown in the text.

vation is not independent of the attitude strength of antis, however, since it is just those with strong positions who appear to respond to such mobilizing efforts. We believe that the interaction of pro-anti position, centrality, and behavior shows how individual dispositions can be related to social organization and social mobilization to produce politically important effects (cf. McCarthy and Zald, 1977). Additional studies will be needed, however, to test these interpretations by means of direct questions on organizational memberships, solicitations, and other mobilizing activities.

Implications

From a methodological standpoint, the three measures of attitude strength are not equally useful for throwing light on the nature of public opinion on this issue. The intensity measure appears to be the least useful of the strength indicators, probably because it is too easy for people to claim to feel strongly about the issue, as indicated by the high proportion of people who say "extremely strong," but also because the measure seems sensitive to context. As a result, it fails entirely to capture the fact that antis are disproportionately represented among those with the strongest opinions on the gun-permit question. The behavioral measure, on the other hand, picks up just this difference to a remarkable extent, and if one is concerned primarily with the political consequences of opinion on an issue, it would seem wise to use questions on letter writing, contributions of money, or other forms of overt activity. The percentage reporting such behaviors is far from trivial, and the contrast between the distribution of pro and anti positions and the distribution of behaviors in support of those positions is pronounced.

The centrality measure provides a more complex picture than either the intensity or the behavior questions. On the one hand, it identifies those most involved in the issue, and for them taps something similar to what is manifested in self-reported behavior. At the same time, the centrality measure picks up an opposite and apparently quite reliable trend: Among those less concerned over the GP issue, there is a greater proportion of antis than of pros. The exact meaning of this latter finding is not clear, but in the interest of providing a full picture of public attitudes, the curvilinear distribution of centrality seems worth obtaining and exploring further. Overall, our experience with the gun-permit issue suggests the value of following pro-anti questions on policy issues with two measures: one registering centrality and the other obtaining reports on relevant behavior. However, some questions about general values cannot be put in terms of actions, and intensity measures are useful for assessing attitude strength in these cases, as we will see in the next chapter.

There remains one issue about the centrality measure, namely, what makes it distinctive. Apparently number of categories alone is not crucial, for we saw in Table 9.2 that centrality and intensity questions perform differently even when both have four categories. A second way in which the centrality item differs from the intensity item has to do with the behavioral reference contained in the former, and our results with the direct question on committed action would seem to indicate that the centrality measure benefitted from its quasi-behavioral nature. Whether other aspects of the wording of the two questions also played a part (such as the objectivity of "important" versus the subjectivity of "feel") can only be a matter of speculation in the absence of experimental variations in exact wording. We return to these methodological considerations after considering the application of the two measures to a second social issue.

ABORTION

The term abortion evokes a set of issues that have divided the public in fiercely emotional ways. Some people oppose abortion under virtually any condition, while others believe that a woman should have the right to have an abortion whenever and for whatever reason she chooses.[11] Unlike the gun-permit issue, we had no reason initially to believe that the minority opinion would be held more strongly than the majority position. But there was good reason to think that public attitudes played a particularly crucial role in a moral issue of this kind, and also good reason to expect the strength of these attitudes to enter importantly into political outcomes. Thus abortion questions seemed likely to be ones where attitude-strength measures might add appreciably to our understanding.

[11]Despite the heat that the debate has produced, we should note that when abortion was listed along with other national issues, it did not rank very high in importance for the public as a whole (e.g., Gallup, 1972: 879–881), though the issue may have come to be seen as more important in recent years. However, the relation between the proportion of people who rate an issue important, the strength with which such ratings are given, and the enduring quality of the ratings are separate issues in need of study.

Intensity, Centrality, and Committed Action

We carried out initial experiments on strength of opinion and abortion questions in two SRC telephone surveys in 1979, March and July. Intensity, centrality, and behavior measures exactly like those used for the gun-permit issue were employed.

In March we used a question on abortion from NORC's General Social Survey, together with a single centrality measure. A split-ballot was not employed, all respondents being asked the two questions in sequence. As Table 9.4 shows, a majority (58%) of respondents favored legal abortions for a married woman, but those opposing such legalization were much more likely to consider this to be a high priority issue. [12] Thus here again is an instance where majority opinion may be counterbalanced by the passion with which the minority holds its view. The results are similar to those for gun permits, but much stronger. We also examined the abortion–centrality association separately for three educational levels, for two age groups, and for both sexes, and found little sign of interaction involving any of these background variables.

The NORC abortion item speaks only of married women. It seemed desirable to generalize the issue further, as well as to make certain that the relation of centrality of opinion to pro–anti position was replicable and to test our other measures of strength. In July, therefore, we used a quite general question about abortion, originally written as part of a balance experiment. On one questionnaire form it was followed by an intensity measure; on the other form by a centrality measure; and after each of these the behavioral question was asked. [13] As Table 9.4 shows, the earlier results for centrality are perfectly replicated, and they also

[12]NORC reports different marginals for this abortion question in 1978, showing a majority opposed to abortion. Part of this difference can be attributed to sample composition differences, but most of it appears to be due to a question-order effect, as demonstrated in Chapter 2. The context effect makes it difficult to say what (if any) true division of opinion on this issue exists in the country, but it is probably close to 50–50.

[13]The behavioral question was added just as the survey began and could not be asked during the first 31 interviews. This accounts for the slightly smaller N when it is included in the analysis. The behavioral item also produces an unexpected borderline three-way interaction ($\chi^2 = 3.77$, $df = 1$, $p < .10$) with position on abortion and type of strength measure in the July 1979 survey: Committed actions are reported less often when the behavioral question follows the intensity measure than when it follows the centrality measure, but only for those who oppose abortion. If meaningful, such an interaction would reflect a complicated context effect, and since it is not quite significant and we can make no sense of it, we treat it as due to chance, but mention it here for completeness. The possibility of context effects on strength measures is raised again at the end of Chapter 10.

TABLE 9.4
Centrality of Opinion by Position on Abortion[a]

SRC–79 March

*Do you think it should be possible
for a pregnant woman to obtain a
legal abortion if she is married and
does not want any more children?*

Centrality	Yes	No
1. One of the most important	3.6%	11.4%
2. Very important	17.6	37.3
3. Somewhat important	37.6	31.8
4. Not too important	41.2	19.4
	100	100
	(279)	(201)

$$\chi^2 = 47.3, \ df = 3$$
$$p < .001$$

SRC–79 July

*Do you feel a woman should be
allowed to have an abortion in
the early months of pregnancy
if she wants one?*

Intensity	Yes	No	Centrality	Yes	No
1. Extremely strong	6.6%	35.6%	1. One of the most important	1.3%	11.5%
2. Very strong	18.4	34.5	2. Very important	16.8	43.6
3. Fairly strong	44.7	24.1	3. Somewhat important	32.3	20.5
4. Not strong at all	30.3	5.7	4. Not important	49.7	24.4
	100	100		100	100
	(152)	(87)		(155)	(78)

$$\chi^2 = 57.6, \ df = 3 \qquad\qquad\qquad \chi^2 = 35.9, \ df = 3$$
$$p < .001 \qquad\qquad\qquad\qquad p < .001$$

Behavior	Yes	No
Written letter	1.5%	8.3%
Given money	4.1	5.6
Both letter and money	1.1	5.6
Neither	93.3	80.6
	100	100
	(270)	(144)

$$\chi^2 = 19.5, \ df = 3$$
$$p < .001$$

[a] See Table 9.2 and p. 240 for wordings of Centrality, Intensity, and Behavior measures.

extend to the other two follow-up indicators of strength of opinion. Majority opinion supports abortion on demand in the early months of pregnancy (65% to 35%), but the minority shows much stronger commitment to its position regardless of whether strength is operationalized as intensity, centrality, or committed action relevant to the issue. These strength differences by pro–anti position are quite large, and given the substantial size of the minority, it is easy to see it winning political battles on the basis of greater dedication.[14]

We do not, however, find the relation of centrality to behavior to differ between pro- and antiabortion respondents—for both groups the relation is moderately strong (gammas of .48 and .44, respectively)—unlike the gun-permit issue. Furthermore, the relation of intensity to behavior is at slightly higher levels (gammas of .60 and .51 for pros and antis, respectively). These findings suggest that it is the greater fervor of the abortion opponents that is politically important, not their distinctive ties to central mobilizing organizations, although the fervor no doubt has its main effects through organized activities.

Implications

From a methodological standpoint, differences among the three indicators of strength prove to be of no importance in the case of the abortion issue. Although centrality continues to identify a much smaller set of fervent people than does intensity, and both are certainly different in nature from the question on behavior, each measure tells the same tale and an investigator can choose whichever seems conceptually more interesting. This conclusion differs from that for gun control, but we believe that the difference has to do with the distinctive relations of these two social issues to strength of opinion. Abortion position shows a monotonic relation to strength, as illustrated in Figure 9.2. Although the three indicators of strength—intensity, centrality, behavior—display different parts of the underlying continuum, all three reveal the same basic relation. Gun-permit position, on the other hand, shows a curvilinear relation to strength, with opponents represented disproportionately at both extremes of the strength dimension. The behavioral measure of strength separates the population only at the high strength end; the

---

[14]The abortion and centrality questions were repeated in panel interviews at two later dates, and also in a third new sample for a different purpose—all of which is discussed in Chapter 10. The basic abortion by centrality relation shown in Table 9.4 is replicated clearly in all these later surveys.

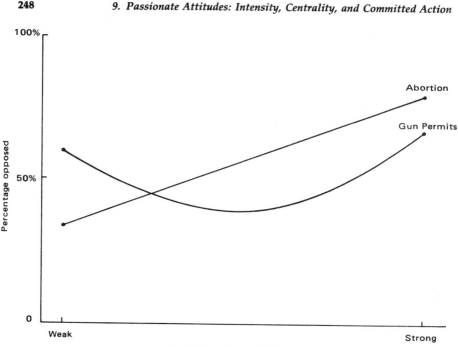

FIGURE 9.2   Hypothetical Relation of Abortion and Gun-Permit Positions to Underlying Strength of Opinion Dimension. (Strength of opinion is assumed to be an underlying dimension that is tapped by such indicators as centrality, intensity, and behavior. For each point on the dimension, the proportion opposed on the issue is shown, though the points are estimated only very approximately.)

intensity measure only at the low-strength end; and the centrality measure manages to divide the population so that the full curve is indicated.

Figure 9.2 is, of course, hypothetical, but our results are generally consistent with assumptions of this type. If approximately correct, then we begin to distinguish issues where varying measures of strength yield essentially the same results and issues where they do not. The important point seems to be the division of the population; verbal distinctions among the subjective measures are important only as they lead to differing divisions. This may be too simple a picture, but it provides a parsimonious hypothesis for future research. Questions on committed action, however, cannot be reduced to simply another measure of attitude strength, since writing letters and giving money are part of the political process, and connect (as Figure 9.1 suggests) to the activities of organizations that are more than the sum of individual attitude strengths.

CONCLUDING DISCUSSION

We have dealt in this chapter with three concepts: intensity, centrality, and what we call committed action. Intensity and centrality are both direct measures of the strength with which attitudes are held. They seem to differ only in that they distinguish different points along the strength scale. As we were able to operationalize them, people find it easier to say that they feel extremely strong about an issue than that they would regard it as one of the most important issues on which to decide their vote. This difference in where they fall along a strength dimension can have important consequences. But otherwise the two measures are generically alike and should be highly correlated, although there is some evidence that the intensity measure is more subject to context-like influence from a preceding question.

Committed action can also be treated as an indicator of attitude strength, but at the same time it takes on additional practical importance, at least to the extent that self-reports of letter writing, donations of money, and other behaviors are accurate. Thus, measures of committed action are doubly valuable to obtain, although their relation to other indicators of attitude strength cannot be assumed, since actions may have sources other than subjective strength.

Both of the issues that we investigated in detail revealed interesting associations between attitude direction and attitude strength. On the abortion issue, those favoring legalization were in the majority for two separate wordings of the question, but opponents held their attitudes with appreciably greater strength. The latter relation was true regardless of which measure of strength was used, and the three measures (intensity, centrality, and committed action) performed about the same. We concluded that opponents of abortion would carry more weight than their numbers imply, and that this would be true today primarily for subjective individual reasons rather than because of special organizational factors, although the strength of attitudes is expressed and made effective through organized activity.

For the gun-permit issue the findings are more complex. There is evidence that opponents of requiring permits include a disproportionate number who feel very strongly about the issue, but also (surprisingly) a disproportionate number who do not feel strongly at all. Although the former group may help to account somewhat for the success of opposition to gun permit laws, the major reason for success appears to lie elsewhere. It is not so much a difference in subjective strength, but rather in the way attitudes connect to action. For those who favor gun-permit laws, there is relatively little evidence of committed action and, furthermore, little indication that such action is related to attitude strength. For opponents of a gun-permit system, however, actions are much more frequent and are substantially correlated with subjective strength. Our interpretation, which admittedly could not be directly tested, is that gun-control opponents are connected to an effective national organization that is able to channel subjective feelings into letter writing and money donations. Thus in this case it is not so much that the two sides differ in subjective strength, but rather that on only one side is this attitude strength converted into effective political behavior.

The implication of our results is that it will often be useful to accompany pro–con items on an issue with measures of attitude strength. We suspect that only a single subjective measure is needed, and that most of the various ways of conceptualizing subjective attitude strength that have been suggested in the literature will come to much the same thing once operationalized. But perhaps further research is needed on this point, using other issues and other strength concepts and measures. A separate indicator of committed action certainly appears worth obtaining, for it proved for both issues studied to be a sensitive discriminator between pro and anti positions.

In closing this chapter, it is interesting to note a more general finding from the use of attitude-strength measures here and elsewhere in the book. If social issues are seen in liberal–conservative terms, as usually defined at present, then the pattern we have found for abortion is true for five of the six social and moral issues that we inquired into during the last half of the 1970s: The conservative position is held with more passion by its supporters than is the liberal position by its supporters. The six issues (with the page on which at least one form of each question appears) are: abortion (p. 246), divorce laws (p. 163), attribution of crime to individuals (p. 208), punishment of criminals (p. 120), laws against marijuana (p. 163). Only for gun permits does what would ordinarily be considered the liberal side have a slightly higher average level of subjective strength and as we have seen the relations for that issue are complex. This is not a matter of status quo versus change, since two of the items were parts of experiments where the present status of laws was contrasted to possible changes in both liberal and conservative directions.[15]

[15]There are also three other types of issues on which we have strength measures: a retrospective question on Vietnam (p. 163), an item on the closed union shop (p. 181), and a general question on whether the government is too powerful (p. 120). The probable liberal side shows greater strength on the first two, less strength on the third. But none is a social issue in the same sense that legalization of abortion or marijuana is.

10
Attitude Strength and the Concept of Crystallization

Crystallize: To give a definite and permanent form to.
—*American Heritage Dictionary of the English Language*

Having developed two measures of attitude strength in the previous chapter and shown their relation to socially relevant behavior, we turn now to the value of strength measures for assessing the reliability of attitude measures themselves. Before beginning these analyses, however, it will be useful to introduce an old idea from survey writing and discuss its relation to attitude strength.

Attitudes have often been characterized as crystallized or uncrystallized. The earliest such usage we have discovered is by Katz (1940), although he indicates (through personal communication) that it probably was employed still earlier by others. Rugg and Cantril (1944) lean heavily on the concept when discussing question-wording effects, but employ the term in a circular manner: They attribute wording effects to lack of opinion crystallization, yet identify lack of opinion crystallization by the occurrence of wording effects. Converse (1964, 1970, 1975) also makes frequent use of the word, but generally treats it as self-evident in meaning and seems not to have provided an explicit definition.

We believe that the term is a valuable one, but that it needs to be clearly defined, adequately operationalized, and systematically related to the notion of attitude strength. With respect to attitudes we believe that what most people mean by crystallized is (*a*) existence prior to measurement and (*b*) persistence in the sense of reliability of measurement. One might also include resistance to systematic change, as implied in the dictionary definition, but we think it more sensible to restrict the definition to one of existence and reliability, and to investigate empirically the relation between degree of crystallization in these senses and the likelihood of change under the influence of persuasion or events.

Existence of an attitude prior to measurement is the less easily operationalized part of our definition, but at least theoretically one can imagine using unobtrusive observation of spontaneous speech across a range of situations. Open questions are also a way of attempting to obtain genuine attitudinal expression with relatively little influence from the measurement procedure itself, although both the open question (see p. 85) and the interview situation (as in Table 2.9) no doubt do some shaping of responses. On the whole, however, prior existence of an attitude is something an investigator typically assumes, and then tests by assessing reliability.

Reliability can be operationalized by measuring an attitude at two or more points in time, provided that both memory of the previous response and true change can be ruled out as important factors affecting response consistency.[1] Given a sufficient time interval, it is unlikely that memory plays an artifactual role in the consistency of individual attitude items, and true change can be distinguished from unreliability by examining aggregate shifts in marginal distributions and by analysis of multiwave data (Heise, 1969; Wiley and Wiley, 1970).

Although prior existence of an attitude is ordinarily difficult to demonstrate, absence of such prior existence would seem to follow from evidence that the attitude is unreliable when measured. Thus, response consistency from one time to another seems a good way of assessing both aspects of crystallization. Of course, judgment is involved in these inferences, since defects in measurement can either decrease or increase consistency artifactually: Failure to give respondents a choice they see as realistic might prevent the expression of genuinely crystallized attitudes (see a possible instance in Chapter 8, pp. 214–217), while systematic biases such as acquiescence might increase reliability spuriously.

The concept of crystallization proposed here and the concept of attitude strength developed in the previous chapter are not the same—either theoretically or operationally—but they should be closely connected. Although it may be possible to think of examples of well-crystal-

---

[1]The term *response consistency*, used by Smith and Stephenson (1979), is purely descriptive, and refers to whether a respondent gives the same response at two or more points in time. The exact interpretation of response consistency or inconsistency—whether in terms of reliability, true change, memory, etc.—requires other evidence or theory. At later points we use the term *over-time correlation* in the same descriptive way.

lized attitudes that are not strongly held, on the whole one expects attitude strength (as measured through self-report) and attitude crystallization (as operationalized by over-time reliability) to be highly correlated. The expectation is indeed so reasonable that one might think it already well documented, but in fact we have not located any demonstration using data on the general population. Thus we treat it as one major hypothesis to be investigated in this chapter. A second hypothesis is that the increase in reliability will cause relevant interitem correlations to be greater among those who show greater attitude strength. In the course of testing these hypotheses, we explore the relations and differences between general and issue-specific measures of attitude strength, as well as the involvement of education both in these measures and in response consistency.

The standard psychometric approach to the problems discussed in this chapter is to construct multi-item indexes or scales (McNemar, 1946). In attitude surveys of the national population, this approach has drawbacks that are both practical (lack of interview time to include enough items for all constructs of interest) and theoretical (such indexes tend to force measurement toward abstract constructs such as gun control, rather than specific issues like gun permits that may be of more direct interest). Moreover, the approach taken here throws light on *who* it is that varies in reliability, and *why*, and the strength measures perform other functions as well, as described in Chapter 9. To be sure, there is no necessary opposition between multi-item and strength approaches, and the two can no doubt be combined in useful ways; but we do argue for treating unreliability as a substantive problem having to do with attitude crystallization, and not simply as a necessary but incidental attribute of measuring instruments.

OVER-TIME CORRELATIONS FOR THE INDIVIDUALS VERSUS SOCIAL CONDITIONS ITEM

The following forced-choice question was asked in SRC–74 Fall of a random one-third of the total sample:

> *Which in your opinion is more to blame for crime and lawlessness in this country—individuals or social conditions?*

Most of the respondents were successfully reinterviewed several months later in SRC–75 February, and exactly the same question was

repeated to the same third of the sample, followed by a simple dichotomous measure of intensity:

How strongly do you feel about that: quite strongly or not so strongly?

Using this item-specific intensity measure, one can examine separately
for high-intensity and low-intensity respondents the over-time correlations for the individuals versus social conditions (I–SC) item.[2]

The item proves to have a moderate correlation over time for the total
sample (phi = .43), but as shown in Table 10.1, the correlation is considerably greater among those who felt "quite strongly" than among those
who felt "not so strongly." The three-way interaction approaches significance ($p < .10$), despite the fact that the number of cases is small for
detecting higher order interactions. In fact, this is a rare instance where
there are compelling theoretical reasons for a directional statistical prediction, in which case $p < .05$. Thus we conclude that the reliability and
therefore the crystallization of this attitude is greater for those who
report more intensity of feeling.[3]

General Strength Measures

Attitude surveys sometimes employ general strength measures over a
range of items, on the assumption that these can serve the same purpose
as more specific measures attached to each issue. Our 1974–1975 panel
data included three such general strength measures, shown in Table
10.2, called News interest, General opinion strength, and Arguing. The
first (asked in SRC–74 Fall) was intended mainly as an indicator of political interest, while the latter two (both asked in SRC–75 February) were
thought of as tapping personality traits or personal style. In addition,
specific intensity measures much like the one asked after the individuals
versus social conditions item followed immediately after substantive

---

[2]There were two other forms of the question, both phrased as agree–disagree statements
rather than in forced-choice form, but they were not repeated in their original form and are
not directly relevant to our present purpose. See Chapter 8 for a discussion of the full
experiment.

[3]It is difficult to separate the substantive interpretation of this result from a statistical
phenomenon connected with it. Presumably those on each side of an issue who feel more
strongly about it are further apart on the dimension that underlies the dichotomous pro–
con choices than are those who feel less strongly. Therefore the former group has greater
variance than the latter, which should affect the size of the correlations. One could argue
that the larger over-time correlation of the strong intensity group merely reflects the
group's greater variance. We are indebted to Philip Converse for raising this point.

TABLE 10.1
Response Consistency Over Time for Individuals–Social Conditions Item by Levels of Intensity

		1. Persons saying: Quite strongly	
		Time 1 (SRC–74 Fall)	
		Individuals	Social conditions
Time 2 (SRC–75 Feb.)	Individuals	71.0%	21.7%
	Social conditions	29.0	78.3
		100	100
		(100)	(120)

$$\chi^2 = 56.04, \, df = 1, \, p < .001$$
$$phi = .49$$

		2. Persons saying: Not so strongly	
		Time 1 (SRC–74 Fall)	
		Individuals	Social conditions
Time 2 (SRC–75 Feb.)	Individuals	55.0%	27.1%
	Social conditions	45.0	72.9
		100	100
		(40)	(48)

$$\chi^2 = 7.16, \, df = 1, \, p < .01$$
$$phi = .28$$

Three-way interaction (time 2 × time 1 × intensity): $\chi^2 = 3.16, \, df = 1, \, p < .10$

questions on three issues: gun permits, the union closed shop, and America's past involvement in Vietnam. (The substantive gun-permit and union questions are treated in Chapter 7, and the Vietnam question in Chapter 6, but here we are interested only in the intensity measure that followed each of them.) To the extent that there is a general attitude strength trait, all these measures should be related to one another.[4]

[4]The general attitude strength items are adapted mainly from ISR Election Studies questions (see Robinson *et al.*, 1968: 661, 450). The specific strength measures were our own, but similar items have been used previously by others. Five of the seven measures were asked in dichotomous form, and the two that were not are dichotomized for the purposes of Table 10.2. (If news interest is maintained at four categories, its correlations

The intercorrelations among all seven measures of strength are shown in Table 10.2. With two exceptions, all the correlations are highly significant, and although General opinion strength lives up to its name by having the highest mean correlation with the others, all the measures appear to tap the same characteristic. Even the four specific measures are significantly correlated with one another, despite the diversity of issues to which they are attached. For example, notwithstanding the fact that the substantive questions on gun permits and Vietnam show no sign of a relation (gamma $= -.01$), the intensity measures attached to them are reliably correlated. At the same time, it is important to note that the three general measures are all significantly associated with education, whereas the four specific measures are unrelated to this major background variable and apparently reflect something quite different.

We substituted for the I–SC intensity measure in Table 10.1 each of the other six strength measures available in the 1974–1975 data set. Not one of these other measures produces more than the faintest trace of the different levels of association shown in Table 10.1. For example, when the General opinion strength item (shown in Table 10.2) is used in Table 10.1, those who say they have *strong opinions about a good many things* produce an over-time correlation (phi) of .44, whereas those who say they are *more in the middle of the road* produce an over-time correlation of .42. Moreover, the largest interaction (obtained by using the Vietnam intensity measure) is in the direction opposite to that predicted (.37, .49). In sum, whatever it is about the I–SC intensity measure that specifies the over-time correlation of the I–SC item, it is not part of the covariation that it shares with the other intensity measures. Our interpretation is that this unique factor is indeed strength of opinion on the particular issue dealt with by the I–SC item.[5]

Thus, although there seems to be a general attitude strength dimen-

---

with other variables tend to go down rather than up because of some irregularities in the relationships.) It will be noted that some of the measures were obtained in the 1974 Fall interviews and some in the 1975 February interviews of the same panel, and this difference in time of measurement might lower their correlations. It is impossible to test this point exactly, but the pattern of the correlations in Table 10.2 does not suggest that time of administration was an important factor. The wordings of the specific intensity items also differ among themselves to some degree, a regrettable but probably not major problem in evaluating their correlations. Note that the N for Table 10.2 is much larger than the N for Table 10.1, because the former is based on the full 1974–1975 panel, whereas the latter is based only on the third of the panel sample that received exactly the same I–SC form twice.

[5]There is some ambiguity in our specific measures over whether they tap strength of feeling about the issue or strength of feeling about one's response to the issue. We suspect that these amount to the same thing for most respondents, but further experimentation on this point would be useful.

TABLE 10.2
Attitude Strength Intercorrelations (Gammas) in 1974–1975 Data[a]

	(1) General opinion strength	(2) News interest	(3) Arguing	(4) I-SC intensity	(5) Guns intensity	(6) Union intensity	(7) Vietnam intensity	Education[b]
(1)	—							−.21
(2)	.36	—						−.20
(3)	.58	.44	—					−.38
(4)	.41	.30	.13[c]	—				.04[c]
(5)	.22	.26	.11[c]	.31	—			.09[c]
(6)	.31	.27	.18	.23	.26	—		−.05[c]
(7)	.28	.34	.35	.26	.25	.28	—	.06[c]
Mean	.36	.33	.30	.27	.24	.26	.29	

Strength Measures

General
- General opinion strength (1975): Some people have strong opinions about a good many things (45.2%). Other people are more in the middle of the road (54.8%). Which kind of person would you say you are? (N = 1077)
- News interest (1974): On the whole, would you say you follow national and international news very closely (28.7%), somewhat closely (48.7%), only a little (20.2%), or not at all (2.4%)? (Dichotomized here: 1 versus 2, 3, and 4, N = 1076)
- Arguing (1975): Some people like to argue about public issues (28.1%). Other people dislike arguing about public issues (71.9%). In general, which kind of person would you say you're closer to? (N = 1077)

Specific
- Intensity (following I-SC, 1975): How strongly do you feel about that: quite strongly (73.5%), or not so strongly (26.5%)? (N = 1018)
- Intensity (following gun permits, 1975): Compared with how you feel on other public issues, are your feelings on this issue extremely strong (47.8%), fairly strong (38.6%), or not very strong (13.5%)? (Dichotomized: 1 versus 2 and 3) (N = 1048)
- Intensity (following unions, 1974): How strongly do you feel about this issue: quite strongly (70.1%), or not so strongly (29.9%)? (N = 1077)
- Intensity (following Vietnam aid, 1974): How strongly do you feel about this issue: quite strongly (67.4%), or not so strongly (32.6%)? (N = 976)

[a] Items were asked of the same SRC sample in either 1974 or 1975. Marginal distributions and Ns for each strength item are shown in parentheses using full 1974–1975 panel sample. The Ns for the correlations range from 932 to 1077. All items are scored so that 1 = high strength.

[b] Education is coded into 5 categories, with 5 = college graduate or more. Negative correlations indicate that high education is associated with greater attitude strength.

[c] All gammas *except* these are significant at p < .02.

sion, it is not useful for understanding the consistency of responses to
the I–SC item. We hesitate on the basis of the results with a single item
to draw too broad a conclusion, and certainly a set of attitude items all of
which have related political content might well have over-time correlations sensitive to a measure of general interest in politics or the news.
But these data do suggest a useful and testable hypothesis: If investigators wish to identify a group of persons showing relatively high
consistency over time, they can do so best by obtaining a measure of
attitude strength that reflects the respondents' involvement in that specific issue, regardless of the person's degree of involvement in public
issues more generally.

Education

It is often assumed that education will be positively related to response consistency over time, a thesis proposed by Converse in his early
writings (e.g., 1964), but largely withdrawn by him at a later point
(1975). As Table 10.3 shows, there is no evidence at all that response
consistency over time on the I–SC item is higher among more educated
persons.[6] Rapoport (1979) points out that over-time correlations omit
respondents who say DK at either point in time, and that since these
respondents will ordinarily be disproportionately low educated, an
analysis such as ours may miss exactly the low-educated people who
tend to create unreliability. This is an important point and may account
for the absence of any relation of education to unreliability for the I–SC
item, although the same bias should occur for the abortion item (discussed next) and therefore probably cannot explain the difference between them. (See Appendix B.4 for further discussion of this problem.)

There is some evidence, moreover, of a curious interaction among
response consistency, education, and intensity. Among respondents
who graduated from high school or had some college, there is—as in the
total sample—a greater consistency for those who feel more strongly
about the issue than for those who feel less strongly. Indeed, the gap is
quite striking. Among the least educated, however, the difference does
not hold and is even reversed slightly. One possible explanation is that
poorly educated respondents are less able to separate attitude strength
toward a specific issue from attitude strength as a personal style. Partial
evidence for this appears when the four specific intensity measures in
Table 10-2 are intercorrelated for each of the three educational levels.
The mean interitem correlations (gamma) are .36, .33, and .16, respec-

---

[6]Age shows a trend for lower reliability with older age, but the trend is not strong or
regular and is not repeated for the abortion item (discussed below).

TABLE 10.3
Response Consistency Over Time for I–SC Item by Education
and I–SC Intensity[a]

A. By education alone:

	Education		
	0–11	12	13+
	.41*	.46*	.38*
	(79)	(119)	(109)

B. By education and intensity:

		Education		
		0–11	12	13+
Intensity	Quite strongly	.37*	.54*	.52*
		(58)	(89)	(73)
	Not so strongly	.52*	.26	.14
		(21)	(30)	(36)

Four-way interaction: linear $\chi^2 = 2.84$, $df = 1$, $p < .10$

*$p < .02$.
[a] Phi coefficients for over-time correlations of individuals versus social conditions item. Base Ns are shown in parentheses.

tively, for the low, medium, and high educated. Thus college-educated respondents are most likely to differentiate among the four issues in terms of strength of feeling, though the sharp contrast between the high school and the less than high school categories in Table 10.3 is not reflected here.

THE ABORTION ISSUE

We obtained additional panel data with a question taken from the NORC General Social Survey:

Do you think it should be possible for a pregnant woman to obtain a legal abortion if she is married and does not want any more children?[7]

[7] This question is subject to an important context effect, as discussed in Chapter 2 (see especially Table 2.6). In the present experiment the item was always asked without any other items on the same issue preceding it, thus maintaining a constant context over the three time-points.

The question was first asked in SRC–79 March (T_1), repeated in SRC–79 September (T_2), and repeated again in SRC–80 March (T_3). Each time it was followed immediately by the same attitude strength measure: the four-point centrality scale discussed in Chapter 9 and shown here in Figure 10.1. Thus an issue that is much more concrete than the I–SC item, a different and more differentiated specific strength measure, and three time points are available for this further investigation. Unfortunately, no general strength measures were included.

Overall response consistency for the abortion question from T_1 to T_2 is quite high, phi $= .71$, as might be expected for a moral issue that has been much debated and requires no special knowledge as a basis for response. Figure 10.1 presents the T_2 by T_1 associations for the abortion item separately by the four levels of the centrality measure obtained at T_1. Consistency rises monotonically with the importance that respon-

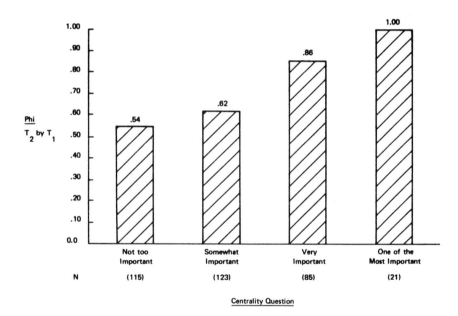

Centrality Question

"How important is a candidate's position on abortion when you decide how to vote in a Congressional election — is it one of the most important factors you would consider, a very important factor, somewhat important, or not too important?"

Three-way interaction (T_2 Abortion response by T_1 Abortion response by Centrality response at T_1)

$\chi^2 = 3.89$, $df = 1$, $p < .05$.

FIGURE 10.1 Response Consistency Over Time (T_1 to T_2) for General Abortion Item by Levels of Centrality. (Based on full sample available at both times 1 and 2 [March 1979, and Sept. 1979].)

dents attribute to the issue, the linear trend for the three-way interaction reaching significance at the .05 level. The phi scale, however, maximizes the monotonic appearance; if gamma is used, both the top two centrality points are 1.0, and if a simple percentage of those consistent out of total respondents is used, the bottom two points are almost identical. Thus the progression upward is not quite so clear-cut as the figure suggests, but the general finding holds.

In order to present results between all three time-points without undue detail, it is useful to note several preliminary findings. First, the centrality measure itself was asked at all three time points and shows a moderate degree of reliability, with no evident loss over time:

	phi
$T_1 - T_2$	.34
$T_2 - T_3$	.37
$T_1 - T_3$	.42

We use one separate and one combined measure of centrality in Table 10.4. The first is the measure from the initial of the two time points in each correlation: T_1 for $T_1 - T_2$ and $T_1 - T_3$, and T_2 for $T_2 - T_3$.

TABLE 10.4
Response Consistency Over Time for Abortion Item by Centrality[a]

$T_1 - T_2$		N	Phi				N	Phi
	Most	18	1.00		High	(3–6)	49	1.00
Centrality (T_1)	Very	70	.85	Combined		(7–8)	70	.72
	Somewhat	99	.62	centrality		(9–10)	86	.57
	Not too	84	.48		Low	(11–12)	69	.43
$T_2 - T_3$		N	Phi				N	Phi
	Most	21	1.00		High	(3–6)	49	.75
Centrality (T_2)	Very	82	.69	Combined		(7–8)	68	.71
	Somewhat	98	.53	centrality		(9–10)	85	.58
	Not too	72	.65		Low	(11–12)	69	.43
$T_1 - T_3$		N	Phi				N	Phi
	Most	18	.72		High	(3–6)	49	.75
Centrality (T_1)	Very	70	.72	Combined		(7–8)	68	.64
	Somewhat	100	.61	centrality		(9–10)	84	.50
	Not too	85	.53		Low	(11–12)	68	.57

[a] All correlations are based on the sample available at all three time-points (March 1979, Sept. 1979, and March 1980). On the left, a single centrality measure is employed, with the time of its administration indicated. On the right, a combination of the T_1, T_2, T_3 centrality measures is employed, as described in the text.

The second is a simple sum of a respondent's rating on each of the three centrality scales, yielding a possible range of 3–12, with 3 scored as high centrality and 12 as low centrality. The scores are collapsed back into four categories, which are constant in meaning for all comparisons. (It will be noted that the centrality measure asks about the importance of the issue, rather than focusing on the particular response given, and thus it maintains the same meaning even if the respondent's views on abortion should change.)

Because of sample attrition between T_2 and T_3, the correlations for $T_1 - T_2$ can be based on a larger N than those that involve T_3. However, since Figure 10.1 presents the $T_1 - T_2$ comparison for the full T_2 sample, in Table 10.4 we restrict all comparisons to the T_3 sample in order to keep the sample constant. (There are still small sample variations where the different centrality measures are used, since these cut the sample differently and also had slightly different amounts of missing data.) A comparison of results in Figure 10.1 with the $T_1 - T_2$ results in Table 10.4 shows that the reduction of the sample by about a fifth makes little difference in the correlations obtained.

Correlations among all three time points for the abortion item are presented in Table 10.4 by levels of centrality. In general, correlations rise for those who say that the abortion issue is more important to them. The increase is not as striking when T_3 is involved as when only T_1 and T_2 are in the picture, and there are some inversions at the low end of the centrality scale, but the results generally support the hypothesis that attitude crystallization, as measured by response consistency over time, is partly a function of self-reported attitude strength.

The relatively low over-time correlations for those who say the abortion issue is "not too important" could arise from either or both of two sources. On the one hand, respondents could simply answer the abortion item carelessly on both occasions, creating random error or unreliability in the traditional sense of the term. On the other hand, these respondents could be especially open to a genuine shift in attitude, and their discrepant responses may represent true change. Although individual attitude changes of the latter kind could conceivably occur in both directions and therefore cancel out at the aggregate level, it is more likely that such changes would be due to larger events and thus would be manifested as a movement upward or downward in the abortion item marginals. There is a slight upward shift in the marginals for the total sample over time (56.2% yes in March, 1979; 58.0% in September, 1979; and 59.0% in March, 1980), but it is small in size and nonsignificant ($\chi^2 = .45$, $df = 1$, for T_1 versus T_3), and it does not hold when those who consider the issue "not too important" are isolated (79.1%, 77.1%,

79.3%). Hence the lower over-time correlations for low-centrality respondents probably reflects unreliability of response almost entirely.

Education

We saw earlier that educational levels did not directly affect over-time correlations for the individuals–social conditions item, though they did seem to interact with our measure of intensity. The results are different for the abortion item, as Table 10.5 indicates. For all three sets of over-time correlations, consistency increases with increased education, and

TABLE 10.5
Consistency Over Time for Abortion Item by Centrality and Education[a]

$T_1 - T_2$		Education		
		0–11	12	13+
Centrality (T_1)	High	1.00 (22)	.69 (29)	1.00 (37)
	Low	.23 (26)	.63 (70)	.67 (90)
$T_2 - T_3$		Education		
		0–11	12	13+
Centrality (T_2)	High	.69 (25)	.80 (31)	.80 (45)
	Low	.18 (22)	.45 (66)	.82 (82)
$T_1 - T_3$		Education		
		0–11	12	13+
Centrality (T_1)	High	.42 (22)	.74 (29)	.80 (37)
	Low	.50 (28)	.58 (67)	.61 (90)
Means		Education		
		0–11	12	13+
Centrality	High	.70	.74	.87
	Low	.30	.55	.70

[a] All correlations (phis) are based on the sample available at all three times. Each centrality measure is divided into high (1 and 2) and low (3 and 4). Base Ns are in parentheses.

with two exceptions the increase is regular when centrality is controlled. Likewise, consistency increases from low to high centrality when education is controlled, again with two exceptions out of the nine comparisons. Moreover, as the pattern of base *N*s in Table 10.5 indicates, education and centrality tend to be *negatively* correlated for the abortion item, so that it is the less educated who feel more strongly about the abortion issue. (The relation is not monotonic, but levels off at the point of high school graduation. If the five-category education variable and the combined centrality measure are used, gamma $= .11$, SE $= .07$; thus the trend does not reach significance.)

Thus each of the two variables—centrality and education—tends slightly to suppress the effects of the other. If values of phi for each cross-classification of education and centrality are averaged for crude summary purposes across the three time-points, as shown at the bottom of the table, then respondents who are low in both education and centrality yield a mean over-time correlation of only .30, whereas respondents who are high in education and centrality produce a correlation of .87. The gap between these two figures for this single item is enormous, with the former revealing only a low–moderate amount of reliability and the latter reaching a level almost equivalent to that of quite lengthy multi-item attitude scales.

We are uncertain why education has different effects on the abortion and individuals–social conditions items, but the fact that it does indicates that a simple generalization about the role of education with regard to attitude crystallization may not be possible. Some of the conflicts in the literature about the effects of education (cf. Converse, 1980) may be due to the fact it does not act in the same way for all issues. In any case, more than the two issues dealt with here are needed for any broad conclusions about the role of education in response consistency. Specific attitude strength, however, is effective for both issues we have examined, and we hypothesize that it should normally specify consistency over time for attitude items regardless of their substantive content.

ATTITUDE STRENGTH AND ASSOCIATIONS AMONG ATTITUDE ITEMS

If the reliability of attitudinal responses over time is higher when the attitudes are held with greater strength, then relations among correlated items should—other things being equal—increase as a function of the strength of one or both of the attitudes (cf. Jackman, 1977). Strength cannot create an association where none exists, but it should enhance even a slight relation where there is a psychologically real connection to begin with.

Our early experiments seldom involved items expected to correlate, since we usually worked with quite different issues in order to avoid context effects. But there were several surveys where two potentially related items were asked and where one item had a strength measure accompanying it. We examined five such pairs. In three, the two items showed little sign of an overall correlation, and in these cases the strength measure had no noticeable specifying effect. But in the two instances where there was a significant overall association, the correlations increased among those higher on the strength measure. One pair consisted of an item on gun permits (followed by a four-category centrality measure) and an item on laws to conserve heating fuel (see Chapter 7 for the wording of the two items). Averaging across question forms (both items were constructed as question-balance experiments but form is unrelated to this result), the gammas from low to high centrality are .04, .29, .25, and .56. The other pair of items, from SRC–79 Sept., dealt with the legalization of abortion (followed by centrality) and the relaxation of divorce laws: The four gammas are .32, .61, .72, and 1.00. Thus these analyses support the hypothesis that interitem correlations are higher for respondents who claim that at least one of the issues is of real importance to them.

Abortion and Divorce

Based on these results we included the divorce item (see Chart 6.1 for the item wording, Omitted form only) and a modified version of the abortion item in SRC–80 June, each followed by its own centrality measure. The abortion item was varied in wording across two split-ballot forms as part of a tone of wording experiment (see Chapter 11):

Do you think it should be possible for a pregnant woman to go to a doctor to end her pregnancy if she is married and does not want any more children?

Do you think it should be possible for a pregnant woman to go to a doctor to have an abortion if she is married and does not want any more children?

The variation in wording may have complicated our results for the present analysis. In any case, the divorce by end-pregnancy correlations on the first form provide results generally in line with prediction, as shown in Table 10.6, though it is odd that it is the second highest rather than

TABLE 10.6
Divorce by Abortion/End-Pregnancy Correlations
(Gamma) by Levels of Centrality[a]

	Form A		Form B	
	By centrality for end pregnancy	By centrality for divorce	By centrality for abortion	By centrality for divorce
One of the most important	.61	.14	−.33	−1.00
	(20)	(11)	(14)	(8)
Very important	.70*	.85*	.53*	.68*
	(62)	(46)	(69)	(39)
Somewhat important	−.02	.26	.34	.27
	(86)	(77)	(98)	(96)
Not too important	.12	.23	.61*	.54*
	(98)	(132)	(113)	(153)

*$p < .01$.
[a] Carried out in SRC–80 June. The N on which each gamma is based is given in parentheses. The forms differed only in the wording of the abortion-end-pregnancy item, as explained in the text.

the highest centrality level that yields the strongest correlations. On the other form, however, the trends are quite unclear, with those saying "most important" again being especially puzzling. Combining the two centrality measures on each form does not clarify the picture, but simply emphasizes that the intercorrelations present different patterns on the two forms, with one pattern generally in line with the hypothesis and the other producing a reverse trend. Since no other results involving the abortion versus end-pregnancy variation reveal an effect of the tone of wording experiment (see Chapter 11), we are reluctant to interpret the form difference in correlations as due to this variation. Moreover, the form that fails to support the hypothesis is the one that is closest to the experiment from SRC–79 Sept. that provided initial support for it.

Abortion and Presidential Preference

It was not possible through other analysis to clarify the conflicting results in Table 10.6, but the same June 1980 survey also included an item on preferences among Presidential candidates that can be used in a further test of the same general hypothesis. Reports from other polls at that point in time indicated that position on the abortion issue was not much correlated with voting preferences, despite the fact that Ronald Reagan supported a Constitutional amendment to ban abortions, whereas John Anderson had clearly advocated free choice on the abor-

TABLE 10.7
Abortion Response by Candidate Preference for High and Low
Centrality Respondents[a]

		High centrality on abortion		
		Candidate preference		
		Reagan	Carter	Anderson
Position on abortion	Favor	32.7%	45.2%	53.6%
	Oppose	67.3	54.8	46.4
		100	100	100
		(55)	(62)	(28)
			gamma = .27, SE = .13, p < .05	

		Low centrality on abortion		
		Candidate preference		
		Reagan	Carter	Anderson
Position on abortion	Favor	76.7%	70.5%	80.2%
	Oppose	23.3	29.5	19.8
		100	100	100
		(163)	(112)	(91)
			gamma = .02, SE = .10, n.s.	

Three-way interaction (preference for Reagan versus others × abortion × centrality):
$\chi^2 = 3.39$, $df = 1$, $p < .10$

[a] SRC–80 June. Centrality levels are collapsed into high (one of the most important, plus very important) and low (somewhat important and not too important).

tion issue and Jimmy Carter leaned toward the free choice side of the issue. We hypothesized that the lack of overall correlation was due mainly to those who considered the issue unimportant, and that a correlation would appear among those who did consider the issue to be important.

The results in Table 10.7 tend to support the hypothesis.[8] For those who characterized the abortion issue as low in centrality, there is no

[8]To obtain the abortion item, we collapsed the abortion and end-pregnancy versions just discussed, after first examining the data separately for each form and finding no indication that the difference in wording affected results with respect to candidate preference. The preference question read: *Suppose the Presidential election were being held today. If Ronald Reagan were the Republican candidate, and Jimmy Carter were the Democratic candidate, and John Anderson of Illinois were an Independent candidate, who would you like to see win?*

relation between position on the issue and candidate preference. But for those who say the issue is high in centrality, support for legalized abortion is greatest among Anderson supporters, medium among Carter supporters, and lowest among Reagan supporters. (If Anderson and Carter supporters are pooled, the three-way interaction of preference by abortion by centrality is: $\chi^2 = 3.39$, $df = 1$, $p < .10$.) Thus, this is an instance where attitude strength may condition not only the association between two attitudes, but between an attitude and a behavioral intention (voting preference). In this respect, it is similar to the interaction reported in Chapter 9 for attitude direction, centrality, and behavior on the gun-permit issue.

RANDOM AND SYSTEMATIC EFFECTS IN MEASUREMENT

In this chapter we have provided evidence that random measurement error is, at least in part, a function of low attitude strength. In earlier chapters we investigated the complementary proposition that systematic measurement effects are also a function of low attitude strength. The latter proposition can be derived from reasoning that respondents are especially susceptible to question form and wording changes when their attitudes are not well crystallized. Indeed, such a hypothesis was stated long ago by Rugg and Cantril (1944:48–49):

> The extent to which the wording of questions affects the answers obtained depends almost entirely on the degree to which the respondent's mental context is solidly structured. Where people have standards of judgment resulting in stable frames of reference, the same answer is likely to be obtained irrespective of the way questions are asked. On the other hand, where people lack reliable standards of judgment and consistent frames of reference, they are highly suggestible to the implications of the phrases, statements, innuendoes or symbols of any kind that may serve as clues to help them make up their minds.

This view is probably held by many social scientists who measure attitudes.

However, only in our study of middle alternatives (Chapter 6) did we find clear evidence for an important role for attitude strength, and in that case attitude strength is really inherent in the dimension for which the middle alternative is the midpoint. In both balance experiments (Chapter 7) and agree–disagree experiments (Chapter 8), by contrast, specific attitude strength did not seem to condition form effects. This suggests that random measurement error and systematic form effects may be fundamentally different in origin, and that only the former is due to poorly crystallized attitudes.

Our data are too sparse to allow adequate testing of this broad conclusion, and we offer it here primarily as a hypothesis for future research. But we have one experiment that allows examination of both random error and systematic form effects simultaneously, and the results in this one case are striking enough to warrant presentation. The focal item is on the union closed shop and was presented earlier in Tables 7.1 and 7.3. It was asked in SRC–74 Fall in three forms (unbalanced, formally balanced, and counterargument), and the first two subsamples were reinterviewed in SRC–75 February using the counterargument form (the third subsample received the formally balanced form on reinterview and is not used in this analysis). Table 10.8 pools the first two subsamples (unbalanced and formally balanced), since they did not differ in results in any way, and cross-classifies their answers on the original form with their answers on the reinterview counterargument form. This is done separately for those who in the original interview had answered a follow-up specific intensity item "quite strongly" or "not so strongly."

Respondents who were not influenced by changes in question form *and* who were consistent over time should have responded to the union item with either pro- or anti-union answers both times it was asked. Thus, the pro–anti combinations (the off-diagonal cells) in Table 10.8 reflect either random error due to unreliability or systematic shifts due to question form. Moreover, the difference between the two gammas (.96 for the "quite strongly" and .68 for the "not so strongly") indicates that whatever change occurred was more marked among those with low attitude strength than among those with high attitude strength. The χ^2 statistic under the subtables shows this three-way interaction to be highly significant.

What is the source of the interaction of response, question form, and time? By comparing the row and column marginals for each subtable, we can observe the systematic effect due to the change in question form. As we would expect from earlier analysis in Chapter 7, anti-union responses increase on the counterargument form, *but* they do so to almost exactly the same extent for the "quite strongly" and the "not so strongly" people. (This interaction of marginal response distribution, question form, and intensity is nil: $\chi^2 = .00$, $df = 1$, n.s.) Thus the difference between the two subtables is *not* due to a difference in systematic form effects.[9] This leaves only random error as the source of the

---

[9]In Table 10.8 the question form comparison involves the same sample at two points in time. But a similar test can be carried out using the SRC–74 Fall cross section, where each form was administered to a separate subsample. In this case, the three-way interaction of response, question form, and intensity yields: $\chi^2 = 1.42$, $df = 1$, n.s.

TABLE 10.8
Responses to the Union Item Over Time and Question Form by Levels of Intensity

A. Quite strongly

Counterargument form (SRC-75 Feb.)	Original form[a] (SRC-74 Fall)			
	Pro-union	Anti-union	N	Percentage
Pro-union	68.1%	3.8%	(125)	26.0
Anti-union	31.9	96.2	(356)	74.0
N	100	100		
	(166)	(315)		
Percentage	34.5	65.5		100

gamma = .96

B. Not so strongly

Counterargument form (SRC-75 Feb.)	Original form[a] (SRC-74 Fall)			
	Pro-union	Anti-union	N	Percentage
Pro-union	41.8%	12.0%	(40)	20.3
Anti-union	58.2	88.0	(157)	79.7
N	100	100		
	(55)	(142)		
Percentage	27.9	72.1		100

gamma = .68

Three-way interaction: $\chi^2 = 21.3$, $df = 1$, $p < .001$

[a] Original form in 1974 was either unbalanced or formally balanced, the two subsamples having been pooled here. The counterargument form in 1975 was identical in both cases.

significant three-way interaction shown in Table 10.8. Those who feel less strongly on the union issue show greater unreliability in their responses.

In sum, for the union item we find that attitude strength is related to random error but not to systematic form effects. Other scattered evidence in our experiments suggests that this conclusion may be a broad one, but our data are too thin to do more than hint at such generality. The point is one of considerable importance and deserves a thorough test.

CONCLUDING DISCUSSION

Crystallized attitudes are those that exist independently of our measurement, and that when appropriately measured show high reliability. Existence independent of measurement is inherently difficult, if not impossible, to assess, but perhaps more can be done along that line by following the recommendations developed in Chapter 3. In any case, estimation of reliability is the primary way of assessing crystallization, and for single items in surveys this can be done with panel data, taking care to avoid confounding the degree of reliability over time with artifacts due to memory or true change.

Our main hypothesis is that attitude crystallization, as indexed by reliability over time, is reflected in self-reports of attitude strength. These are obtainable by means of simple questions on intensity of feeling or importance of an issue. Results for two series of experiments generally support the hypothesis. Those who felt strongly about the individuals–social conditions issue showed greater response consistency over time than those who did not feel strongly. And those who considered the issue of abortion to be more important showed appreciably higher consistency than those who regarded it as unimportant. Thus the relatively low over-time correlations for single survey items arise partly from the fact that many respondents do not care much one way or the other about the issues.

The point of particular interest and importance is that respondents are generally able and willing to report their strength of concern for a particular issue. It is often assumed that a great many people will not admit to lacking an attitude on an issue, and this is certainly true if their only way of doing so is to insist on a don't know response. But perhaps it is unrealistic to expect this kind of assertion of ignorance, since many people doubtless do have some vague feeling about almost any issue that can be posed (see Chapter 5). However, if we ask them to report the strength of their attitude on an issue, they are generally quite willing to do so. Indeed, on the abortion issue the majority claimed that it was *not* a central issue for them in terms of political decisions.[10]

Three other findings in this chapter deserve both emphasis and further research. First, the usefulness of an attitude strength measure with respect to response consistency over time seems to be a function of its being closely tied to the issue at hand. It is possible to construct measures of a general attitude strength trait, but they may not bear much on the problem of item reliability. Correspondence in level of specificity between the issue and the strength measure seems to be of critical importance for this problem. It is also quite interesting to note that general attitude strength measures are significantly related to education, and may indeed be thought of as one type of psychological mediator of education's effects on attitudes. Specific attitude strength measures typically do *not* relate to education, but presumably arise from an individual's personal involvement in a particular issue. Their value, we suspect, lies precisely in this fact.

Second, the effect of education on reliability is not simple. For one of our items it had no direct effect, although it did interact in a puzzling way with intensity. For the other item, however, higher levels of education were directly associated with greater reliability. We suspect that education does not have the simple, uniform effect on reliability that is often assumed, and that investigations should focus on what kinds of items show effects and what kinds do not. It may be useful to recognize that higher education can increase ambivalence and uncertainty as well as decrease ignorance and confusion.

A further hypothesis for which there was some but not unequivocal evidence is that if two attitude items are correlated at all, the correlation will be higher among those who report greater attitude strength for one or both of the items. Two secondary analyses of past data supported the hypothesis, a strong direct test of it using abortion and divorce items produced mixed results difficult to interpret, and still another test using vote preference was clearly positive. The hypothesis is thus largely but not entirely supported. Moreover, although it seems to be theoretically reasonable, all other things being equal, it is possible to imagine other

---

[10]It would be very convenient from a practical standpoint, as well as theoretically illuminating, if those who reported low attitude strength on an item were exactly the same people that chose "no opinion" when a DK filter was provided. As noted in Chapter 4, such an association does occur, but it is not strong enough to consider the two responses interchangeable.

things not being equal, so that higher strength on one or even both items does not imply a stronger connection between them. In any case, further systematic studies are needed before firm conclusions can be drawn on this issue.

This chapter and the previous one have presented arguments and evidence for the usefulness of attitude strength measures in surveys. Yet some cautions are also needed as we try to treat such measures as independent variables much like education or age. Attitude strength questions are themselves subjective to a considerable degree, and they therefore are open to influence from other features of a survey and other characteristics of the people who report them. We found evidence in Chapter 9 that an intensity measure was affected by context, which is not surprising since such specific measures must ordinarily be placed immediately after the issue question they are intended to modify. Earlier in this chapter we also noted evidence that the less educated do not distinguish among issues as sharply as the more educated when asked to report attitude strength. [11]

Despite these difficulties, the addition of measures of attitude strength to an attitude survey can deepen our understanding both substantively and methodologically of public values and of the public's response to issues. It is not enough to know pro and con divisions, even allowing for wording problems in obtaining such information. For both pros and antis we need to know with what passion—or absence of passion—positions are taken and held.

[11]This also shows up in two split-ballot experiments that administered an intensity measure to half the sample and a centrality measure to the other half. One experiment was in SRC–78 August where the two types of measures followed gun-permit questions. The other was in SRC–79 July where the same two types of strength measures followed a question on abortion. As reported in Chapter 9, the proportion of persons claiming strong views is much lower on centrality than intensity measures, presumably because the centrality question stimulates respondents to consider their priorities more carefully, rather than claiming too readily to feel strongly about every issue. Further analysis shows that in both experiments this difference is significantly ($p < .05$) greater for higher-educated than for less-educated respondents: The former discriminate more sharply between the two types of measures than do the latter.

11
Tone of Wording

... Words strain,
Crack and sometimes break, under the burden,
Under the tension, slip, slide, perish,
Decay with imprecision, will not stay in place,
Will not stay still.
        —T. S. Eliot, *Burnt Norton*

Warnings about the ease with which minor changes in question phrasing may affect results appear in many discussions of survey research. For example, Davis writes: "Slight changes in question wordings can produce distinct effects on item distributions [1976, p. 33]." Most often such warnings refer not to systematic variations in question form of the type we have considered in preceding chapters, but to unique changes in the choice of words for a particular item. Sometimes the concern is over the possibility of bias or loading (Payne, 1951); at other times, as in the quotation from Davis, what is involved is a more general observation about the sensitivity of survey responses to all kinds of nuances in wording. In either case, the warnings testify to the fact that ideas must be embodied in words and that words have a life—and an influence—of their own.

As explained in Chapter 1, our major effort in this research was not on idiosyncratic and probably ineluctable problems of wording individual items. But we did decide to carry out several experiments on choice or tone of wording where the verbal variation appeared to have implications beyond the single item involved. This is especially true for key words that occur time and again in survey items, either because they provide a common linguistic framework for posing issues or because they involve social symbols of enduring significance. The present chapter describes five such sets of experiments, takes note of past research on similar problems of question wording, and moves from this collection of ad hoc results toward a broader hypothesis about when changes in tone of wording will affect responses and when they will not.

TO FORBID OR TO NOT ALLOW

One of the most interesting examples of the apparent impact of tone of wording was reported four decades ago by Rugg (1941). He found in a split-ballot experiment (carried out by Elmo Roper in 1940) that support for free speech in the United States was 21 percentage points higher when respondents were asked *Do you think the United States should forbid public speeches against democracy* than when they were asked *Do you think the United States should allow public speeches against democracy?* In addition to our interest in learning whether this large difference due to wording could be replicated in the 1970s, the words "allow" and "forbid" have wide applicability where surveys inquire into moral issues such as abortion or use of marijuana. All such issues can be phrased in terms of whether a particular practice or behavior should be allowed or should be forbidden, and if the way the issue is posed influences responses about free speech, it may do so about other issues as well.

We began by replicating exactly the original forbid–allow experiment. Univariate results from three replications in 1974 and 1976, as well as from the original 1940 experiment, are presented in Table 11.1. Three important conclusions emerge from the comparisons. First, the original wording effect reported by Rugg (1941) is replicated in all three of our experiments: Americans are much more willing to not allow speeches than they are to forbid them, although the two actions would appear to be logically equivalent in this instance. Readers who doubt the equivalence should ask themselves whether it is possible both to allow and forbid a speech at the same time, or to not allow and yet not forbid it in practice. Of course, the two terms have different connotations, as discussed below, but their operational implications are the same in this case.

Second, there has been a sharp increase in willingness to tolerate "public speeches against democracy" on both forms of the question—a result consistent with other data on changes in the area of civil liberties (cf. Davis, 1975, and Nunn, Crockett, and Williams, 1978). The generality of this conclusion has recently been challenged by Sullivan, Pierson, and Marcus (1979) on the grounds that it may reflect only a reduction in concern over Communists and other symbols of the left. The Rugg question is not open to this objection, however, especially since in the 1940

TABLE 11.1
Four Experiments with Forbid–Allow Speeches against Democracy

	Forbid form					Allow form				
	Do you think the United States should forbid public speeches against democracy?					*Do you think the United States should allow public speeches against democracy?*				
	1940[a]	SRC-74 Fall	SRC-76 Feb.	SRC-76 Spring			1940[a]	SRC-74 Fall	SRC-76 Feb.	SRC-76 Spring
Yes (forbid)	54%	28.1%	20.1%	21.4%	No (not allow)		75%	43.9%	45.2%	47.8%
No (not forbid)	46	71.9	79.9	78.6	Yes (allow)		25	56.1	54.8	52.2
N	100 (1300?)	100 (936)	100 (586)	100 (1475)			100 (1300?)	100 (494)	100 (591)	100 (1375)

Response × form

1974 Fall: $\chi^2 = 35.75$, $df = 1$, $p < .001$
1976 Feb.: $\chi^2 = 85.50$, $df = 1$, $p < .001$
1976 Spring: $\chi^2 = 223.2$, $df = 1$, $p < .001$

[a] The 1940 results are from Rugg (1941). Exact Ns for 1940 are not provided by Rugg, but from information given in Cantril (1940) we assume that the percentages shown here are based on about 1300 respondents for each version. All DK responses are omitted, but see footnote 1 (p. 278).

context Americans no doubt thought of right-wing as well as of left-wing threats to democracy.

Finally, the two versions of the question record the increase in tolerance so similarly that there is little sign of interaction of response, question form, and time. (The three-way interaction [collapsing the 1974–1976 data and assuming 1300 cases for Rugg's data] is: $\chi^2 = 1.14$, *df* $= 1$, n.s.) Thus, unlike the context effect on the Reporter questions examined in Chapter 2, the wording effect here does not create a problem in assessing attitude change over time, *provided* that the question wording is kept constant at all time points.[1]

Education

On the assumption that the allow and forbid versions of the question are logically equivalent, we expected the form difference to be located primarily among the less educated, who would more easily be misled by superficial variations in wording.[2] Rugg (1941) does not provide data that allow this point to be tested, but results by education in 1974 and 1976 show the predicted interaction, twice significantly ($p < .05$) and once as a nonsignificant trend ($p < .20$). It should be emphasized, however, that although question wording significantly alters the strength of

[1]Despite the general stability of results over time, there is significant variation among the three recent replications. The 95% confidence interval calculated for the forbid–allow percentage difference in 1974 is approximately 11% to 21%, yet the differences in 1976 fall outside this range. Thus, although the basic direction of the orginal Rugg effect is replicated in all cases, the recent data show a vexing tendency not to conform neatly to statistical expectations (see Appendix A for a general discussion of this problem). We are uncertain why the form effect is larger in 1976 than in 1974, but one factor that can probably be rejected is the change in mode of administration from face-to-face to telephone. The second 1976 experiment was carried out partly by telephone and partly face-to-face, and this experimental comparison produced no relevant significant difference in the size of the wording effect (see Appendix B.2). Thus the results by mode of administration have been combined here.

An important difference not shown in Table 11.1 is a marked decline in don't know responses. Rugg (1941) reports DK levels of 17% and 15%, respectively, for the forbid and allow versions in 1940, whereas our later replications show DK levels of about 6% for both forms. This difference in levels apparently extends beyond the present items, since other items discussed in Rugg and Cantril (1944) and Rugg (1941) also tend to show higher DK levels than are common today, although these are confounded with differences in subject matter. Some part of the DK decline is probably due to the rise in education over the past 40 years, and some part to a difference in survey organization practices (p. 114).

[2]Gafke and Leuthold (1979) show that misleading, confusing, and difficult ballot titles affect the least educated disproportionately.

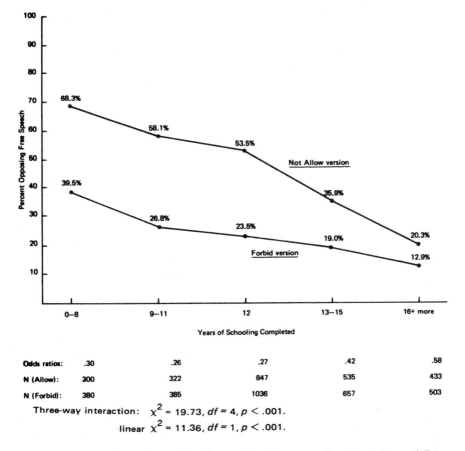

FIGURE 11.1 Opposition to Speeches against Democracy by Education and Form (Combined data from SRC–74 Fall, SRC–76 Feb., and SRC–76 Spring).

association between education and libertarianism—there is a sharper relation between response and education on the allow form than on the forbid form—it does not change the direction of the relation: Using either version one would conclude that education is positively related to support for free speech.

Figure 11.1 combines our three replications and breaks the education variable into five categories. Examination of the figure suggests that the interaction is not linear but involves a constant difference between the two question versions for persons of 0–12 years of schooling, then decreasing differences with some college and college graduation. The fact that higher education is associated with a decline in the form difference supports our assumption that the terms forbid and not allow amount to the same thing logically, and that it is verbal confusion rather than verbal precision that leads to a difference in response. At the same time, even college graduates show a significant form difference ($\chi^2 = 9.30$, *df* = 1, $p < .01$), so the effect must be considered both powerful and widespread.

Generalizing the Effect

The forbid–allow effect has now been established as substantial, quite stable over several decades, and related to but not fully accounted for by education. What causes it? And does it extend to items that differ in subject matter from the original Rugg questions?

There are at least three possible sources to the effect. First, and most obvious, are the differing connotations of the words "forbid" and "allow": the former sounds harsher and may therefore be more difficult to endorse, whereas the latter in some contexts might seem to encourage a deviant behavior and therefore may invite opposition. Thus what we have called tone of wording could be the sole source of the effect.[3] Second, the two terms create different grammatical structures. To forbid speeches against democracy, for example, may be confused with forbidding democracy itself, and the negation of allow also has its complexities. Third, whatever the main source of the effect, it may work in the Rugg items only because "speeches against democracy" is an abstract phrase that is not salient or clear to respondents. With a more concrete issue or one with greater salience, so this explanation goes, the effect should disappear. It will be noted that all three explanations could lead to the prediction of the interaction with education reported earlier (Figure 11.1), since it is the least educated who might be hypothesized to be most easily confused by emotional tone, by grammatical complexity, and by abstract issues. The three explanations are also not mutually exclusive, and each could play a part in creating the large effects shown in Table 11.1.

We tested the grammatical interpretation by changing the words "against democracy" to "in favor of Communism." This also switches symbols, of course, but maintains a fairly abstract level. When we in-

---

[3]Adams (1956) proposed that respondents tend to inhibit strong unfavorable judgments to all questions. His test of the hypothesis, however, produced no evidence for it. For the present, we assume that the forbid–allow effect is restricted to these verbs, though it may well extend to synonyms such as "permit" and "prohibit."

cluded this new experiment in DAS-76, the not allow response was 16 percentage points higher than the forbid response (see Table 11.2). This is at the low end of the previous range of effects but not radically different, and it suggests that the original effect extends to other symbols and other grammatical structures. At the same time, however, the interaction with education disappears entirely, and both versions show the same positive relation to years of schooling. Evidently low education is not a requisite for producing the generic forbid–allow effect, although it may accentuate the effect in the Rugg versions, perhaps because of the difficult grammatical structure created by those items.

Next we designed two experiments with more concrete subject matters, though in one case using an issue we believed to be of fairly high salience (X-rated movies), in the other an issue we thought to be of lesser salience (cigarette advertisements on television). If both these experimental items produced a forbid–allow response difference similar to the earlier ones, we could rule out interpretations dependent on interaction with certain types of subject matter and generalize the findings to a

TABLE 11.2
Forbid–Allow Speeches in Favor of Communism[a]

Forbid form		Allow form	
Do you think the United States should forbid public speeches in favor of communism?		*Do you think the United States should allow public speeches in favor of communism?*	
Yes (forbid)	39.3%	No (not allow)	56.3%
No (not forbid)	60.1	Yes (allow)	43.8
	100		100
	(409)		(432)

Response × form: $\chi^2 = 22.73$, $df = 1$, $p < .001$

By education

	0–11	12	13+	
Forbid	54.2%	42.8%	23.3%	gamma = .40
	(120)	(159)	(129)	SE = .07
				$p < .001$
Not allow	72.9%	57.2%	41.1%	gamma = .41
	(129)	(152)	(151)	SE = .07
				$p < .001$
Odds ratios:	.44	.56	.43	

Response × education × form interaction: linear $\chi^2 = .00$, $df = 1$, n.s.

[a] Carried out in DAS-76.

wide range of issues. On the other hand, if there were no forbid–allow response differences with either or both experiments, then we could reject the hypothesis that there is something about the connotations of forbid and allow in and of themselves sufficient to produce a response difference regardless of issue.

As may be seen in Tables 11.3 and 11.4, neither comparison reveals a clear marginal effect. Although there are trends in the same direction as our earlier results, they are small (5% and 4%) and of uncertain reliability. There is also not much sign of an interaction with education in either case. If forbid and not allow (or not forbid and allow) convey somewhat different meanings, the effect of the verbal difference taken alone is not large. For the alternative formulations to have much impact, it would appear that they have to be joined to abstract issues like free speech or Communism.

There is one other possible clue to the different degrees of wording effect found for the four types of forbid–allow content that we used. The don't know (DK) level is highest on the speeches-against-democracy item (where the mean DK percentage is 5.8), next highest on the speeches-in-favor-of-Communism item (3.9), third on the X-rated-movies item (2.4); and lowest on the cigarette-advertisements item

TABLE 11.3
Forbid–Allow X-Rated Movies (SRC–77 Aug.)

Forbid form		Allow form	
Do you think the government should forbid the showing of X-rated movies?		*Do you think the government should allow the showing of X-rated movies?*	
Yes (forbid)	41.0%	No (not allow)	46.4%
No (not forbid)	59.0	Yes (allow)	53.6
	100		100
	(547)		(576)

Response × form: $\chi^2 = 3.33$, $df = 1$, $p < .10$

	By education			
	0–11	12	13+	
Forbid	65.3%	41.8%	30.7%	gamma = .40
	(101)	(189)	(254)	SE = .06
				$p < .001$
Not allow	66.1%	53.4%	31.0%	gamma = .47
	(127)	(174)	(261)	SE = .06
				$p < .001$
Odds ratios:	.97	.62	.98	

Response × education × form: linear $\chi^2 = .00$, $df = 1$, n.s.

TABLE 11.4
Forbid–Allow Cigarette Ads (SRC–79 Sept.)

Forbid form		Allow form	
Do you think the government should forbid cigarette advertisements on television?		*Do you think the government should allow cigarette advertisements on television?*	
Yes (forbid)	50.6%	No (not allow)	54.9%
No (not forbid)	49.4	Yes (allow)	45.1
	100		100
	(607)		(297)

Response × form: $\chi^2 = 1.48$, $df = 1$, n.s.

By education

	0–11	12	13+	
Forbid	50.0%	46.8%	53.4%	gamma = .07
	(118)	(216)	(251)	$SE = .07$, n.s.
Not allow	62.5%	50.5%	55.7%	gamma = .04
	(58)	(99)	(131)	$SE = .10$, n.s.
Odds ratios:	.60	.86	.91	

Response × education × form: linear $\chi^2 = 1.10$, $df = 1$, n.s.

(1.3). In other words, the higher the DK level the larger the forbid–allow effect. This fits a suggestion by Gallup that the effect of a "difference in wording . . . tends to decrease to zero as the no opinion vote tends to zero [1941:261]." However, the sizes of form effects reported in other chapters (for example, response-order effects in Chapter 2) do *not* show any relation to DK levels. Thus, the apparent association here (based on only four forbid–allow variants) may be due to chance; or if not, it is probably restricted to a narrow range of wording effects.

At this point it seems that the forbid–allow effect can best be attributed to a subtle interaction between words and subject matter, with grammatical structure perhaps playing an additional role in creating an educational difference in some instances. But these interpretations are too much after the fact to be offered with great confidence, and given the large size and uncertain scope of the effect, further work on it would be desirable. Indeed, its nonobvious nature offers a challenge to students of survey research.[4]

[4]Still another complication has appeared, based on a recent study by Duane Alwin, Susan Stephens, and Richard Serpe (personal communication, 1980). These investigators

COMMUNISM AND QUESTION WORDING

A quite different type of wording change, but one that also may have some generality was noted by John Mueller in his review of public opinion data on the Korean and Vietnam wars. Mueller (1973:44, 112) observed that support for American intervention seemed to rise when a Communist threat was mentioned as part of the question.[5] Since the observation was based, however, on a comparison of questions that varied in other respects also, the reported variation of about 15% could have come from other sources. To provide a more rigorous test of Mueller's thesis, as well as to consider interactions between this question form difference and relevant background and attitude variables, we carried out an experiment using a Gallup question cited by Mueller:

> If a situation like Vietnam were to develop in another part of the world,
> do you think the United States should or should not send troops?
> [Gallup Opinion Index, 29, 1967]

This item constituted one form of a split-ballot included in the SRC–74 Fall survey. The other form of the question consisted of exactly the same words, but with the addition of the phrase: *to stop a Communist take-over?* The experiment was repeated in SRC telephone surveys in 1976 and 1978, so replication data are available for most of our analyses.

---

replicated the forbid–allow "speeches against democracy" experiment in Indianapolis in 1979, and followed it by two further experiments on forbidding–allowing abortions and forbidding–allowing ownership of unregistered hand guns. All three experiments show significant differences in the predicted direction, despite a total sample size of only about 325. (Because of the small sample, breaks by education are not very practical, but there is little sign of three-way interaction.) Their evidence, therefore, is that the forbid–allow effect does generalize across issues, including two that are quite concrete and salient for the public. One way to reconcile the Alwin *et al.* results with those we obtained for X-rated movies and cigarette advertisements is to note that the former were asked in sequence (democracy first) and to hypothesize an order effect that transfers the forbid–allow wording impact from one item to another. In addition, the Alwin *et al.* new items are worded in a quite difficult fashion, and it is possible that grammatical confusion by respondents contributed to the effects they discovered.

Blankenship (1940b) also discusses an experiment quite close to the forbid–allow problem. He compared results for five versions of a question on race track gambling in New Jersey with subsequent referendum results on the same issue. Two of his forms use "permit" and "prohibit" as key terms; the latter shows a trend toward higher predictive validity. The greatest validity, however, is shown by a form that combines both verbs, as we might have done by asking respondents whether they would *allow or forbid speeches against democracy*. This last approach seems a sensible one, but it is impossible to evaluate Blankenship's own claim about validity because he does not present the wording of the referendum itself.

[5]Barron and Immerwahr (1979) report a similar difference for questions about South Africa.

TABLE 11.5
Response to Another Vietnam by Question Form

Original question		Communist Takeover version	
*If a situation like Vietnam were to develop in another part of the world, do you think the United States **should** or **should not** send troops?*		*If a situation like Vietnam were to develop in another part of the world, do you think the United States **should** or **should not** send troops to stop a communist takeover?*	
SRC–74 Fall			
Send troops	18.3%	Send troops	33.2%
Not send troops	81.7	Not send troops	66.8
	100		100
	(459)		(871)
	$\chi^2 = 34.54$, $df = 1$, $p < .001$		
SRC–76 Feb.			
Send troops	15.6%	Send troops	27.9%
Not send troops	84.4	Not send troops	72.1
	100		100
	(575)		(549)
	$\chi^2 = 24.93$, $df = 1$, $p < .001$		
SRC–78 Fall			
Send troops	18.3%	Send troops	36.7%
Not send troops	81.7	Not send troops	63.3
	100		100
	(885)		(449)
	$\chi^2 = 52.67$, $df = 1$, $p < .001$		

Results

Univariate distributions for the two forms of the "another Vietnam" question are shown in Table 11.5.[6] A highly significant form difference, quite similar in size to that reported by Mueller, appears in all three experiments. Approximately one seventh of the public evidently will choose sides differently on the issue of American intervention depending upon whether or not threat of a Communist takeover is explicitly mentioned.

We had hypothesized that more-educated respondents would assume that reference to Vietnam already implied a Communist threat of some sort, and therefore that the additional "Communist takeover" phrase

[6]Missing data (DK, NA, other) are omitted from all tables for simpler presentation. In 1974 missing data (especially NA) were significantly more frequent on the Communist takeover form, but there was no difference in 1976 or 1978. No explanation for the difference is apparent.

would not appreciably change the question for them. As can be seen in Table 11.6, there is some evidence for the hypothesis, but it is not strong and is restricted to the first two surveys. In both 1974 and 1976, college graduates show only a tiny effect (3%) of question form, whereas those with the least education (0–8 years) show the largest effect (19–25%). The intermediate educational categories are generally intermediate in effect, but there are inconsistencies in trend that do not fit the hypothesis. Furthermore, in the 1978 survey, education is unrelated to the form effect, despite the fact that the marginal difference in 1978 is very similar to those in the first two studies.[7] The status of the hypothesis is at best uncertain, and if there is an education effect it is doubtless small.

We also hypothesized that the version of the Vietnam item mentioning Communism would be related to other items referring to Communism, but that this would be less true or not true at all for the original Gallup question. In order to test this hypothesis we included a constant item about domestic Communism in the 1978 survey that replicated the another-Vietnam experiment. As shown in Table 11.7, people who favor removing a book by a Communist are slightly more likely to favor intervening in another Vietnam, but this occurs to the same extent on both question forms. (The split-ballot for this experiment employed different subsample sizes, and this accounts for the difference in the bivariate significance levels.) Thus those people affected by the form of the Vietnam item, although obviously sensitive to the mention of Communism in an international context, do not seem to be disproportionately concerned about Communism at home.

Other standard background factors (age, sex, race, religion) and several other attitude items were also analyzed in relation to the another-Vietnam experiment. In no case was a significant interaction produced, and in fact the effect of the Communist takeover addendum is remarkably uniform over all the categories examined in each such analysis. This seems to be an instance where a highly reliable difference in marginals shows very little sign of altering relations with other variables.

Different Versions or Different Questions?

It is important to recognize that varying theoretical interpretations can be given to the addition of the "Communist takeover" phrase to the

---

[7] The four-way interaction, response by education by form by survey (1974 plus 1976 versus 1978) is of borderline significance ($\chi^2 = 8.77$, $df = 4$, $p < .10$). The response by education by form interactions do not differ between 1974 and 1976 ($\chi^2 = 2.41$, $df = 4$, n.s.).

TABLE 11.6
Percentage "Send Troops" by Education and Form

	Education				
	0-8	9-11	12	13-15	16+
SRC-74 Fall					
Original question	15.0% (80)	20.8% (53)	20.8% (154)	16.2% (99)	16.7% (72)
			gamma = .02, SE = .08, n.s.		
Question with *Communist takeover*	39.9% (148)	32.8% (122)	34.1% (299)	35.4% (178)	20.2% (119)
			gamma = .13, SE = .05, $p < .02$		
Odds ratios:	.27	.54	.51	.35	.79
	Response × form × education: linear χ^2 = 2.26, df = 1, n.s.				
SRC-76 Feb.					
	0-8	9-11	12	13-15	16+
Original question	17.1% (76)	20.9% (91)	13.9% (187)	13.1% (107)	15.8% (114)
			gamma = .07, SE = .08, n.s.		
Question with *Communist takeover*	35.7% (70)	22.9% (70)	31.4% (194)	27.3% (121)	19.1% (94)
			gamma = .13, SE = .07, $p < .10$		
Odds ratios:	.37	.89	.35	.40	.79
	Response × form × education: linear χ^2 = .36, df = 1, n.s.				
SRC-78 Fall					
	0-8	9-11	12	13-15	16+
Original question	21.6% (74)	27.0% (100)	21.7% (323)	16.0% (188)	10.1% (189)
			gamma = .25, SE = .06, $p < .001$		
Question with *Communist takeover*	37.5% (48)	61.2% (49)	35.7% (154)	37.3% (110)	24.7% (81)
			gamma = .20, SE = .07, $p < .01$		
Odds ratios:	.46	.23	.50	.32	.34
	Response × form × education: linear χ^2 = .06, df = 1, n.s.				

TABLE 11.7
The Association of "Another Vietnam" and "Communist Book"
by Form (SRC–78 Fall)

Communist book

*This next question is about a man who admits he is a communist.
Suppose he wrote a book which is in your public library. Somebody
in your community suggests the book should be removed from the
library. Would you favor removing the book, or not?*[a]

Original another Vietnam question

	Favor	Not favor
Send troops	21.7%	16.0%
Not send troops	78.3	84.0
	100.0	100.0
	(244)	(595)

$\chi^2 = 3.82$, $df = 1$, $p < .10$,
gamma = .19

Another Vietnam with Communist takeover

	Favor	Not favor
Send troops	41.3%	34.0%
Not send troops	58.7	66.0
	100.0	100.0
	(121)	(303)

$\chi^2 = 1.99$, $df = 1$, n.s.,
gamma = .16

Three-way interaction: $\chi^2 = .05$, $df = 1$, n.s.

[a] This question is taken from Stouffer (1955). Here it is used only in the original wording, but in a later section it becomes the subject of an experiment.

another-Vietnam item. Mention of Communism can be seen as simply a rhetorical flourish, leaving the substance of the question unaltered, and this interpretation was the basis for our experiments with the item. But the two versions can also be seen as basically different questions: Mention of a Communist threat specifies the reason for intervention and distinguishes (for some people) a needed American action from one not needed. Other interpretations between these two extremes also seem possible, and it is unlikely that the ambiguity of what is happening can easily be resolved.[8] Nevertheless, whether the results are treated as

[8]Much the same problem arises with an early experiment reported by Cantril (1940). Respondents on one form were asked *Do you think the U.S. should do more than it is now doing to help England and France?* On a parallel form the phrase *in their fight against Hitler?* was added. The latter form raised the percentage saying yes from 13% to 22%, significant

methodological or substantive in nature, it is of considerable interest that support for American military intervention can be increased by 15% when a question—or a speech by a President?—points to a Communist threat.

LOADED STOUFFER ITEMS?

The judgment as to whether certain words or phrases bias an item or are instead legitimate specification of the issue is rarely a simple matter. Consider the following two questions from Stouffer's well-known study of *Communism, Conformity, and Civil Liberties* (1955):

> *There are always some people whose ideas are considered bad or dangerous by other people. For instance, somebody who is against all churches and religion. If such a person wanted to make a speech in your (city/town/community) against churches and religion, should he be allowed to speak, or not?*

> *This next question is about a man who admits he is a Communist. Suppose he wrote a book which is in your public library. Somebody in your community suggests the book should be removed from the library. Would you favor removing the book, or not?*

The introductory sentence in the first question, implying that atheists are "bad or dangerous," may strike some readers as gratuitously loading the item against the free speech position. Similarly, the reference in the second question to "somebody suggests the book should be removed" might seem to unfairly tilt responses in the intolerant direction. Yet when Stouffer wrote these questions he apparently did not regard them as biased. Indeed, he might have claimed that they accurately embodied the libertarian issues of interest: One wants to know if people are willing to extend free speech even to those thought bad or dangerous, and likewise to know if citizens are willing to preserve unpopular books even in the face of pressures from others. Since the investigator's basic aims are involved, there may be no definitive resolution to this issue, but what we can do is to determine how much, if at all, such additions to questions influence responses.

The two Stouffer items quoted previously (which also are asked regularly in the NORC General Social Survey) were used as one form of a

---

for the sample used; the shift is said to be slightly greater for women, people over 40, and those with lower incomes. Clearly the mention of Hitler can be regarded as further information, rather than as emotional loading.

split-ballot experiment in 1974. In a second form we simply removed the offending words:

> *There are some people who are against all churches and religion. If such a person wanted to make a speech in your (city/town/community) against churches and religion, should he be allowed to speak, or not?*

> *This next question is about a man who admits he is a Communist. Suppose he wrote a book which is in your public library. Would you favor removing the book, or not?*

In still a third form of each question, we added words to tilt the items in the pro-libertarian direction (bold face shows the additions, but the bold face itself was not included in the questionnaire):

> *There are some people who are against all churches and religion. If such a person wanted to make a speech in your (city/town/community) against churches and religion, should he be allowed **the freedom** to speak, or not?*

> *This next question is about a man who admits he is a Communist. Suppose he wrote a book which is in your public library. Somebody in your community suggests the book should be removed from the library. **Somebody else in your community says this is a free country and it should be allowed to remain.** Would you favor removing the book, or not?*

All three versions of each item were included in SRC–74 Fall, and the first and third versions were replicated in SRC–76 February.

For the atheist item it appears that Stouffer's "bad or dangerous" introduction had no effect in 1974 on item marginals, but that addition of a reference to "freedom" shifted some respondents in the civil libertarian direction (see Table 11.8). It may be that the former is too blatant and unreasoned a characterization, whereas the latter is a more subtle reminder of the basis for allowing unpopular speeches. When the two extreme forms were repeated in 1976, the difference increased in size, although without the neutral form we cannot be certain that the effect is due only to adding the word "freedom" and not also to removing the negative introduction.[9]

[9]Both here and for the book item, the form effect in 1976 is so much larger than in 1974 that the three-way interaction with time reaches borderline significance ($\chi^2 = 3.47$, $df = 1$, $p < .06$ for the atheist item). In both cases the interaction stems from a sharp increase in libertarian sentiment on the form that leans in the liberal direction, combined with no change on the original form. Since it seems unlikely that much real attitude change occurred over the 2-year period, sampling error is probably responsible for the difference; note that the same trend occurs with the forbid–allow item in Table 11.1.

TABLE 11.8
Free Speech for Atheists by Question Wording

	a. Original Stouffer question	b. Neutral modification	c. Modification in liberal direction
SRC–74 Fall			
Yes, allowed to speak	66.3%	65.8%	71.7%
No, not allowed	33.7	34.2	28.3
	100.0	100.0	100.0
	(508)	(503)	(487)

a versus b: $\chi^2 = .03$, $df = 1$, n.s.   b versus c: $\chi^2 = 3.95$, $df = 1$, $p < .05$

	a. Original Stouffer question		c. Modification in liberal direction
SRC–76 Feb.			
Yes, allowed to speak	68.7%		80.1%
No, not allowed	31.3		19.9
	100.0		100.0
	(629)		(612)

$\chi^2 = 21.2$, $df = 1$, $p < .001$

For the book item there are no meaningful response differences among any of the three versions in 1974 (see Table 11.9). In 1976 there is a small but just significant difference between the original form and the more balanced form. In the absence of further replication, the most sensible strategy is probably to combine the results from the 2 years, in which case there is only a 2% difference between the two extreme versions of the book item.

We also examined response differences by education on the assumption that less-educated respondents would be most influenced by the wording changes. None of the three-way interactions for the atheist comparisons approaches significance, though there are small trends for the more educated to show less effect from wording changes. The education relation for the original Stouffer version of the book item is significantly different in 1974 from the relations on the modified versions; but the interaction is difficult to interpret (both high-and low-educated respondents show an effect, but in opposite directions) and there is no trace of it in 1976. Thus at present we conclude that education does not play an important role in these wording variations.

In sum, there is not much evidence that Stouffer's original loaded wordings influence respondents to answer in a more conservative (or any other) direction on these two items. However, there is fairly strong evidence that our more subtle addition in the liberal direction did influ-

TABLE 11.9
Removal of a Communist's Book by Question Wording

	a. Original Stouffer question	b. Neutral modification	c. Modification to opposite direction
SRC–74 Fall			
Favor removing	30.9%	35.6%	32.6%
No, not favor	69.1	64.4	67.4
	100	100	100
	(495)	(481)	(469)

a versus b: $\chi^2 = 2.37$, $df = 1$, n.s.   b versus c: $\chi^2 = .91$, $df = 1$, n.s.

	a. Original Stouffer question		c. Modification to opposite direction
SRC–76 Feb.			
Favor removing	28.9%		23.8%
No, not favor	71.1		76.2
	100		100
	(615)		(601)

$\chi^2 = 4.16$, $df = 1$, $p < .05$

ence responses on the atheist item in 1974, and somewhat more ambiguous evidence that the same can occur for the Communist book item as well. Thus the assertion that changes in wording may affect response is stated in the right way: They may, but they also may not. Moreover, it would have been difficult to predict in advance which type of change would have an effect. In hindsight, it appears that more subtle forms of influence may be more effective, especially if there is positive emphasis on widely accepted values (freedom, in this instance), whereas a crude negative appeal (bad and dangerous) may have no impact. This seems an hypothesis worth pursuing in future experiments on question wording. Finally, there is not much evidence that any of the effects interact meaningfully with education. Response marginals, but perhaps not much else, are changed by the kinds of verbal variations discussed in this section.

ABORTION VERSUS ENDING PREGNANCY

An antiabortion advertisement in The New York Times in 1974 claimed that some polls showing support for legalization of abortion did so by substituting the words "end pregnancy" for "abortion" in their question. This might be considered an example of use of euphemisms, especially if we assume that the terms are equivalent in ordinary English and are so understood by almost everyone who understands the meaning of either one separately.

We tested the claim in a split-ballot experiment in SRC–80 June:

Do you think it should be possible for a pregnant woman to go to a doctor to end her pregnancy if she is married and does not want any more children?

Do you think it should be possible for a pregnant woman to go to a doctor to have an abortion if she is married and does not want any more children?

The results do not provide much evidence for the hypothesis that the end-pregnancy version of the question will elicit the greater support or have other effects. In fact, a slightly larger proportion of the population said yes to the abortion version (63.4%) than to the end-pregnancy version (62.9%), though the difference does not approach significance (*N*'s are 315 and 319, respectively). A centrality measure followed each item, for reasons discussed in Chapter 10, and the distributions on the measure do not differ significantly by form, nor do they relate differently to the two versions of the question. There are also no significant differences between responses to the abortion and end-pregnancy versions by sex, education, or age. A possible four-way interaction involving form that is discussed in Chapter 10 prevents us from ruling out completely any effect from the wording change. But if there is such an effect—and we doubt its reliability—it does not influence the level of univariate distributions where it would be most obvious, and it thus works in mysterious ways. For most practical purposes, "ending pregnancy" and "having an abortion" seem to be interchangeable phrases in a survey question at present.

TONE OF WORDING AND ATTITUDE STRENGTH

Most of the experimental items discussed in this chapter were first included in SRC–74 Fall. For these early experiments and certain later ones, we have available all or some of the three general attitude strength indicators presented in Table 10.2 and discussed in Chapter 10. A plausible hypothesis is that persons reporting stronger attitudes generally (e.g., liking to argue over public issues) will be less likely than others to be affected by changes in tone of wording. However, there is no convincing evidence in support of this hypothesis for the data dealt with in the present chapter. Neither the another-Vietnam nor the Communist book item shows any sign of such specification when the general attitude strength items are introduced as third variables along with question form and response. Both the forbid–allow and the atheist item experiments do show some evidence of a significantly increased wording effect for those with less strong attitudes, but in each case the significant effect disappears when education is controlled.

Unfortunately, only one tone of wording experiment was accompanied by a specific strength measure, but there are few signs in analysis reported in preceding chapters that such specific items influence systematic wording effects, as distinct from random error. There is no particular reason to expect a different outcome where tone of wording is involved.

CONCLUDING DISCUSSION

We have considered five experiments (plus replications of most of these) that deal with unique wording changes: the forbid–allow contrast; addition of a Communist threat reference to an item about American intervention in another Vietnam; alterations in two of Stouffer's 1955 civil liberties questions; and avoidance of the word "abortion." Most of the experiments show reliable shifts in marginals—some of the shifts being quite large in percentage terms. Yet it would surely be a mistake to assume from our results that any change in the wording of an attitude question will shift marginals noticeably. Our experiments were deliberately carried out on questions where we had reason—empirical or intuitive—to expect a wording effect. From this standpoint, the most striking results may actually have been the *failure* to obtain such effects when we removed seemingly important sentences from the two Stouffer items. Evidently not every sizable change in wording shifts marginals significantly. And even fewer, to judge from our results, affect the association of an item with other key variables.

Similar conclusions can be drawn from a review of past research on wording effects. The largest collection of experiments appears in Rugg and Cantril (1944) under the heading of "Deviations from 'Objective' Wording," and includes mainly experiments on prestige symbols, along with several other types of rather specialized wording changes. Presumably most of the experiments were also done because split-ballot differences seemed likely. Some did produce reliable effects, but others did not, and the authors are not very clear as to the proportion of each type. With regard to prestige symbols, for example, they give two examples where introduction of Franklin Roosevelt's name affected responses to foreign policy questions, but they also note that "On a number of other questions . . . there was in no single case a significant difference due to the prestige effect of using President Roosevelt's name [p. 40]." They also mention that one of their two positive results failed to replicate decisively, a point of some interest given our own occasional problems with replication.[10] Moreover, where effects do occur, their direction is often hard to predict in advance, as in the case of a boomerang effect noted by Cantril (1940) when Roosevelt's name was added to a question.[11]

In other chapters, we have felt it useful to conceptualize a universe to which results from our sample of items can be generalized, however vague the boundaries of the universe and however imprecise the definition of its elements. Perhaps the same thing could be attempted for prestige symbols, but if we think in terms of the broader sphere of wording changes exemplified by the experiments in this chapter, it becomes impossible to conceive of a larger universe of variations in even the most metaphoric terms. The problem becomes still more difficult when one recognizes that some wording changes—as in the another-Vietnam experiment—may involve changes in the issue itself and not simply alterations in wording the same issue. Thus it becomes foolish to

[10]For another largely unsuccessful replication in the area of prestige effects, see Tarantino and Jedner (1972). These authors failed to replicate Asch's (1952) well-known display of an effect due to attributing a statement on rebellion to Jefferson or Lenin, and although they interpret this as a sign of cultural change, simple unreliability of the original finding seems at least as plausible.

[11]We also obtained an unexpected, though understandable, boomerang effect in a 1977 experiment using University of Michigan undergraduates. One half of the sample was told (correctly) that the university's president had recently stated that a major complaint he heard was of too much teaching being done by graduate teaching assistants (TAs) rather than professors. The respondents were then asked whether they thought professors and TAs differed as instructors and if so which group was better. The other half of the sample was asked the same question, but without the prefatory statement by the university president. Respondents were significantly less likely to report TAs to be inferior to professors (on a five-point scale) when they were first exposed to the president's statement of this position (gamma = .23, SE = .07, $p < .01$). An even more unusual set of findings is reported by Navazio (1977), where white-collar workers were influenced in one direction by preparatory additions to questions and blue-collar workers in the opposite direction. The additions were quite artificial from the standpoint of question construction (which was not the purpose of the experiment), but the results remind us that negative findings in a split-ballot experiment can result from two opposing trends that cancel out.

try to talk about the proportion of wording changes that yields response effects and the proportion that does not.

A more practical and probably more useful goal is to develop principles that discriminate between wording changes that have effects and those that do not. Our results, together with past research, suggest a general hypothesis of considerable interest: The more blatant the attempt to influence a respondent, the less likely it will succeed. Stouffer's characterization of atheists as bad or dangerous seems to have no effect whatever. Likewise, in chapter 7, a highly emotional counterargument against abortion had no discernible impact on respondents, and avoidance of the word "abortion" did not alter responses in the experiment reported in this chapter. Paradoxically, it may be that the most obvious examples of bias in wording—the ones that would be seized on most quickly by the survey profession as grossly improper—are the least harmful in actual practice. [12]

The opposite of blatant is less clear, but it is noteworthy that the largest wording effect we have discovered (and the only one interacting with education) comes from the forbid–allow contrast, where we are hard put to see any obvious source for the effect. Evidently such effects can be especially strong where they are most subtle. [13]

[12]There is probably less talk today within survey research about the general problem of biased wording than there was in earlier years, for it is now widely recognized that bias in wording cannot really be separated from the goals of a study and the interpretation of the resulting data. We do not hear so much now, for example, about identifying and perhaps excluding "danger words" (Roper, 1940; Blankenship, 1940a).

[13]One negative piece of evidence on this hypothesis should be noted. Rugg (1941) reports no significant difference in marginals for an experiment that interchanged *Brazil's relations with Germany* and *Germany's relations with Brazil* in a question about American foreign policy at the beginning of World War II. This is the kind of subtle difference in phrasing that one might expect (and Rugg did expect) to influence responses.

12

Some Final Thoughts on Survey Research and Research on Surveys

Distrust all generalizations, including this one.
—adapted from Alexandre Dumas fils

Despite the technical and technological changes that have moved survey research from a largely hand-counting tabular operation in the early half of the century to an increasingly streamlined process symbolized by such acronyms as RDD, CATI, and LISREL, questions and answers exchanged between people remain at the heart of surveys. This book has attempted to deal with central issues associated with the question-answer process by conceptualizing and classifying them, developing hypotheses, and constructing and reconstructing experiments. In doing so, we have tried not to become so procrustean that we lose sight of the living qualities of language and of the human responses that language embodies.

This final chapter is not a systematic summary of the earlier chapters, but assumes at least passing familiarity with what went before. Readers who wish a detailed summary are advised to read the opening parts of Chapter 1 and the concluding sections of the other chapters. Here we use our results to address a few broader themes and problems. In doing so we do not distinguish sharply between conclusions and hypotheses, for most of our conclusions *are* hypotheses. There is none that we cannot imagine being overturned by future work on the boundless universe of possible questions.

QUESTION FORM

In Chapter 1, we outlined a series of research problems, most of which involved two or more different ways of asking questions. On the whole that scheme, which was a development of earlier classifications by others (cf. Tamulonis, 1947), has proved serviceable. Basically, it can be reformulated here to comprise five broad classes of problems: open versus closed questions; encouragement or discouragement of don't know responses; middle alternatives and neutral positions; balance and imbalance in question form and content; strength of attitudes. The measurement of attitude strength is often treated as a part of the middle alternative area, but we prefer to approach it as a distinctive domain, as discussed in Chapters 9 and 10.

The scheme is only a first approximation. For one thing, each of the classes is itself internally differentiated in various ways. Some of these subclasses can also be formalized, for example, methods of assessing don't know responses through filter questions can be nicely divided into full filters and quasi-filters, and in Chapter 4 we show that this formal distinction makes a difference in results. In other cases, however, such distinctions are much harder to systematize in any formal way. For instance, in the balance experiments in Chapter 7, variations in the content of counterarguments sometimes had an effect on responses, yet there seems to be no formal way to classify different counterarguments.

In addition, beyond these five broad classes of problems, there are other useful ways to consider questions, which we treated only partially or tangentially, for example, tone of wording, question length, difficulty of vocabulary, and types of subject matter. Our own classification was intended mainly to identify research problems in a way that connected them with actual decisions survey practitioners confront, and for this purpose the classification should continue to provide a useful guide.

THE RULES OF THE GAME

The classification scheme is also valuable because it describes what respondents face in interviews and questionnaires. They are confronted with a question that is *either* open or closed, provides or does not provide a don't know alternative, and so on. This is a feature of surveys of some importance, since the form of a question places an enormous constraint on respondents. One of the clearest findings that runs through this book is the extent to which people, once they have agreed to be interviewed, accept the framework of questions and try earnestly to work within that framework. If we do not provide a particular substantive alternative to a closed question, people rarely give it. If we omit a don't know category or a middle alternative, people ordinarily do not volunteer one—let alone insist on it. Question constraints are not absolute, and in extreme situations, as when (in Chapter 5) we ask people questions about objects they have never heard of, the majority will rebel. But for most questions people accept the "rules of the game," as they are conveyed by the form of the question.

QUESTION CONSTRAINT AND
RESPONSE PERSUASION

The concept of *question constraint* provides a useful starting point in attempting to understand the effects of question form on response marginals. The largest of these effects can be viewed as a result of the omission of categories that many respondents would like to use if they are available. This is most obvious for two of the forms we studied: don't know (DK) filters and middle alternatives (MA). For the former, the choice of don't know is higher by an average (median across items) of about 22% when the don't know alternative is read to respondents; in the latter case, the choice of a middle alternative increases by an average of about 15% when it is offered. It seems sensible to regard these increments as representing respondent preferences and to assume that it is the *decreases* on the versions that omit such alternatives that represent artificial constraint by question form. This is not to argue that the constraint is unreasonable from the standpoint of the investigator's goals, but only that it is indeed a constraint. Moreover, these estimates are minimal ones, for our experiments always included instructions to interviewers to accept DK and MA responses when they were given spontaneously: Without such instructions the form differences would certainly be greater, although by how much we do not know.

Question constraint plays an equally strong role in open–closed question comparisons, but its effects there are double-edged. The most obvious impact is that responses on a closed question are largely limited to the substantive alternatives listed, whereas an open version of the same question produces a much wider array of responses. Even where we took great pains to maximize comparability between the main open codes and closed alternatives, a noticeable proportion of open responses fell outside the codes common to the two forms. Yet, paradoxically, the completely open form of a question can also be constraining, even though in theory almost any response to it is acceptable. This is because the question itself inevitably implies a frame of reference, and this frame can be defined more broadly for respondents by listing alternatives that they did not realize were legitimate (see Chapter 3, p. 85).

In a sense even the absence of attitude strength measures in a questionnaire is constraining, since this prevents respondents from indicating qualifications to a response and thus forces answers to sound more black and white than they often are.

Only in the case of the balance problem are we unsure as to whether question constraint as such plays a role. If what we have called formal balance (p. 180) increased "no" responses appreciably, one might argue that the absence of an explicit negative alternative in unbalanced questions is constraining. However, if one regards the addition of "or oppose" in a question as similar to the addition of "don't know" or a middle alternative, then our evidence is that the former has virtually no effect, whereas the latter, as already indicated, have substantial impact. Thus unbalanced questions apparently imply the omitted negative category so clearly that its absence from the wording of the question imposes no constraint. The further step of adding a counterargument, which does have an effect, seems better seen as introducing a second force, that of persuasion, into the question–answer process. The counterargument carries an informational, logical, or emotional message that influences the respondent toward a different answer. Although this might also be considered a kind of constraining pressure, it is rather different from the previous cases, which were based on defining alternatives as within or outside the question frame of reference.

Agree–disagree statements, however, raise a further complication, for one way of conceptualizing the phenomenon labeled acquiescence is that some respondents feel constrained to agree with an assertion offered by the interviewer. In that case the substitution of a forced-choice form can be seen as freeing respondents from constraints imposed by the joint operation of the agree–disagree form and an acquiescent tendency by the individual. Moreover, since in two experiments we found that interrogative forms are not less acquiescence-prone than statements, the same argument can be made for all one-sided questions. In sum, even where a purely formal negative alternative (disagree) is offered to respondents, there *may* still be constraint imposed by the affirmative thrust of the question.

The resolution of this issue is difficult but important. It is clear that question constraint plays a critical role in defining what is a legitimate response in a simple "rules of the game" or definition of the situation sense. We believe that persuasion of a more active sort also affects responses, but the evidence is not quite so self-evident in interpretation.[1] And the mixture of the two processes—of question constraint and response persuasion—is even less well understood. A direct attempt to distinguish the two processes would be valuable.

Primary and Secondary Effects on Marginals

There is one further issue having to do with marginal distributions that is peculiar to don't know and middle-alternative experiments: The effect on the main substantive alternatives of the form variation. For don't know and middle alternative experiments, the response that is varied is usually not the primary concern of the research, and it is possible for its proportion to change substantially without altering the *relative* distribution of other responses. In fact, this is exactly what occurs: For most don't know and middle alternative comparisons, the relative proportions choosing the substantive alternatives (e.g., pro and con on an issue) are much the same on both question forms, although there are a few exceptions that prevent complete generalization.

The situation is different for the other types of question form variations that we studied. In these cases the variation directly involves a substantive alternative, hence an effect produces by its very nature a change in substantive marginals. If a counterargument is added to a question, or an agree–disagree item transformed into a forced-choice item, any effect that occurs has an immediate impact on the primary response marginals.

These considerations lead to some qualification of the common belief among experienced survey researchers that almost any change in question wording will affect question marginals. For although inclusion of a don't know or middle alternative certainly changes the proportion of persons taking that choice—often shifting more than a quarter of the sample—there is usually no other detectable change in question margi-

---

[1]Under unintended response persuasion one might include presumed effects due to variation in the social desirability of closed alternatives. But here also the evidence is not strong, for our attempts in Chapter 3 to isolate such an artifact were unsuccessful. More positive evidence on persuasion due to wording effects appears in Chapter 11, where the nonsubstantive addition of the word "freedom" to a question has an impact that seems to involve a kind of persuasion.

nals. The effect of the change in wording is localized, and does not spread to other choices. We had hypothesized at the beginning of the research that persons affected by question form were unlikely to constitute a random subsample of all respondents. But for DK and MA question variations, it appears that persons affected by form—we call them floaters—do tend to be random in relation to substantive alternatives. If floaters were being drawn disproportionately from one substantive alternative, overall marginals would shift. They seldom do.

Even DK (don't know) and MA (middle alternative) responses themselves do not seem to be interdependent to the extent sometimes assumed. It is often supposed, for example, that many persons who give an MA response do so as a way of saying don't know. Our data indicate that this is true to a statistically significant degree, but that the overlap is nevertheless very small. DK proportions do not change greatly in MA experiments between Omitted and Offered forms. Since we did not pursue this problem in depth, our conclusions here are quite tentative, but it appears that DK and MA responses are not interchangeable, and instead carry different meanings for respondents. A more systematic effort is needed to clarify these two concepts, perhaps leading also to clarification of the words used to operationalize the concepts in the questioning process.

FORM-RESISTANT CORRELATIONS

Survey research specialists have been nearly unanimous in offering explicit warnings about the effects of question form and wording variations on univariate distributions, but have said little about the possible effects of such variations on associations. Implicitly the assumption has usually been one we have termed "form-resistant correlations." Despite the shifting of marginals as a result of different question wordings, the relation of one such question to another has been assumed to remain essentially invariant, as discussed in Chapter 1.

We investigated this assumption along three lines: associations between different forms of an attitude question and background variables such as education; associations between an attitude question and another attitude question where one or both vary in form; and differences between question forms as a function of variations in attitude strength. The first two are treated immediately below, the third in the next section because it can usefully be cast in a different way and leads to other research problems.

Background Variables

Contrary to our hypothesis, neither education nor other background variables that we employed generally interacted significantly with either DK or MA question variations. There are exceptions to this conclusion under special conditions (e.g., the obscure issues dealt with in Chapter 5), but although such evidence contributes importantly to our understanding of the processes underlying form effects, the processes are apparently multiple and complex and do not translate into simple or visible three-way interactions across all or even most items. Thus within the limits of the DK and MA experiments we carried out—a fairly large number in each area—the assumption of form-resistant correlations holds up well in practice for these types of question form variation, despite the fact that they produce large (but usually localized) marginal effects.

Open–closed question variations, on the other hand, generally yielded important interactions with several background factors, and the type of balancing variation that involves addition of a counterargument sometimes produced interactions and sometimes did not. For both these types, however, the interactions are content-specific, rather than involving a general tendency of the less educated, or men, or some other background category to invariably be influenced by question form. (This also seemed to be true of tone of wording variations: Some do but some do not interact with education.) Only in the case of agree–disagree balance variations is there evidence of a systematic tendency for low education to accompany a general, rather than content-specific, type of question effect, but even here the evidence is not without some ambiguity.

It is also important to note that whereas form differences in marginal effects do not always or even usually signify differences in association with background variables, the absence of marginal effects does not preclude the presence of such differences in associations. The individuals–social conditions experiments analyzed in Chapter 8 show two forms of the question to yield quite similar marginal distributions, yet the two forms differ significantly in their relations to education. Associational differences by form must be investigated in their own terms, and cannot be assumed to exist or not to exist on the basis of what happens to the marginal distributions of the items involved.

In sum, neither the assumption of form-resistant correlations, nor our original hypothesis of pervasive and systematic effects of education appears to hold. Survey questions are fairly robust in terms of background relationships, especially in the face of large marginal variations such as those produced by don't know filters. Yet there certainly are relationships with background variables that differ by question form, in some cases only in degree (as for the forbid–allow example in Chapter 10), but in others to the extent that conclusions about the very existence of a relationship hinge on which form is used (the gun-permit balance experiment in Chapter 7, and the Security response to the work-values item in Chapter 3). Whether one regards this mixture of evidence as showing the robustness or the vulnerability of survey results probably depends on one's starting point, prejudices, and temperament.

Between-Attitude Correlations

Several striking interactions of question form with interitem associations were demonstrated in earlier chapters, but they tended not to be replicable across time. This suggests that other variables for which time was a proxy introduced further conditions that affected responses differentially by form. The Arab–Russia association, analyzed extensively in Chapter 4, provides the most interesting and convincing example of an association that is conditioned by question form, but also by marginal distributions that were themselves shifting in response to real events. Our analysis in that chapter, and again in Chapter 5, provided intriguing evidence that persons affected by the presence or absence of don't know filters—persons we named DK floaters—produced relations among items by drawing on quite broad attitudes, rather than on more specific attitudes toward the subject matter of the particular items. A general positive or negative view of politics and government appeared, in both chapters, to provide DK floaters with a world view that gave meaning to attitude objects they otherwise knew little or nothing about.

For other kinds of question form variations we seldom found interitem associations that challenged the form-resistant correlation assumption. We believe such challenges to be rare, but there were enough cases to indicate that it would be dangerous to expect the assumption to hold in all instances for any type of question form variation.

ATTITUDE STRENGTH

We initially expected variations in question form to occur most readily among those who felt least intensely about issues or regarded them as relatively unimportant. One could also imagine more complex relations to attitude strength, for example a curvilinear one where question variations had their greatest effect among those of middling strength, since the strongest would be too heavily committed to be changed and the weakest too uninvolved to pay attention to nuances in question wording. Whatever the theory, we do not find much clear evidence that attitude strength is implicated as an important variable in response to question form variations—an exception being the fairly clear trends for middle alternative effects to occur most readily among those showing the least intensity.

What we did find, and discuss at length in Chapter 10, is that random error is significantly and appreciably lower among those with greater attitude strength. In any effective variation of question forms there are two types of movement going on: One type that is systematic and caused by the form of the question, and a second that is essentially random, probably the result of uncrystallized attitudes and best treated as independent of question form. Attitude strength appears to be directly connected to the latter of these, but to have little or no relation to the former. So far as we can tell, those who feel strongly about an issue or regard it as highly important are much less apt to give random responses to a question about the issue, but they are *not* less apt to be influenced by form effects (except on middle-alternative variations). This is a surprising conclusion, but if it holds up, an important one.[2]

The fact that measures of attitude strength help us to understand unreliability justifies obtaining them even if they do not contribute to knowledge of systematic question effects. Their usefulness is further enhanced by the considerable light they throw on the relation of attitudes to politically meaningful actions and outcomes. In Chapter 9, we discussed various types of attitude strength measures and present evidence on their sometimes subtle differences and connections. Measures of intensity and of centrality (importance) differ in the way they divide the population, with centrality isolating a much smaller and presumably more passionate set of single-issue people than does intensity. Measures of committed action, such as letter writing, add data not only about overt behavior but also provide suggestive evidence on organizational mobilization. The combination of strength measures throws light on what is happening in the United States today with regard to two important social issues: abortion and gun control. For the first issue, the subjective strength component seems to be more critical in stimulating political action; for the second, organizational factors appear crucial.

The preceding discussion of attitude strength refers to measures obtained in relation to specific issues, for example, how important a re-

[2]After completion of this book, we became aware of an analysis of nonexperimental data by Judd and Krosnick (1981) that reports the opposite results: The relation of attitude strength measures to systematic but not random effects.

spondent considers abortion to be as an issue when voting in an election. This kind of specific strength measure needs to be distinguished from more general measures of attitude strength, which can be obtained either from a collection of specific strength measures or from summary questions about general interest or involvement in public issues. It is only the specific strength measures that we found useful in relation to reliability, which indicates that involvement in issues can be and often is highly particularized. It is also interesting that general strength measures were significantly associated with respondent education, whereas specific strength measures were typically unrelated to education. A useful way of conceptualizing these and other findings is to view attitude strength as composed of a general factor and a set of specific issue-related factors, with the latter being useful both because they are not redundant with educational level and because they are linked much more directly to the degree to which any particular attitude is crystallized for any particular respondent.

ORDER EFFECTS

In the early stages of our research we did not believe order effects to be of great importance either as a methodological problem in its own right or as a complication to experiments on question form. The literature on order effects available in 1974 did not make them seem frequent or large, and earlier experiments through the Detroit Area Study did not point to context as very important. Our first context experiments in 1974 and 1975 also yielded no detectable effects.

We continue to believe that order effects are not pervasive in surveys, as borne out by a systematic search for them through an entire questionnaire in one survey. But they are clearly more common, greater in magnitude, and more varied in direction than we had thought, and they constitute a serious problem for surveys and an important complication to our own research. Without attempting to review the extensive evidence presented in Chapter 2, the following important points can be noted:

1. Order effects can be large, nearly 20% in several cases.
2. Although usually in the direction of creating consistency, a clear case of contrast is documented.
3. Order effects seem to occur especially with general or summary type questions, though they are not limited to these.

4. Order effects sometimes interact with background factors and in one instance with a measure of ambivalence toward the issue.

Order effects have their most important implications for trend studies. In tracing attitude change over time, response marginals constitute the dependent variable and time the independent variable. In Chapter 2, we document several cases where order effects could seriously confound inferences about change based on items asked in different contexts. The most telling of these is one dealing with allowing Communist reporters into the United States, where conclusions are diametrically opposed if context is varied, as it easily might be. Indeed, in the case of the Communist reporter item, even holding context constant does not produce unequivocal conclusions about the direction of change, because the direction of change itself is complex. In this sense, the context effect is not really a survey artifact, but reveals fundamental ambiguities of both language and thought.

In the previous paragraphs we used the term "order" to refer to question order, but we also document in Chapter 2 several instances of response-order effects, especially recency effects whereby the last listed alternative within a question elicits a significant increment in choice due to its position. Although this is not as serious a problem as question-order effects, it complicates results from any experiment that involves an alternative (such as a logical middle alternative) that is added to a question. Furthermore, response-order effects force us to recognize in still another way the vulnerability of survey results to variations in question form.

OBSTACLES TO GENERALIZATIONS
ABOUT QUESTION EFFECTS

The goal of this research was to combine the inferences that experimentation allows about causality with the inferences that probability sampling provides about population values. Having now carried out several hundred experiments in 34 surveys, we are aware not only of the advantages of the combination, but also of the obstacles in the way of higher levels of generalization. Experiments do not always produce interpretable results, nor always cumulate to yield general conclusions, nor always even replicate well (see Appendix A). Some of these obstacles to generalization have been touched on in previous pages, but it may be useful to bring together what seem to be the main difficulties with which any program of research on question effects must contend.

Variability in Results Due to Chance

Although this first problem is obvious for virtually all social science research, it is worth emphasizing here. We have many effects that fall in the borderline region between compelling evidence for statistical significance and probable chance effects. Often this leads us to replication, but even replications are not always decisive. In addition, there are other ways in which sampling variation operates (e.g., through variations in samples of interviewers) that are not adequately handled by ordinary sampling error statistics. All in all, constructing a theory in the face of the degree of variability inherent in survey data can at times seem like building castles out of sand. Not really, for with enough understanding and replication, results do move toward clarification, despite the large amount of interfering noise. This obstacle is a large one, however.

Chance also enters this research in another way in the form of what is generally labeled random measurement error, although we are in agreement with Converse (1980) in seeing this as some sort of combination of limitations in the measures and limitations in the people being measured. Initially we did not adequately conceptualize this source of random error, and even at this point we are not certain of exactly how it operates in all situations where systematic form effects are being tested. We have generally treated such error as one of the "other things equal" when comparing form effects across split-ballot subsamples. But we are not certain that this is always the case, and can imagine situations where analyses of systematic effects are distorted if measurement error occurs differentially among subgroups or question forms. In any case, it will be useful in future experimentation to obtain better estimates of this form of error to combine in a more complete picture with systematic question effects. Chapter 10 tries to move in this direction, and we consider another aspect of the problem below.

Order Effects

Having already discussed order effects in this chapter, it is necessary only to indicate the likelihood that some of our methodological results are contingent on context in ways that are not visible or are visible only in the form of contradictory findings. The whole effort to generalize about question form must usually pretend that each question can be viewed in isolation, but of course this is incorrect. It will be a difficult process to combine question effects with context effects in the interest of larger generalizations, but it must eventually be attempted. For now we can simply note that the results in Chapters 3 through 11 of this book depend in often unknown ways on the phenomena treated in Chapter 2.

Interactions between Form Effects

It is also possible that the several types of form variations that we have studied depend on each other in crucial ways. For example, counterarguments may have effects mainly for standard but not filtered DK questions. Since most of our chapters examine only one effect at a time, we have little data on this point. Factorial designs that introduce this level of complexity would be useful, provided that they do not become so artificial as to be removed from the realities of survey questioning.[3]

Time

Just as question form is ordinarily and unrealistically viewed apart from questionnaire context, so both form and context must ordinarily be treated as static, despite our awareness that the effects of events on attitudes cannot be dismissed as either small or incidental. For some of

---

[3]Our one nonfactorial attempt at a multi-form experiment was not very successful. We chose an item from the Anomia scale (Srole, 1956), *In spite of what some people say, the lot of the average man is getting worse, not better,* and constructed a second version that transformed the item into forced-choice form and added both a middle alternative and a don't know option: *Do you think the lot of the average man is getting worse, getting better, staying about the same, or don't you have enough information to say?* Both question forms were included as a split-ballot experiment in DAS–76, but because of time pressure and because the original item had been used many times by other researchers (e.g., NORC, 1980) we violated the first rule of questionnaire construction and did not pretest the experiment. Whatever its past use, the item turned out, according to interviewer reports, to be poorly understood by a great many respondents. The word "lot" is archaic, and respondents interpreted the phrase "lot of the average man" variously to refer to a lot of average men, to housing lots, even in one case to cemetery lots! Because of this confusion we cannot place much weight on this single attempt at multi-form variation, but the results are worth noting. The newly constructed version showed significant increments of DK and MA responses, as expected. It did not show the expected signs of acquiescence in terms of marginals ("worse" was chosen slightly more often on the forced-choice form than was "agree" on the original question), but the (negative) relation of the pessimistic response to education was significantly stronger for the agree–disagree form than for the forced-choice form (linear $\chi^2 = 3.94$, $df = 1$, $p < .05$). The latter finding suggests that acquiescence continued to occur even after removal of DK and MA respondents. (A similar pattern of no marginal effects but an education interaction occurs for forms B and C of the individuals versus social conditions experiment in Chapter 8.)

our simplest generalizations, such as the incremental effect of don't know filters, changes over time may not be crucial. But for more complex relations and interactions, shifts in marginals that reflect aggregate attitude change almost certainly both create and destroy question effects. We generally avoided working with highly topical issues, but most of our questions concern matters that are changing to some degree, and none of our generalizations is immune to this movement of reality. A science of question wording cannot avoid being to some degree a kind of natural history: Its generalizations are subject to change because the data deal with change. It is far too early to know just how enduring generalizations about question effects can be, but we suspect that time is a more potent variable in relation to question effects than we or others have recognized (cf. Gergen, 1973).

Other Sources of Instability

In Appendix B we consider several other possible types of effects that must be considered artifacts from our present standpoint: mode of administration, response rates, cluster effects, previous interview experience. Evidence is presented that most of these can upset generalizations, but we do not at this point see any as a major hurdle. Still, they contribute further complications to the search for simple truths in this research.

Other Ways of Distinguishing Survey Questions

We have treated *attitudes* as a generic term covering all kinds of subjective questions. But it is also useful for certain purposes to make conceptual distinctions within this realm, as for example between attitudes narrowly defined as evaluative or affective responses for or against objects, and *beliefs* defined as propositions linking objects to attributes (cf. Fishbein and Ajzen, 1975). Our assumption has been that the effects of question form variations are the same for both attitudes and beliefs. Although the assumption still seems to us reasonable, it deserves systematic testing.

Language

Last, but hardly least, is the fact that language is not a set of formal classes or boxes, but as Fleming (1967) asserts, a medium in which we exist. When we speak about don't know filters, for example, we are abstracting from the particular words used or usable to legitimize don't know options in questions. As some of the examples in Chapter 11 indicate, the alteration of one seemingly innocuous word may—though it may not—shift meaning in unintended ways. Thus every attempt to design experiments that deal with generic question forms flies in the face of the fact that every question is unique. Experiments on form seek to draw generalizations from a material that resists generalization, that is particular and plastic and seamless. This may well be the greatest obstacle of all.

Each of the preceding problems is serious enough taken alone, but in combination and interaction they obviously add to and multiply the difficulties of scientific work in this area. We suspect that for this reason progress will be slow and uneven. There is also a danger of proliferating isolated experimental question results that are of little cumulative value. It is desirable to try at this point to chart a course for both research and practice that will be as fruitful as possible. We close this last chapter with some thoughts along both these lines.

IMPLICATIONS FOR PRACTICE

Our research provides few simple or straightforward rules for the practice of surveys. It would be easy to justify omitting such recommendations entirely, and tempting to do so because any advice offered is likely to seem either so obvious as not to need offering here, or so unobvious as to need too much qualification to be useful. Yet there are certainly some implications for practice in the preceding pages, and in the absence of strong reasons to the contrary, the following suggestions at least merit consideration when a survey questionnaire is being developed. Some are familiar guidelines from years past, but where they are supported by new evidence, they are mentioned nonetheless.

1. Context effects are a serious hazard and any attempt to compare marginal results from one survey to another, whether to study change over time or for some other purpose, should avoid removing a single question from a context of related items, or else build in a way of assessing the effects of doing so.

2. General summary type questions are especially susceptible to context effects and should probably be avoided if the needed information can be built up from more specific questions.

3. Important questions should be developed first by using an open question form in a sufficiently large pilot study, then in most cases turned into closed questions on the basis of the main open codes needed to summarize the open data. Departure from this process should be justified theoretically.

4. Don't know filters should be used if informed opinion on a particular issue is the goal, but standard (unfiltered) questions are useful if basic values, ideologies, or general attitudes are wanted.

5. Balanced questions, rather than agree–disagree items, are to be preferrred, although the investigator should realize that the content of the balancing contributes to the definition of the question and thus affects responses.

6. If attitudes are important to measure, it is almost always worth obtaining some indication of the self-reported strength with which they are held. Centrality measures are of more value (where appropriate) than intensity measures, and scales with more than two or three categories are useful because they allow identification of small sets of highly involved people. For policy issues, behavioral measures of committed action should be included.

Beyond specific advice of this type, some traditional survey wisdom is reenforced by our investigation, but also qualified by it. Absolute marginal proportions are to be greatly distrusted, for relatively innocuous changes in wording or context can result in considerable change in proportions. Yet in many cases the marginal change in response to such a question variation is slight or nonexistent. The basic problem is *not* that every wording change shifts proportions—far from it—but that it is extraordinarily difficult to know in advance which changes will alter marginals and which will not. For this reason, a trend study that compares results for even slightly different wordings of questions asked at different points in time invites major error.[4]

For the same and additional reasons it is dangerous to work with single items on any important issue. Enough question effects have been discovered to indicate that conclusions based on a single item may be influenced in unexpected ways. Since the influences tend to go in different directions, several items in *different forms, wordings* and *contexts*, will ordinarily reduce greatly the danger. The advice here is not the

---

[4]In Chapter 7, we proposed one possible exception to this otherwise firm rule. But the exception is based on empirical results with a special type of wording variation, and not merely on a priori reasoning about the triviality of the change. In fact, in Chapter 11 we suggest that subtle or even unwitting changes in wording may have substantial effects on response, whereas large attempts to bias questions may have no effects at all.

same as that of McNemar (1946) simply to build scales, for scales constructed from items of the same form may still cumulate unwanted effects—as well as obscure important substantive differences among items—but rather to look at the results produced by different types of measures (and contexts) intended to operationalize the same construct. Even two or three items will be far better than reliance on a single one.

Finally, split-ballot comparisons have a place in substantive research where an investigator wants to be assured that something important is not being missed. We feel we learned about the limitations of the most-important-problem question (Chapter 3) by comparing the traditional open version with a closed form, and elsewhere an experimental approach was highly informative in a substantive way about an easily overlooked meaning of words or context. Split-ballots should be included in major investigations as a way of helping researchers escape their own limited frames of reference.

IMPLICATIONS FOR RESEARCH ON SURVEYS

Between Payne's (1951) book and our early work in 1974, very little systematic research on survey question form was published, excepting the large specialized literature on agreeing response bias. Already there is evidence that this is changing. Since split-ballot experiments are not difficult to create, especially in connection with telephone surveys, which are themselves relatively easy to mount, it is not hard to imagine an outpouring of experiments on survey questions. Some consideration of how such work should most fruitfully proceed is in order.

Our own experience has emphasized the need for replication, both literal replication in independent surveys and replication across items in order to clarify constructs. We hope that some of our own work will be subjected to further test by others and that likewise new experiments will ordinarily not be published in too isolated or premature a fashion.

What is needed most is theoretically directed research, but exactly what this means is not so clear. It is sometimes suggested that research on survey questions should draw its theory from cognitive or social psychology, from linguistics or psycholinguistics, or from one of the other basic social sciences. We are skeptical of this recommendation, having tried it ourselves. Psychological theory has developed largely through a kind of controlled laboratory experimentation that is usually far removed from the encounters with ordinary people that characterize surveys. Linguistics is even more remote from the level and sampling of natural language used in surveys. One can find in these disciplines interesting scholarly parallels to problems discussed in these pages, but theoretical guidance to their solution or even improved definition is much harder to locate. This is not to say that psychologists, linguists, and other social scientists cannot contribute substantially to survey research, but we suspect that this will happen only if they become directly involved in studying survey data, not because the latest theories in psychology or elsewhere can be applied to survey research with profound implications.

Theorizing in survey research will have to begin by formulating problems that arise more directly from its own data, methods, and ideas. This was one lesson to be learned from Converse's (1964) influential paper on mass beliefs: Although cognizant of general social psychological ideas, it drew its real strength from reflection on data unique to survey research. In fact, what should have happened was an influence from this kind of survey theorizing back on to psychology, but it is noteworthy that McGuire's (1969) encyclopedic review of the nature of attitudes and attitude change did not mention the Converse paper, and even today much of social psychology proceeds in blithe ignorance of the kind of data Converse and others deal with.

We will end by noting two broad problems that seem to us to arise out of our research and that of others, problems that are far from solved but that can usefully serve as theoretical guides for work on the question-answer process.

Measuring Crystallized Attitudes

In Chapter 10 we conceptualized crystallized attitudes as those that exist before being measured. In Chapter 8 we suggested that a question on crime may have evoked attitudes not adequately contained within the closed alternatives offered and that this in turn may have led to unreliability when the closed question was repeated several months later. This raises a difficult issue that is almost epistemological in nature: Can we learn about attitudes before we measure them? Although this may seem a contradiction in terms, a combination of open and closed questions might allow some handle on the problem, especially since both attitude strength measures and the use of over-time reliability can serve as touchstones for success. The basic hypothesis is that alternatives that focus with more precision on the attitudes people actually have will produce responses that are held with greater strength and greater reliability. Stated in this way, the hypothesis may seem almost self-evident, but in fact it has never to our knowledge been seriously investigated, and it will not be easy to do so. But such tests should lead to useful results both methodologically and theoretically.

Discovering Who Changes

In Chapter 4 we ask whether floaters on one item and floaters on another item are largely the same people. In other chapters also we try to determine who shifts as a result of changes in wording, form, or context. Indeed, throughout the book we have searched for distinctive characteristics of those most readily influenced by nonsubstantive alterations in questions. The Snark has never been found, nor even sighted very clearly from a distance. Yet it seems likely that the question and answer process in survey research would be illuminated if sure identification could be made. At the very least, it would be helpful to know how many different species of Snarks we are after: whether each type of question or even each unique question produces a different kind of person who shifts; whether indeed the persons can be classified in any way.

One obvious distinction is between those who on a given question contribute random error and those who do not. Some might hypothesize that it is the former who change most readily; some, the latter. As far as our evidence goes, which is not very far, we are uncertain that shifters can be identified with either type, since attitude strength was associated with reliability but not with resistance to shifting. In any case, these hypotheses deserve investigation in an effort to understand better what part of the population changes—and why— when question forms are altered.

These two theoretical problems do not by any means exhaust those raised by issues discussed in earlier pages. But they provide examples of how research on survey questions might proceed beyond repeatedly demonstrating the fact that some changes in wording affect some results and others do not. They also suggest that more complex approaches may be needed than simple split-ballots. Combinations of open and closed questions and of between- and within-experimental designs will be required to identify the hypothesized attitudes and people.[5] In that

[5]Within-subject designs have two great advantages for research on question effects: They allow estimates of response consistency when a question is repeated exactly and they enable precise identification of persons who shift or do not shift as a result of a variation in question wording. However, such designs also have serious weaknesses: Used in the same interview they court artifacts due to memory and used in a panel they introduce possible bias due to both sample attrition and true change. Thus within and between designs are best used in combination.

sense, this book may represent a transition between the work of Cantril and others in the early days of survey research and a type of future work that combines theory and method in a way that more fully elucidates the nature of survey questions.

As we remarked at the beginning of the first chapter, asking questions and giving answers are ancient ways of exchanging information. But they take on new meanings within the setting of a large-scale survey. Although our book has concentrated on the problems that confront those who seek to use survey data, we do not doubt the power and the promise of the survey method. Numerous illustrations of both appear in the course of the book. At an obvious level, the chapter on passionate attitudes illustrated the usefulness of survey data for increasing our understanding of variations in the political impact of public opinion. But even such problems as context effects provide opportunities to deepen one's understanding. To discover that answers to a question about allowing Communist reporters into the United States are determined not only by attitudes toward Communism but also by a norm of reciprocity is to gain insight into the complexity of public responses. Always, the challenge is to allow ourselves to learn more from the answers gathered so readily today by large-scale surveys. In a positive as well as negative sense, there are many unanswered questions about both questions and answers.

A

Mysteries of Replication and Non-Replication

> What I tell you three times is true.
> —Lewis Carroll, *The Hunting of the Snark*

Survey research does not have a tradition of replicating results in order to establish their reliability and generality beyond a single survey. Where items are asked more than once, this is usually done with questions and time intervals such that any statistically significant difference can be attributed to true change in attitude. In the course of our research, however, we carried out many replications, usually of relationships not expected to change over the relatively short time intervals involved. Many of the replications have been reassuring, but there have been some striking failures that are difficult to explain.

We recognize, of course, that "statistically significant differences" can occur as a result of chance, and that an analyst testing a number of hypotheses within a single data set may capitalize on sampling error by treating seriously the one out of 20 tests that reaches the .05 level of significance. (The theory underlying this assumption is more complex, since it really assumes 20 independent samples, but it seems to apply approximately to multiple tests in a single sample where items show relatively low intercorrelations.) At the same time, we also recognize that failure to reject a null hypothesis does not prove its truth. Even after qualification along both these lines, however, as well as other lines suggested by problems discussed in Appendix B, the following examples remain for us mysterious.

A striking instance is provided in Chapter 7 where we consider whether there is a difference in results between unbalanced and formally balanced question forms such as the following:

> Unbalanced: *If there is a serious fuel shortage this winter, do you think there should be a law requiring people to lower the heat in their homes?*
>
> Formally balanced: *If there is a serious fuel shortage this winter, do you think there should be a law requiring people to lower the heat in their homes, or do you oppose such a law?*

In SRC–74 Fall this experiment showed a highly significant form difference ($\chi^2 = 8.90$, $df = 1$, $p < .01$). Although the difference was in the direction most would predict (opposition to a law increased by 8.9% when *"or do you oppose such a law"* was added), we were skeptical of its reliability because it was not in accord with results from three similar experimental items (see Table 7.1, p. 181), nor with our prior reasoning. We therefore replicated the fuel experiment just shown, not once but three times: once in 1977 and twice in 1978. None of these replications, taken separately or together, reproduced the original finding, although the pooled replication sample does yield a 2.8% difference in the same direction as the original finding ($\chi^2 = 2.24$, $df = 1$, n.s., based on 2668 cases). The difference between the original finding and the three replications (pooled) approaches significance: $\chi^2 = 3.48$, $df = 1$, $p < .10$.

What then do we make of the original highly significant finding? On the basis of all related results, both those with other similar experiments and those based on later replications of the fuel item, we choose in Chapter 7 to treat the anomalous significant difference as due to sampling error, in this case to the one out of more than a hundred differences that is to be expected by chance. We are not comfortable with this decision, however, and recognize that there are at least two other related possibilities. One is that there is a real effect that is smaller than our first finding but larger than later findings, perhaps best estimated by the mean of the four trials. The other possibility is that the later three surveys were different in some way from the first survey, and that all the results should be taken at face value. And true enough, there are differences, for example, all the later surveys were done by telephone, whereas the 1974 survey was face-to-face. Other evidence suggests that this is not the explanation, since another item included in the 1974 face-to-face survey showed essentially no formal balance effect whatever. Yet we certainly cannot demonstrate the point conclusively, anymore than we can rule out other types of interactions, for example, with the year or even the season of the survey.[1] All we can say is that the original 1974 difference could not be replicated with other items or on other occasions, and was therefore not a pervasive or enduring effect.

Another comparison involving the same 1974 fuel experiment complicates the problem, as well as illustrating the other side of the coin: the finding of a nonsignificant trend where a significant one was hypothesized, followed by replication that produced the originally expected result. The two fuel items already presented were actually parts of a tripartite split-ballot experiment, with the third version as follows:

> *If there is a serious fuel shortage this winter, do you think there should be a law requiring people to lower the heat in their homes,* **or** *do you think this should be left to individual families to decide?*

We expected this third version, with its added counterargument, to produce a reliable shift toward the negative position, in comparison to the formally balanced version. But the change, as shown in more detail in Table 7.3, was slight (3.5%) and nonsignificant ($p > .20$). Again we were skeptical of the result and therefore repeated the experiment in SRC–78 Fall. This time the formal versus counterargument comparison produced a highly significant difference of 13% ($\chi^2 = 18.80$, $df = 1$, $p < .001$), and the three-way interaction of response, form, and time (1974 versus 1978) is also significant: $\chi^2 = 4.65$, $df = 1$, $p < .05$. The later result, supplemented by evidence of a counterargument effect on other items, suggests that the original finding was misleading, perhaps due to sampling error. Yet is is disquieting to realize how different our conclusions would be if only one of the two results were available.[2]

Perhaps the previous two examples can be dismissed as quirks (especially since sampling error with a single question form could account for both), but a third example resists such an easy interpretation. In our 1974 SRC face-to-face survey we discovered that question form (in par-

---

[1]Context, at least in a simple sense, can be ruled out, since the fuel experiment was the first one administered in 1974. Since the questionnaire was constant up to that point, one would have to assume an interaction between a prior set of uniform questions and the two different question forms of the fuel item. This seems highly unlikely, although of course not impossible.

[2]The percentages opposing the fuel law in 1974 were 61.7%, 70.6%, and 74.1%, respectively, on the unbalanced, formally balanced, and counterargument forms. Note that if the formally balanced version percentages had been about 5% lower in that experiment, *neither* of the discrepancies discussed thus far would have appeared. The unbalanced to formally balanced differences would have produced a χ^2 of only 1.60, whereas the formal to counterargument χ^2 would have been 8.34 ($p < .01$).

ticular whether a middle alternative was offered or omitted) dramatically affected the relationship between liberal–conservative self-identification and a retrospective question about support for the Vietnam War (see Chapter 6 for exact questions and detailed results). Opinions were unrelated on the Omitted forms of the two items ($\chi^2 = .11$), but were clearly related on the Offered forms, liberals being more likely than conservatives to say the United States gave too much aid to the Vietnamese ($\chi^2 = 5.73$, $df = 1$, $p < .02$). The three-way interaction testing the difference between the two associations was significant beyond the .05 level ($\chi^2 = 4.53$, $df = 1$).

Because of our experience with other statistically significant findings that failed to replicate, we repeated the liberal–conservative and Vietnam experiments in a February 1978 survey. Despite the fact that over 3 years had elapsed since the 1974 survey, and the new survey was carried out by phone rather than face-to-face, the findings replicated almost exactly. Once again there was no association on the Omitted forms ($\chi^2 = .33$), a significant association in the same direction as before on the Offered forms ($\chi^2 = 10.19$, $df = 1$, $p < .002$), and the null hypothesis of no three-way interaction could be rejected even more clearly ($\chi^2 = 8.46$, $df = 1$, $p < .01$).

The closeness of the two sets of findings seemed to justify considerable confidence in the result. Because of their importance, however, and also to obtain additional interpretive data through follow-up open questions, we replicated the two experiments once again 6 months later in an August 1978 telephone survey. To our dismay, this new survey produced not a trace of the original interaction. The two items were not significantly associated on either form! In the hope that this was a freakish result we repeated the experiment yet again barely 2 months later and obtained the same negative finding: no relation on either form. These nonreplications occurred despite the fact that the marginals for the two sets of items showed essentially no change between the first two surveys and the second two. The probability of this difference between pairs of surveys (i.e., the four-way interaction, response by response by form by first two studies combined versus second two combined), given the null hypothesis, is two out of a thousand ($\chi^2 = 9.64$, $df = 1$).

One further and even more complex example of nonreplication is given in Chapter 4 and others of lesser importance or of a more explicable nature appear in other sections of this book. Those who follow these results in detail will find that the abstract debates that have occurred from time to time over the meaning of significance testing (Morrison and Henkel, 1970) become practical and vivid as one attempts to establish as solidly reliable a set of findings about question effects. Yet the reader who at this point is tempted to see either this area of research, or indeed all survey research, as consisting of untrustworthy findings—of findings that become "losings" the next time around—is even more misguided than the person who regards the .01 level of significance with awe. The majority of our findings do replicate well, as the following examples illustrate.

In 1974 we repeated the forbid–allow comparison first reported by Rugg in 1941 and found much the same higher choice of not allow than forbid that he reported (see Chapter 11, p. 276). Moreover, we subsequently repeated the experiment in two separate surveys (one of which compared telephone and face-to-face interviewing experimentally), and in both found the same basic and quite significant effect, although the magnitude of the effect also varies significantly among the three replications. Thus despite wide differences in sample design (the 1941 data doubtless were based on quota sampling of an unknown nature) and mode of administration, as well as a 35-year time gap, we draw basically the same conclusions today as Rugg did. Much the same is true for our replications of Hyman and Sheatsley's (1950) finding on question order and Payne's (1951) results on response order, both reported in Chapter 2: In each case conclusions from many years ago, based on different sampling designs, modes of administration, and of course organizations, are shown to hold today in our own surveys.

A more complex example of successful replication is presented in Chapter 3, where open and closed versions of a question on work values are compared. In 1977 we found that a response emphasizing security (little danger of being laid off the job) was given significantly more often to the closed form of the question, and moreover that this effect was negatively related to the educational level of respondents. These findings led to an important interpretation of open–closed question differences, and it was therefore critical that we replicate both the marginal difference and the three-way interaction (response by education by form). Both results were replicated significantly and at quite similar percentage levels a year and a half later, and exactly the same conclusion would be drawn from either survey. (In Appendix B.3 we qualify this conclusion, but not in terms of replication from one survey to another.) Many other examples of successful replication will be found throughout this book.

SOME CONCLUSIONS

Where do our examples of failure to replicate leave us with regard to the reliability of results in this volume and in surveys more generally?

First, we doubt that our experience with nonreplication is peculiar to this research (cf., Williams, 1978). Rather, most survey investigators have been spared the shock of having a cherished conclusion upset by the failure to replicate because most survey reports are based on a single data set.[3] Possibly that will change as the growth of telephone surveys encourages investigators to think more naturally in terms of replication.

Second, there is the issue of why nonreplications occur in surveys such as the ones we have used. An obvious answer is that sampling error will occasionally produce an apparently significant result and that it is these that fail to replicate on the next go-round. It is our strong sense that we encountered more, as well as more extreme, nonreplications than can be accounted for by this purely statistical explanation, although we have not made exact calculations on this point and would find it very difficult to do so. Another possibility is that of real changes over time, and for at least two or three of our important nonreplications there is reason to believe this explanation, although it is inherently almost impossible to test. But most of our experiments seem unlikely to have been so sensitive to external events over the several years that we worked. A third possibility has to do with variations in nonresponse rates, modes of interviewing, and other extrinsic features of the surveys. We deal with these in more detail in Appendix B, and will merely note here that none of them seems to be a systematic factor in nonreplication, although they may play a role. The fact that we are able to replicate quite well results from the 1940s carried out by different organizations using different procedures suggests that these features are not as critical as is sometimes assumed. A fourth possibility is that the structure of the questionnaire itself may be implicated in nonreplications—that question order interacts with question content to influence results in unexpected ways. This possibility is considered at length in Chapter 2 and there is certainly some evidence for it. We cannot locate plausible context effects for our most startling nonreplications, but it is impossible to be certain of their absence.

We suspect that in the end each of these factors may occasionally play a part and that there is no single explanation for failures to replicate. But at this point we are mystified more than confident as we try to make sense out of nonreplications.[4] Most important, we have come to regard it as essential to try to replicate at least once and preferably twice all

---

[3]The work of Hyman and his colleagues is one exception to the general lack of replication in survey research. See Hyman, Wright and Reed (1975) and Hyman and Wright (1979).

[4]Processing errors are always a possibility and in cases of serious nonreplication we have normally checked carefully to make certain that questionnaires, codes, and data are consis-

results on which we wish to place much weight. We have not been able to follow this precept in all instances, and our overall stance toward any finding is guided by some combination of its degree of statistical significance, its magnitude, its interpretability, and its replicability. But given the large number of factors that can confound results, in making the claim for the reliability of a finding there is no substitute for an independent replication—the more independent the better.[5] As Cook and Campbell (1979: 25) write:

> In some areas ... the difficulties of replicating experimental results are so great that ... perhaps such areas should put ... less emphasis on elaborate theorization until there are indeed dependable factual puzzles worthy of the theoretical effort.

---

tent. On several occasions computer output has been compared to raw questionnaire responses. Although mistakes have occurred on occasion (almost always in the process of recoding), none of our failures to replicate has been explicable in this way.

[5] By independent we mean repeating precisely the same experimental form variation, but with alterations in those survey conditions believed to be not relevant to the effect expected. Such irrelevant conditions ordinarily include not merely a new sample, but different questionnaire contexts, modes of administration, survey organizations, and investigators. Replication can also involve attempts to show that a theoretical effect can be obtained with different questions, as we do in every chapter of this book (e.g., the sequence of forbid-allow experiments reported in Chapter 11), but more exact replication is a prior necessity. For a discussion of different types of replication, see Lykken, 1968. For a discussion of the generic issue of deviant results, see the article on "Outliers" by Anscombe (1968).

Special Sampling and
Interviewing Problems

In the course of this research, we drew on more than 30 surveys. Technical differences among these surveys and special features of several of them could have contributed to variations in our results. In this appendix we present available evidence on the more important of these problems: sample design, mode of administration, response rate, and reinterviewing of previously interviewed respondents.

1. SAMPLING DESIGN

Because the design of most of our samples involved some clustering, statistical tests based on simple random sampling (SRS) assumptions are, strictly speaking, inappropriate. To assess the effects of this clustering on bivariate analyses, we computed more exact sampling errors for all such analyses (response by question form) from our first large national face-to-face survey, SRC–74 Fall. Computations were carried out with the University of Michigan Population Studies Center Program "SAM," using paired selection. (There were 51 strata based on the 62 nonself-representing PSUs plus 40 pseudo-PSUs formed from the 12 self-representing areas.)

In all cases, results taking into account clustering yielded the same conclusions about the effect of form on response as did SRS tests. A typical example, and one involving an important result from Chapter 7 (also discussed in Appendix A), is the comparison between unbalanced and formally balanced versions of the fuel-shortage item. Assuming SRS, the χ^2 testing the 8.9% difference between forms is 8.90, $df = 1$, $p < .01$. The design effect in this instance is 1.23 and the more exact estimate of the standard error of the 8.9% difference is plus or minus 3.3%. On the other items in the SRC–74 Fall survey, the design effect for the difference in proportions between question forms ranged from .70 to 1.40, with about an equal number falling on either side of 1.00. Thus there was no evidence that relying on SRS tests produced any systematic effect on conclusions about the influence of question form on item marginals.

Other important analysis in this book examines the effect of form on bivariate associations (i.e., three-way interactions). One of the most crucial instances involves the relation between items on the Middle East (Arabs) and Russia, using filtered and standard question forms (see Chapter 4). Since the difference in associations discovered in 1974 disappears in a later replication, the reader may wonder if the original significance levels were inflated because the statistics assumed simple random sampling. In order to test this possibility, it was necessary to estimate chi square from variances of odds ratios, using the Wald χ^2 statistic. Table B.1 shows the original likelihood-ratio χ^2 values for SRS reported in Chapter 4, the Wald χ^2 values assuming SRS, and the Wald χ^2 values assuming complex sampling. While the calculation using the Wald statistic itself produces some difference in χ^2 estimates, the movement from SRS to complex sampling calculations actually increases the value of the χ^2 for the three-way interaction. In substantive terms, none of the differences affects conclusions importantly, and there is no evidence that our use of the SRS formula inflates significance levels in this instance.[1]

2. MODE OF ADMINISTRATION: TELEPHONE VERSUS FACE-TO-FACE INTERVIEWING

The earliest surveys in which we worked were carried out on a face-to-face basis, but most of the later surveys were done by telephone. This

---

[1]The analysis shown in Table B.1 was carried out by James M. Lepkowski of the Sampling Section, Institute for Social Research. His 1979 dissertation, *Design Effects for Multivariate Categorical Interactions*, includes a number of other analyses of our 1974 data in terms of SRS and complex sampling comparisons, and the results indicate that on the average three-way interactions have design effects closer to 1.0 than do estimates of proportions and differences of proportions.

TABLE B.1
Comparison of χ^2 Values for SRS and Complex Sampling[a]

	Likelihood-ratio χ^2, SRS	Wald χ^2, SRS	Wald χ^2, complex sampling
Arabs × Russia, for filtered form	.03	.03	.04
Arabs × Russia, for standard form	22.0	18.3	18.3
Arabs × Russia × form (3-way)	8.8	8.8	12.1

[a] All χ^2 values have one degree of freedom.

means that changes in our results from one survey to another could be due to changes in mode of administration, a possibility that we have examined with some care.

Much of what is known about the difference in national samples between telephone and face-to-face surveys comes from an experimental comparison carried out in 1976 by Groves and Kahn (1979). We were fortunate in being invited to include in that SRC–76 Spring study four of our own experiments. Before reporting the results of these, it is important to note that telephone versus face-to-face differences are complex, and by no means limited to the interviewing process as such. There are small differences produced by noncoverage in the telephone survey of households with no phones (just under 10% of the population), and less easy to document losses to face-to-face surveys of other kinds of households (e.g., some very recent housing construction). Response rates seem to be lower on the telephone (by 5% or more), though this is hard to determine precisely because the status of some unanswered telephone numbers cannot be ascertained. Moroever, even when overall response rates are about the same, this does not mean that sources and types of nonresponse are the same. There is also evidence that the more one dimensional and impersonal nature of the telephone interview leads to a less relaxed and less trusting atmosphere. One of the most striking findings in the Groves and Kahn study was that more telephone respondents expressed impatience for the interview to end, despite the fact that in the 1976 survey the telephone questionnaire was actually shorter than that used in the face-to-face interview. Finally, it should be mentioned that the Groves and Kahn (1979) telephone survey employed an interviewing staff newly recruited and located in Ann Arbor and subject to centralized supervision, whereas the face-to-face staff was an experienced one spread across the country.

The main visible result of these variations appears in demographic characteristics. The Groves and Kahn telephone respondents were noticeably younger and better educated than the face-to-face respondents, even when comparisons are made only among households having telephones. Thus 15.6% of the face-to-face sample reported 8 years or less of schooling, as compared to 9.5% of the telephone sample—this being one of the largest discrepancies (Groves and Kahn, 1979, Table 4.6, p. 95). Despite such variations in background characteristics, plus all the other differences in procedure described above, the investigators found very few effects on attitude items of the type we are concerned with in this book. Although there was evidence of some decrease in willingness to provide personal information (e.g., on income) on the telephone, most of the wide range of attitude questions that were included in the comparison failed to show significant differences between modes of administration, and of course some of the differences that do appear may be due to chance.

The four experimental attitude items included in SRC–76 Spring were ones we had developed previously to represent important types of question form differences. We chose a DK experiment (the Arabs item in Chapter 4), a middle alternative experiment (the liberal–conservative item, Chapter 6), an agree–disagree experiment (women in politics, Chapter 8), and a tone of wording experiment (forbid–allow, Chapter 11). Univariate results are shown in Table B.2, separately by form and by mode of administration.

For two of the experiments (liberal–conservative and women in politics) there is no sign that mode of administration affects separate item distributions or form comparisons. In the forbid–allow experiment, the allow item does show significantly more libertarian responses on the phone than face-to-face ($\chi^2 = 4.19$, $df = 1$, $p < .05$), but the forbid item reveals no similar trend and the three-way interaction (response by form by mode) does not approach significance ($\chi^2 = 1.41$, $df = 1$). It seems best to treat this significant effect as due to chance, though replication of the experiment would be desirable. There is also no evidence of four-way interactions between mode, form, education, and response for any of these three experiments (data not shown).

The Arab item, by contrast, does show a highly significant three-way interaction of response by form by mode ($\chi^2 = 11.94$, $df = 2$, $p < .01$). The overall interaction can best be thought of as composed of two separate effects. The first involves DK versus opinion (agree and disagree combined): $\chi^2 = 5.96$, $df = 1$, $p < .02$. On the filtered form the DK response goes up on the telephone survey, while on the standard form the DK response goes down on the telephone survey, both of these in comparison with the face-to-face survey. A possible interpretation is that the changes are due to the greater impatience felt by respondents

TABLE B.2
Four Experimental Comparisons by Form and Telephone versus Face-to-Face Interviewing[a]

	Telephone		Face-to-Face	
Arab nations (DK experiment)	Standard	Filtered	Standard	Filtered
Agree	31.0%	10.9%	20.1%	12.0%
Disagree	37.4	21.7	43.5	24.0
DK, no opinion	31.5	67.4	36.4	64.0
	100	100	100	100
	(802)	(825)	(711)	(803)
Liberal–conservative (middle alternative)	Omitted	Offered	Omitted	Offered
Liberal	32.3%	17.9%	31.4%	15.6%
Middle-of-the-road	12.6	52.1	13.7	56.4
Conservative	55.1	30.0	55.0	28.0
	100	100	100	100
	(715)	(747)	(717)	(654)
Women in politics (agree–disagree)	Agree version	Forced choice	Agree version	Forced choice
Men better suited	48.0%	38.0%	48.3%	38.7%
Men and women equally suited[b]	52.0	62.0	51.7	61.3
	100	100	100	100
	(743)	(777)	(673)	(786)
Forbid–allow (tone of wording)	Forbid version	Allow version	Forbid version	Allow version
Forbid, not allow	21.2%	45.2%	21.6%	50.7%
Not forbid, allow	78.8	54.8	78.4	49.3
	100	100	100	100
	(735)	(713)	(740)	(663)

[a] From SRC–76 Spring. Exact wording of the questions appears in the text (Arab, p. 117, liberal, p. 163, women, p. 221, forbid, p. 277). Missing data have been omitted after examination of the full tables showed no meaningful differences in these categories. Our results differ slightly from the tables in Groves and Kahn (1979) because they changed the final disposition of two cases in the face-to-face sample after our analysis was complete.

[b] The forced-choice percentages include the response "women more suited than men" whereas that is implicit in the negative position for the agree–disagree version. See pages 220–221.

when interviewed on the telephone. Confronted with a difficult question on the phone, respondents wishing to get the interview over with quickly might well be more apt to say DK when it is offered (as it is on the filtered form), and less apt to say DK when it is not offered but must be volunteered. However, a control for interviewer reports of signs of impatience by respondents does not specify the original effect and thus leaves the interpretation in doubt. It is nevertheless worth pursuing in future comparison of modes of administration, since it would have wide implications for telephone surveys.

The effect of mode of administration on substantive responses (agree versus disagree) for the different forms of the Arab item is even more reliable than for DK versus opinion, despite being based on fewer cases: $\chi^2 = 6.61$, $df = 1$, $p < .02$. One might hypothesize some sort of relation between mode of administration and agreeing-response set (Jordan, Marcus, and Reeder, 1980), but the similarly formatted women in politics item fails to show even a sign of an agreeing effect by mode, though it does show such an effect by form. In the absence of a tenable interpretation we are inclined to regard the interaction as due to chance, an explanation that finds some support in the total results for the Arab item in 1976 and in other surveys. When agree and disagree responses in 1976 are repercentaged omitting DK categories, three of the mode–form combinations are very similar (32–33%), the exception being the standard form on the telephone (45%). We have two other independent surveys in which both forms of the Arab item were asked and when all four sets of results are listed chronologically, the 1976 standard telephone results are again the exception:

| | | Percentage agree | |
Date	Mode	Standard	Filtered
1974	F	21.8	18.4
1976	F	31.6	33.2
1976	T	45.4	33.4
1978	T	46.4	51.4

Note that the percentage agreeing (pro-Arab) rises generally from 1974 to 1978. If the time variable is important, as we think it is because of changing events in the Middle East, then the results for the filtered form make good sense. The anomaly is the 1976 telephone standard percentage-agree. If that anomaly is to be attributed to something about the telephone, then it is difficult to understand why the same relative increase did not occur in the 1978 telephone survey.

When we stand back and look at all our surveys as a whole, we do not have a sense that differences among them correspond in any consistent way to whether telephone or face-to-face interviewing was used. This, plus the difficulty of interpreting the isolated results reported above, leads to our belief that mode of administration has no systematic effects on our experiments, with the possible exception of a greater tendency on the phone for respondents to avoid answers that might lengthen the interview. Nevertheless, the puzzling findings for the Arab experiment indicate that further research is desirable on possible interactions involving question form, response, and mode of administration.[2]

3. RESPONSE RATES AND REINTERVIEWS

For most surveys, the failure to interview all members of the target sample constitutes a potentially serious bias, since the goal is to generalize to the total population sampled. This is not a problem for our research, however, since our goal is to generalize to other sample surveys. Indeed, it is an advantage for us to have response rates typical for national surveys, which during the 1970s have usually ranged from 65 to 75%. Much of our data come from surveys with such response rates (see Table 1.1).

For some of our SRC telephone surveys, however, the overall response rate is noticeably lower, because only part of the sample consists of new random digit dial (RDD) respondents. The other part consists of callbacks to respondents interviewed some months earlier, and in these cases the final response rate is reduced because not all of the original RDD respondents agreed to participate in the reinterview or could be reached.[3] In general, we would have preferred to restrict our use of these samples to the initial RDD portion, and often did so, but in a number of instances we felt that an increase in total size of sample (by

[2]We also cross-tabulated the four experimental items with one another, separately by form and mode. The Arab item is unrelated to the others in all cases, but the remaining three are significantly associated in a number of instances. There are significant three-way interactions of form, item 1, and item 2 for the face-to-face mode, but never the telephone mode. We are inclined to regard these trends as due to chance, since none of the four-way interactions (mode by form by item 1 by item 2) is significant, but note them here for completeness.

[3]The recontact design is used because a prime purpose of monthly SRC surveys is to assess consumer sentiments and the panel data from the reinterviews provide an efficient measure of change. The final response rate for the reinterview sample is the product of the original RDD response rate times the reinterview response rate (or rates if there is more than one reinterview).

using both RDD and reinterview cases) was preferable to restricting ourselves to use of only new RDD cases. This is the familiar problem of balancing known sampling error against possible nonresponse bias. (In some cases, e.g., SRC–74 Fall and SRC–75 February, we ourselves used an original RDD sample and its later reinterviews to construct the within-subject experiments reported in Chapter 10 and elsewhere.)

Where reinterviews are included in our data, two issues are raised: a response rate lower than typical of current surveys and use of respondents who had been interviewed once or sometimes twice before. The two issues are largely confounded in these surveys, since the lowered response rate results from the inclusion of reinterview cases. Nevertheless, it is possible to a limited extent to treat the issues separately.

Low Response Rates

In order to guard against results due to the low response rate of a reinterview sample, we disaggregated all data sets containing both RDD and reinterview subsamples, and examined all important findings separately for each subsample.[4] In one such instance we found that a form difference was restricted entirely to a reinterview subsample, which led us to drop the reinterview subsample; in a second instance reported below a similar but less extreme sample difference occurs. In virtually all other instances findings are quite similar for both subsamples. This is somewhat surprising, given the fairly large response rate differences and the obvious self-selection of respondents who consent to be reinterviewed a second or even a third time. Apparently the answers and associations we investigate are largely unrelated to factors affecting these response rate differences.

Tables B.3 and B.4 present examples of results for RDD and reinterview subsamples in the same surveys, using experiments of importance to our research. In Table B.3, representative question-form differences in marginals are shown separately for RDD and reinterview subsamples from three surveys. Our primary interest here is whether the form differences themselves are different between the two subsamples, that is, is there a three-way interaction of response by form by subsample? In no instance in Table B.3 does the three-way interaction approach significance ($p > .20$), whether for distributions as a whole or for meaningful partitions (e.g., DK versus opinion on the Russia item).

---

[4]In our first reinterview survey in 1975 we also computed results with age, income, and education weights to make the recontact sample resemble the original one, but in no case did this change a finding.

TABLE B.3

Comparison of RDD and Reinterview Distributions for Three Experiments

		RDD		Reinterviews	
DK filter: Russia (SRC-78 Spring)		Standard	Filtered	Standard	Filtered
(see p. 117 for wording)	1. Agree	51.0%	27.0%	58.0%	34.3%
	2. Disagree	36.0	24.1	31.3	23.3
	3. DK, no opinion	13.0	48.9	10.7	42.4
		100	100	100	100
		(308)	(307)	(319)	(309)
Middle alternative: marijuana (SRC-77 August)		Offered	Omitted	Offered	Omitted
(see p. 163 for wording)	1. More strict	42.3%	50.0%	42.8%	51.1%
	2. Less strict	30.4	44.9	31.8	41.5
	3. Same	27.3	5.1	25.3	7.4
		100	100	100	100
		(260)	(274)	(292)	(311)
Balance: fuel (SRC-77 February)		Unbalanced	Formal balance	Unbalanced	Formal balance
(see p. 181 for wording)	1. Yes, a law	50.7%	49.7%	53.6%	52.6%
	2. No, no law	49.3	50.3	46.4	47.4
		100	100	100	100
		(211)	(183)	(366)	(361)

We present a more complex set of relations in Table B.4: the basic findings about Security from our main open–closed comparison of work values in Chapter 3. The reported findings there are that the Security category is chosen more often on the closed form than it is given spontaneously on the open form and, furthermore, that it shows a sharp negative relation to education on the closed form—but little or no relation to education on the open form. Our main evidence for these findings came from open–closed comparisons in two different surveys (SRC-77 February and SRC-78 August), each of which comprised both an RDD and a reinterview subsample. In Chapter 3 these data are pooled, but in Table B.4 the results (dichotomizing Security versus four other categories collapsed) are presented separately by subsample and by survey. Our main interest is in whether RDD and reinterview data lead to similar conclusions. We tested the significance of various effects in this five-way table, although the table itself is fairly clear to visual inspection.

TABLE B.4

Security versus Other Categories by Form, Education, Subsample, and Survey[a]

SRC–78 August

			RDD Subsample					
	Closed form				Open form			
Education:	0–11	12	13+	Total	0–11	12	13+	Total
Security	33%	16%	11%	16%	10%	18%	13%	14%
Other four categories	67	84	89	84	90	82	87	86
	100	100	100	100	100	100	100	100
	(27)	(64)	(83)	(174)	(21)	(34)	(47)	(102)

			Reinterview Subsample					
	Closed form				Open form			
Education:	0–11	12	13+	Total	0–11	12	13+	Total
Security	49%	22%	11%	24%	16%	18%	15%	16%
Other four categories	51	78	89	76	84	82	85	84
	100	100	100	100	100	100	100	100
	(90)	(129)	(160)	(379)	(58)	(73)	(101)	(232)

SRC–77 February

			RDD Subsample					
	Closed form				Open form			
Education:	0–11	12	13+	Total	0–11	12	13+	Total
Security	33%	23%	6%	18%	5%	26%	11%	15%
Other four categories	67	77	94	82	95	74	89	85
	100	100	100	100	100	100	100	100
	(43)	(82)	(86)	(211)	(22)	(35)	(45)	(102)

			Reinterview Subsample					
	Closed form				Open form			
Education:	0–11	12	13+	Total	0–11	12	13+	Total
Security	32%	20%	20%	22%	5%	18%	7%	9%
Other four categories	68	80	80	78	95	82	93	91
	100	100	100	100	100	100	100	100
	(85)	(128)	(158)	(371)	(41)	(62)	(121)	(224)

The marginal difference for the Security response depends more heavily than we would like on the reinterview data, although trends are similar for both subsamples in both surveys and the χ^2 for the response by form by subsample interaction, controlling for survey, is only of borderline significance ($\chi^2 = 3.55$, $df = 1$, $.05 < p < .10$). Indeed, the response by form relation (controlling for both survey and subsample) is highly significant ($\chi^2 = 19.51$, $df = 1$, $p < .001$). Still, our conclusion in Chapter 3 that the Security response is given more often to the closed than the open form must be considered more uncertain as far as RDD interviews go, even though we are inclined to think that a small difference does exist.[5] Our more important conclusion about Security, however, was that its relation to education is quite different for open and closed forms of the question, and that conclusion holds up extremely well in all comparisons in Table B.4. On the closed form, education is negatively related to response, whereas on the open form there seems to be no relation—or possibly a slight curvilinear relation between education and response. (Response by education by form, controlling for survey and subsample: $\chi^2 = 26.81$, $df = 2$, $p < .001$). Finally, the variable representing time of survey does not play a significant role in the relations just discussed, and the five-way interaction itself does not approach significance ($\chi^2 = 2.94$, $df = 2$, $p > .20$).

We have deliberately presented work-values results for the RDD and reinterview samples that are somewhat more problematic than is usually the case in our data. In most instances, as is evident in Table B.3, the RDD–reinterview distinction makes no difference in marginal results. And of course, in the majority of our surveys there is no reinterview component at all, or where there is we have checked in order to assure ourselves that important conclusions are not distorted by being based partly on a subsample atypical in response rate or past interview experience.

The Reinterview Experience

Thus far we have discussed reinterview subsamples that were problematic mainly due to their low response rate, and secondarily to their having been interviewed before in another SRC survey, though not in

---

[5]This means that our statement on p. 100 about lack of "social desirability" effects needs to be qualified slightly, but we do not withdraw it because such an effect would have shown *reduced* Security responses on the RDD closed forms, which does not occur; furthermore, the greater percentages for the reinterview subsample on the closed form are themselves meaningful, even if representative of only part of the original sample.

most cases one in which we had prior experiments. It is also of interest to ask what happens when respondents whom we ourselves interviewed in one survey were reinterviewed using a smilar question at a slightly later point in time. One such piece of evidence can be reported based on the SRC–74 and 75 panel. After being asked the Arabs item in SRC–75 February, all respondents were asked: *When you answered that question about the Arab nations did you recall having been asked it before?* Of those who had been asked the item a few months before in SRC-74 Fall, only 24% said yes. Moreover, the 1975 sample included a component that had *not* received our 1974 interview, although it had received another previous SRC interview, and 8% of those people also said (incorrectly) yes. Thus the true proportion of persons who remembered the Arab item is probably only some 16%.[6] In any case, when persons who had been interviewed in 1974 are divided into those claiming and those not claiming

[6]We also looked at these recollections of the Arabs item by age and education. Older respondents who had been asked the item were significantly less likely to recall it, whereas there is a trend for older respondents who had *not* been asked the item to be more likely to recall (incorrectly) having heard it. Less-educated respondents who had been asked the item were significantly less apt to recall it; only the college educated appeared less likely to recall incorrectly having heard it. There are also suggestive departures from monotonicity in most of these relations, as shown below.

The results are summarized by showing percentages reporting that they recalled the item, the base in parenthesis for each percentage, and measures of association. "Correct yes" refers to the subsample that had actually been asked the item several months earlier; "incorrect yes" refers to the subsample that had not been asked the item several months earlier.

	Age								
	18–24	25–34	35–44	45–54	54–65	65+	gamma	SE	p
Correct yes	23.2%	33.3%	27.6%	21.3%	16.4%	11.2%	.21	.05	.001
	(155)	(273)	(174)	(183)	(152)	(116)			
Incorrect Yes	7.3%	2.8%	7.3%	10.0%	7.3%	14.0%	−.23	.15	n.s.
	(55)	(72)	(41)	(40)	(41)	(43)			

	Education							
	0–8	9–11	12	13–15	16+	gamma	SE	p
Correct yes	14.2%	19.5%	25.8%	27.7%	25.4%	−.14	.05	.01
	(141)	(118)	(383)	(231)	(181)			
Incorrect yes	8.6%	12.5%	7.6%	9.1%	2.0%	.22	.15	n.s.
	(35)	(32)	(119)	(55)	(51)			

The interaction of response (yes–no), correctness (correct–incorrect), and age (linear trend) yields: $\chi^2 = 8.87$, $df = 1$, $p < .01$. The equivalent interaction with education replacing age

such a memory in 1975, the two groups do not differ significantly in the latter year in their answers to the Arab question.

4. BIAS DUE TO VARIOUS FORMS OF NONRESPONSE

Rapoport (1979) has raised an important point about possible bias due to nonresponse when education or other "sophistication" variables are used in analysis. His focus is on those *within* a survey who say DK to a question either when it is asked originally or in a recontact interview. If such responses are more common among persons low in education, interest, or sophistication, then the final sample of substantive responses to such a question will underrepresent these people. Moreover, he implies that the persons missing from any given category of education, interest, or sophistication will be even less educated, less interested, or less sophisticated than those present. Hence bias will be introduced when, say, educational categories are compared with respect to reliability of response over time, since the proportion missing from the lower categories is greater. In particular, our analysis in Chapter 10 of responses to the individual versus social conditions item seemed to show no relation of unreliability to education, but this could be because our low-educated respondents are an elite rather than representative subsample of their educational category and therefore achieve a level of reliability comparable to that of the high-educated category. Rapoport's hypothesis is that an analysis for the whole population would show the low educated to manifest lower reliability than the high educated.

As we considered Rapoport's basic point, it became clear that there are a number of different ways in which persons varying along educational and other sophistication dimensions can be lost from a survey. Among the more important possibilities are:

1. Nonresponse (complete omission) from an initial face-to-face sample
2. Nonresponse from an initial telephone sample
3. Nonresponse in a recontact (telephone or face-to-face) sample
4. DK response to a specific item in an initial survey
5. DK response to an item in a recontact survey

---

yields: $\chi^2 = 4.43$, $df = 1$, $p < .05$. (Cases are too few to allow adequate testing of the four-way interaction.) If "correct yes" is regressed on both age and education, only the coefficient for age is significant ($p < .001$), the coefficient for education becoming borderline ($p = .10$).

The possibilities are thus complicated, especially when considered together, and we have not been able to carry out a thorough analysis. But it appears that much of the potential bias occurs at points 2, 3, and 4. First, telephone surveys underrepresent low education and similar categories on other sophistication dimensions more than do face-to-face surveys. This shows up not only in the Groves and Kahn (1979) experimental comparison noted earlier, but also in other nonexperimental phone versus face-to-face comparisons we were able to make (e.g., see p. 36). Second, there is a quite noticeable differential loss along the same lines when people are contacted for a second interview. Third, for most attitude items DK responses occur more frequently at low education, interest, and sophistication levels, though there are some exceptions (see Chapter 4, footnote 20, p. 145). It is probably at these three points that the danger emphasized by Rapoport is greatest, and our data suggest that the losses are additive to at least some extent.

To take one example of the loss due to reinterview by telephone, in SRC–74 Fall we asked the following question on news interest:[7]

> *On the whole, would you say you follow national and international news very closely, somewhat closely, only a little, or not at all?*

In the 1975 attempt to recontact those respondents, there was a sharp differential loss by 1974 news interest categories:

	Percentage not reinterviewed in 1975	Number originally interviewed in 1974
Not at all	60.0	65
Only a little	35.0	334
Somewhat	24.8	697
Very	26.7	419

It is interesting to note, however, that specific strength measures attached to items on unions (Chapter 7) and Vietnam aid (Chapter 6) in 1974 did not show a differential reinterview loss, for example, of those who felt "quite strongly" on the union issue, 25.4% were not successfully reinterviewed, whereas of those who felt "not so strong," the figure was 25.3%. Thus specific item-related intensity measures do not

---

[7]Although this example seems to reflect loss of respondents due only to recontact, we believe this to be but one factor. Also important is loss of the least-educated part of the population when telephone is the mode of administration, regardless of whether first or second contact is involved. In the 1974–75 panel data from which the news-interest item comes, mode of administration and recontact cannot be separated.

seem to be subject to the same form of differential loss as a general measure such as interest in the news, probably because the former are not related to education (see Table 10.2)

It is still possible that despite the differential loss of persons from news-interest categories, those remaining in each category are entirely representative of those who dropped out. If so, when we examine our data in terms of these categories, bias can be eliminated or at least estimated. In order to test this point, we compared the mean educational and informational levels of those remaining within each news-interest category in the 1975 reinterview with the original mean of all respondents in the 1974 sample (see Table B.5). Not only is there a decrease in means in all cases, but the decrease is greatest for the categories representing least interest. It appears from this evidence that the loss of respondents in this and similar studies does introduce bias into the data, and that the bias cannot be eliminated or controlled in a simple way.

Even on the basis of the previous evidence, we cannot be certain that the lack of relation of education to reliability for the individuals versus social conditions item in Chapter 10 is artifactual to any important degree. None of the evidence in this section touches the point directly, and our estimate is that even the assumption of moderate bias in that case would not change the reliability figures very noticeably. But the general problem raised by loss to surveys of less-educated, less-interested, and less-informed respondents is an important one. Gross response rates do not adequately reflect the problem, partly because they do not tell us who the nonrespondents are and partly because they do not even record as nonrespondents those who agree to be interviewed but fail to answer

TABLE B.5
Mean Education and Information Levels for News Interest Categories in 1974 and 1975 Data

	News Interest			
	Very	Somewhat	Little	Not at all
1974 Education Mean[a]	3.25	3.17	2.65	2.02
1975 Education Mean	3.35	3.25	2.88	2.23
Difference	.10	.08	.23	.21
1974 Information[a]	5.20	5.81	6.98	7.90
1975 Information	5.08	5.69	6.80	7.46
Difference	.12	.12	.18	.44

[a] Educational level is a 5-point scale, 1–5 with 5 = High. Information is a 7-point scale, 3–9, with 3 = High. See Appendix C for a description of both codes.

particular questions. In this book we have simplified tables by omitting DK responses except in chapters where they play a central role. Although we do not think that this practice compromised our conclusions to an important extent, it may at certain points have led us to underestimate the effects of missing data of all kinds on associations involving education and related variables. Especially as telephone surveys and panel studies become increasingly common, research on these issues deserves high priority.

CONCLUSIONS

We have no evidence that use of SRS formulas with complex samples affected our results to any important degree. Conclusions are less certain for mode of administration and inclusion of reinterview subsamples, since each presents some significant effects that we cannot explain. But the effects appear to be either isolated or small and whatever their origin we doubt that they point to major problems running through our data. Indeed, as noted in Appendix A, some of our most striking replications involve surveys vastly different from one another, while some of our most puzzling failures to replicate involve surveys carried out in essentially the same way.

Education and Information Measures

In this appendix we briefly describe two independent variables used throughout our analysis:

EDUCATION

In most of our SRC surveys the measure of education is based on the following questions:

What is the highest grade of school or year of college you completed?

Grades of school   College

[00] [01] [02] [03] [04] [05] [06] [07] [08] [09] [10] [11] [12] [13] [14] [15] [16] [17+]

Did you get a high school diploma or pass a high school equivalency test?		Do you have a college degree?
YES NO		YES NO

In early analyses we used a five-category variable coded: 0–8, 9–11, 12, 13–15, and 16+, with respondents who had passed a high school equivalency test included in the third category, regardless of the actual number of years they had completed. Results based on this variable were almost always quite similar to those based on collapsing the first category with the second and the fourth with the fifth. Thus in the majority of reported analyses we present this three category variable (those without a high school diploma or who did not pass a high school equivalency test; those with a high school diploma or equivalency certificate who had never been to college; those with at least some college). In a few cases, all five categories are presented because they could or do exhibit an unusual trend. In analyses of NORC and DAS data, the same three or five summary categories were constructed, but they are based on exact number of years of school completed.

INFORMATION

Measures of information about political figures are available in two SRC surveys. In SRC–74 Fall respondents were asked:

> *In this next question we're interested in how well-known several men are. Don't worry if they are unfamiliar to you. Can you tell me what each of these men does or did?*
> a. Henry Kissinger _____
> b. William O. Douglas _____
> c. William C. Westmoreland _____

Answers were coded as correct (e.g., *Douglas is a Supreme Court Justice*), partly correct (*some kind of judge*), or incorrect (usually DK, but also extremely vague or wrong responses). The intercorrelations between items ranged from .46–.52 ($\bar{X}$ = .48), and a simple summative index was constructed producing scores from 0–6, with 6 = high information. In most analyses these were collapsed into (0–1), (2–4), and (5–6). The same procedure was repeated in SRC–78 Fall with the names Walter Mondale, Warren Burger, and Robert Byrd.

Education and information are correlated .50 in SRC–74 Fall and .45 in SRC–78 Fall. In most cases where education specifies the relation between form and response, information does much the same. For example, a three-way education interaction ($p < .10$) for the fuel item in SRC–74 Fall (Table 7.6, p. 193) is paralleled by a comparable three-way information interaction for that experiment. Similarly, in most instances where one measure does not produce an interaction, neither does the other. Furthermore, combining the two indicators into a single information–education index does not generally add explanatory power over either taken singly, nor is there evidence that controlling for the effect of one variable specifies the effect of the other (i.e., we discovered no four-way interactions). It appears that the cost of including a measure of information, at least information about political persons, is not offset by returns to the analysis greater than those provided by a simpler standard measure of years of schooling, although for some theoretical purposes it might be useful to treat information as a mediating psychological variable between education and a response such as don't know.

Additional Items and Codes
Bearing on Acquiescence

COMPARISONS OF AGREE–DISAGREE FORMS
WITH OTHER FORMS

As noted in Chapter 8, we constructed 14 experimental comparisons involving agree–disagree items. Only two of the comparisons (involving individuals versus social conditions and women in politics) were analyzed in that chapter. We have decided that the others were insufficiently controlled for content, that is, the two forms allowed differences in item content and thus confounded any attempt to infer the presence or absence of acquiescence. Table D.1 presents the 12 experiments not covered in Chapter 8. Marginals and significance tests are included, along with identification of the survey in which the experiments appeared. Missing data have been omitted, but in no case does this change results importantly.

The first seven experiments (as well as the eleventh) draw on sets of items from ISR Election surveys. All of these but the eleventh were included in the DAS–76 survey, and constituted an attempt to construct scales using different question forms in order to determine whether form effects cumulate. The housing item (Item 7) was later also used in a response-order experiment reported in Chapter 2.

The three foreign affairs experiments were part of a tripartite split-ballot in SRC–74, and are drawn on in Chapter 4 on DK filters. What are

TABLE D.1
Agree–Disagree and Other Form Comparisons[a]

Agree–Disagree	Forced-choiced

Political efficacy (DAS–76)

1. Officials

I don't think public officials care much what people like me think.

Would you say that public officials care much what people like you think, or that they don't care much?

Percentage agree	64.2 (452)	Percentage don't care much	67.9 (421)

$$\chi^2 = 1.38, \; df = 1, \; \text{n.s.}$$

2. Voting

Voting is the only way that people like me can have any say about how the government runs things.

Do you think voting is the only way that people like you can have any say about how the government runs things, or that there are other ways that you can have a say?

Percentage agree	51.4 (451)	Percentage voting is only way	40.8 (417)

$$\chi^2 \; 9.95, \; df = 1, \; p < .01$$

3. Complicated

Sometimes politics and government seem so complicated that a person like me can't really understand what's going on.

Would you say that sometimes politics and government seem so complicated that a person like you can't really understand what's going on, or that you really can understand what's going on all the time?

Percentage agree	71.4 (455)	Percentage seems complicated	77.8 (423)

$$\chi^2 = 4.67, \; df = 1, \; p < .05$$

4. Say

People like me don't have any say about what the government does.

Do you think that people like you have any say about what the government does, or that you don't have any say at all?

Percentage agree	53.2 (449)	Percentage don't have any say	52.4 (424)

$$\chi^2 = .07, \; df = 1, \; \text{n.s.}$$

Welfare (DAS–76)

5. Job

The federal government should see to it that every person has a job and a good standard of living.

Some people feel that the federal government should see to it that every person has a job and a good standard of living. Others think the government should just let each person get ahead on his own. Which comes closest to how you feel?

Percentage agree	52.4 (431)	Percentage government see to it	42.7 (452)

$$\chi^2 = 8.40, \; df = 1, \; p < .01$$

(continued)

Agree-Disagree	Forced-choiced

6. Medical

The federal government should see to it that every person receives adequate medical care.

How about medical care: Should the federal government see to it that every person receives adequate medical care, *or* should everyone be responsible for his own medical care? Which comes *closest* to how you feel?

Percentage agree	79.1 (426)	Percentage government see to it	76.5 (438)

$$\chi^2 = .86, \ df = 1, \ \text{n.s.}$$

7. Housing[b]

The federal government should see to it that all people have adequate housing.

Some people feel the federal government should see to it that all people have adequate housing, while others feel each person should provide for his own housing. Which comes *closest* to how you feel about this?

Percentage agree	59.8 (423)	Percentage government see to it	37.1 (434)

$$\chi^2 = 44.64, \ df = 1, \ p < .001$$

Foreign Affairs (SRC–74 Fall)

8. Russia

Here are some questions about other countries. Do you agree or disagree with this statement: The Russian leaders are basically trying to get along with America.

Here are some questions about other countries. Would you say that the Russian leaders are basically trying to get along with America, or that they are basically trying to dominate America?

Percentage agree	58.9 (423)	Percentage Russians get along	49.0 (398)

$$\chi^2 = 8.06, \ df = 1, \ p < .01$$

9. Portugal

How about this statement: The new Portuguese military government is trying to maintain its own control without concern for democracy in Portugal. Do you agree or disagree?

In your opinion, is the new Portuguese military government trying to move toward democracy, *or* is it trying to maintain its own control without concern for democracy in Portugal?

Percentage agree	59.6 (183)	Percentage military maintain control	74.6 (122)

$$\chi^2 = 7.48, \ df = 1, \ p < .01$$

10. Arabs

The Arab nations are trying to work for a real peace with Israel. Do you agree or disagree?

Do you think the Arab nations are trying to defeat Israel, *or* are they trying to work for a real peace with Israel?

Percentage agree	21.8 (377)	Percentage Arabs for peace	15.4 (350)

$$\chi^2 = 4.80, \ df = 1, \ p < .05$$

(continued)

TABLE D.1—*Continued*

Agree–Disagree	Forced-choiced
	Other Experiments

11. Officials (SRC–76 Feb.)

Here is a statement: Public officials really care about what people like me think. Do you strongly agree, agree, disagree, or strongly disagree with that?	*Here is a statement: I don't think public officials care much about what people like me think. Do you strongly agree, agree, disagree, or strongly disagree with that?*
SA: 4.4%, A: 40.0, D: 45.1, SD: 10.4 (607)	SD: 4.4%, D: 36.1, A: 44.8, SA: 14.7 (593)

linear $\chi^2 = 1.48$, $df = 1$, n.s.

12. Unions (SRC–79 August)

Please tell me if you agree or disagree with this statement: Labor unions are more to blame than businesses for inflation.	*Please tell me if you agree or disagree with this statement: Businesses are more to blame than labor unions for inflation.*
Percentage agree 49.1 (291)	Percentage agree 38.9 (298)

$\chi^2 = 7.10$, $df = 1$, $p < .01$

---

[a] Base Ns are shown in parentheses.

[b] This comparison was replicated in SRC–79 Sept. as part of a tripartite experiment on response order effects. The results are presented in Chapter 2, footnote 18 .

here called agree–disagree forms are also "standard" in the sense of not offering DK responses; they are also presented with their filtered equivalents in Table 4.1.

The union item was constructed on the model of the individuals versus social conditions item extensively analyzed in Chapter 8. However, we now believe that the apparent form effect for the union item occurs because a fair number of respondents reject *both* sides of the issue as framed—that the "coin-on-edge" possibility mentioned in Chapter 8 becomes important for the union item. If so, the failure to create genuine reversals in this case provides a good example of how easy it is to go astray when attempting to produce experimental variations involving acquiescence.

FULL CODES FOR INDIVIDUALS–SOCIAL CONDITIONS FOLLOW-UP

In Chapter 8, abbreviated codes were presented for the follow-up open question (*Would you tell me why you feel that way?*) to the individuals versus social conditions item. The full codes are given in Table D.2.

TABLE D.2
Codes for Open Question to Individual–Social Conditions Item

Would you tell me why you feel that way?

Code *main* mention if one factor clearly predominates. (Judge by number of words if necessary.) If no main factor, code *first* mention.

Code answer to probe without reference to choice in previous question.

10. Religion
    Man was born in original sin.
    It's just sinfulness of people.
    People aren't following the Bible anymore.
    People aren't being good Christians.
20. Individual controls his behavior, or should
    Everyone is responsible for his own actions.
    People should know the difference between right and wrong.
    It's the individual's decision if he wants to commit crimes.
    A person doesn't have to commit crimes just because he has bad conditions.
21. Well-off and powerful commit crimes (too)
    Rich people break the law all the time.
    Little people do the purse-snatching but big guys make money illegally too.
    The politicians in Washington are corrupt.
22. People are selfish, too concerned with themselves.
25. People don't want to get involved in reporting crime.
30. Law enforcement is lax or lenient
    Punishment should be more strict.
    The courts are going to let them off so they don't care what they do.
40. Family socialization or other early childhood experiences.
    (Include schools.)
    It's their upbringing; children don't get the right training at home or at school.
    It's the home environment.
    Parents can't give their children enough love and guidance because they both work.
50. Moral decay, social change in values or expectations.
    (Include here references to drugs and to deviant individuals or subgroups.)
    It's the permissive society.
    People want so much today.
    Young people have bad morals to contend with nowadays.
    Times have changed so—the crimes and TV violence and pornography all around.
60. Inequality of laws, treatment, or wealth (unjust system)
    Some people have so much more money than others—it leads to resentment.
    Laws are enforced unfairly—punishment depends on who you are, not what you've done.
    Blacks are treated unfairly.
70. Poverty, economic difficulties and other specific social conditions.
    (Include here references to overpopulation and congestion.)
    Poverty breeds crime.
    When a man cannot get a job, he has to steal.
    It's slums and overcrowding and unemployment.
80. The environment controls the individual
    (No specific factors are mentioned.)
    Man is the product of his environment.

(continued)

TABLE D.2—*Continued*

It's the bad environment that's to blame.
People cannot really shape their own lives in a complex society like ours.
90. Denies the concept of social conditions as existing apart from individuals
   Individuals make up the society so it has to be individuals who are to blame.
91. No real reason given; repeat of words in question
   You can't blame it on the individual.
   You can't blame it on social conditions.
   It's more the social conditions than the individuals.
97. Other
98. DK
99. NA

References

Abelson, R. P., and M. J. Rosenberg
    1958   "Symbolic psychologic: A model of attitudinal cognition" *Behavioral Science* 3: 1–8.
Adams, J. S.
    1956   "An experiment on question and response bias" *Public Opinion Quarterly* 20: 593–598.
Adorno, T. W., E. Frenkel-Brunswik, D. J. Levinson, and R. N. Sanford
    1950   *The Authoritarian Personality*. New York: Harper.
Allport, F. H., and D. A. Hartman
    1925   "The measurement and motivation of atypical opinion in a certain group," *The American Political Science Review* 19: 735–760.
Allport, G. W.
    1935   "Attitudes." In C. Murchison (ed.), *A Handbook of Social Psychology*. Worcester, Mass.: Clark University Press.
    1954   "The historical background of modern social psychology." In G. Lindzey (ed.), *Handbook of Social Psychology*. Cambridge, Mass.: Addison-Wesley.
Anscombe, F. J.
    1968   "Outliers," *International Encyclopedia of the Social Sciences* 15. New York: Macmillan and Free Press.
Asch, S. E.
    1946   "Forming impressions of personality," *Journal of Abnormal and Social Psychology* 41: 258–290.
    1952   *Social Psychology*. New York: Prentice Hall.
Bailey, K. D.
    1978   *Methods of Social Research*. New York: Free Press.
Barron, D., and J. Immerwahr
    1979   "The public views South Africa," *Public Opinion* 2: 54–59.

Becker, S. L.
  1954   "Why an order effect," *Public Opinion Quarterly,* 18: 271–278.
Belson, W. A.
  1966   "The effects of reversing the presentation order of verbal rating scales," *Journal of Advertising Research* 6: 30–37.
Belson, W. A., and J. A. Duncan
  1962   "A comparison of the check-list and the open response questioning systems," *Applied Statistics* II: 120–132.
Bem, D. J.
  1970   *Beliefs, Attitudes, and Human Affairs.* Belmont, Calif: Brooks-Cole (Wadsworth).
Bianchi, S. M.
  1976   *Sampling Report for the 1976 Detroit Area Study.* Ann Arbor: Detroit Area Study, University of Michigan.
Bishop, G. F., R. W. Oldendick, and A. J. Tuchfarber
  1978   "Effects of question wording and format on political attitude consistency," *Public Opinion Quarterly* 42: 81–92.
  1980   Experiments in using survey filter questions with American public affairs issues," Paper presented at Midwest Political Science Association Meeting. Chicago, Ill.
Bishop, G. F., R. W. Oldendick, A. J. Tuchfarber, and S. E. Bennett
  1980   "Pseudo-opinions on public affairs," *Public Opinion Quarterly* 44: 198–209.
Blankenship, A. B.
  1940a   "The choice of words in poll questions," *Sociology and Social Research* 25: 12–18.
  1940b   "Does the question form influence public opinion poll results," *Journal of Applied Psychology* 24: 27–30.
Bogart, L.
  1967   "No opinion, don't know, and maybe no answer," *Public Opinion Quarterly* 31: 331–345.
Boulding, E.
  1960   "Orientation toward achievement or security in relation to consumer behavior," *Human Relations* 13: 365–383.
Bradburn, N. M.
  1978   "Response effects," (Chap. 10) Draft. (To appear in P. H. Rossi, J. D. Wright, and C. Anderson (eds.), *The Handbook of Survey Research.* New York: Academic Press (in press).
Bradburn, N. M., and W. M. Mason
  1964   "The effect of question order on responses," *Journal of Marketing Research* 1: 57–61.
Bradburn, N. M., S. Sudman, and Associates
  1979   *Improving Interview Method and Questionnaire Design.* San Francisco: Jossey-Bass.
Brannon, R., G. Cyphers, S. Hesse, S. Hesselbart, R. Keane, H. Schuman, T. Viccaro, and D. Wright
  1973   "Attitude and action: A field experiment joined to a general population survey," *American Sociological Review* 38: 625–636.
Brook, D., and G. J. G. Upton
  1974   "Biases in local government elections due to position on the ballot paper," *Applied Statistics* 23: 414–419.
Burnstein, E., and A. Vinokur
  1977   "Persuasive argumentation and social comparison as determinants of attitude polarization," *Journal of Experimental Social Psychology* 13: 315–332.

Campbell, A. A.
1945   "Two problems in the use of the open question," *Journal of Abnormal and Social Psychology* 40: 340–343.
Campbell, A., P. E. Converse, W. E. Miller, and D. E. Stokes
1960   *The American Voter*. New York: Wiley.
Campbell, D. T., and P. J. Mohr
1950   "The effect of ordinal position upon responses to items in a check list," *Journal of Applied Psychology* 34: 62–67.
Campbell, D. T., C. R. Siegman, and M. B. Rees
1967   "Direction-of-wording effects in the relationship between scales," *Psychological Bulletin* 68: 292–303.
Cannell, C. F., L. Oksenberg, and J. M. Converse
1977   "Striving for response accuracy: Experiments in new interviewing techniques," *Journal of Marketing Research* XIV: 306–315.
Cantril, H.
1940   "Experiments in the wording of questions," *Public Opinion Quarterly* 4: 330–332.
1942   "Public opinion in flux." *The Annals of the American Academy of Political and Social Science* March.
Cantril, H. (Ed.)
1944   *Gauging Public Opinion*. Princeton: Princeton University Press.
Carp, F. M.
1974   "Position effects on interview responses," *Journal of Gerontology* 29: 581–587.
Carpenter, E. H., and L. G. Blackwood
1979   "The effect of question position on responses to attitudinal questions," *Rural Sociology* 44: 46–72.
Carr, L. G.
1971   "The Srole items and acquiescence," *American Sociological Review* 36: 287–293.
Clancy, K. J., and R. A. Wachsler
1971   "Positional effects in shared-cost surveys," *Public Opinion Quarterly* 35: 258–265.
Clogg, C. C.
1980   "Using Association Models in Sociological Research: Some examples." Unpublished paper.
Converse, J. M.
1976–1977 "Predicting 'no opinion' in the polls," *Public Opinion Quarterly* 40: 515–530.
Converse, J. M. and H. Schuman
1981   "The manner of inquiry: An analysis of survey question form across organizations and over time," Paper prepared for the Panel on Survey Measurement of Subjective Phenomena, National Research Council.
Converse, P. E.
1964   "The nature of belief systems in mass publics." In D. E. Apter (ed.), *Ideology and Discontent*. New York: Free Press.
1970   "Attitudes and non-attitudes: Continuation of a dialogue." In E. R. Tufte (Ed.), *The Quantitative Analysis of Social Problems*. Reading, Mass.: Addison-Wesley.
1972   "Change in the American electorate." In A. Campbell and P. E. Converse (Eds.), *The human meaning of social change*. New York: Russell Sage Foundation.
1975   Public opinion and voting behavior. In F. I. Greenstein and N. W. Polsby (eds.), *Handbook of Political Science* 4. Reading, Mass.: Addison-Wesley.
1980   "Rejoinder to Judd and Milburn," *American Sociological Review* 45: 644–646.
Converse, P. E., A. Clausen, and W. E. Miller
1965   "Electoral myth and reality," *The American Political Science Review* 59: 321–336.

Converse, P. E., and G. B. Markus
1979 "Plus ca change...: The new CPS election study panel," *The American Political Science Review* 73: 32-49.

Cook, T. D., and D. T. Campbell
1979 *Quasi-Experimentation: Design and Analysis Issues for Field Settings.* Chicago: Rand McNally.

Coombs, C. H., and L. Coombs
1976-1977 "Don't know: Item ambiguity or respondent uncertainty?," *Public Opinion Quarterly* 40: 497-514.

Couch, A., and K. Keniston
1960 "Yeasayers and naysayers: Agreeing response set as a personality variable," *Journal of Abnormal and Social Psychology* 60: 151-174.

Cowan, C. D., L. R. Murphy, and J. Wiener
1978 "Effects of supplemental questions on victimization estimates from the national crime survey," *1978 Proceedings of the Section on Survey Research Methods.* Washington, D.C.: American Statistical Association.

Crutchfield, R. S., and D. A. Gordon
1947 "Variations in respondents' interpretations of an opinion poll question," *International Journal of Opinion and Attitude Research* I: 1-12.

Dahl, R. A.
1956 *A Preface to Democratic Theory.* Chicago: The University of Chicago Press.

Davis, J. A.
1975 "Communism, conformity, cohorts, and categories: American tolerance in 1954 and 1972-73," *American Journal of Sociology* 81: 491-513.
1976 "Are surveys any good, and if so, for what?" In H. W. Sinaiko and L. A. Broedling (eds.), *Perspectives on Attitude Assessment: Surveys and Their Alternatives.* Champaign, Ill.: Pendleton.
1978 "Trends in NORC General Social Survey items 1972-1977," *General Social Survey Technical Report,* No. 9: Chicago: NORC.

DeLamater, J., and P. MacCorquodale
1975 "The effects of interview schedule variations on reported sexual behavior," *Sociological Methods and Research* 4: 215-236

Dohrenwend, B. S.
1965 "Some effects of open and closed questions on respondents' answers," *Human Organization* 24: 175-184.

Dotson, L. E., and G. F. Summers
1970 "Elaboration of Guttman scaling techniques," In G. F. Summers (ed.), *Attitude Measurement.* Chicago: Rand McNally.

Duncan, B., and O. D. Duncan
1978 *Sex Typing and Social Roles: A Research Report.* New York: Academic Press.

Duncan, O. D.
1979 "Indicators of sex typing: Traditional and egalitarian, situational and ideological responses," *American Journal of Sociology* 85: 251-260.

Duncan, O. D., and H. Schuman
1976 "An experiment on order and wording of attitude questions," unpublished manuscript.
1980 "Effects of question wording and context: An experiment with religious indicators," *Journal of the American Statistical Association* 75: 269-275.

Duncan, O. D., H. Schuman, and B. Duncan
1973 *Social Change in a Metropolitan Community.* New York: Russell Sage Foundation.

Duvall, E. M.
  1946   "Conceptions of parenthood." *American Journal of Sociology* 52: 193–203.
Duverger, M.
  1964   *Introduction to the Social Sciences.* London: George Allen and Unwin.
Evers, M.
  1974   *Changes in subjective social class identification in Detroit between the 1950s and 1971,* Ph.D. dissertation, Ann Arbor: University of Michigan.
Faulkenberry, G. D., and R. Mason
  1978   "Characteristics of nonopinion and no opinion response groups," *Public Opinion Quarterly* 42: 533–543.
Fay, R., and L. A. Goodman
  1973   "ECTA program description for users," unpublished manuscript.
Ferber, R.
  1952   "Order bias in a mail survey," *The Journal of Marketing* 17: 171–178.
Fischer, E. M.
  1974   "Change in anomie in Detroit from the 1950s to 1971," Ph.D. dissertation, Ann Arbor: University of Michigan.
Fishbein, M., and I. Ajzen
  1975   *Belief, Attitude, Intention and Behavior.* Reading, Mass.: Addison-Wesley.
Fleming, D.
  1967   "Attitude: The history of a concept." In *Perspectives in American History* 1. Cambridge, Mass.: Charles Warren Center in American History, Harvard University.
Francis, J. D., and L. Busch
  1975   "What we know about 'I don't knows,'" *Public Opinion Quarterly* 39: 207–218.
Gafke, R., and D. Leuthold
  1979   "The effect on voters of misleading, confusing and difficult ballot titles," *Public Opinion Quarterly* 43: 394–401.
Gallup, G. H.
  1941   "Question wording in public opinion polls." *Sociometry* 4: 259–268.
  1947   "The quintamensional plan of question design," *Public Opinion Quarterly* 11: 385–393.
  1972   *The Gallup Poll, Public Opinion 1935–71,* 3. New York: Random House.
  1976–1977   *The Gallup Poll, Public Opinion 1972–1977,* 2. New York: Random House.
Geertz, C.
  1976   "From the native's point of view: On the nature of anthropological understanding." In K. H. Basso and H. A. Selby (eds.), *Meaning in Anthropology.* Albuquerque: University of New Mexico Press.
Gergen, K. J.
  1973   "Social psychology as history," *Journal of Personality and Social Psychology* 26: 309–320.
Gibson, C., G. M. Shapiro, L. R. Murphy, G. J. Stanko
  1978   "Interaction of survey questions as it related to interviewer-respondent bias." *1978 Proceedings of the Section on Survey Research Methods.* Washington D.C.: American Statistical Association.
Gill, S.
  1947   "How do you stand on sin?," *Tide* (March 14): 72.
Goffman, E.
  1959   *The Presentation of Self in Everyday Life.* Garden City, N.Y.: Doubleday.
Goldberg, D., H. Sharp, and R. Freedman
  1959   "The stability and reliability of expected family size data," *Milbank Memorial Fund Quarterly* 37: 369–385.

Goodman, L. A.
   1975   "The relationship between modified and usual multiple-regression approaches
           to the analysis of dichotomous variables." In D. R. Heise (ed.), *Sociological
           Methodology 1976*. San Francisco: Jossey-Bass.
   1978   *Analyzing Qualitative/Categorical Data: Log-Linear Models and Latent-Structure
           Analysis*. Reading, Mass.: Addison-Wesley.
Gouldner, A. W.
   1960   "The norm of reciprocity: A preliminary statement," *American Sociological Review*
           25: 161–178.
Green, B. F.
   1954   "Attitude measurement." In G. Lindzey (ed.), *Handbook of Social Psychology*.
           Cambridge, Mass.: Addison-Wesley.
Groves, R. M., and R. L. Kahn.
   1979   *Surveys by Telephone: A National Comparison with Personal Interviews*. New York:
           Academic Press.
Guttman, L., and E. A. Suchman
   1947   "Intensity and a zero point for attitude analysis," *American Sociological Review* 12:
           57–67.
Harris, L., and Associates
   1976   *The Harris Survey Yearbook of Public Opinion 1973*. New York: Louis Harris and
           Associates.
Hartley, E.
   1946   *Problems in Prejudice*. New York: Kings Crown Press.
Hayes, D. P.
   1964   "Item order and Guttman scales," *American Journal of Sociology* 70: 51–58.
Hedges, B. M.
   1979   "Question wording effects: Presenting one or both sides of a case," *The Statisti-
           cian* 28: 83–99.
Heise, D. R.
   1969   "Separating reliability and stability in test-retest correlation," *American Sociologi-
           cal Review* 34: 93–101.
Hitlin, R.
   1976   "On question wording and stability of response," *Social Science Research* 5: 39–41.
Hyman, H. H.
   1944   "Do they tell the truth?," *Public Opinion Quarterly* 8: 557–559.
   1953   "The value systems of different classes: A social psychological contribution to
           the analysis of stratification." In R. Bendix and S. M. Lipset (eds.), *Class Status
           and Power*. Glencoe, Ill.: The Free Press.
Hyman, H. H., and P. B. Sheatsley
   1950   "The current status of American public opinion." In J. C. Payne (ed.), *The
           Teaching of Contemporary Affairs*. Twenty-first Yearbook of the National Council
           of Social Studies, 1950, 11–34.
   1954   "The authoritarian personality—a methodological critique." In R. Christie and
           M. Jahoda (eds.), *Studies in the Scope and Method of "the Authoritarian Personality."*
           Glencoe, Ill.: Free Press.
Hyman, H. H., and C. R. Wright
   1979   *Education's Lasting Influence on Values*. Chicago: University of Chicago Press.
Hyman, H. H., C. R. Wright, and J. S. Reed
   1975   *The Enduring Effects of Education*. Chicago: University of Chicago Press.
Interviewer's Manual (Revised Edition)

1976   Ann Arbor: Survey Research Center, Institute for Social Research.
Jackman, M.
1973   "Education and prejudice or education and response set?," *American Sociological Review* 38: 327–339.
1977   "Prejudice, tolerance, and attitudes toward ethnic groups," *Social Science Research* 6: 145–169.
Jordan, L. A., A. C. Marcus, and L. G. Reeder
1980   "Response styles in telephone and household interviewing: A field experiment," *Public Opinion quarterly* 44: 210–222.
Judd, C. M., and J. A. Krosnick
1981   Attitude centrality, organization, and measurement. *Journal of Personality and Social Psychology* (in press).
Kalton, G., M. Collins, and L. Brook
1978   "Experiments in wording opinion questions," *The Journal of the Royal Statistical Society Series C* 27: 149–161.
Kalton, G., J. Roberts, and D. Holt
1980   "The effects of offering a middle response option with opinion questions," *The Statistician* 29: 11–24.
Katz, D.
1940   "Three criteria: Knowledge, conviction, and significance," *Public Opinion Quarterly* 4: 277–284.
1944   "The measurement of intensity." In H. Cantril (ed.), *Gauging Public Opinion.* Princeton: Princeton University Press.
Key, V. O., Jr.
1961   *Public Opinion and American Democracy.* New York: Alfred A. Knopf.
Kiecolt, J.
1978   Instructor's Manual. To accompany K. D. Bailey's *Methods of Social Research.* New York: Free Press.
Kirchner, W. K., and W. H. Uphoff
1955   "The effect of grouping scale items in union–attitude measurement," *The Journal of Applied Psychology* 19: 182–183.
Kish, L.
1959   "Some statistical problems in research design," *American Sociological Review* 24: 328–338.
Klopfer, F. J., and T. M. Madden
1980   "The middlemost choice on attitude items: Ambivalence, neutrality, or uncertainty?," *Personality and Social Psychology Bulletin* 6: 97–101.
Kohn, M. L.
1969   *Class and Conformity: A Study in Values* Homewood, Ill.: Irwin-Dorsey
Kornhauser, A. W.
1946–1947 "Are public opinion polls fair to organized labor?," *Public Opinion Quarterly* 10: 484–500.
Kraut, A. I., A. D. Wolfson, and A. Rothenberg
1975   "Some effects of position on opinion survey items," *Journal of Applied Psychology* 60: 774–776.
Kruskal, W. H.
1968   "Significance tests," *International Encyclopedia of the Social Sciences* 14. New York: Macmillan and Free Press.
Lane, R. E.
1962   *Political Ideology.* New York: Free Press.

Lazarsfeld, P. E.
  1944   "The controversy over detailed interviews—an offer for negotiation," *Public Opinion Quarterly* 8: 38–60.
Lemon, N.
  1973   *Attitudes and Their Measurement.* New York: Halsted Press (Wiley).
Lenski, G. E.
  1963   *The Religious Factor.* Garden City, N.Y.: Anchor.
Lenski, G. E., and J. C. Leggett
  1960   "Caste, class, and deference in the research interview," *American Journal of Sociology* 65: 463–467.
Lepkowski, J. M.
  1980   *Design effects for multivariate categorical interactions.* Ph.D. dissertation, Ann Arbor: University of Michigan.
Likert, R.
  1932   Excerpts from "A technique for the measurement of attitudes," *Archives of Psychology,* 140. Reprinted in M. Fishbein (ed.), *Readings in Attitude Theory and Measurement.* New York: Wiley.
Lindzey, G. E., and L. Guest
  1951   "To repeat—check lists can be dangerous," *Public Opinion Quarterly* 15: 355–358.
Link, H. C.
  1946   "The psychological corporation's index of public opinion," *Journal of Applied Psychology* 30: 297–309.
Lipset, S. M.
  1960   *Political Man.* New York: Doubleday.
Lykken, D. T.
  1968   "Statistical significance in psychological research," *Psychological Bulletin* 70: 151–159.
McCarthy, J. D., and M. N. Zald
  1977   "Resource mobilization and social movements: A partial theory," *American Journal of Sociology* 82: 1212–1241.
McDill, E. L.
  1959   A comparison of three measures of attitude identity, *Social Forces* 38: 95–99.
McFarland, S. G.
  1981   "Effects of question order on survey responses," *Public Opinion Quarterly* 45: 208–215.
McGuire, W. J.
  1969   "The nature of attitudes and attitude change." In G. Lindzey and E. Aronson (eds.), *The Handbook of Social Psychology,* Second Ed., 3. Reading, Mass.: Addison-Wesley.
McKennell, A. C.
  1974   *Surveying Attitude Structures.* Amsterdam: Elsevier.
McNemar, Q.
  1946   "Opinion-attitude methodology," *Psychological Bulletin* 43: 289–374.
  1969   *Psychological Statistics.* New York: Wiley.
Marquis, K. H., J. Marshall, and S. Oskamp
  1972   "Testimony validity as a function of question form, atmosphere, and item difficulty," *Journal of Applied Social Psychology* 2: 167–186.
Martin, E.
  1980   "The effects of item contiguity and probing on measures of anomia," *Social Psychology Quarterly* 43: 116–120.

Metzner, H., and F. Mann
  1952   "Effects of grouping related questions in questionnaires," *Public Opinion Quarterly* 16: 136–141.
Morrison, D., and R. E. Henkel
  1970   *The Significance Test Controversy*. Chicago: Aldine.
Moser, A. C., and G. Kalton
  1971   *Survey Methods in Social Investigation*, Second Ed. London: Heinemann.
Mueller, J. E.
  1970   "Choosing among 133 candidates," *Public Opinion Quarterly* 34: 395–402.
  1973   *War, Presidents and Public Opinion*. New York: Wiley.
  1979   "Public expectations of war during the cold war," *American Journal of Political Science* 23: 301–329.
Nakamura, C. Y.
  1959   "Salience of norms and order of questionnaire items: Their effect on responses to the items," *The Journal of Abnormal Social Psychology* 59: 139–142.
National Opinion Research Center
  1972   "A brush-up on interviewing techniques," unpublished memo.
  1980   *General Social Surveys, 1972–1980: Cumulative Codebook*. Chicago: NORC, University of Chicago.
Navazio, R.
  1977   "An experimental approach to bandwagon research," *Public Opinion Quarterly* 41: 217–225.
Newcomb, T. M., R. H. Turner, and P. E. Converse
  1965   *Social psychology*. New York: Holt, Rinehart and Winston,
Noelle-Neumann, E.
  1970–1971   "Wanted: Rules for wording structured questionnaires," *Public Opinion Quarterly* 34: 191–201.
Nunn, C. A., H. J. Crockett, and J. A. Williams
  1978   *Tolerance for Nonconformity*. San Francisco: Jossey-Bass.
Nunnally, J. C.
  1978   *Psychometric Theory*. New York: McGraw-Hill.
Payne, J. D.
  1971   "The effects of reversing the order of verbal rating scales in a postal survey." *Journal of the Market Research Society* 14: 30–44.
Payne, S. L.
  1951   *The Art of Asking Questions*. Princeton: Princeton University Press.
Peabody, D.
  1961   "Attitude content and agreement set in scales of authoritarianism, dogmatism, anti-semitism, and economic conservatism," *Journal of Abnormal and Social Psychology* 63: 1–11.
  1962   "Two components in bipolar scales: Direction and extremeness," *Psychological Review* 69: 65–73.
Peak, H.
  1953   "Problems of objective observation." In L. Festinger and D. Katz (eds.), *Research Methods in the Behavioral Sciences*. New York: Holt, Rinehart and Winston.
Peterson, K. K., and J. E. Dutton
  1975   "Centrality, extremity, intensity," *Social Forces* 54: 393–414.
Piazza, T.
  1980   "The analysis of attitude items" *American Journal of Sociology* 86: 584–603.
Powers, E. A., P. Morros, W. J. Goudy, and P. M. Keith
  1977   "Serial order preference in survey research," *Public Opinion Quarterly* 41: 80–85.

Presser, S.
1977   *Survey question wording and attitudes in the general public.* Ph.D. dissertation, Ann Arbor: University of Michigan.
Presser, S., and H. Schuman
1975   "Question wording as an independent variable in survey analysis: A first report," *Proceedings of the Social Statistics Section,* American Statistical Association, 16–25.
1980   "The measurement of a middle position in attitude surveys," *Public Opinion Quarterly* 44: 70–85.
Quinn, S. B., and W. A. Belson
1969   *The Effects of Reversing the Order of Presentation of Verbal Rating Scales in Survey Interviews.* London: Survey Research Centre.
Rapoport, R. B.
1979   "What they don't know can hurt you," *American Journal of Political Science* 23: 805–815.
Robinson, D., and S. Rohde
1946   "Two experiments with an anti-semitism poll," *Journal of Abnormal and Social Psychology* 41: 136–144.
Robinson, J. P., and P. R. Shaver
1968   *Measures of Social Psychological Attitudes.* Ann Arbor: Institute for Social Research.
Roll, C. W., and A. H. Cantril
1980   *Polls: Their Use and Misuse in Politics.* Cabin John, Md.: Seven Locks Press.
Roper Center
1975   *Survey Data for Trend Analysis.* The Roper Public Opinion Research Center, Williams College.
Roper, E.
1940   "Problems and techniques," *Public Opinion Quarterly* 4: 129–130.
Rorer, L. G.
1965   "The great response-style myth," *Psychological Bulletin* 63: 129–156.
Rugg, D.
1941   "Experiments in wording questions: II," *Public Opinion Quarterly* 5: 91–92.
Rugg, D., and H. Cantril
1944   "The wording of questions." In H. Cantril (ed.), *Gauging Public Opinion.* Princeton: Princeton University Press.
Sayre, J.
1939   "A comparison of three indices of attitude toward radio advertising," *Journal of Applied Psychology* 23: 23–33.
Schuman, H.
1966   "The random probe: A technique for evaluating the validity of closed questions," *American Sociological Review* 21: 218–222.
1969   "Free will and determinism in public beliefs about race," *Transaction* 7: 44–48.
1973   "Attitudes vs. action *versus* attitudes vs. attitudes," *Public Opinion Quarterly* 36: 347–354.
Schuman, H., and J. Converse
1971   "The effects of black and white interviewers on black responses in 1968," *Public Opinion Quarterly* 35: 44–68.
Schuman, H., and O. D. Duncan
1974   "Questions about attitude survey questions," In H. L. Costner (ed.), *Sociological Methodology 1973–74* San Francisco: Jossey-Bass.
Schuman, H., and J. Harding
1964   "Prejud ce and the norm of rationality," *Sociometry* 27: 353–371.

Schuman, H., and S. Presser
1977–1978 "Attitude measurement and the gun control paradox," *Public Opinion Quarterly* 41: 427–438.
1977 "Question wording as an independent variable in survey analysis," *Sociological Methods and Research* 6: 151–170.
1978 "The assessment of no opinion in attitude surveys." In K. Schuessler (ed.), *Sociological Methodology 1979*. San Francisco: Jossey-Bass.
1979 "The open and closed question," *American Sociological Review* 44: 692–712.
1980 "Public opinion and public ignorance: The fine line between attitudes and nonattitudes," *American Journal of Sociology* 85: 1214–1225.
1981 "The attitude-action connection and the issue of gun control." *The Annals of the American Academy of Political and Social Science* 455: 40–47.

Schuman, H., S. Presser, and J. Ludwig
1981 "Context effects on survey responses to questions about abortion." *Public Opinion Quarterly* 45: 216–223.

Scott, W. A.
1968 "Attitude measurement." In G. Lindzey and E. Aronson (eds.), *The Handbook of Social Psychology*, Second Ed., 2. Reading, Mass.: Addison-Wesley.

Searle, J. R.
1979 *Expression and Meaning*. New York: Cambridge University Press.

Sherif, M., and C. W. Sherif
1969 *Social Psychology*. Evanston, Ill.: Harper and Row.

Sigelman, L.
1981 "Question-order effects on presidential popularity," *Public Opinion Quarterly* 45: 199–207.

Smith, M. B., J. S. Bruner, and R. W. White
1956 *Opinions and Personality*. New York: Wiley.

Smith, T. W.
1978 "In search of house effects: A comparison of responses to various questions by different survey organizations." *Public Opinion Quarterly* 42: 443–463.
1979 "Happiness: Time trends, seasonal variations, inter-survey differences, and other mysteries," *Social Psychology Quarterly* 42: 18–30.
1980 "The 75% solution: An analysis of the structure of attitudes on gun control, 1959–1977, *The Journal of Criminal Law & Criminology* 71: 300–316.
1981 "Can we have confidence in confidence? Revisited." In Denis Johnston (Ed.) *Measurement of Subjective Phenomena*. Washington, D.C.: U.S. Government Printing Office, Forthcoming.

Smith, T. W., and C. B. Stephenson
1979 "An analysis of test–retest experiments in the 1972, 1973, 1974, and 1978 General Social Surveys," *General Social Survey Technical Report No. 14*. Chicago: NORC.

Srole, L.
1956 "Social integration and certain corollaries: An exploratory study," *American Sociological Review* 21: 709–716.

Stember, H., and H. Hyman
1949–1950 "How interviewer effects operate through question form," *International Journal of Opinion and Attitude Research* 3: 493–512.

Stouffer, S. A.
1933 "A technique for analyzing sociological data classified in non-quantitative groups," *American Journal of Sociology* 31: 180–193.
1955 *Communism, Conformity, and Civil Liberties*. Garden City, N.Y.: Doubleday.

Stouffer, S. A., and L. C. DeVinney
  1949   "How personal adjustment varied in the army—by background characteristics of the soldiers." In S. A. Stouffer, E. A. Suchman, L. C. DeVinney, S. A. Star and R. M. Williams, Jr. (eds.), *The American Soldier: Adjustment during Army Life.* Princeton: Princeton University Press.
Suchman, E. A.
  1950   "The intensity component in attitude and opinion research." In S. A. Stouffer, L. Guttman, E. A. Suchman, P. F. Lazarsfeld, S. A. Star, J. A. Clausen (eds.), *Measurement and Prediction.* Princeton: Princeton University Press.
Sudman, S., and N. Bradburn
  1974   *Response Effects in Surveys.* Chicago: Aldine.
Sullivan, J. L., J. Pierson, and G. E. Marcus
  1979   "An alternative conceptualization of political tolerance: Illusory increases 1950s–1970s *The American Political Science Review* 73: 781–794.
Surveys of Consumer Attitudes
  1980   Unpublished paper. Monitoring Economic Change Program, Survey Research Center, Institute for Social Research, Ann Arbor, Michigan.
Tamulonis, V.
  1947   *"The effects of question variations in public opinion surveys,"* Masters thesis. Denver: University of Denver.
Tarantino, S. J., and R. E. Jednak
  1972   "A re-examination of factors influencing the evaluation of assertions," *Public Opinion Quarterly* 36: 109–113.
Thumin, F. J.
  1962   "Watch for those unseen variables," *Journal of Marketing* 26: 58–60.
Turner, C. F., and E. Krauss
  1978   "Fallible indicators of the subjective state of the nation," *American Psychologist* 33: 456–470.
Verba, S., and R. A. Brody
  1970   "Participation, policy preferences, and the war in Vietnam," *Public Opinion Quarterly* 34: 325–332.
Weissberg, R.
  1976   *Public Opinion and Popular Government.* Englewood Cliffs, N.J.: Prentice-Hall.
Wendt, J. C.
  1979   "Canonical correlations as an exploratory technique of attitude scale construction," *Public Opinion Quarterly* 43: 518–531.
Whitehead, A. N.
  1925   *Science and the Modern World.* New York: Macmillan.
Wiley, D. E., and J. A. Wiley
  1970   "The estimation of measurement error in panel data," *American Sociological Review* 35: 112–117.
Williams, W. H.
  1978   "How bad can 'good' data really be?" *The American Statistician* 32: 61–65.
Willick, D. H., and R. K. Ashley
  1971   "Survey question order and the political party preferences of college students and their parents," *Public Opinion Quarterly* 35: 189–199.

Index

Entries in italics *are pages where an exact question wording appears.*
Entries for certain subjects *(e.g., chi square, replication) are given only where an initial or major discussion appears.*

About the Authors

Howard Schuman is a research scientist in the Survey Research Center of the Institute for Social Research and a professor of sociology at the University of Michigan. His main research interests are in survey methods (especially the question-answer process); collective memory; and race and ethnic relations. In 1996 he plans to retire from teaching, to live primarily on the Maine coast, and to continue his research through the Survey Research Center in Ann Arbor. He is presently revising an earlier book, *Racial Attitudes in America: Trends & Interpretations* (Harvard University Press, 1985), and writing a new book titled *Collective Memories*. His professional positions have included editor of *Social Psychology Quarterly* (1977-1979) and of *Public Opinion Quarterly* (1986-1993), director of the Survey Research Center (1982-1990), and president of the American Association for Public Opinion Research (1985-1986). He has received a Guggenheim Fellowship, been a Fellow at the Center for Advanced Study in the Behavioral Sciences, a Resident at the Bellagio Center, and is presently a Fellow of the American Academy of Arts and Sciences.

Stanley Presser is the director of the Survey Research Center and a professor of sociology at the University of Maryland, College Park. He was director of the Joint Program in Survey Methodology from its founding in 1992 through 1995 and currently serves as editor of *Public Opinion Quar-*

terly. He was president of the American Association for Public Opinion Research during 1993-1994 and is an elected Fellow of the American Statistical Association. His other books include *Survey Questions: Handcrafting the Standardized Questionnaire* (with Jean Converse) and *Survey Research Methods: A Reader* (edited with Eleanor Singer).